Securities and Exchange Commission v. Cuban

A Trial of Insider Trading

Marc I. Steinberg

Radford Professor of Law
SMU Dedman School of Law

Titles in the Deep Dive Series

Administrative Law
Chevron U.S.A., Inc. v. Natural Resources Defense Council, Inc., by Kristin Hickman and Samuel Estreicher

Constitutional Law
McCulloch v. Maryland, by Michael P. Malloy

Constitutional Law
Steel Seizure Case (*Youngstown Sheet & Tube Co. v. Sawyer*), by Samuel Estreicher and Steven Menashi

Criminal Procedure
Miranda v. Arizona, by Amos N. Guiora and Louisa M.A. Heiny

Evidence
Crawford v. Washington, by Jay Tidmarsh

Federal Courts/Civil Rights
Juidice v. Vail, by Jane Bloom Grise and Michelle C. Grise

First Amendment
New York Times v. Sullivan, by Eric B. Easton

Immigration
Jean v. Nelson, by Irwin P. Stotzky

Patents
J.M. Smucker Co. v. Albie's Foods, Inc., by Thomas C. Folsom

Securities
Securities and Exchange Commission v. Cuban, by Marc I. Steinberg

Securities and Exchange Commission v. Cuban

A Trial of Insider Trading

Marc I. Steinberg

Radford Professor of Law
SMU Dedman School of Law

TWELVE TABLES PRESS
XII

Dedication

I am delighted to dedicate this book to U.S. District Court Judge (ret.) Stanley Sporkin. Judge Sporkin is having a superlative career—as the Director of the SEC's Division of Enforcement, General Counsel of the CIA, a federal district court judge, and an attorney in the private sector representing high profile clients. As SEC Enforcement Director, Judge Sporkin presided over the Division during the period that the Division may well have been most revered.

A couple of years after my graduation from law school, Judge Sporkin hired me as an enforcement attorney in the SEC's home office in Washington, D.C. That position commenced my career in securities law, one of which I have thoroughly enjoyed. Through the journey in the decades that followed, Judge Sporkin has been a wonderful mentor and good friend.

It is fitting that this book is dedicated to Judge Sporkin. After all, this case focuses on an SEC enforcement action for alleged violation of the insider trading prohibition. During Judge Sporkin's tenure as SEC enforcement director, the Commission pursued alleged insider trading violators with vigor. Thus, a book that focuses on this subject is deservedly dedicated to Judge Stanley Sporkin.

Thank you Stan for all of your friendship, mentoring, and support through the years.

About the Author

Marc I. Steinberg is the Rupert and Lillian Radford Professor of Law at the Southern Methodist University (SMU) Dedman School of Law. He is the Director of SMU's Corporate Directors' Institute, the Director of the SMU Corporate Counsel Externship Program, the former Senior Associate Dean for Academics, and the former Senior Associate Dean for Research at the Law School. Prior to becoming the Radford Professor, Professor Steinberg taught at the University of Maryland School of Law, the Wharton School of the University of Pennsylvania, the National Law Center of the George Washington University, and the Georgetown University Law Center. His experience includes appointments as a Visiting Professor, Scholar and Fellow at law schools outside of the United States, including at Universities in Argentina, Australia, China, England, Finland, Germany, Israel, Italy, Japan, New Zealand, Scotland, South Africa, and Sweden. In addition, he has been retained as an expert witness in several significant matters, including Mark Cuban, Enron, Martha Stewart, and Belnick (Tyco).

In addition to his University appointments, Professor Steinberg has lectured extensively both in the United States and abroad, including at the Lauterpacht Centre of International Law at the University of Cambridge, the Aresty Institute of Executive Education at the University of Pennsylvania, The American Bar Association's Annual Meeting, the PLI Annual Institute on Securities Regulation, the University of Texas Annual Securities Law Conference, the International Development Law Institute in Rome, the Hong Kong Securities and Futures Commission, the Taiwan "SEC" in Taipei, the New Zealand Securities Commission, the Australian Law Council Section on International Law in Melbourne, the David Hume Institute in Edinburgh, the German-American Lawyers' Association in Munich, the International Law Society of South Africa, the Buenos Aires Stock Exchange, the Finnish Banking Lawyers Association in Helsinki, the Swedish Banking Lawyers Association in Stockholm, and the Ministry of Internal Affairs, Economic Crimes Department of the Russian Federation in Moscow. He also has served as a member of the FINRA National Adjudicatory Council (NAC).

Professor Steinberg received his undergraduate degree at the University of Michigan and his law degrees at the University of California, Los Angeles (J.D.) and Yale University (LL.M.). He clerked for Judge Stanley N. Barnes of the U.S. Court of Appeals for the Ninth Circuit, extern clerked for Judge Anthony J. Celebrezze of the Sixth Circuit, was legislative counsel to U.S. Senator Robert P. Griffin and served as the adviser to former U.S. Supreme

Court Justice Arthur J. Goldberg for the Federal Advisory Committee Report on Tender Offers.

Professor Steinberg was an enforcement attorney at the U.S. Securities and Exchange Commission, and thereafter became special projects counsel. In that position, he directly assisted the SEC's General Counsel in a wide variety of projects and served as the General Counsel's confidential legal adviser.

Professor Steinberg has authored approximately 40 books and 150 law review articles, is editor-in-chief of The International Lawyer, editor-in-chief of The Securities Regulation Law Journal, and is an adviser to The Journal of Corporation Law. Professor Steinberg is a member of the American Law Institute.

Contents

Note from the Author

Given that the materials generated in *Securities and Exchange Commission v. Mark Cuban* amounted to thousands of pages, a challenge was presented to condense these materials in a meaningful manner. In undertaking this endeavor, I have attempted to preserve the flavor of the contentious litigation that occurred—from the SEC's investigation through the conclusion of trial. I have included excerpts of many of the pleadings and motions that were made by the parties as well as excerpts of the testimony of each witness who testified at trial.

Due to the need to condense these thousands of pages, hopefully to make the book user-friendly and to enhance consistency, I have made certain modifications. These editorial modifications include for example: using excerpts of testimony given as well as other materials that were filed or otherwise made available; using multiple periods (. . . .) after a sentence or answer to a question when other words or paragraphs that follow are not included in the book due to being omitted in the editing process; and using an individual's correct name where the record reflected inconsistencies (such as Fauré, not Faure).

The Foreword to the book that follows is written by Mr. George Anhang who served as one of Mr. Cuban's attorneys. I thank Mr. Anhang for authoring this Foreword. For disclosure and fairness purposes, members of the SEC staff who were involved in this litigation and Mr. Cuban separately were invited to author a Foreword—they declined the invitation.

In the analysis set forth in this book, the views expressed herein solely are my own. Readers understandably may disagree with a number of my positions. Throughout this process, particularly recognizing that I served as an expert witness on Mr. Cuban's behalf, I diligently have sought to maintain an objective perspective.

I hope that the book proves to be enjoyable and worthwhile—both as an experiential resource and as a scintillating account of one of the foremost sagas of securities litigation.

Foreword

BY GEORGE ANHANG[1]

Securities and Exchange Commission v. Mark Cuban was an improbable case. There was *no* judicial precedent for the SEC's insider trading claim against Mark Cuban, *no* support for it in the plain meaning of governing federal statutes, and *no* solid evidence in the record for the factual allegations on which the claim depended—yet the SEC pushed on against Cuban nonetheless. That the SEC's claim lacked legal and factual basis is not only what Cuban and his legal team thought. It is what the presiding federal district judge apparently thought when he initially threw out the case. And it is what the members of the jury clearly all thought, given they deliberated and reached a complete verdict in Cuban's favor so swiftly.

It likewise was improbable that the SEC's lawsuit would be litigated for as long as it was—1,795 days, to be exact—and took a trial to resolve. Confronted with the might of the SEC, and the burdens (financial and otherwise) of drawn-out litigation against the government, many defendants submit to a negotiated settlement early on, even if it means forfeiting the chance to clear their name.

Not only was the case's length extraordinary, its prehistory was almost as long. The SEC's case was built upon an eight-minute phone call between Mark Cuban and Mamma.com CEO Guy Fauré that took place on June 28, 2004. The SEC did not file its complaint against Cuban until more than four years later. Of note, at the trial that took place almost five years after that, Fauré was nowhere to be found, despite the SEC's claim that Cuban had defrauded him and Mamma.com. Victims of fraud are usually eager to help bring the perpetrator to justice. Fauré's unwillingness to fly to Dallas to testify at trial—and submit to cross-examination before the jury—spoke volumes.

That one may think that *SEC v. Cuban* should not have been filed in the first place, or that once filed, should have reached an earlier or different resolution, makes the need for this book no less compelling. On the contrary, that such a case *was* filed and then could *not* be resolved except in the manner it was, makes this book with all its illuminating power that much *more*

---

1. George Anhang represented Mark Cuban in *SEC v. Cuban.* He is Counsel at Shearman & Sterling LLP, a global law firm, where he is resident in the Washington, DC office. The views he expresses herein are his own.

essential. I hope that many will read it. Those who do may be surprised at what they learn.

Not that the book sets out to prove a point about the case. It is one of its (many) virtues that it does not. Without advocating a position or sitting in judgment, the book methodically sets out the key filings, factual and legal issues, and procedural maneuverings in the case. The presentation of the subject matter benefits enormously from the intimacy of Marc Steinberg's knowledge of the suit (the result of his serving as one of Cuban's expert witnesses), and the subterranean depths of his expertise in insider trading law (Steinberg is one of the country's preeminent securities law scholars).

While this book is generally dispassionate about *SEC v. Cuban*, I am not. I was privileged to be on the team of lawyers that represented Mark Cuban.[2] That privilege was accompanied by an acute desire to do right by him. My belief that the SEC's suit was baseless, and not brought in good faith, also bred pressure. When you represent a client in a case you think had no business being filed, and your client should never have had to retain your services, winning seems like the least you should do.

I have referred to certain improbabilities—that *SEC v. Cuban* was filed at all, and once filed, was not resolved until years later. What explains them, in large part, is the identity of the defendant. Without a doubt, who Mark Cuban is factored into the SEC's decision to pursue a case against him. In the eyes of the SEC, Cuban was not just another investor. Hardly.

---

2. Other members of the defense team included, at the law firm where I practiced at the time, Lyle Roberts, and, at other law firms, lead trial counsel Thomas Melsheimer, Stephen Best, and Christopher Clark. I learned much from Lyle (who it is my good fortune to have as my colleague again, at Shearman & Sterling LLP), Tom, Steve, and Chris, and I am indebted to each of them.

Although, as I noted before, people who find themselves staring down the barrel of an SEC enforcement action are inclined to seek refuge in an early negotiated settlement, the SEC's pursuit of Cuban had no such effect upon him. Cuban believed, to the core of his being, that he had done nothing wrong. He was not about to enter into a settlement with the SEC that suggested otherwise. He also saw the litigation as capable of providing a window into certain excesses in SEC enforcement practices and policies. By vigorously defending the case, Cuban thought that he could bring into the open what he regarded as an abuse of enforcement authority by some within the SEC. Sunlight is the best disinfectant, he knew. All market participants, the public at large, even the SEC itself, stood to benefit.

Cuban's belief that the litigation could serve a salutary purpose reflected Cuban's high regard for the legal system, most especially the role of the jury.

Juries are complicated, and by reputation, unpredictable. In no jury trial would any sensible lawyer guarantee his or her client a particular outcome. No matter the strength of the evidence in one's favor, there is always an element of uncertainty. A negotiated settlement before trial is the only way to avoid that uncertainty. That is one of the main reasons settlements are as common as they are.

Cuban was a realist about the jury process, but at the same time supremely hopeful. Because, in a word, he *trusted* the jury in the case. He trusted the jury as much as he had come to *distrust* the SEC (which he believed, with reason, had targeted him unfairly). Cuban trusted the members of the jury to set aside preconceived notions they may have, and to consider all the evidence with an open mind. To be fair. To apply common sense. To spot the flaws in the SEC's case that the SEC sought strenuously to obscure. To faithfully apply governing law as the judge stated it, to the facts as the jury found them. In doing so, to reject the SEC's efforts to use the case to create new insider trading law, and deploy it retroactively to punish Cuban for conduct he would have reasonably understood at the time to be lawful.

I am referring here to the proposition that the SEC sought (without precedent) to advance in the case that securities *fraud*—which insider trading must amount to, the Supreme Court has held, in order to be actionable—can be established through the violation of a bare confidentiality agreement. The SEC could not seriously argue that when Mark Cuban sold his Mamma.com shares in 2004, he knew (or should have known) *then* that his stock sale ran afoul of the novel legal position that the SEC would pursue in a suit against him in 2008. In any event, the record in the case did *not* show that Cuban intended to make an agreement to keep information about the company whose stock he sold (Mamma.com) confidential, let alone that his stock sale would have violated an agreement of that kind. The case that the SEC presented to the jury thus fit neither existing law nor the established facts.

Cuban's trust in the jury was not misplaced. Once the case went to the jury, it deliberated only briefly before coming back with a complete verdict in Cuban's favor.

It was clear from the verdict, and the speed with which it was rendered, that the jury rejected the SEC's case from top to bottom. It was especially evident from a form that the judge directed the jury to complete. To establish its insider trading claim, there were a number of discrete elements the SEC was required to prove. The jury was provided a form listing these elements, with an instruction from the judge to indicate, at the conclusion of its deliberations, whether the SEC had satisfied its burden of proof as to each element.

The jury found, and specified in the form, that the SEC failed to meet its burden as to every one of the contested elements of its insider trading claim. The jury concluded the SEC had not shown *any* of the following: that Mark Cuban received information from Mamma.com that was material and nonpublic;[3] *or* that he agreed to keep any such information confidential; *or* that he agreed not to trade on it, or otherwise use it for his own benefit; *or* that he traded on the information in the sale of his Mamma.com stock; *or* that before trading, he did not disclose to Mamma.com that he planned to trade; *or* that he engaged in improper conduct knowingly or with severe recklessness.

In short, the SEC failed to convince the jury of anything of significance to its case. The jury determined, and indicated in the jury form, that after litigating against Mark Cuban for almost five years (and investigating him for several years before that), all the SEC could show in support of its claim was that Cuban traded his shares of Mamma.com, and thereby engaged in interstate commerce. Of course, these were unremarkable facts that, standing on their own, were of no legal moment. Besides that, no case was even needed for them to become known. After selling his Mamma.com stock in June 2004, Cuban immediately disclosed to the SEC and the public that he had done so.

In my office is a photograph inscribed by Mark Cuban. It shows him and members of his legal team after the conclusion of the trial. At the bottom of the photo, Cuban signed his name and scrawled in large letters: "Trust the Jury!" Indeed.

* * *

I conclude with a disclaimer. I was not asked to suppress here the unfavorable view I have of the SEC's suit against Mark Cuban. I set out some observations above that reflect that view, in the hope they may be instructive. I am grateful for the opportunity to do so. Perhaps in giving me free rein in this regard, Marc Steinberg had in mind a line that a colleague of his at the SEC (and later of mine, coincidentally, in private practice)—Ralph Ferrara, the eminent former General Counsel of the SEC—was wont to quote: "you cannot do *Hamlet* without Hamlet." In other words, a book on *SEC v. Cuban* would seem fundamentally incomplete without an appearance from someone who was in Cuban's camp in the case. All the more so given that it was Cuban's

---

3. The SEC's specific allegation, which the jury rejected, was that in his June 28, 2004 telephone call with Guy Fauré, Cuban received material, non-public information about an impending Mamma.com transaction known as a "private investment in public equity," or "PIPE."

position that the jury adopted. In examining the jury's verdict, one should consider the views that informed and inspired it.

The disclaimer to be made is that those views are not necessarily shared by Marc Steinberg. He may even have opposing views. Whatever Steinberg's views are, as I noted before, he has chosen not to impose them upon the reader. He does not use the book to relitigate the case for the SEC (where he once served as an enforcement attorney), nor to be a champion of Cuban's cause. Like many great authors, Steinberg wants his readers to make up their own minds. In this book, Steinberg presents in ingenious and elegant fashion the substance that readers need to do just that. That is something on which both sides in the exceedingly contentious case to which the book is devoted could agree.

Acknowledgments

This has been an interesting and fun project. Its successful completion was facilitated by the input of several individuals who I wish to thank. First, I express my appreciation to my wonderful friend George Anhang, a superb attorney, who has authored the Foreword of this book. Mr. Anhang was instrumental in providing me with certain key public documents that otherwise would have been more challenging to access. Second, my research assistants are deserving of kudos—Miles Abell, G. Adrian Galvan, David Watson, and Logan Weissler. Third, I express my gratitude to the outstanding attorneys who provided comments on the manuscript—Roger Bivans, Robert Hart, and Frank Razzano. Fourth, I thank SMU Law School Dean Jennifer Collins for her support of my scholarship, Associate Dean for Library and Technology Greg Ivy for his research contributions, and Carolyn Yates for her excellent administrative assistance. And fifth, I received a generous research grant from the Fred E. Tucker Endowment for Faculty Excellence Fund for this book project for which I am appreciative.

I am delighted to be a faculty member of this outstanding law school. In these Acknowledgments, I thank SMU and the Law School for supporting my scholarship through the years.

Securities and Exchange Commission v. Cuban

A Trial of Insider Trading

Marc I. Steinberg

Radford Professor of Law
SMU Dedman School of Law

CHAPTER 1

Setting the Stage

This experiential book focuses on the Securities and Exchange Commission's (SEC) enforcement action against Mr. Mark Cuban, a well-respected U.S. entrepreneur, businessman and investor whose ownership interests include the National Basketball Association's (NBA) Dallas Mavericks. Mr. Cuban also is known as a celebrity on "Dancing with the Stars" and as one of the principal investors on the reality television program, "Shark Tank." His net worth is valued in the billions of dollars.

The author (Marc I. Steinberg) was retained as an expert witness on Mr. Cuban's behalf. Accordingly, I had the opportunity to experience this litigation, at least to some degree, from the playing field rather than as a spectator. These insights hopefully will enhance the book's substance and vitality.

The government's case against Mr. Cuban alleged that he sold his Mamma.com stock (a publicly-traded company) while aware of material, non-public information. Prior to his trades, Mr. Cuban owned over six percent of Mamma.com stock. The alleged material, non-public information involved Mr. Cuban being selectively informed by the Company's chief executive officer (CEO) and its investment banker of a forthcoming securities offering at a substantial discount to its then-current trading price which Mr. Cuban viewed as harmful to the company's shareholders—referred to as a "Private Investment in Public Equity" or "PIPE" transaction.[1] Prior to the formal public disclosure of this offering, Mr. Cuban opted to sell his stock in the public markets. The SEC contended that Mr. Cuban had entered into a confidentiality agreement with the

---

1. Generally, a "PIPE" Transaction (Private Investment in Public Equity) involves "the purchase of securities in an issuer private placement (such as pursuant to § 4(a)(2) or Rule 506), the issuer's subsequent registration of the restricted stock with the SEC, and, upon effectiveness of the registration statement, the ability of the PIPE investors to resell immediately their stock into the public markets." Marc I. Steinberg, *Understanding Securities Law* 492 (7th ed. 2018).

company as a condition of receiving the material, non-public information and thereby had agreed both to maintain the information's confidentiality and to abstain from trading until adequate information regarding the offering was publicly disclosed.

The government's position is seen by an alleged phone conversation between Mr. Cuban and Mr. Guy Fauré, Mamma.com's then chief executive officer. *Before the SEC enforcement staff, Mr. Fauré testified regarding the call with Mr. Cuban:*

[Mr. Fauré]: To the best of my recollection, ... I mentioned to him [Mr. Cuban] that I had confidential information to convey to him. I told him that we [Mamma.com] were finalizing a private placement and asked him if he was interested in participating in the private placement.

[Ms. Julie Riewe, SEC Enforcement Attorney]: And did Mr. Cuban say anything during the call to indicate that he understood that the information you were conveying was to be kept confidential?

[Mr. Fauré]: Yes. Because at the end of the call, or near the end of the call, he said, "Well, now, I'm screwed. I can't sell."

[Ms. Riewe]: Do you remember whether those were his exact words?

[Mr. Fauré]: Pretty much.[2]

Second, an email described the conversation between Mr. Fauré and Mr. Cuban as follows:

Today ... Guy [Fauré] spoke to Mark Cuban about this equity raise [PIPE transaction] and whether or not he would be interested in participating. As anticipated, [Cuban] initially 'flew off the handle' and said he would sell his shares (recognizing that he was not able to do anything until we announce the equity [PIPE transaction])....[3]

---

2. Testimony of Guy Fauré, In the Matter of Mamma.com Financing Transaction, at page 19 (Jan. 11, 2007).

3. Email from David Goldman to Daniel Bertrand, et al., dated June 28, 2004.

Interestingly, whether to invite Mr. Cuban to participate in the PIPE transaction was a matter of discussion among Mamma.com participants and was addressed in an email to Mr. Fauré in the following way:

Should we ask Cuban if he wants to participate? My off the cuff answer:
He [Cuban] is against these instruments . . . .
He could blow up at an inconvenient time.
He would be privy to information not available to other shareholders.[4]

In his defense, Mr. Cuban denied that: the information was non-public; he entered into a confidentiality agreement; or agreed not to sell his stock prior to the formal public announcement of the PIPE offering. After Mamma.com formally announced the PIPE offering, Mr. Cuban went public that he had sold his shares.[5] The price of Mamma.com's stock tumbled 15% on news of the PIPE transaction as well as Mr. Cuban's exit as a Mamma.com investor. Not mincing words, Mr. Cuban asserted:

I hate when companies do PIPES-type transactions to raise money. . . . It's dilutive, and I hate being diluted . . . that simple.[6]

After conducting an investigation, the SEC determined to bring an enforcement action against Mr. Cuban alleging that he engaged in illegal insider trading—avoiding losses of $750,000 by selling his Mamma.com shares prior to the company's public disclosure of the PIPE offering. Adamantly contesting the Commission's charges, Mr. Cuban mounted an impressive defense, with an array of premier global law firms serving as his counsel. Asserting that he made no such agreement not to trade and that the information imparted to

---

4. Email from David Goldman to Guy Fauré dated June 23, 2004.

5. Mr. Cuban was required publicly to disclose his sales in SEC filings as he beneficially owned over 5% of the company's stock.

6. Paul Shread, *Mark Cuban Sells Mamma.com Stake*, InternetNewsBureau.com, *available at* http://www.internetnews.com/bus-news/print.php/3376981 (July 2, 2004).

him was publicly known,[7] Mr. Cuban asserted that he "refuse[d] to be bullied" by the feds.[8] After prolonged discovery, motions, and pre-trial orders, the case was tried before a jury which found Mr. Cuban not liable of all charges. In the aftermath of the verdict, Mr. Cuban attacked the SEC's enforcement action against him, claiming "[t]his is a horrific example of how the government does work."[9]

After suffering years of government investigation, litigation, and attacks challenging his integrity and business ethics, Mr. Cuban's reaction is understandable. Nonetheless, although its investigative and enforcement acumen have been criticized during the past few decades,[10] the SEC remains as a premier federal agency.[11] The Commission, through its Enforcement Division, vigorously pursues alleged violators and seeks meaningful relief with the objectives of enhancing investor protection and law compliance.[12] At times, the SEC misses "red flags" and institutes unwarranted enforcement actions. Rarely, however, is the good faith of the Commission at issue; simply, like other decision-makers, the SEC at times makes mistakes: in determining when prosecution is justified; and in the implementation of effective litigation (including trial) strategy. This assessment, in my view, is accurate. It is affected by my serving for four years as an attorney at the SEC, including in the Division of Enforcement.

In this book, I have tried to capture why the SEC brought this case and why Mr. Cuban defended so vigorously and at such great expense by extracting for the reader key excerpts of the actual record of the investigation, the pleadings filed by the parties, the discovery taken, and the record of the trial. By doing so, it is my hope that you will be able to determine what actually occurred by examining not only the participants' actions, but their motivations and

---

7. See Erin Fuchs, *Why the SEC Lost Its Big Case Against Mark Cuban*, Business Insider, *available at* http://www.businessinsider.com/how-mark-cuban-defeated-the-sec-2013-10 (June 12, 2011); Jess Krochtengel, *Cuban Denies He Promised to Keep Deal Info Confidential*, Law 360, *available at* https://www.law360.com/articles/477905/print?section=media (Oct. 3, 2013).

8. David Koenig, *Mark Cuban: 'I Refuse to be Bullied' by the Feds*, *available at* https://www.usatoday.com/story/money/business/2013/10/07/mark-cuban-insider-trading-trial/2939663 (Oct. 7, 2013).

9. Jess Krochtengel, *Jury Hands Cuban The Win In SEC's Insider Trading Case*, Law 360, *available at* https://www.law360.com/articles,480898/print?section=corporate (Oct. 16, 2013).

10. See Roberta Karmel, *Regulation by Prosecution—The Securities and Exchange Commission Versus Corporate America* (1982); Paul G. Mahoney, *Wasting a Crisis—Why Securities Regulation Fails* (2015); Stephen Labaton, *SEC Facing Deeper Trouble*, N.Y. Times, Dec. 1, 2002, at D1.

11. See Joel Seligman, *The Transformation of Wall Street—A History of the Securities and Exchange Commission and Modern Corporate Finance* (1982); Judith Miller, *SEC: Watchdog 1929 Lacked*, N.Y. Times, Oct. 31, 1979, at D1; Symposium, *In Honor of [Former SEC Enforcement Director] Stanley Sporkin*, 43 Sec. Reg. L.J. No. 1 (2015).

12. For two books by the author covering this subject, see Marc I. Steinberg, *The Federalization of Corporate Governance* (Oxford Univ. Press 2018); Marc I. Steinberg and Ralph C. Ferrara, *Securities Practice: Federal and State Enforcement* (2d ed. 2001 and 2018-2019 supp.).

credibility from the very sources that the judge and jurors had available to them. As we will see, the SEC contended that Mr. Cuban acted fraudulently to avoid losses, while Mr. Cuban claimed the evidence showed that he acted without any deceptive intent. Like many cases that go to trial in white-collar proceedings, several of the key facts themselves were undisputed—such as in this litigation, Mr. Cuban got a call from the CEO of Mamma.com and promptly sold his stock. The crux of the parties' dispute in this case, as in any white-collar case, is what those facts mean and the credibility of the witnesses who testified.

Ultimately, Mr. Cuban prevailed and the SEC lost. By reading these documents, you will be placed in a similar position that the jurors found themselves when they adjourned to deliberate. While you will not see the witnesses testify, you can, by reading their transcripts, draw conclusions about credibility and determine how you would have decided the case. When you finish the book, see if your conclusions differ from those of the jury, or my own, which I set forth in the final chapter.

Finally, for the lawyers, students, investors, business persons, and others reading this book you will see, as the facts unfold, many decision points. As you identify those decision points, ask yourself whether you would have acted differently. To help in this task, I have provided a short primer on insider trading in Chapter 2, since, in making any decision in this area, some grounding in the law, even a law as vague and ambiguous as insider trading, is necessary.

A "Glimpse" at the Law of Insider Trading

The law of insider trading should be aptly covered in one's business enterprises and securities regulation courses. Treatises have been written on this subject.[1] This book does not focus on the intricacies of insider trading law. However, some basic principles are necessary to better understand the SEC's case against Mr. Cuban.

Insider trading occurs when one, who has a duty not to trade, does so while aware of *material* and *non-public* information. The term "material" generally means that a reasonable person would consider such information important in making his or her investment decision.[2] The term "non-public" generally connotes that the subject information has not been adequately disseminated to the investing public.[3]

In many of the world's developed securities markets, one cannot trade or convey (tip) material non-public information to others if he or she is in knowing possession of or has unequal access to such information.[4] In the United States, that standard applies only in the tender offer setting[5] (which, of course,

---

1. The author has written a treatise on this subject. See Marc I. Steinberg and William K.S. Wang, *Insider Trading* (Oxford Univ. Press 3d ed. 2010).

2. See Matrixx Initiatives, Inc. v. Siracusano, 563 U.S. 27 (2011); Basic, Inc. v. Levinson, 485 U.S. 224 (1985); TSC Industries, Inc. v. Northway, Inc., 426 U.S. 438 (1976). In applying this standard with respect to contingent events, the probability/magnitude test is applied whereby materiality "will depend at any given time upon a balancing of both the indicated probability that the event will occur and the anticipated magnitude of the event in light of the totality of the company activity." SEC v. Texas Gulf Sulphur Co., 401 F.2d 833, 849 (2d Cir. 1968) (en banc).

3. See SEC v. Mayhew, 121 F.3d 44 (2d Cir. 1997).

4. See Regulation (EU) No. 596/2014 of the European Parliament and of the Council (Market Abuse Regulation); Australia Corporations Law §1043A; Ontario Securities Act, ch. S-5, §76.

5. SEC Rule 14e-3 (setting forth that one cannot trade or tip material non-public information concerning a tender offer when the person knows or has reason to know that such information

was not the situation for the Cuban trades). Moreover, under Section 16(b) of the Securities Exchange Act, if an insider—meaning an officer, director, or shareholder owning more than ten percent of the subject company's stock—buys and sells or sells and buys an equity security of the company within a six-month period, such insider must disgorge all profits made when an action is brought by the company or by a company shareholder in a derivative action.[6]

Ordinarily, insider trading prosecutions are pursued under Section 17(a) of the Securities Act, Section 10(b) of the Securities Exchange Act, and SEC Rule 10b-5. As interpreted by the U.S. Supreme Court, one is liable for trading on material non-public information if he or she owes a fiduciary duty or has a relationship of trust or confidence to the subject corporation or its shareholders (*the "classical" theory*).[7] By trading on such information, insiders—such as officers and directors—breach their fiduciary duty. Likewise, temporary insiders, including attorneys and investment bankers who knowingly receive confidential information from their corporate client, are subject to liability under the classical theory when they trade in breach of this duty owed to the corporation and its shareholders.[8] *The "classical" theory was not implicated in the SEC's action against Mr. Cuban because he was neither a traditional nor a temporary insider of Mamma.com.*

Alternatively, an individual may be liable for insider trading by trading in breach of a fiduciary duty or a relationship of trust and confidence owed to the *source* of the information (*the "misappropriation" theory*).[9] For example, an employee who receives material non-public information from his or her employer with the understanding that it must be kept confidential and not traded upon prior to public disclosure of such information is subject to liability under the misappropriation theory by breaching that understanding. According to the SEC under its Rule 10b5-2, a person may be deemed to have a relationship of trust and confidence under the misappropriation theory when such individual enters into an agreement to maintain the confidentiality

---

was received, directly or indirectly, from the bidder, target, or financial intermediary), upheld in, United States v. O'Hagan, 521 U.S. 642 (1997). Generally, a tender offer is "a means frequently used to acquire control of a corporation characterized by active solicitation to purchase a substantial percentage of the target's stock from the target's shareholders at a premium over the market price, offered for a limited period of time and that may be contingent upon the tender of a specific number of shares." Marc I. Steinberg, *Understanding Securities Law* 500 (7th ed. 2018).

6. See Kern County Land Co. v. Occidental Petroleum Corp., 411 U.S. 582 (1973); Whittaker v. Whittaker Corp., 639 F.2d 516 (9th Cir. 1981); Peter Romeo and Alan Dye, *Section 16 Treatise and Reporting Guide* (2018).

7. See Chiarella v. United States, 445 U.S. 222 (1980).

8. Dirks v. Securities and Exchange Commission, 463 U.S. 646, 677 n. 14 (1983).

9. United States v. O'Hagan, 521 U.S. 642 (1997).

of the subject information.[10] *Significantly, this rationale was relied upon by the SEC in its case against Mr. Cuban.*

Lastly, one can be liable for insider trading by breaching his or her fiduciary duty by knowingly communicating material non-public information to a tippee with the motivation of receiving a personal benefit or conveying a gift. A tippee who receives the information and thereupon trades, knowing of the tipper's breach, is likewise liable.[11] *This rationale was not invoked by the SEC in its enforcement action because Mr. Fauré did not convey the information to Mr. Cuban for Mr. Fauré's personal benefit or for purposes of providing a gift to Mr. Cuban.*

As will be covered later in the book, Judge Sidney A. Fitzwater, a highly respected judge, granted Mr. Cuban's motion to dismiss the SEC's Complaint. Thus, it appeared that the SEC's enforcement action had ended. However, on appeal, the U.S. Court of Appeals for the Fifth Circuit vacated and remanded. Because the Fifth Circuit's decision provides a succinct overview of the classical and misappropriation theories of insider trading, crystallizing certain issues raised in this litigation, it is included at this point in the text.

Securities and Exchange Commission v. Cuban
United States Court of Appeals
620 F.3d 551 (5th Cir. 2010)

Higginbotham, Circuit Judge:

This case raises questions of the scope of liability under the misappropriation theory of insider trading. Taking a different view from our able district court brother of the allegations of the complaint, we are persuaded that the case should not have been dismissed ... and must proceed to discovery.

Mark Cuban is a well-known entrepreneur and current owner of the Dallas Mavericks and Landmark theaters, among other businesses. The SEC brought this suit against Cuban alleging he violated [the federal securities laws] by trading in Mamma.com stock in breach of his duty to the CEO and Mamma.com—amounting to insider trading under the misappropriation theory of liability. The core allegation is that Cuban received confidential information from the CEO of Mamma.com, a Canadian search engine company in which Cuban was a large minority stakeholder, agreed to keep the information confidential, and acknowledged he could not trade on the information. The SEC alleges that, armed with the inside information regarding a private investment of public equity (PIPE) offering, Cuban sold his stake in the company in

---

10. See Securities Exchange Act Release No. 43154 (2000). A family relationship, such as husband and wife, as well as a meaningfully close personal friendship, also are within the scope of Rule 10b5-2.

11. See Salman v. United States, 137 S.Ct. 420 (2016); Dirks v. Securities and Exchange Commission, 463 U.S. 646 (1983).

an effort to avoid losses from the inevitable fall in Mamma.com's share price when the offering was announced.

Cuban moved to dismiss the action. The district court found that, at most, the complaint alleged an agreement to keep the information confidential, but did not include an agreement not to trade. Finding a simple confidentiality agreement to be insufficient to create a duty to disclose or abstain from trading under the securities laws, the court granted Cuban's motion to dismiss. The SEC appeals, arguing that a confidentiality agreement creates a duty to disclose or abstain and that, regardless, the confidentiality agreement alleged in the complaint also contained an agreement not to trade on the information and that agreement would create such a duty. . . .

The SEC alleges that Cuban's trading constituted insider trading .... The Supreme Court has interpreted section 10(b) [of the Securities Exchange Act] to prohibit insider trading under two complementary theories, the "classical theory" and the "misappropriation theory."

The classical theory of insider trading prohibits a "corporate insider" from trading on material nonpublic information obtained from his position within the corporation without disclosing the information. According to this theory, there exists "a relationship of trust and confidence between the shareholders of a corporation and those insiders who have obtained confidential information by reason of their position with that corporation." Trading on such confidential information qualifies as a "deceptive device" under section 10(b) because by using that information for his own personal benefit, the corporate insider breaches his duty to the shareholders. The corporate insider is under a duty to "disclose or abstain"—he must tell the shareholders of his knowledge and intention to trade or abstain from trading altogether.

There are at least two important variations of the classical theory of insider trading. The first is that even an individual who does not qualify as a traditional insider may become a "temporary insider" if by entering "into a special confidential relationship in the conduct of the business of the enterprise [he/she is] given access to information solely for corporate purposes." Thus underwriters, accountants, lawyers, or consultants are all considered corporate insiders when by virtue of their professional relationship with the corporation they are given access to confidential information. The second variation is that an individual who receives information from a corporate insider may be, but is not always, prohibited from trading on that information as a tippee. "[T]he tippee's duty to disclose or abstain is derivative from that of the insider's duty" and the tippee's obligation arises "from his role as a participant after the fact in the insider's breach of a fiduciary duty." Crucially, "a tippee assumes a fiduciary duty to the shareholders of a corporation not to trade on material nonpublic information only when the insider has breached his fiduciary duty to the shareholders by disclosing the information to the tippee and the tippee knows or should know there has been a breach." The insider breaches his fiduciary duty when he receives a "direct or indirect personal benefit from the disclosure."

Both the temporary insider and tippee twists on the classical theory retain its core principle that the duty to disclose or abstain is derived from the corporate insider's duty to his shareholders. The misappropriation theory does not rest on this duty. It rather holds that a person violates section 10(b) "when he misappropriates confidential information for securities trading purposes, in breach of a duty owed to the source of the information." The Supreme Court first adopted this theory in *United States v. O'Hagan*. There, a lawyer traded the securities of a company his client was targeting for a takeover. O'Hagan could not be liable under the classical theory as he owed no duty to the shareholders of the target company. Nevertheless, the Court found O'Hagan violated section 10(b). The Court held that in trading the target company's securities, O'Hagan misappropriated the confidential information regarding the planned corporate takeover, breaching "a duty of trust and confidence" he owed to his law firm and client. Trading on such information "involves feigning fidelity to the source of information and thus utilizes a 'deceptive device' as required by section 10(b)." The Court stated that while there is "no general duty between all participants in market transactions to forgo actions based on material nonpublic information," the breach of a duty to the source of the information is sufficient to give rise to insider trading liability.... Because the duty flows to the source of the information and not to shareholders "if the fiduciary discloses to the source that he plans to trade on the nonpublic information, there is no 'deceptive device' and thus no § 10(b) violation."

While *O'Hagan* did not set the contours of a relationship of "trust and confidence" giving rise to the duty to disclose or abstain and misappropriation liability, we are tasked to determine whether Cuban had such a relationship with Mamma.com. The SEC seeks to rely on Rule 10b5-2(b)(1), which states that a person has "a duty of trust and confidence" for purposes of misappropriation liability when that person "agrees to maintain information in confidence." In dismissing the case, the district court read the complaint to allege that Cuban agreed not to disclose any confidential information but did not agree not to trade, that such a confidentiality agreement was insufficient to create a duty to disclose or abstain from trading under the misappropriation theory, and that the SEC overstepped its authority under section 10(b) in issuing Rule 10b5-2(b)(1). We differ from the district court in reading the complaint and need not reach the latter issues.

The complaint alleges that, in March 2004, Cuban acquired 600,000 shares, a 6.3% stake, of Mamma.com. Later that spring, Mamma.com decided to raise capital through a PIPE offering on the advice of the investment bank Merriman Curhan Ford & Co. At the end of June, at Merriman's suggestion, Mamma.com decided to invite Cuban to participate in the PIPE offering. "The CEO was instructed to contact Cuban and to preface the conversation by informing Cuban that he had confidential information to convey to him in order to make sure that Cuban understood—before the information was conveyed to him—that he would have to keep the information confidential." [SEC Complaint at Paragraph 12]

After getting in touch with Cuban on June 28, Mamma.com's CEO told Cuban he had confidential information for him and Cuban agreed to keep whatever information the CEO shared confidential. The CEO then told Cuban about the PIPE offering. Cuban became very upset "and said, among other things, that he did not like PIPEs because they dilute the existing shareholders." "At the end of the call, Cuban told the CEO 'Well, now I'm screwed. I can't sell.'" [SEC Complaint at Paragraph 14]

The CEO told the company's executive chairman about the conversation with Cuban. The executive chairman sent an email to the other Mamma.com board members updating them on the PIPE offering, [stating:]

> Today, after much discussion, [the CEO] spoke to Mark Cuban about this equity raise [the PIPE Offering] and whether or not he would be interested in participating. As anticipated he initially "flew off the handle" and said he would sell his shares (recognizing that he was not able to do anything until we announce the [offering]) but then asked to see the terms and conditions which we have arranged for him to receive from one of the participating investor groups with which he has dealt in the past.

The CEO then sent Cuban a follow up email, writing "[i]f you want more details about the private placement please contact ... [Merriman]."

Cuban called the Merriman representative and they spoke for eight minutes. "During that call, the salesman supplied Cuban with additional confidential details about the PIPE. In response to Cuban's questions, the salesman told him that the PIPE was being sold at a discount to the market price and that the offering included other incentives for the PIPE investors." It is a plausible inference that Cuban learned the off-market prices available to him and other PIPE participants.

With that information and one minute after speaking with the Merriman representative, Cuban called his broker and instructed him to sell his entire stake in the company. Cuban sold 10,000 shares during the evening of June 28, 2004, and the remainder during regular trading the next day.

That day, the executive chairman sent another email to the board, updating them on the previous day's discussions with Cuban, stating, "'we did speak to Mark Cuban ... to find out if he had any interest in participating.... His answers were: he would not invest, he does not want the company to make acquisitions, he will sell his shares which he cannot do until after we announce [the PIPE offering].'"

After the markets closed on June 29, Mamma.com announced the PIPE offering. The next day, Mamma.com's stock price fell 8.5% and continued to decline over the next week, eventually closing down 39% from the June 29 closing price. By selling his shares when he did, Cuban avoided over $750,000 in losses. Cuban notified the SEC that he had sold his stake in the company and publicly stated that he sold his shares because Mamma.com "was conducting a PIPE, which issued shares at a discount to the prevailing market price and also would have caused his ownership position to be diluted."

In reading the complaint to allege only an agreement of confidentiality, the [district] court held that Cuban's statement that he was "screwed" because he "[could not] sell" "appears to express his belief, at least at that time, that it would be illegal for him to sell his Mamma.com shares based on the information the CEO provided." But the court stated that this statement "cannot reasonably be understood as an agreement not to sell based on the information." The court found "the complaint asserts no facts that reasonably suggest that the CEO intended to obtain from Cuban an agreement to refrain from trading on the information as opposed to an agreement merely to keep it confidential." Finally, the court stated that "the CEO's expectation that Cuban would not sell was also insufficient" to allege any further agreement.

Reading the complaint in the light most favorable to the SEC, we reach a different conclusion. In isolation, the statement "Well, now I'm screwed. I can't sell" can plausibly be read to express Cuban's view that learning the confidences regarding the PIPE forbade his selling his stock before the offering but to express no agreement not to do so. However, after Cuban expressed to the CEO the view that he could not sell, he gained access to the confidences of the PIPE offering. According to the complaint's recounting of the executive chairman's email to the board, during his short conversation with the CEO regarding the planned PIPE offering, Cuban requested the terms and conditions of the offering. Based on this request, the CEO sent Cuban a follow up email providing the contact information for Merriman. Cuban called the salesman, who told Cuban "that the PIPE was being sold at a discount to the market price and that the offering included other incentives for the PIPE investors." Only after Cuban reached out to obtain this additional information, following the statement of his understanding that he could not sell, did Cuban contact his broker and sell his stake in the company.

The allegations, taken in their entirety, provide more than a plausible basis to find that the understanding between the CEO and Cuban was that he was not to trade, that it was more than a simple confidentiality agreement. By contacting the sales representative to obtain the pricing information, Cuban was able to evaluate his potential losses or gains from his decision to either participate or refrain from participating in the PIPE offering. It is at least plausible that each of the parties understood, if only implicitly, that Mamma.com would only provide the terms and conditions of the offering to Cuban for the purpose of evaluating whether he would participate in the offering, and that Cuban could not use the information for his own personal benefit.[12] It would require additional facts that have not been put before us for us to conclude that the parties could not plausibly have reached this shared understanding. Under Cuban's reading, he was allowed to trade on the information but prohibited from telling others—in effect providing him an exclusive license to trade on the material nonpublic information. Perhaps this was the understanding, or perhaps Cuban mislead the CEO regarding the timing of his sale in order to obtain a confidential look at the details of the PIPE. We say only that on this factually sparse record, it is at least equally plausible that all sides understood there was to be no trading before the PIPE.[13] That both Cuban and the CEO expressed the belief that Cuban could not trade appears to reinforce the plausibility of this reading.

[12.] The parties dispute Mamma.com's motive in providing the information to Cuban. Cuban contends that the offering was already oversubscribed and that this demonstrates the sole purpose of the phone call was to prevent Cuban from trading ahead of the offering. We express no opinion on this factual dispute or the potential implications of Cuban's allegations if they are true. At the motion to dismiss stage we must view all the facts in light most favorable to the SEC and assume that Mamma.com had a legitimate reason for contacting Cuban.

[13.] Such an arrangement would raise serious tipper/tippee liability concerns were it explicit. If the CEO knowingly gave Cuban material nonpublic information and arranged so he

... [W]e VACATE the judgment dismissing the case and REMAND to the court of first instance for further proceedings including discovery, consideration of summary judgment, and trial, if reached.[14]

With this overview, the law of insider trading—especially with respect to Mr. Cuban's trades—is sufficiently introduced. As the litigants' filings and motions are excerpted in later chapters of this book, the issues implicated will be further developed. The next step is to ascertain the process by which the SEC gained information in order to determine whether to institute an enforcement action against Mr. Cuban. Accordingly, the following chapter explores, prior to filing the case, the Commission's investigation of Mamma. com and Mr. Cuban.

---

could trade on it, it would not be difficult for a court to infer that the CEO must have done so for some personal benefit—e.g., goodwill from a wealthy investor and large minority stakeholder. "A reputational benefit that translates into future earnings, a quid pro quo, or a gift to a trading friend or relative all could suffice to show the tipper personally benefitted." *SEC v. Yun*, 327 F.3d 1263, 1277 (11th Cir. 2003). This of course is not to suggest any such improprieties occurred; rather, it simply reinforces the plausibility of the interpretation of the alleged facts as evidencing an understanding that the agreement included an agreement by Cuban not to trade.

[14.] [Note that the decision as edited omits citations.]

CHAPTER 3

The SEC'S Investigation

The SEC issued a formal order of investigation concerning the trading of Mamma.com securities. The Commission has broad investigative authority to decide whether a violation of the federal securities laws is transpiring or has occurred. An SEC investigation is a fact-finding process; it is issued as a non-public order and without notice to potential targets. As stated by the U.S. Supreme Court, the securities statutes

> empower the SEC to conduct investigations which, in the opinion of the Commission, are necessary and proper for the enforcement [of the federal securities laws] ... and to require the production of any books, papers, or other documents which the Commission deems relevant or material to the inquiry.... It appears, in short, that Congress intended to vest the SEC with considerable discretion in determining when and how to investigate possible violations of the statutes administered by the Commission.[1]

I. ISSUANCE OF SEC SUBPOENA TO MR. CUBAN

Upon initiating its investigation, the SEC issued subpoenas to several persons, including Mark Cuban. Consistent with its customary practices, the subpoena issued to Mr. Cuban required that he personally testify before the SEC staff and produce documents as called for by the subpoena. Attached to the subpoena was "supplemental information" focusing on the Commission's

---

1. Securities and Exchange Commission v. Jerry T. O'Brien, Inc., 467 U.S. 735, 744-745 (1984).

disclosures and warnings regarding this investigative process. *The SEC subpoena issued to Mr. Cuban and its attachment follow.*

▬▬▬▬

SUBPOENA
UNITED STATES OF AMERICA
SECURITIES AND EXCHANGE COMMISSION

In the Matter of Mamma.com Financing Transactions (HO-10576)

To: Mark Cuban

X   **YOU MUST PRODUCE** everything specified in the Attachment to this subpoena to officers of the United States Securities and Exchange Commission, at the place, date, and time specified below.

100 F Street, N.E., Washington, D.C. 20549 at 2:00 p.m. on Tuesday, March 27, 2007

X   **YOU MUST TESTIFY** before officers of the United States Securities and Exchange Commission, at the place, date, and time specified below.

100 F Street, N.E., Washington, D.C. 20549 at 9:30 a.m. on Tuesday, April 3, 2007

FEDERAL LAW REQUIRES YOU TO COMPLY WITH THIS SUBPOENA
Failure to comply may subject you to a fine and/or imprisonment

By: *[Signed]*   Date: *3/12/07*
       Julie M. Riewe
       Senior Counsel
       100 F. Street, N.E.
       Washington, D.C. 20549-6041
       (202) 551-4546

I am an officer of the Securities and Exchange Commission authorized to issue subpoenas in this matter. The Securities and Exchange Commission has issued a formal order authorizing this investigation pursuant to Section 20(a) of the Securities Act of 1933 and Section 21(a) of the Securities Exchange Act of 1934.

NOTICE TO WITNESS: If you claim a witness fee or mileage, submit this subpoena with the claim voucher.

ATTACHMENT TO SUBPOENA ISSUED TO MARK CUBAN

In the Matter of Mamma.com Financing Transactions (HO-10576)

Date: March 12, 2007
To: Mark Cuban

I.   DEFINITIONS

1. **COMMUNICATIONS.** As used in this attachment, the term "communications" means all written and oral communications, including, but not limited to, email messages, blackberry messages, voicemail messages, instant messages, Bloomberg instant messages, letters, notes, memoranda, and facsimiles.

2. **CONCERNING.** As used in this attachment, the term "concerning" means relating to, referring to, describing, evidencing, or constituting.

3. **DOCUMENTS.** As used in this attachment, the term "documents" means all records and other tangible forms of expression, whether originals, drafts, finished versions, or non-identical copies including annotated copies, however and by whomever created, produced, or stored (manually, mechanically, electronically, or otherwise), including, but not limited to, books, papers, files, notes, account statements, confirmations, internal or external correspondence and communications, memoranda, ledger sheets, reports, electronic mail, instant messages, tape recordings or electronic recordings of any kind (including back-up tapes, disks, microfilm, microfiche, and storage devices), telegrams, telexes, telecommunications whether intra-network or inter-network, facsimiles, telephone logs, phone messages, notes or records of conversations or meetings, contracts, agreements, calendars, date books, bank statements, checks, wire transfers, drafts for money, records of payment, working papers and supporting materials and analyses, desk files, personal files, and engagement, representation or retention letters.

4. **MAMMA.COM INC.** As in this attachment, the term "Mamma.com Inc." means Mamma.com Inc. and all entities in which it has or has had an interest, and all subsidiaries, predecessors, successors, and affiliated entities of Mamma.com Inc., and any joint ventures, partnerships for which Mamma.com Inc. serves as a general or limited partner, and the present and former directors, officers, principals, employees, agents, representatives, general partners, and limited partners of the foregoing entities.

5. **MERRIMAN CURHAN FORD & CO.** As in this attachment, the term "Merriman Curhan Ford & Co." means Merriman Curhan Ford & Co. and all entities in which it has or has had an interest, and all subsidiaries, predecessors, successors, and affiliated entities of Merriman Curhan Ford & Co., and any joint ventures, partnerships for which Merriman Curhan Ford

& Co. serves as a general or limited partner, and the present and former directors, officers, principals, employees, agents, representatives, general partners, and limited partners of the foregoing entities.

6. **YOU and YOURS.** As used in this attachment, the terms "you" and "your" refer to the person to whom this subpoena is directed, Mark Cuban, and any of his family members, agents, employees, or representatives, and all entities in which he has or has had a direct or indirect ownership interest.

II. INSTRUCTIONS/RULES OF CONSTRUCTION

1. If, after the service of your responses to this subpoena, you become aware of any other document responsive to this subpoena, you shall promptly furnish such additional document to the staff.

2. If the attorney-client privilege, work product doctrine, or any other privilege or immunity is claimed as to anything called for by this subpoena, you shall state: (i) the date that any such document was prepared; (ii) the identity of each person who prepared it; (iii) its subject matter; (iv) the identity of each person to whom it was directed or circulated; (v) the identity of each person who has custody of it; (vi) the nature of each objection; (vii) any and all facts and reasons that you claim support each objection; (viii) the reason or reasons for the preparation of the document; and (ix) the identity of each person who has knowledge of any of the facts or reasons that you claim support such objection or any of the reasons for the preparation of the document.

3. You must produce each document in your actual or constructive possession, custody, or control.

4. The following rules of construction apply to this attachment:
   a. The terms "all" and "each" shall be construed as all and each;
   b. The connectives "and" and "or" shall be construed either disjunctively or conjunctively as necessary to bring within the scope of the attachment all responses that might otherwise be construed to be outside of its scope; and
   c. The use of the singular form of any word includes the plural and vice versa.

III. REQUIRED PRODUCTION

Please produce the following documents in your possession, custody, or control:

1. For the period January 1, 2004 through the present, any and all communications to, from, or concerning Mamma.com Inc.

2. For the period January 1, 2004 through the present, any and all communications to, from, or concerning Merriman Curhan Ford & Co.

3. For the period January 1, 2004 through the present, any and all public statements regarding Mamma.com Inc., including, but not limited to, any statements concerning Mamma.com Inc. that appear or have appeared on the website www.blogmaverick.com.

4. For the period January 1, 2004 through August 31, 2004, documents sufficient to identify all telephone numbers assigned to you or used by you, in a personal and/or business capacity, including home telephone number(s),

business phone number(s), cellular and/or mobile telephone number(s), and "direct ring" or similar direct line numbers.

5. For each telephone number identified in response to item (4), documents sufficient to identify all incoming and outgoing telephone calls, the numbers of dialed and incoming calls, call times, call durations, and persons called for the period June 27, 2004 through June 30, 2004.

6. For the period January 1, 2004 through August 31, 2004, documents sufficient to identify all brokerage accounts in any account in your name or in any account in which you share or shared a beneficial interest or in any account controlled by you or for which you have or have had trading authority.

7. For the period January 1, 2004 through August 31, 2004, all documents concerning any trades in Mamma.com Inc., including, but not limited to, trade confirmations and cancellations, order tickets, order instructions, and monthly and/or periodic account statements.

8. For the period June 27, 2004 through June 30, 2004, documents reflecting your daily activities, including, but not limited to, diaries, desk calendars, appointment books, time sheets, and work summaries.

9. For period June 27, 2004 through June 30, 2004, documents sufficient to identify all golf outings, including, but not limited to, course location, tee times, and the identities of any persons with whom you played.

SECURITIES AND EXCHANGE COMMISSION

Washington, D.C. 20549

Supplemental Information for Persons Requested to Supply Information Voluntarily or Directed to Supply Information Pursuant to a Commission Subpoena

---

False Statements and Documents

Section 1001 of Title 18 of the United States Code provides as follows:

> Whoever, in any matter within the jurisdiction of any department or agency of the United States knowingly and willfully falsifies, conceals or covers up by any trick, scheme, or device a material fact, or makes any false, fictitious or fraudulent statements or representations, or makes or uses any false writing or document knowing the same to contain any false, fictitious or fraudulent statement or entry, shall be fined under this title or imprisoned not more than five years, or both.

Testimony

If your testimony is taken, you should be aware of the following:

1. *Record.* Your testimony will be transcribed by a reporter. If you desire to go off the record, please indicate this to the Commission employee taking your testimony, who will determine whether to grant your request. The reporter will not go off the record at your, or your counsel's, direction.

2. *Counsel.* You have the right to be accompanied, represented and advised by counsel of your choice. Your counsel may advise you before, during and after your testimony; question you briefly at the conclusion of your testimony to clarify any of the answers you give during testimony; and make summary notes during your testimony solely for your use. If you are accompanied by counsel, you may consult privately.

    If you are not accompanied by counsel, please advise the Commission employee taking your testimony whenever during your testimony you desire to be accompanied, represented and advised by counsel. Your testimony will be adjourned to afford you the opportunity to arrange to do so.

    You may be represented by counsel who also represents other persons involved in the Commission's investigation. This multiple representation, however, presents a potential conflict of interest if one client's interests are or may be adverse to another's. If you are represented by counsel who also represents other persons involved in the investigation, the Commission will assume that you and counsel have discussed and resolved all issues concerning possible conflicts of interest. The choice of counsel, and the responsibility for that choice, is yours.

3. *Transcript Availability.* Rule 6 of the Commission's Rules Relating to Investigations, 17 CFR 203.6, states:

    > A person who has submitted documentary evidence or testimony in a formal investigative proceeding shall be entitled, upon written request, to procure a copy of his documentary evidence or a transcript of his testimony on payment of the appropriate fees: *Provided, however,* That in a nonpublic formal investigative proceeding the Commission may for good cause deny such request. In any event, any witness, upon proper identification, shall have the right to inspect the official transcript of the witness' own testimony.

    If you wish to purchase a copy of the transcript of your testimony, the reporter will provide you with a copy of the appropriate form. Persons requested to supply information voluntarily will be allowed the rights provided by this rule.

4. *Perjury.* Section 1621 of Title 18 of the United States Code provides as follows:

    > Whoever ... having taken an oath before a competent tribunal, officer, or person, in any case in which a law of the United States authorizes an oath to be administered, that he will testify, declare,

depose, or certify truly .... willfully and contrary to such oath states or subscribes any material matter which he does not believe to be true ... is guilty of perjury and shall, except as otherwise expressly provided by law, be fined under this title or imprisoned not more than five years or both....

5.   *Fifth Amendment and Voluntary Testimony.* Information you give may be used against you in any federal, state, local or foreign administrative, civil or criminal proceeding brought by the Commission or any other agency.

You may refuse, in accordance with the rights guaranteed to you by the Fifth Amendment to the Constitution of the United States, to give any information that may tend to incriminate you or subject you to fine, penalty or forfeiture.

If your testimony is not pursuant to subpoena, your appearance to testify is voluntary, you need not answer any question, and you may leave whenever you wish. Your cooperation is, however, appreciated.

6.   *Formal Order Availability.* If the Commission has issued a formal order of investigation, it will be shown to you during your testimony, at your request. If you desire a copy of the formal order, please make your request in writing.

Submissions and Settlements

Rule 5(c) of the Commission's Rules on Informal and Other Procedures, 17 CFR 202.5(c), states:

> Persons who become involved in ... investigations may, on their own initiative, submit a written statement to the Commission setting forth their interests and position in regard to the subject matter of the investigation. Upon request, the staff, in its discretion, may advise such persons of the general nature of the investigation, including the indicated violations as they pertain to them, and the amount of time that may be available for preparing and submitting a statement prior to the presentation of a staff recommendation to the Commission for the commencement of an administrative or injunction proceeding. Submissions by interested persons should be forwarded to the appropriate Division Director, Regional Director, or District Administrator with a copy to the staff members conducting the investigation and should be clearly referenced to the specific investigation to which they relate. In the event a recommendation for the commencement of an enforcement proceeding is presented by the staff, any submissions by interested persons will be forwarded to the Commission in conjunction with the staff memorandum.

The staff of the Commission routinely seeks to introduce submissions made pursuant to Rule 5(c) as evidence in Commission enforcement proceedings, when the staff deems appropriate.

Rule 5(f) of the Commission's Rules on Informal and Other Procedures, 17 CFR 202.5(f), states:

> In the course of the Commission's investigations, civil lawsuits, and administrative proceedings, the staff, with appropriate authorization, may discuss with any person involved the disposition of such matter by consent, by settlement, or in some other manner. It is the policy of the Commission, however, that the disposition of any such matter may not, expressly or impliedly, extend to any criminal charges that have been, or may be, brought against any such person or any recommendation with respect thereto. Accordingly, any person involved in an enforcement matter before the Commission who consents, or agrees to consent, to any judgment or order does so solely for the purpose of resolving the claims against him in that investigative, civil, or administrative matter and not for the purpose of resolving any criminal charges that have been, or might be, brought against him. This policy reflects the fact that neither the Commission nor its staff has the authority or responsibility for instituting, conducting, settling, or otherwise disposing of criminal proceedings. That authority and responsibility are vested in the Attorney General and representatives of the Department of Justice.

Freedom of Information Act

The Freedom of Information Act, 5 U.S.C. 552 (the "FOIA"), generally provides for disclosure of the information to the public. Rule 83 of the Commission's Rules on Information and Requests, 17 CFR 200.83, provides a procedure by which a person can make a written request that information submitted to the Commission not be disclosed under the FOIA. That rule states that no determination as to the validity of such a request will be made until a request for disclosure of the information under the FOIA is received. Accordingly, no response to a request that information not be disclosed under the FOIA is necessary or will be given until a request for disclosure under the FOIA is received. If you desire an acknowledgment of receipt of your written request that information not be disclosed under the FOIA, please provide a duplicate request, together with a stamped, self-addressed envelope.

Authority for Solicitation of Information

Persons Directed to Supply Information Pursuant to Subpoena. The authority for requiring production of information is set forth in the subpoena. Disclosure of the information to the Commission is mandatory, subject to the valid assertion of any legal right or privilege you might have.

Persons Requested to Supply Information Voluntarily. One or more of the following provisions authorizes the Commission to solicit the information requested: Sections

19 and/or 20 of the Securities Act of 1933; Section 21 of the Securities Exchange Act of 1934; Section 321 of the Trust Indenture Act of 1939; Section 42 of the Investment Company Act of 1940; Section 209 of the Investment Advisers Act of 1940; and 17 CFR 202.5. Disclosure of the requested information to the Commission is voluntary on your part.

Effect of Not Supplying Information

Persons Directed to Supply Information Pursuant to Subpoena. If you fail to comply with the subpoena, the Commission may seek a court order requiring you to do so. If such an order is obtained and you thereafter fail to supply the information, you may be subject to civil and/or criminal sanctions for contempt of court. In addition, if the subpoena was issued pursuant to the Securities Exchange Act of 1934, the Investment Company Act of 1940, and/or the Investment Advisers Act of 1940, and if you, without just cause, fail or refuse to attend and testify, or to answer any lawful inquiry, or to produce books, papers, correspondence, memoranda, and other records in compliance with the subpoena, you may be found guilty of a misdemeanor and fined not more than $1,000 or imprisoned for a term of not more than one year, or both.

Persons Requested to Supply Information Voluntarily. There are no direct sanctions and thus no direct effects for failing to provide all or any part of the requested information.

Principal Uses of Information

The Commission's principal purpose in soliciting the information is to gather facts in order to determine whether any person has violated, is violating, or is about to violate any provision of the federal securities laws or rules for which the Commission has enforcement authority, such as rules of securities exchanges and the rules of the Municipal Securities Rulemaking Board. Facts developed may, however, constitute violations of other laws or rules. Information provided may be used in Commission and other agency enforcement proceedings. Unless the Commission or its staff explicitly agrees to the contrary in writing, you should not assume that the Commission or its staff acquiesces in, accedes to, or concurs or agrees with, any position, condition, request, reservation of right, understanding, or any other statement that purports, or may be deemed, to be or to reflect a limitation upon the Commission's receipt, use, disposition, transfer, or retention, in accordance with applicable law, of information provided.

Routine Uses of Information

The Commission often makes the files available to other governmental agencies, particularly United States Attorneys and state prosecutors. There is a likelihood that information supplied by you will be made available to such agencies where appropriate. Whether or not the Commission makes its files available to other governmental agencies is, in general, a confidential matter between the Commission and such other governmental agencies.

Set forth below is a list of the routine uses which may be made of the information furnished.

1. To coordinate law enforcement activities between the SEC and other federal, state, local or foreign law enforcement agencies, securities self-regulatory organizations, and foreign securities authorities.

2. By SEC personnel for purposes of investigating possible violations of, or to conduct investigations authorized by, the federal securities laws.

3. Where there is an indication of a violation or potential violation of law, whether civil, criminal or regulatory in nature, and whether arising by general statute or particular program statute, or by regulation, rule or order issued pursuant thereto, the relevant records in the system of records may be referred to the appropriate agency, whether federal, state, or local, a foreign governmental authority or foreign securities authority, or a securities self-regulatory organization charged with the responsibility of investigating or prosecuting such violation or charged with enforcing or implementing the statute or rule, regulation or order issued pursuant thereto.

4. In any proceeding where the federal securities laws are in issue or in which the Commission, or past or present members of its staff, is a party or otherwise involved in an official capacity.

5. To a federal, state, local or foreign governmental authority or foreign securities authority maintaining civil, criminal or other relevant enforcement information or other pertinent information, such as current licenses, if necessary to obtain information relevant to an agency decision concerning the hiring or retention of an employee, the issuance of a security clearance, the letting of a contract, or the issuance of a license, grant or other benefit.

6. To a federal, state, local or foreign governmental authority or foreign securities authority, in response to its request, in connection with the hiring or retention of an employee, the issuance of a security clearance, the reporting of an investigation of an employee, the letting of a contract, or the issuance of a license, grant or other benefit by the requesting agency, to the extent that the information is relevant and necessary to the requesting agency's decision on the matter.

7. In connection with proceedings by the Commission pursuant to Rule 102(e) of its Rules of Practice, 17 CFR 201.102(e).

8. When considered appropriate, records in this system may be disclosed to a bar association, the American Institute of Certified Public Accountants, a state accountancy board or other federal, state, local or foreign licensing or oversight authority, foreign securities authority, or professional association or self-regulatory authority performing similar functions, for possible disciplinary or other action.

9. In connection with investigations or disciplinary proceedings by a state securities regulatory authority, a foreign securities authority, or by a self-regulatory organization involving one or more of its members.

10. As a data source for management information for production of summary descriptive statistics and analytical studies in support of the function for which the records are collected and maintained or for related personnel management functions or manpower studies, and to respond to general requests for statistical information (without personal identification of individuals) under the Freedom of Information Act or to locate specific individuals for personnel research or other personnel management functions.

11. In connection with their regulatory and enforcement responsibilities mandated by the federal securities laws (as defined in Section 3(a)(47) of the Securities Exchange Act of 1934, 15 U.S.C. 78c(a)(47)), or state or foreign laws regulating securities or other related matters, records may be disclosed to national securities associations that are registered with the Commission, the Municipal Securities Rulemaking Board, the Securities Investor Protection Corporation, the federal banking authorities, including but not limited to, the Board of Governors of the Federal Reserve System, the Comptroller of the Currency, and the Federal Deposit Insurance Corporation, state securities regulatory or law enforcement agencies or organizations, or regulatory law enforcement agencies of a foreign government, or foreign securities authority.

12. To any trustee, receiver, master, special counsel, or other individual or entity that is appointed by a court of competent jurisdiction or as a result of an agreement between the parties in connection with litigation or administrative proceedings involving allegations of violations of the federal securities laws (as defined in Section 3(a)(47) of the Securities Exchange Act of 1934, 15 U.S.C. 78c(a)(47)) or the Commission's Rules of Practice, 17 C.F.R. 202.100-900, or otherwise, where such trustee, receiver, master, special counsel or other individual or entity is specifically designated to perform particular functions with respect to, or as a result of, the pending action or proceeding or in connection with the administration and enforcement by the Commission of the federal securities laws or the Commission's Rules of Practice.

13. To any person during the course of any inquiry or investigation conducted by the Commission's staff, or in connection with civil litigation, if the staff has reason to believe that the person to whom the record is disclosed may have further information about the matters related therein, and those matters appeared to be relevant at the time to the subject matter of the inquiry.

14. To any person with whom the Commission contracts to reproduce, by typing, photocopy or other means, any record within this system for use by the Commission and its staff in connection with their official duties or to any person who is utilized by the Commission to perform clerical or stenographic functions relating to the official business of the Commission.

15. Inclusion in reports published by the Commission pursuant to authority granted in the federal securities laws (as defined in Section 3(a)(47) of the Securities Exchange Act of 1934, 15 U.S.C. 78c(a)(47)).

16. To members of advisory committees that are created by the Commission or by the Congress to render advice and recommendations to the Commission

or to the Congress, to be used solely in connection with their official designated functions.

17. To any person who is or has agreed to be subject to the Commission's Rules of Conduct, 17 CFR 200.735-1 to 735-18, and who assists in the investigation by the Commission of possible violations of federal securities laws (as defined in Section 3(a)(47) of the Securities Exchange Act of 1934, 15 U.S.C. 78c(a)(47)), in the preparation or conduct of enforcement actions brought by the Commission for such violations, or otherwise in connection with the Commission's enforcement or regulatory functions under the federal securities laws.

18. Disclosure may be made to a Congressional office from the record of an individual in response to an inquiry from the Congressional office made at the request of that individual.

19. To respond to inquiries from Members of Congress, the press and the public which relate to specific matters that the Commission has investigated and to matters under the Commission's jurisdiction.

20. To prepare and publish information relating to violations of the federal securities laws as provided in 15 U.S.C. 78c(a)(47), as amended.

21. To respond to subpoenas in any litigation or other proceeding.

22. To a trustee in bankruptcy.

23. To any governmental agency, governmental or private collection agent, consumer reporting agency or commercial reporting agency, governmental or private employer of a debtor, or any other person, for collection, including collection by administrative offset, federal salary offset, tax refund offset, or administrative wage garnishment, of amounts owed as a result of Commission civil or administrative proceedings....

II. INVESTIGATIVE TESTIMONY

In taking investigative testimony, the SEC staff is not limited by the rules of evidence. Relevance to the matter being investigated ordinarily is broadly construed. Of course, a witness may invoke his or her constitutional rights, including one's Fifth Amendment right against self-incrimination. Simply put, the Commission staff is undertaking a fact-finding mission in conducting an investigation and is given broad leeway, so long as it exercises good-faith.[2]

Excerpts of three investigative transcripts follow: The first is the testimony of Mr. Guy Fauré, Mamma.com's chief executive officer; the second is Mr. Arnold Owen who was a key employee with Merriman Curhan Ford & Co. (hereafter referred to as Merriman or MCF)—MCF served as the financial intermediary or placement agent for the Mamma.com PIPE capital raising transaction; and the third is Mr. Cuban.

---

2. See Marc I. Steinberg and Ralph C. Ferrara, *Securities Practice: Federal and State Enforcement* § 3:01 et seq. (2d ed. 2001 & 2018-2019 supp.).

As seen by the testimony below, Mr. Fauré's testimony was helpful to the Commission in determining whether to bring an enforcement action against Mr. Cuban. Note that the SEC, of course, also relied on email communications and other documentary evidence. One such email is excerpted in Chapter 1 of this book.

Mr. Fauré's testimony follows:

[SEC Enforcement Attorney Ms. Julie Riewe]: You testified previously that the Mamma.com Board instructed you to contact Mr. Cuban about the PIPE, is that right?

[Mr. Fauré]: That's right....

[Ms. Riewe]: Do you recall what the [Mamma.com Board] discussion was?

[Mr. Fauré]: I was instructed ... to give a call to Mr. Cuban, inform him that we had confidential information for him, and then proceed to invite him to participate in this PIPE transaction.

[Ms. Riewe]: Do you recall whether the Board discussed specifically what you should say to Mr. Cuban when you contacted him?

[Mr. Fauré]: No.

[Ms. Riewe]: Would it be fair to say, even if you don't recall the specific Board discussion ..., that the point of discussion about inviting Mr. Cuban to participate ... was to make sure that he understood you had to keep the PIPE information confidential before you told it to him?

[Mr. Fauré]: Right. Yes....

[Ms. Riewe]: You testified previously that Mr. Cuban called you on your cell phone as you were walking through Mamma.com's Montreal headquarters on June 28, 2004. Is that right?

[Mr. Fauré]: Right.

[Ms. Riewe]: And you also testified that you prefaced the conversation by informing Mr. Cuban that you had confidential information to convey to him?

[Mr. Fauré]: Yes.

[Ms. Riewe]: Do you recall any of the words you used besides confidential? For instance, privileged or something like that?

[Mr. Fauré]: No.

[Ms. Riewe]: Do you recall what Mr. Cuban said in response when you told him you had confidential information to convey to him?

[Mr. Fauré]: I don't remember exact words. But there was some type of acknowledgment. If not, I wouldn't have proceeded. So it might have been "uh-hmm", "yes", "go ahead."

[Ms. Riewe]: So is it fair to say to summarize what you just said, that you would not have conveyed the PIPE information to Mr. Cuban if he had not said something, even though you don't recall what the exact words were, at the beginning of the call to indicate that he would keep the information confidential?

[Mr. Fauré]: Right.

[Ms. Riewe]: So after you told Mr. Cuban you had confidential information to convey to him, you said something—again, not recalling the exact words you used—to acknowledge that he would keep the information you were going to convey to him confidential?

[Mr. Fauré]: Well, again, I don't remember the exact words. But there was certainly an acceptance which said okay, yeah, go ahead. I understand you're going to give me confidential information....

[Ms. Riewe]: Do you recall whether you told [Mamma.com's Chairman of its Board of Directors] Mr. Goldman that Mr. Cuban had said something along the lines of "Well, now I'm screwed. I can't sell" during the phone call?

[Mr. Fauré]: Yes.

[Ms. Riewe]: Do you remember specifically what you told him?

[Mr. Fauré]: I'm sure I used the exact words. It was sort of a strong sentence, and then that's why it's one sentence I remember today....

[After the telephone call, Mr. Fauré sent an e-mail to Mr. Cuban providing him with the telephone number of Mr. Owen from MCF, the placement agent for the PIPE transaction.]

[Ms. Riewe]: At the time that you sent this email [to Mr. Cuban] were you relying on the fact that Mr. Cuban had acknowledged that he was restricted from trading in Mamma.com securities until the PIPE was publicly announced?

[Mr. Fauré]: Yes.... [I]n the same way when I called him and said I got confidential information....

[Ms. Riewe]: And is it fair to say conversely that if Mr. Cuban had not acknowledged in some way ... that he would keep the PIPE information confidential, you would not have sent this follow-up e-mail to him?

[Mr. Fauré]: Right.

[Ms. Riewe]: Do you recall at the time that you sent this e-mail what type of information you expected Mr. Owen [of MCF] to provide to Mr. Cuban?

[Mr. Fauré]: Not necessarily. But Mr. Owen was the gatekeeper of the information and our documents. So ... he could answer any question that Mr. Cuban would have had regarding that transaction....

[Ms. Riewe]: At the time that you sent this e-mail to Mr. Cuban ..., did you also rely on the fact that Mr. Cuban had acknowledged when he said something along the lines of "Now, I'm screwed, I can't sell" that he was restricted from trading in Mamma.com until the PIPE was publicly announced?

[Mr. Fauré]: Yes. I would say that was my understanding....

[Ms. Riewe]: Were you surprised [subsequently] to learn that [Mr. Cuban] had sold [his Mamma.com stock] before the PIPE was publicly announced?

[Mr. Fauré]: ... Yes.

[Ms. Riewe]: And why were you surprised?

[Mr. Fauré]: Because he had confidential information before this [PIPE transaction] was publicly announced....

[Ms. Riewe]: Were you also surprised because he told you in sum or substance that he wasn't going to sell before the public announcement?

[Mr. Fauré]: I assumed "I'm screwed, I can't sell" to mean ... that he knew that with confidential information he could not sell. Yes. I was surprised when I learned that he sold his shares.

[Ms. Riewe]: Because he had told you that he wouldn't?

[Mr. Fauré]: Right.[3]

Contrasted with the testimony of Mr. Fauré, the testimony of Mr. Arnold Owen of MCF (which served as the placement agent for the Mamma.com PIPE transaction) seemed more helpful to Mr. Cuban than to the SEC. Excerpts of Mr. Owen's SEC investigative testimony follow:

[Ms. Riewe]: Can you tell us what you remember from your [telephone] conversation with Mr. Cuban?

[Mr. Owen]: I just remember that he was very upset and I wanted to be off the call as quickly as possible....

[Ms. Riewe]: What is your understanding of why Mr. Cuban was upset?

[Mr. Owen]: I explained that ... we were effecting a transaction for Mamma. com and he got very upset about that.

[Ms. Riewe]: Was it your impression that Mr. Cuban knew about the PIPE information before you conveyed it to him?

[Mr. Owen]: Not that I'm aware of....

[Ms. Riewe]: Generally, do you remember anything [Mr. Cuban] said during the call apart from his tone?

[Mr. Owen]: Specific words, no.

[Ms. Riewe]: Okay. How about generally?

[Mr. Owen]: I'm just telling you the demeanor that he had, and that's what I remember.

[Ms. Riewe]: I'm trying to make sure there wasn't anything else you remember generally about what [Mr. Cuban] said. I appreciate the demeanor. You said he sounded angry.

[Mr. Owen]: I don't want to make up words. I don't want to make up words.

[Ms. Riewe]: I don't want you to make up words, but I need you to answer the question, whether you remember anything generally that he said during the call.

[Mr. Owen]: I'd be making up words....

[Ms. Riewe]: Did you preface the conversation with Mr. Cuban by telling him you had confidential information to convey to him?

[Mr. Owen]: No, I did not.

[Ms. Riewe]: Did anyone from Mamma.com ever tell you that Mr. Cuban had been asked to maintain the information about the impending PIPE transaction in confidence?

[Mr. Owen]: No.[4]

[3.] SEC Investigative Testimony of Guy Fauré at pages 7-10, 18, 26-29 (Sept. 27, 2007).

[4.] SEC Investigative Testimony of Arnold Owen at pages 41-44, 50 (Oct. 17, 2007).

In his SEC investigative deposition, Mr. Cuban testified that he neither agreed to maintain the confidentiality of the forthcoming Mamma.com PIPE transaction nor did he agree to refrain from selling his stock prior to the public disclosure of the transaction. Excerpts of Mr. Cuban's testimony follow.

[Ms. Riewe]: How did you learn about the [Mamma.com] PIPE ....?

[Mr. Cuban]: I had a conversation with a guy from MCF.... I asked questions to kind of get the facts because to me a PIPE is a ... huge red flag, and I was trying to determine that ... something's not kosher....

[Ms. Riewe]: Did the sales rep [Mr. Owen of MCF] ask you to participate in the PIPE?

[Mr. Cuban]: In the offering, yes.

[Ms. Riewe]: Did the sales rep [Mr. Owen of MCF] ask you to keep the information about the PIPE confidential?

[Mr. Cuban]: No, absolutely not.

[Ms. Riewe]: Did he use the word 'confidential' during that discussion?

[Mr. Cuban]: No....

[Ms. Riewe]: Did you have an understanding that you could not trade on the information that [Mr. Owen of MCF] was conveying to you until [the PIPE transaction] was publicly announced?

[Mr. Cuban]: No, no....

[Ms. Riewe]: ... Did you speak to anyone from Mamma.com about the PIPE at any point?

[Mr. Cuban]: I don't remember. I saw the reference in the documents ... that said I called [Mamma.com] about the PIPE, but I don't remember that conversation about it at all or if there was a conversation....

[Ms. Riewe]: [After showing Mr. Cuban an e-mail that Mr. Fauré sent to him that had Mr. Owens's telephone number, Ms. Riewe asks:] Does this refresh your recollection about whether you spoke to Mr. Fauré about the private placement?

[Mr. Cuban]: No, it doesn't....

[Ms. Riewe]: Do you have a recollection of telling Mr. Fauré something along the lines of "Now, I'm screwed. I can't sell."?

[Mr. Cuban]: No, no, absolutely not.[5]

III. WELLS SUBMISSION

A target of an investigation may submit a written statement (called a "Wells Submission"), often taking on the character of a brief, to the SEC's Division of Enforcement setting forth why an enforcement action should not be instituted

---

[5.] SEC Investigative Testimony of Mark Cuban at pages 36, 40, 42, 43, 47, 50, 60 (April 3, 2007).

against the target (irrespective of whether the target is an institution (such as a corporation or brokerage firm) or an individual). With respect to this process, the SEC has stated that a Wells Submission is helpful to the Commission "in connection with questions of policy and, on occasion, questions of law."[6] But nonetheless, "where a disagreement exists between the staff and a prospective defendant as to factual matters, it is likely that this [disagreement] can be resolved in an orderly manner only through litigation."[7] Hence, tactical considerations must be assessed as the making of a Submission can adversely affect the target—for example, the Submission "can reveal deficiencies in the [target's] case if the SEC elects to initiate an enforcement action, or it may later be used as an admission or for impeachment purposes."[8]

Mr. Cuban opted to provide a Wells Submission. In the Submission, he pointed out that he did not enter into an enforceable nondisclosure agreement. This failure, Mr. Cuban posited, contravened the terms of Mamma. com's engagement letter with its placement agent MCF and was not consistent with custom and practice. These circumstances, the Submission asserted, showed that Mamma.com did not have a reasonable expectation of confidentiality in transmitting the information regarding the forthcoming PIPE transaction to Mr. Cuban. *The pertinent language from Mr. Cuban's Wells Submission follows:*

> MCF was required under its Engagement Letter with Mamma.com to "obtain Nondisclosure Agreements" with potential investors in the PIPE transaction. To the extent Mamma.com believed Mr. Cuban was a potential investor . . . , Mamma.com was aware by reason of the Engagement Letter that obtaining a nondisclosure agreement with Mr. Cuban was necessary. Finally, Mamma.com knew or should have known that it was the [company's] burden (which it was under both U.S. and Canadian law) to obtain an explicit confidentiality agreement with Mr. Cuban. Indeed, the business and legal need for an explicit confidentiality agreement with Mr. Cuban could not have been more obvious. . . .[9]

---

6. SEC Securities Act Release No. 5310 (1972).

7. *Id.*

8. Marc I. Steinberg and Ralph C. Ferrara, *Securities Practice: Federal and State Enforcement* § 3:59 (2d ed. 2001).

[9.] Wells Submission of Mark Cuban at page 21 (Sept. 21, 2007). Interestingly, SEC Regulation FD, with certain exceptions, prohibits a company from making selective disclosure of material non-public information to financial intermediaries and its shareholders. One such exception is disclosure made pursuant to a confidentiality agreement whereby the recipient covenants not to convey the information or trade prior to adequate public dissemination of the information. In any event, Regulation FD was not applicable to Mamma.com as it was a Canadian company and a "foreign private issuer." See Securities Exchange Act Release No. 43154 (2000); Marc I. Steinberg, *Understanding Securities Law* § 11.08 (7th ed. 2018).

IV. SEC DECISION TO INSTITUTE ENFORCEMENT ACTION

After considering the pertinent facts and circumstances, the SEC determined to file an enforcement action against Mr. Cuban in federal district court. In that lawsuit, the Commission alleged that Mr. Cuban committed securities fraud when he engaged in illegal insider trading by selling his Mamma.com stock prior to public disclosure of the PIPE transaction. The next chapter of the book focuses on the SEC's Complaint as well as filings and motions related thereto.

CHAPTER 4

The SEC's Initiation of Litigation and Mark Cuban's Response

I. THE SEC'S COMPLAINT

After completing its investigation, the SEC decided to bring an enforcement action against Mr. Cuban in federal district court for allegedly engaging in illegal insider trading. The SEC requested a finding that Mr. Cuban committed securities fraud and sought an order that he be subject to disgorgement of amounts improperly made from the illegal trades, prejudgment interest, a money penalty, and injunctive relief. *The SEC's Complaint follows:*

IN THE UNITED STATES DISTRICT COURT
FOR THE NORTHERN DISTRICT OF TEXAS
DALLAS DIVISION

SECURITIES AND EXCHANGE COMMISSION   :

               Plaintiff,   :

v.   :

MARK CUBAN,   :

               Defendant.   :

COMPLAINT

Plaintiff Securities and Exchange Commission ("Commission") alleges as follows:

SUMMARY OF ALLEGATIONS

    1.   The Commission charges Defendant Mark Cuban ("Cuban") with committing securities fraud by engaging in illegal insider trading. Despite agreeing in June 2004 to keep material, non-public information about an impending stock offering by Mamma.com Inc. confidential, Cuban sold his entire stake in the company—600,000 shares—prior to the public announcement of the offering. By selling when he did, Cuban avoided losses in excess of $750,000.

    2.   By conduct detailed in this Complaint, Cuban violated Section 17(a) of the Securities Act of 1933 ("Securities Act") [15 U.S.C. § 77q(a)] and Section 10(b) of the Securities Exchange Act of 1934 ("Exchange Act") [15 U.S.C. § 78j(b)] and Rule 10b-5 thereunder [17 C.F.R. § 240.10b-5]. Unless enjoined, Cuban is likely to commit such violations again in the future.

    3.   The Commission seeks a judgment from the Court: (a) enjoining Cuban from engaging in future violations of the antifraud provisions of the federal securities laws; (b) ordering Cuban to disgorge, with prejudgment interest, the losses avoided as a result of the actions described herein; and (c) ordering Cuban to pay a civil money penalty pursuant to Section 21A of the Exchange Act [15 U.S.C. § 78u-1].

JURISDICTION AND VENUE

    4.   The Commission brings this action pursuant to Sections 20(b) and 20(d) of the Securities Act [15 U.S.C. §§ 77t(b) and 77t(d)], and Section 21(d) of the Exchange Act [15 U.S.C. § 78u(d)].

5.   The Court has jurisdiction over this action under Sections 20(b), 20(d), and 22(a) of the Securities Act [15 U.S.C. §§ 77t(b), 77t(d), and 77v(a)] and Sections 21(d), 21(e), 21A, and 27 of the Exchange Act [15 U.S.C. §§ 78u(d), 78u(e), 78u-1, and 78aa].

6.   Cuban, directly or indirectly, used the means of instruments of interstate commerce, the mails, or the facilities of a national securities exchange in connection with the acts described herein.

7.   Venue is proper because certain of the transactions, acts, practices, and courses of business occurred within this judicial district.

DEFENDANT

8.   **Mark Cuban**, age 50, resides in Dallas, Texas. Among other things, he owns the NBA's Dallas Mavericks franchise, HDNet, a national high-definition television network, and Landmark Theaters.

OTHER RELEVANT ENTITY

9.   **Mamma.com Inc.** was a foreign private issuer headquartered in Montreal, Québec, Canada. On June 8, 2007, Mamma.com Inc. shareholders voted to change the company's name from Mamma.com Inc. to Copernic Inc., and on June 21, 2007 the company's NASDAQ ticker symbol changed from MAMA to CNC.

STATEMENT OF FACTS

10.   In March 2004, Cuban acquired 600,000 shares of Mamma.com, a 6.3% stake in the company. After his acquisition, the company's chief executive officer and president ([Guy Fauré] "the CEO") was Cuban's primary point of contact at Mamma. com.

11.   During Spring 2004, Merriman Curhan Ford & Co. ("Merriman"), an investment bank, suggested that Mamma.com should consider raising capital through a private placement known as a PIPE ("private investment in public equity") offering. After consideration, the company decided to proceed with the PIPE and engaged Merriman to serve as the placement agent.

12.   At the end of June 2004, as the PIPE progressed toward closing, Mamma. com, at Merriman's suggestion, decided to invite Cuban, the company's then-largest known shareholder, to participate in the PIPE. The CEO [Fauré] was instructed to contact Cuban and to preface the conversation by informing Cuban that he had confidential information to convey to him in order to make sure that Cuban understood—before the information was conveyed to him—that he would have to keep the information confidential.

13.   On June 28, 2004, the CEO sent an email message to Cuban titled "Call me pls," in which he asked Cuban to call him "ASAP" and provided both his cellular and office telephone numbers. Cuban called four minutes later from the American Airlines Center in Dallas, home of the NBA's Dallas Mavericks, and spoke to the CEO [Fauré] for eight minutes and thirty-five seconds.

14. The CEO [Fauré] prefaced the call by informing Cuban that he had confidential information to convey to him, and Cuban agreed that he would keep whatever information the CEO intended to share with him confidential. The CEO, in reliance on Cuban's agreement to keep the information confidential, proceeded to tell Cuban about the PIPE offering. Cuban became very upset and angry during the conversation, and said, among other things, that he did not like PIPEs because they dilute the existing shareholders. At the end of the call, Cuban told the CEO "Well, now I'm screwed. I can't sell."

15. After speaking to Cuban, the CEO [Fauré] told the company's then-executive chairman about his conversation with Cuban, including the fact that Cuban was very upset and angry about the PIPE. Shortly thereafter, the executive chairman sent an email to the other Mamma.com board members updating them on various PIPE-related items, including the fact that the CEO had spoken to Cuban:

> Today, after much discussion, [the CEO] spoke to Mark Cuban about this equity raise and whether or not he would be interested in participating. As anticipated he initially "flew off the handle" and said he would sell his shares (recognizing that he was not able to do anything until we announce the equity) but then asked to see the terms and conditions which we have arranged for him to receive from one of the participating investor groups with which he has dealt in the past.

16. In reliance on Cuban's acceptance of a duty of confidentiality and his acknowledgment that he could not sell until after the public announcement, the CEO, several hours after their conversation, sent Cuban a follow-up email in which he wrote: "If you want more details about the private placement please contact ... [Merriman]" In his email, the CEO provided the Merriman sales representative's [Mr. Owen's] telephone number.

17. Using that telephone number, Cuban called the Merriman sales representative [Owen] later that afternoon and spoke to him for eight minutes about the PIPE. During that call, the salesman supplied Cuban with additional confidential details about the PIPE. In response to Cuban's questions, the salesman told him that the PIPE was being sold at a discount to the market price and that the offering included other incentives for the PIPE investors. Cuban was very upset and angry about the PIPE during the call.

18. One minute after hanging up with the Merriman sales representative, Cuban called his broker in Dallas and told the broker to sell his entire 600,000 share Mamma.com position. He told the broker "sell what you can tonight and just get me out the next day."

19. During after-hours trading on June 28, 2004, Cuban sold 10,000 of his 600,000 Mamma.com shares at an average cost per share of $13.4990.

20. The following morning, June 29, 2004, Mamma.com's executive chairman sent another email to the board. He wrote that "we did speak to Mark Cuban ... to find out if he had any interest in participating to the extent of maintaining his

[Mamma.com stock ownership] interest. His answers were: he would not invest, he does not want the company to make acquisitions, he will sell his shares which he cannot do until after we announce."

21. On June 29, 2004, Cuban sold his remaining 590,000 Mamma.com shares during regular trading at an average cost per share of $13.2937.

22. On June 29, 2004, at 6:00 p.m. after the markets had closed, Mamma.com publicly announced the PIPE offering.

23. On June 30, 2004, the first trading day following the public announcement, trading in Mamma.com opened at $11.89—down $1.215, or 9.3%, from the June 29, 2004 closing price of $13.105. The stock price on June 30, 2004 ultimately closed at $11.99, down $1.115, or 8.5%, from the June 29, 2004 closing price. Mamma.com continued to decline over the next week, closing at $8.00 on July 8, 2004 (down 39% from the June 29, 2004 closing price).

24. By selling his Mamma.com shares prior to the public announcement of the PIPE, Cuban avoided losses in excess of $750,000.

25. Cuban later publicly stated that he had sold his Mamma.com shares because the company was conducting a PIPE, which issued shares at a discount to the prevailing market price and also would have caused his ownership position to be diluted. Cuban never disclosed to Mamma.com that he was going to sell his shares prior to the public announcement of the PIPE.

26. Cuban sold his Mamma.com securities on the basis of material, non-public information he received from the CEO, and subsequently, from the Merriman sales representative. Cuban knew or was reckless in not knowing that he had received material, non-public information from Mamma.com and that he breached a duty of trust or confidence that he owed to Mamma.com when he sold on the basis of that information.

27. As a result of the conduct described herein, Cuban violated Section 17(a) of the Securities Act and Section 10(b) of the Exchange Act and Rule 10b-5 thereunder.

FIRST CLAIM
INSIDER TRADING IN CONNECTION WITH THE
PURCHASE OR SALE OF SECURITIES

Violations of Section 10(b) of the Exchange Act and Rule 10b-5 Thereunder

28. The Commission realleges and reincorporates paragraphs 1 through 27 as if fully set forth herein.

29. Cuban, with scienter, by use of the means or instrumentalities of interstate commerce or of the mails, in connection with the purchase or sale of securities: (a) employed devices, schemes, or artifices to defraud; (b) made untrue statements of material fact or omissions to state material facts necessary in order to make the statements made, in light of the circumstances under which they were made, not misleading; and/or (c) engaged in acts, practices or courses of business which operated or would operate as a fraud or deceit.

30. By reason of the actions alleged herein, Cuban violated Section 10(b) of the Exchange Act [15 U.S.C. § 78j(b)] and Rule 10b-5 thereunder [17 C.F.R. § 240.10b-5].

SECOND CLAIM
INSIDER TRADING IN THE OFFER OR SALE OF SECURITIES
Violations of Section 17(a) of the Securities Act

31. The Commission realleges and reincorporates paragraphs 1 through 30 as fully set forth herein.

32. Cuban, with scienter, by use of the means or instrumentalities of interstate commerce or of the mails, in the offer or sale of securities: (a) employed devices, schemes or artifices to defraud; (b) obtained money or property by means of untrue statements of material fact or omissions to state material facts necessary in order to make the statements made, in light of the circumstances under which they were made, not misleading; and/or (c) engaged in acts, practices or courses of business which operated or would operate as a fraud or deceit upon the purchasers of the securities offered and sold by Cuban.

33. By reason of the actions alleged herein, Cuban violated Section 17(a) of the Securities Act [15 U.S.C. § 77q(a)].

PRAYER FOR RELIEF

WHEREFORE, the Commission respectfully requests that the Court enter a judgment:

(i) Finding that Cuban violated the antifraud provisions of the federal securities laws as alleged herein;

(ii) Permanently enjoining Cuban from violating Section 17(a) of the Securities Act [15 U.S.C. § 77q(a)] and Section 10(b) of the Exchange Act [15 U.S.C. § 78j(b)] and Rule 10b-5 thereunder [17 C.F.R. § 240.10b-5];

(iii) Ordering Cuban to disgorge the losses avoided as a result of the actions alleged herein and to pay prejudgment interest thereon;

(iv) Ordering Cuban to pay a civil monetary penalty pursuant to Section 21A of the Exchange Act [15 U.S.C. § 78u-1]; and

(v) Granting such other relief as this Court may deem just and proper.

Dated: November 17, 2008

Respectfully submitted,

[Signed]

Kevin P. O'Rourke

. . . .

Securities and Exchange Commission
100 F Street, N.E.
Washington, D.C. 20549

II. THE CUBAN FRONTAL CHALLENGE

As anticipated, Mr. Cuban filed an Answer to the SEC's Complaint, deny-ing the Commission's substantive allegations that he engaged in illegal insider trading. In addition, he mounted a frontal challenge to the impartiality and fairness of the Commission's conduct, asserting in his Amended Answer:

> The SEC's claims for injunctive relief are barred by the doctrine of unclean hands because the SEC and its agents engaged in egregious acts of miscon-duct in connection with the investigation of its claims against Cuban to the prejudice of Mr. Cuban. Indeed, the SEC staff conducted its investigation in an unfair, biased and improper manner designed to prevent Mr. Cuban from being able to (a) successfully persuade the Commission not to bring this action and (b) mount an effective defense to the claims against him.

Thereupon, Mr. Cuban's Answer went into detail charging the SEC and its staff with misconduct. *First,* Mr. Cuban asserted that the SEC enforcement staff who investigated him "were committed to bringing this action against [him], regardless of what their investigation actually revealed." *The Amended Answer presented the following examples:*

> [1] Email correspondence among those in supervisory roles within the SEC Enforcement Division evidences a significant bias against Mr. Cuban, made manifest even before the SEC sought any formal action against him. Indeed, two weeks before the formal order of investigation was issued in this case, the SEC staff member supervising the investigation of Mr. Cuban sent an email with an unflattering set of photos of Mr. Cuban to the Director of Enforce-ment and the Chief Counsel of the Enforcement Division, prompting email responses of "charming" and "Now I feel fully informed. The picture with the money is particularly helpful and certainly speaks a 1,000 words (if not more)."

> [2] Prior to meeting with many of the critical witnesses in this matter, an SEC staff member responded to a comment by one of Mr. Cuban's lawyers regard-ing Mr. Cuban's sale of Mamma.com stock by stating that "Mr. Cuban takes irrational and silly risks every day."[1]

Second, Mr. Cuban asserted that the SEC staff "deliberately undermined and abused the Wells [Submission] process," thereby depriving Mr. Cuban of a fair opportunity to persuade the Commission from instituting an action against him. Mr. Cuban set forth the alleged misconduct as follows:

> [1] In May 2007, the SEC staff initiated a Wells call to Mr. Cuban's counsel. On that call, the staff announced that it planned to recommend [that] the Commission bring a civil enforcement action against Mr. Cuban. The staff told Mr. Cuban's counsel that its recommendation was supported by the evi-dentiary record. In particular, the staff stated, during a June 28, 2004 call between Mr. Cuban and Mr. Fauré (Mamma.com's CEO), Mr. Cuban agreed

---

[1.] Amended Answer of Mark Cuban at page 7 (Feb. 4, 2011).

to keep the information he received confidential and Mr. Fauré then created a contemporaneous document reflecting the existence of that agreement. In fact, the SEC did not have any evidence that Mr. Cuban entered into a confidentiality agreement and Mr. Fauré did not create any such contemporaneous document. Mr. Cuban's first Wells submission (setting forth the reasons why the Commission should not bring an action against him) assumed the existence of this supposed evidence.

[2] The SEC staff's decision to recommend the Commission bring a civil enforcement action against Mr. Cuban was made before the SEC's investigation was "substantially complete"—in contravention of procedures in the SEC Enforcement manual.

[3] Mr. Cuban's counsel submitted a second Wells submission in September 2007, while the SEC staff was still conducting witness interviews. Nevertheless, the staff informed Mr. Cuban's counsel that there could be no assurance that the submission would be given to the Commission. Although the staff, as part of this litigation, has informed Mr. Cuban that the submission was given to the Commission, Mr. Cuban has never received confirmation that the Commission actually reviewed and considered the document as part of its deliberative process.[2]

Third, as a final salvo, Mr. Cuban set forth a litany of illustrations where he alleged that the SEC staff "engaged in acts of outright investigative and litigation misconduct." As alleged in Mr. Cuban's Answer, these transgressions encompassed:

[1] An SEC staff member discouraged a key witness's counsel from making the witness available to speak with Mr. Cuban's counsel. The SEC was informed of this misconduct in September 2007, but apparently never conducted an investigation.

[2] The SEC staff threatened this same witness with perjury when, during his sworn testimony, the witness was unable to clearly recall certain statements he supposedly had made to the SEC in a phone interview conducted ten months before.

[3] In September 2007, the SEC staff sent a letter to Mamma.com stating that the SEC's separate investigation of the company had been closed. Less than two weeks later, the SEC staff took the sworn testimony of Mr. Fauré for the second time in an apparent effort to get him to change his earlier testimony concerning his June 28, 2004 call with Mr. Cuban.

[4] The SEC staff filed a complaint in this action asserting that Mr. Cuban had entered into a confidentiality agreement, despite the lack of any evidentiary support for the existence of such an agreement.[3]

[2.] Amended Answer of Mark Cuban at page 8 (Feb. 4, 2011).

[3.] Amended Answer of Mark Cuban at pages 8-9 (Fe. 4, 2011).

As detailed above, Mr. Cuban asserted the "unclean hands" defense against the SEC in his Amended Answer. In granting the Commission's motion to strike this affirmative defense of unclean hands, Judge Fitzwater held:

> The court concludes that this affirmative defense [of unclean hands] is not barred as matter of law. But to the extent it is available, it is only in strictly limited circumstances when the SEC's misconduct is egregious, the misconduct occurs before the SEC files the enforcement action, and the misconduct results in prejudice to the defense of the enforcement action that rises to a constitutional level and is established through a direct nexus between the misconduct and the constitutional injury. The court holds that Cuban has not adequately pleaded the prejudice prong of unclean hands under this exacting standard, and it grants the SEC's motion to strike.[4]

Accordingly, Mr. Cuban's "unclean hands" defense failed. Nonetheless, it represented "a shot across the bow," confirming to the SEC that contentious litigation would ensue.

III. *PRO HAC VICE*

Many of the attorneys who represented the SEC and Mr. Cuban were not licensed in the state of Texas. These attorneys also were not admitted in the federal district court for the Northern District of Texas where the case was being tried. From the SEC, several attorneys were from the Commission's "home" office in Washington D.C. Many of Mr. Cuban's lawyers were practicing in New York City and Washington D.C. Accordingly, each such lawyer was required to apply for admission *pro hac vice*—referring "to a lawyer who has not been admitted to practice in a particular jurisdiction but who is admitted there temporarily for the purpose of conducting a particular case."[5] The application below was that of Mr. Ralph C. Ferrara who represented Mr. Cuban in this litigation. Mr. Ferrara, who was my supervisor at the SEC, is having an illustrious career—as General Counsel of the SEC in the 1980s and thereafter as an esteemed partner in a number of prestigious global law firms.

[4.] Memorandum Opinion and Order at page 1 (July 18, 2011).

5. *Black's Law Dictionary* 1405 (10th ed. 2014).

IN THE UNITED STATES DISTRICT COURT
FOR THE NORTHERN DISTRICT OF TEXAS
DALLAS DIVISION

SEC	
Plaintiff,	
v.	**3:08-CV-02050-D** **Case Number**
MARK CUBAN,	
Defendant.	

APPLICATION AND ORDER FOR ADMISSION *PRO HAC VICE*

I.   Applicant is an attorney and a member of the law firm of (or practices under the name of)

    Dewey & LeBoeuf LLP, with offices at 1101 New York Avenue, NW,
                                          (Street Address)
    Washington,   D.C.,   20005,   202 346 8000.
      (City)   (State) (Zip Code) (Telephone No.)

II.   Applicant will sign all pleadings with the name Ralph C. Ferrara.

III.   Applicant has been retained personally or as a member of the above-named firm by Mark Cuban.

(List All Parties Represented)

to provide legal representation in connection with the above-styled matter now pending before the United States District Court, for the Northern District of Texas.

IV.   Applicant is a member in good standing of the bar of the highest court of the state of Wash. D.C. [and other states], where Applicant regularly practices law.

    Bar license number: ----------   Admission date: 11/23/70

V.   Applicant has also been admitted to practice before the following courts:

Court:	Admission Date:	Active or Inactive
[States listed]	[Dates listed]	[Status listed]

VI.   Applicant has never involuntarily lost, temporarily or permanently, the right to practice before any court or tribunal, or resigned in lieu of discipline, except as provided below:

      N/A

VII.   Applicant has never been subject to grievance proceedings or involuntary removal proceedings—regardless of outcome—while a member of the bar of any state or federal court or tribunal that requires admission to practice, except as provided below.

      N/A

VIII.   Applicant has not been charged, arrested, or convicted of a criminal offense or offenses, except as provided below (omit minor traffic offenses):

      N/A

IX.   Applicant has filed for *pro hac vice* admission in the United States District Court for the Northern District of Texas during the past three (3) years in the following matters:

      Date of Application   Case No. And Style

      _____   _____

      _____   _____

(If necessary, attach statement of additional applications.)

X.   Local counsel of record associated with Applicant in this matter is <u>Paul Coggins</u> who has offices at <u>1717 Main Street, Suite 5000, Dallas, Texas 75201</u>

                                       (Address)

      <u>214-747-5070</u>
      (Telephone No.)

XI.   Check the appropriate box below.

For Application in a Civil Case

✓   Applicant has read *Dondi Properties Corp. v. Commerce Savs. & Loan Ass'n,* 121 F.R.D. 284 (N.D. Tex. 1988) (en banc), and the local civil rules of this court and will comply with the standards of practice adopted in *Dondi* and with the local civil rules.

For Application in a Criminal Case

___   Applicant has read and will comply with the local criminal rules of this court.

XII.   Applicant respectfully requests to be admitted to practice in the United States District Court for the Northern District of Texas for this cause only.

SIGNED this <u>21</u> day of <u>November, 2008</u>.

                                <u>Ralph C. Ferrara</u>
                                Printed Name of Applicant

                                [Signed]
                                Signature

I hereby certify that I have served a true and correct copy of this document upon each attorney of record and the original upon the clerk of court accompanied by a $25.00 filing fee on this <u>24th</u> day of <u>November, 2008</u>.

Ralph C. Ferrara
Printed Name of Applicant

[Signed]
Signature

ORDER

The Court, having considered the above Application for Admission *Pro Hac Vice*, orders that:

  ✓ the application be granted. The Clerk of Court shall deposit the application fee to the account of the Non-Appropriated Fund of this Court.

      the application be denied. The Clerk of Court shall return the admission fee to the Applicant.

<u>November 25, 2008</u>

[Signed]
JUDICIAL OFFICER
Sidney A. Fitzwater

In the application *pro hac vice*, the applicant confirms that he or she (1) has read the *Dondi Properties* decision as well as the court's local civil rules and (2) will comply with the standards of practice enunciated in *Dondi Properties* as well as with the local civil rules. In *Dondi Properties*, the federal district court for the Northern District of Texas convened en banc and adopted the following standards of practice to be followed by lawyers who appear in civil actions in that District:

(A) In fulfilling his or her primary duty to the client, a lawyer must be ever conscious of the broader duty to the judicial system that serves both attorney and client.

(B) A lawyer owes, to the judiciary, candor, diligence and utmost respect.

(C) A lawyer owes, to the opposing counsel, a duty of courtesy and cooperation, the observance of which is necessary for the efficient administration of our system of justice and the respect of the public it serves.

(D) A lawyer unquestionably owes, to the administration of justice, the fundamental duties of personal dignity and professional integrity.

(E) Lawyers should treat each other, the opposing party, the court, and members of the court staff with courtesy and civility and conduct themselves in a professional manner at all times.

(F) A client has no right to demand that counsel abuse the opposite party or indulge in offensive conduct. A lawyer shall always treat adverse witnesses and suitors with fairness and due consideration.

(G) In adversary proceedings, clients are litigants and though ill feeling may exist between clients, such ill feeling should not influence a lawyer's conduct, attitude, or demeanor towards opposing lawyers.

(H) A lawyer should not use any form of discovery, or the scheduling of discovery, as a means of harassing opposing counsel or counsel's client.

(I) Lawyers will be punctual in communications with others and in honoring scheduled appearances, and will recognize that neglect and tardiness are demeaning to the lawyer and to the judicial system.

(J) If a fellow member of the Bar makes a just request for cooperation, or seeks scheduling accommodation, a lawyer will not arbitrarily or unreasonably withhold consent.

(K) Effective advocacy does not require antagonistic or obnoxious behavior and members of the Bar will adhere to the higher standard of conduct which judges, lawyers, clients, and the public may rightfully expect.[6]

IV. THE FAILED ATTEMPT AT SETTLEMENT RESOLUTION

Pursuant to Rule 26(f) of the Federal Rules of Civil Procedure, the parties conferred to consider the possibility of settlement. Not surprisingly, no such resolution was reached. In the Rule 26(f) report and proposal submitted by the SEC and Mr. Cuban to the federal district court, the parties explained:

> The parties discussed settlement but were unable to reach a mutually agreeable resolution. Counsel for the Plaintiff SEC stated that any proposed settlement would be subject to review and approval by the full Commission. Counsel for the Plaintiff further stated that a settlement would need to be consistent with the Commission's insider trading enforcement standards. Defendant Cuban stated that settlement on the SEC's terms was unacceptable. The parties recognize that they have an obligation to the Court to continue to give good faith consideration to settlement. Defendant Cuban

---

[6.] *Dondi Properties Corp. v. Commerce Savings & Loan Association*, 121 F.R.D. 284, 287-288 (N.D. Tex. 1988) (en banc). See Marc I. Steinberg, *Lawyering and Ethics for the Business Attorney* (4th ed. 2016) (West Academic Press).

believes that if either party changes its settlement stance, the parties should discuss settlement further.

. . . .

The parties agreed that it is not advisable to refer this case for alternative dispute resolution or to conduct a court-supervised settlement conference at this stage of the litigation.[7]

V. MOTION FOR JUDICIAL NOTICE

In connection with filing his motion to dismiss the SEC's Complaint, Mr. Cuban also filed a motion for the Court to take judicial notice of certain documents. This motion was granted by Judge Fitzwater. *Mr. Cuban's Motion for Judicial Notice follows.*

MARK CUBAN'S MOTION FOR JUDICIAL NOTICE

Mark Cuban files this motion requesting that the Court take judicial notice of certain documents cited in his motion to dismiss the Complaint pursuant to Federal Rule of Civil Procedure 12(b)(6) ("motion to dismiss"). Mr. Cuban's motion to dismiss is being filed on the same day as the instant motion.

In deciding Mark Cuban's motion to dismiss, the Court may consider matters of which it may take judicial notice. See Fed. R. Evid. 201(f) ("Judicial notice may be taken at any stage of the proceeding."). The Fifth Circuit has held that when deciding a motion to dismiss a claim for securities fraud on the pleadings—such as Mr. Cuban's motion to dismiss—a court may consider "public disclosure documents required by law to be, and that have been, filed with the SEC, and documents that the plaintiffs either possessed or knew about and upon which they relied in bringing the suit" without converting the motion into one for summary judgment. . . . In addition, "[w]hen a plaintiff quotes from a document used as a foundation for allegations in the complaint, the Court may examine the entire document to review a motion to dismiss." . . .

In considering Mr. Cuban's motion to dismiss, Mr. Cuban requests that the Court take judicial notice of the following documents attached as exhibits to this motion:

1. Excerpt of Mamma.com Inc., Annual Report (Form 20-F) (May 14, 2004) (Ex. 1) [filed with the SEC];

[7.] Rule 26(f) Report and Proposal at pages 1-2 (Feb. 12, 2009).

2. Mark Cuban Schedule 13G (March 15, 2004) (Ex. 2) [filed with the SEC];
3. E-mail from David Goldman on June 28, 2004 (cited in Compl. ¶ 15) (Ex. 3);
4. Excerpt of Mamma.com Inc., Annual Report (Form 20-F) (May 27, 2005) (Ex. 4) [filed with the SEC];
5. Mark Cuban Schedule 13G (July 1, 2004) (Ex. 5) [filed with the SEC].

Exhibits 1, 2, 4, and 5 above are relevant public disclosure documents which were required to be filed and were filed with the SEC, and are therefore appropriate for the Court's consideration [with respect to ruling on Mr. Cuban's motion to dismiss the Complaint]. . . . Exhibit 3 above is an e-mail quoted in the Complaint (but was not attached to the Complaint). It is appropriate for the Court to take judicial review of the e-mail because it is a document the SEC knew about and relied upon in bringing this suit against Mr. Cuban, and the SEC quoted from it as a foundation of its allegations in the Complaint. . . .

In the event that the Court is of the opinion that consideration of any of the documents that are the subject of this motion would require the Court to treat Mr. Cuban's motion to dismiss as a motion for summary judgment under Rule 56, Mr. Cuban withdraws his request for judicial notice of those documents and asks that the Court not consider them in deciding his motion to dismiss. . . .

Under clear Fifth Circuit precedent, the Court may take judicial notice of SEC filings and the e-mail quoted in the Complaint in deciding Mark Cuban's motion to dismiss without converting his motion into a summary judgment motion. Therefore, Mark Cuban respectfully requests that the Court grant his motion and take judicial notice of the documents listed above in considering his motion to dismiss.

VI. THE MOTION TO DISMISS THE SEC'S COMPLAINT

Mr. Cuban filed a motion to dismiss the SEC's Complaint which the Commission opposed. *Excerpts of the briefs submitted to the district court follow.*

[A] SEC's Position

In its Memorandum of Law opposing Mr. Cuban's motion to dismiss, the SEC asserted:

This case involves the application of well-settled insider trading principles to straightforward allegations of fraud. As alleged in the Complaint, Mamma.com Inc. ("Mamma.com") contacted defendant Mark Cuban, the company's then-largest known shareholder, to ask—confidentially—if he wished to participate in a private offering. Cuban agreed to keep the offering information confidential. In reliance on

Cuban's acceptance of a duty of confidentiality, the company conveyed material, nonpublic offering information to the defendant. Upset and angry that Mamma.com was conducting the offering, Cuban breached his agreement of confidentiality and promptly sold his entire 600,000 share Mamma.com position before the offering was publicly announced. In so doing, defendant fraudulently avoided losses in excess of $750,000 when Mamma.com's stock price declined after the public announcement. Cuban's trading in Mamma.com took advantage of precisely the type of informational advantage stemming from contrivance, as opposed to research or skill, with which the Supreme Court was concerned when it adopted the misappropriation theory of insider trading under Section 10(b) of the Securities Exchange Act of 1934....

Cuban mischaracterizes this case as a "test case" attempting to "impermissibly expand the scope" of misappropriation law. Yet, the reality is that Cuban's agreement to keep the offering information confidential and his immediate and bold breach of that agreement is a textbook example of unlawful misappropriation. This case involves no new theory of liability or expansion of existing law; the Court need only apply black letter law and an unambiguous rule consistent with that law. Indeed, defendant's motion—by inappropriately focusing primarily on irrelevant state law fiduciary principles, choice of law, and agency rule promulgation—essentially concedes the impossibility of his task under well-settled misappropriation law.

As demonstrated conclusively herein, under that well-settled law and a clear Commission rule, a confidentiality agreement establishes a duty under the misappropriation theory.[8]

[B] Mr. Cuban's Position

Mr. Cuban's position that his motion to dismiss should be granted is succinctly stated in the opening paragraph of his reply brief:

Even assuming the truth of the facts as alleged in the [SEC's] Complaint, Mark Cuban did not engage in insider trading when he sold his Mamma.com stock because a confidentiality agreement alone does not establish a fiduciary or fiduciary-like duty. The SEC spends its entire Opposition distorting or ignoring controlling Supreme Court precedent and Texas precedent on this issue. That should tell the Court all it needs to know about the strength of the SEC's position. Mr. Cuban's motion to dismiss should be granted with prejudice.[9]

[8.] Plaintiff Securities and Exchange Commission's Memorandum of Law in Opposition to Defendant Mark Cuban's Motion to Dismiss at pages 1-2 (Feb. 27, 2009).

[9.] Reply Brief of Mark Cuban in Support of Motion to Dismiss at page 1 (March 20, 2009).

[C] Brief of *Amici Curiae* Supporting the Motion to Dismiss

It is relatively unusual that a brief of *amici curiae* is filed at the federal district court level when a motion to dismiss is pending. In this case, five law professors with superb credentials (Professors Steven Bainbridge—UCLA, Alan R. Bromberg—SMU, Allen Ferrell—Harvard, M. Todd Henderson—Chicago, and Jonathan R. Macey—Yale) filed a brief of *amici curiae* supporting Mr. Cuban's Motion to Dismiss. *This relatively short brief targeted the key issue at stake in the motion to dismiss and is included at this point.*

AMENDED BRIEF OF *AMICI CURIAE* IN SUPPORT OF DEFENDANT'S MOTION TO DISMISS

Section 10(b) of the Securities Exchange Act of 1934 creates fraud liability for conduct involving a "deceptive device or contrivance" used "in connection with" the purchase or sale of securities. In *U.S. v. O'Hagan*, 521 U.S. 642 (1997), the U.S. Supreme Court found that Section 10(b) permits liability for insider trading based on the misappropriation theory. Under that theory, "a fiduciary's undisclosed, self-serving use of a principal's information to purchase or sell securities, in breach of a duty of loyalty and confidentiality, defrauds the principal of the exclusive use of that information." The [Supreme] Court emphasized, consistent with its earlier insider trading rulings, that *only* if the defendant has breached a fiduciary or similar relationship of trust and confidence can the defendant be found to have engaged in the requisite deception through nondisclosure.

In the context of a business relationship, a confidentiality agreement alone is insufficient to create a fiduciary or similar relationship of trust and confidence between the parties. Under both state and federal common law, a confidentiality agreement alone creates only an obligation to maintain the secrecy of the information, not a fiduciary or fiduciary-like duty to act loyally to the source of the information. In the absence of any other facts or circumstances indicating the existence of a fiduciary or similar relationship of trust and confidence, there can be no insider trading liability based on the misappropriation theory pursuant to Section 10(b).

After the *O'Hagan* decision, the Securities and Exchange Commission (SEC) promulgated Rule 10b5-2. The adopting release states that the rule was designed to address when "a breach of a family or other non-business relationship may give rise to liability under the misappropriation theory of insider trading." Federal courts likewise have found that Rule 10b5-2 does not apply in the context of business relationships.

Rule 10b5-2 purports to provide a non-exclusive list of three situations in which a person is deemed to have a "duty of trust or confidence" for purposes of applying the theory. The first situation in which a person is deemed to have a "duty of trust or confidence" is "[w]henever a person agrees to maintain information in confidence."

Assuming that Rule 10b5-2(b)(1) is even applicable to business relationships, a confidentiality agreement alone would be insufficient to establish the existence of a fiduciary or similar relationship of trust and confidence. The SEC's use of the phrase "trust or confidence" in Rule 10b5-2(b)(1), as opposed to the *O'Hagan* standard of "trust and confidence," suggests that the SEC sought to go beyond the *O'Hagan* articulation of the misappropriation theory. If Rule 10b5-2(b)(1) creates potential liability based *solely* on the existence of a confidentiality agreement, the rule is an invalid exercise of the agency's rulemaking authority. Interpreted in this manner, Rule 10b5-2(b)(1) directly contradicts the Supreme Court's rulings on the scope of Section 10(b) liability for insider trading because it would create liability without the existence of a fiduciary or similar relationship of trust and confidence. The SEC does not have the authority to adopt rules that impermissibly expand the scope of Section 10(b) liability.[10]

[D] The District Court Grants the Motion to Dismiss

After reviewing the briefs submitted and hearing oral argument, Judge Fitzwater granted Mr. Cuban's motion to dismiss but allowed the SEC to replead. *In his Order, Judge Fitzwater opined:*

> Because [SEC] Rule 10b5-2(b)(1) attempts to predicate misappropriation theory liability on a mere confidentiality agreement lacking a non-use component, the SEC cannot rely on it to establish Cuban's liability under the misappropriation theory. To permit liability based on Rule 10b5-2(b)(1) would exceed the SEC's § 10(b) authority to proscribe conduct that is deceptive....
>
> Because the SEC has failed to allege that Cuban undertook a duty to refrain from trading on information about the impending PIPE offering, and because the SEC cannot rely on the duty imposed by Rule 10b5-2(b)(1) alone, Cuban cannot be held liable under the misappropriation theory of insider trading liability, even accepting all well-pleaded facts as true and viewing them in the light most favorable to the SEC. The court therefore grants Cuban's motion to dismiss the complaint under Rule 12(b)(6).[11]

[E] The SEC's Appeal and the Fifth Circuit's Reversal

Not surprisingly, the SEC opted to appeal the district court's dismissal of its Complaint against Mr. Cuban. *The SEC's Notice of Appeal follows.*

[10.] Amended Brief of *Amici Curiae* in Support of Defendant's Motion to Dismiss (Feb. 5, 2009) (citations omitted).

11. SEC v. Cuban, 634 F. Supp. 2d 713, 731 (N.D. Tex. 2009).

IN THE UNITED STATES DISTRICT COURT
FOR THE NORTHERN DISTRICT OF TEXAS
DALLAS DIVISION

SECURITIES AND EXCHANGE COMMISSION	:
Plaintiff,	:
v.	: Civil Action N.: 3-08-CV-2050-D (SAF)
MARK CUBAN,	:
Defendant.	:

PLAINTIFF SECURITIES AND EXCHANGE COMMISSION'S
NOTICE OF APPEAL

Notice is hereby given that the Securities and Exchange Commission, plaintiff in the above-named case, hereby appeals to the United States Court of Appeals for the Fifth Circuit from the final judgment entered on August 13, 2009, as amended and then entered on August 14, 2009.

Dated: October 7, 2009

Respectfully submitted,

s/ Kevin P. O'Rourke

Kevin P. O'Rourke (D.C. Bar No. _____)

Toby M. Galloway

Texas Bar No. _____

Securities and Exchange Commission

Burnett Plaza, Suite 1900

801 Cherry Street, Unit 18

Fort Worth, TX 76102

Julie M. Riewe (D.C. Bar No. _____)

Adam S. Aderton (D.C. Bar No. _____)

Securities and Exchange Commission

100 F Street, N.E.

Washington, D.C. 20549

Attorneys for Plaintiff

Securities and Exchange Commission

The U.S. Court of Appeals for the Fifth Circuit vacated and remanded the district court's order granting Mr. Cuban's motion to dismiss. The Fifth Circuit's decision—*SEC v. Cuban*, 620 F.3d 551 (5th Cir. 2010)—is contained in Chapter 2 of the book and may be reviewed at this time.

The Fifth Circuit's decision thus signified that the SEC's enforcement action against Mr. Cuban would proceed. Accordingly, the next chapter focuses on the discovery phase of this litigation.

CHAPTER 5

Onward to Discovery

This chapter focuses on a number of subjects related to the conducting of discovery by the parties. Excerpts of deposition transcripts are few due to the book's length limitations and that many of these witnesses also testified at trial. The chapter begins with a look at the Scheduling Order.

I. THE SCHEDULING ORDER

The Scheduling Order was entered by the federal district court on January 6, 2011. Although it was subsequently amended to modify certain of the dates originally set forth, the January 6th Scheduling Order is excerpted below as it appears to be the most comprehensive version. *The Scheduling Order, as excerpted, follows.*

SCHEDULING ORDER

Pursuant to Fed. R. Civ. P. 16(b) and 26(f), the court's Civil Justice Expense and Delay Reduction Plan, and the local civil rules now in effect, and after having considered any proposals submitted by the parties, the court enters this scheduling order. If a date specified in this order falls on a Saturday, Sunday, legal holiday, or date on which the clerk's office is closed by direction of the court or is otherwise inaccessible, the deadline is the next day that is not one of the aforementioned days.

1. ELECTRONIC FILING OPTIONAL/"JUDGE'S COPY" REQUIREMENTS

Pursuant to N.D. Tex. Civ. R. 5.1(e), the court grants the parties the option of filing pleadings, motions, or other papers on paper. Filing by electronic means is permitted, not required.

Pursuant to N.D. Tex. Civ. R. 5.1(b), when a pleading, motion, or other paper is submitted on paper, the party must file an original and one judge's copy with the clerk. When a pleading, motion, or other paper is filed by electronic means, the party must submit the judge's copy—i.e., a paper copy of the electronic filing—using the procedures for Chief Judge Fitzwater specified on the court's website....

A party making an electronic filing should assume that the court is unaware of the filing until the judge's copy has been physically received in chambers, even if the filing requests "emergency," "expedited," or similar relief or provides for agreed relief concerning a fast-approaching deadline. When such relief is sought, counsel should arrange to have the judge's copy promptly delivered to chambers and should alert the court's staff telephonically to expect the delivery.

II. PRETRIAL SCHEDULE

The parties must comply with each of the following deadlines unless a deadline is modified by court order upon a showing of good cause....

A. Joinder of Parties

A party must file a motion for leave to join other parties no later than **March 1, 2011**.

B. Expert Witnesses

A party with the burden of proof on a claim or defense must designate expert witnesses and otherwise comply with Rule 26(a)(2) no later than **June 1, 2011**.

C. Rebuttal Expert Witnesses

A party who intends to offer expert evidence "intended solely to contradict or rebut evidence on the same subject matter identified by another party under Rule 26(a)(2)(B)" must designate expert witnesses and otherwise comply with Rule 26(a)(2) no later than **August 1, 2011**.

D. Amendment of Pleadings

A party must file a motion for leave to amend pleadings no later than **August 30, 2011**.

E. Completion of Discovery, Filing of Joint Estimate of Trial Length and Status Report

The parties must complete discovery and file a joint estimate of trial length and joint status report concerning the progress of settlement negotiations no later than **September 30, 2011**.

F. Summary Judgment Motions

A party must file a motion for summary judgment no later than **October 31, 2011**.

. . . .

G. Motions Not Otherwise Covered

A party must file a motion not otherwise covered by this order no later than **February 1, 2012**. . . .

III. TRIAL SETTING ORDER

The court will set the case for trial by separate order. The order will establish trial-type deadlines. It will also contain modifications to the requirements of the local civil rules regarding such matters as submitting the joint pretrial order, and filing witness lists, exhibit lists, and deposition excerpt designations.

IV. TRIAL LIMITS

Section VII of the court's Civil Justice Expense and Delay Reduction Plan permits the presiding judge to "limit the length of trial, the number of witnesses each party may present for its case, the number of exhibits each party may have admitted into evidence, and the amount of time each party may have to examine witnesses." Rule 16(c)(15) permits the court to take appropriate action to "establish[h] a reasonable limit on the time allowed for presenting evidence[.]" Before commencement of the trial of this case, the court will impose time limits on the presentation of evidence, and may set other limits permitted by the Plan. In conducting discovery and other pretrial proceedings in this case, counsel should account for the fact that such limitations will be imposed. . . .

SO ORDERED
January 6, 2011.

[Signed]
SIDNEY A. FITZWATER
CHIEF JUDGE

II. INADVERTENT PRODUCTION OF PRIVILEGED DOCUMENTS— STIPULATED PROTECTIVE ORDER

In litigation, the inadvertent production to adverse parties of materials that come within the attorney-client privilege, work product doctrine, or other ground of exemption from discovery occurs with some frequency. To avoid issues of waiver of privilege or waiver of other protective evidentiary doctrine, the parties commonly execute a protective order that ensures that such inadvertent production will not constitute a waiver. *The Stipulated Protective Order in this case follows.*

STIPULATED PROTECTIVE ORDER

WHEREAS, the parties have agreed to produce documents, including electronically stored information ("ESI"), and information responsive to each other's discovery requests that are not privileged or otherwise exempted from discovery under the Federal Rule of Evidence, the Federal Rules of Civil Procedure, or other federal or state statutes or the common law;

WHEREAS, the parties acknowledge that, despite each party's best efforts to conduct a thorough preproduction review of all documents and ESI, some privileged, work product, or other material exempted from discovery may be inadvertently disclosed to the other party during the course of this litigation;

WHEREAS, the parties desire to establish a mechanism to avoid waiver of privilege or any other applicable protective evidentiary doctrine as a result of the inadvertent disclosure and to avoid time-consuming, expensive and wasteful motion practice;

IT IS HEREBY STIPULATED, AGREED AND ORDERED:

1. If documents or other information subject to a claim of attorney-client privilege, work product protection, or any other immunity from disclosure is produced or otherwise provided to the opposing party (hereinafter "inadvertently disclosed information"), such disclosure shall in no way constitute a waiver or forfeiture of any claim of privilege or work-product protection or other immunity for such information and/or its subject matter.

2. No party shall claim a waiver of any evidentiary privileges based on the fact that it has received inadvertently disclosed information.

3. In the event the producing party discovers that it had inadvertently disclosed privileged, work product or other information immune from discovery, the producing party shall have ten (10) days from the date of its discovery to notify the receiving party if it wishes to assert claims of privilege or other protection to that information;

4. In the event the producing party is informed by the receiving party that the producing party inadvertently disclosed privileged, work product or other information immune from discovery, the producing party shall have ten (10) days from the date it is informed to review the inadvertently produced information and notify the receiving party if it wishes to assert claims of privilege or other protection to that information;

5. If the producing party asserts a claim of privilege or other protection to inadvertently disclosed information, the receiving party shall immediately return or destroy all copies of or notes or other records that reflect

the inadvertently disclosed information, unless the receiving party decides to challenge the claim of privilege or other protection;

6. In the event that the receiving party challenges a claim of privilege or other protection to inadvertently disclosed information, the receiving party may retain one (1) copy of the inadvertently produced information for the sole purpose of seeking a court determination of the issue;

7. This agreement shall survive the final termination of this case regarding any retained documents or the contents thereof.

III. FRCP RULE 26(a) INITIAL DISCOVERY DISCLOSURES

With certain exceptions, a party must disclose to the other parties under Rule 26(a)(1) of the Federal Rules of Civil Procedure, "without awaiting a discovery request," specified information, including:

[T]he name and, if known, the address and telephone number of each individual likely to have discoverable information—along with the subjects of that information—that the disclosing party may use to support its claims or defenses, unless the use would be solely for impeachment; [and]

[A] copy—or a description by category and location—of all documents, electronically stored information, and tangible things that the disclosing party has in its possession, custody, or control and may use to support its claims and defenses, unless the use would be solely for impeachment. . . .

The excerpt that follows is the SEC's initial discovery disclosures pursuant to F.R.C.P. Rule 26(a) to Mr. Cuban.

PLAINTIFF SECURITIES AND EXCHANGE COMMISSION'S RULE 26(a) INITIAL DISCOVERY DISCLOSURES

Plaintiff Securities and Exchange Commission (the "SEC") makes its initial disclosures pursuant to Rule 26(a) of the Federal Rules of Civil Procedure.

1. Pursuant to Rule 26(a)(1)(A), plaintiff provides, as Attachment A, a list of individuals believed to have discoverable information that the SEC may use to support its claims, along with the last known address and telephone number of each individual so identified. Where any such individual has been represented by counsel, plaintiff provides counsel's name, address and telephone number.

2.   Pursuant to Rule 26(a)(1)(B), plaintiff provides, as Attachment B [not contained herein], an index of source documents obtained from Mark Cuban, source documents and data obtained by the SEC from non-governmental third parties, and transcripts of investigative testimony (and exhibits thereto) in the SEC's investigation, *In the Matter of Mamma.com Financing Transactions*, HO-10576. These documents are available in their original format (whether paper or electronic) for inspection and copying. The SEC has imaged these documents, and is producing them in a Concordance-ready format on the enclosed DVD Bates-stamped SEC-MC-DVD000001 (containing documents Bates-stamped SEC-MC0000001 through SEC-MC0003187 and SEC-MC-E0000001 through SEC-MC-E0007829).

3.   Pursuant to Rule 26(a)(1)(C), plaintiff submits that the requirement for a computation of damages is inapplicable. In addition to injunctive relief, plaintiff seeks disgorgement under the federal securities laws in an amount to be determined, but believed to be in excess of $750,000 plus prejudgment interest, and also seeks statutory penalties.

4.   Pursuant to Rule 26(a)(1)(D), plaintiff submits that it has no insurance agreements in connection with any judgment entered in this action....

ATTACHMENT A
PLAINTIFF'S LIST OF INDIVIDUALS BELIEVED TO HAVE DISCOVERABLE INFORMATION THAT PLAINTIFF MAY USE TO SUPPORT ITS CLAIMS

1.   Mark Cuban
c/o Paul E. Coggins, Esq.
Fish & Richardson LLP
1717 Main Street
Suite 5000
Dallas, TX 75201
(214) 292-4003

c/o Lyle Roberts, Esq.
Dewey & LeBoeuf LLP
1101 New York Avenue, N.W.
Washington, DC 20005
(202) 346-8020

Cuban is believed to have discoverable information related to his conduct alleged in the complaint.

2.   Mamma.com Inc.
c/o Michael E. Storck, Esq.
Lippes Mathias Wexler Friedman LLP
655 Main Street, Suite 300
Buffalo, NY 14203
(716) 853-5100

Mamma.com Inc. ("Mamma.com") was a foreign private issuer headquartered in Montreal, Québec, Canada. On June 8, 2007, Mamma.com shareholders voted to change the company's name from Mamma.com Inc. to Copernic Inc. ("Copernic"), and on June 21, 2007 the company's NASDAQ ticker symbol changed from MAMA to CNIC. Mamma.com is believed to have discoverable information concerning Cuban's investment in Mamma.com; Mamma.com's June 2004 private investment in public equity ("PIPE") offering; and Cuban's communications with Mamma.com.

3.   Guy Fauré
c/o Jason Brown, Esq.
Ropes & Gray LLP
1211 Avenue of the Americas
New York, NY 10036-8704
(212) 841-0478

Fauré is the former chief executive officer and president of Mamma.com. Fauré is believed to have discoverable information concerning the following subjects of information: the operation, management, and performance of Mamma.com; Mamma.com's June 2004 PIPE offering; and Cuban's communications with Mamma.com.

4.   David Goldman
c/o David C. Gustman, Esq.
Freeborn & Peters LLP
311 South Wacker Drive
Suite 3000
Chicago, IL 60606
(312) 360-6515

Goldman is the former executive chairman of Mamma.com and is the current chairman of Copernic. Goldman is believed to have discoverable information concerning the following subjects of information: the operation, management, and performance of Mamma.com; Mamma.com's June 2004 PIPE offering; and Cuban's communications with Mamma.com.

5.   **Daniel Bertrand**
       c/o David U. Gourevitch, Esq.
       Law Office of David U. Gourevitch, P.C.
       150 E. 58th Street, 34th Floor
       New York, NY 10017
       (212) 355-1300

Bertrand is the former chief financial officer and executive vice president of Mamma.com. Bertrand is believed to have discoverable information concerning the following subjects of information: the operation, management, and performance of Mamma.com; Mamma.com's June 2004 PIPE offering; and Cuban's communications with Mamma.com.

6.   **Irwin Kramer**
       c/o Michael E. Storck, Esq.
       Lippes Mathias Wexler Friedman LLP
       655 Main Street - Suite 300
       Buffalo NY 14203
       (716) 853-5100

Kramer is a former Mamma.com board member and current Copernic board member. Kramer is believed to have discoverable information concerning the following subjects of information: the operation, management, and performance of Mamma.com; Mamma.com's June 2004 PIPE offering; and Cuban's communications with Mamma.com.

7.   **Claude Forget**
       c/o Michael E. Storck, Esq.
       Lippes Mathias Wexler Friedman LLP
       655 Main Street - Suite 300
       Buffalo NY 14203
       (716) 853-5100

Forget is a former Mamma.com board member and current Copernic board member. Forget is believed to have discoverable information concerning the following subjects of information: the operation, management, and performance of Mamma.com; Mamma.com's June 2004 PIPE offering; and Cuban's communications with Mamma.com.

8.   **Dr. David Schwartz**
       c/o Michael E. Storck, Esq.
       Lippes Mathias Wexler Friedman LLP
       655 Main Street - Suite 300
       Buffalo NY 14203
       (716) 853-5100

Schwartz is a former Mamma.com board member and current Copernic board member. Schwartz is believed to have discoverable information concerning the following subjects of information: the operation, management, and performance of Mamma.com; Mamma.com's June 2004 PIPE offering; and Cuban's communications with Mamma.com.

9.   Robert Raich
c/o Ira L. Sorkin, Esq.
Dickstein Shapiro LLP
1177 Avenue of the Americas
New York, NY 10036-2714
(212) 277-6576

Raich is a former Mamma.com board member. Raich is believed to have discoverable information concerning the following subjects of information: the operation, management, and performance of Mamma.com; Mamma.com's June 2004 PIPE offering; and Cuban's communications with Mamma.com.

10.   Merriman Curhan Ford & Co.
c/o Christopher Aguilar, Esq.
General Counsel/Chief Compliance Officer
600 California Street, 9th Floor
San Francisco, CA 94108
(415) 248-5634

Merriman Curhan Ford & Co. ("Merriman") is a registered broker-dealer. Merriman is believed to have discoverable information concerning Mamma.com's June 2004 PIPE offering and Cuban's communications with Mamma.com and Merriman.

11.   Arnold Owen
c/o Christopher Aguilar, Esq.
General Counsel/Chief Compliance Officer
600 California Street, 9th Floor
San Francisco, CA 94108
(415) 248-5634

Owen is a former managing director at Merriman. Owen is believed to have discoverable information concerning Mamma.com's June 2004 PIPE offering and Cuban's communications with Mamma.com and Merriman.

12.   UBS Financial Services Inc.
c/o Lawrence B. Carlson, Esq.
Associate General Counsel
UBS Financial Services Inc.
51 West 52nd Street, 16th Floor
New York, NY 10019
(212) 882-5033

UBS Financial Services Inc. ("UBS") is a registered broker-dealer. UBS is believed to have discoverable information concerning Cuban's purchase and sale of Mamma. com shares.

13. Charles McKinney
c/o Lawrence B. Carlson, Esq.
Associate General Counsel
UBS Financial Services Inc.
51 West 52nd Street, 16th Floor
New York, NY 10019
(212) 882-5033

McKinney is a former senior vice president at UBS. McKinney is believed to have discoverable information concerning Cuban's purchase and sale of Mamma.com shares.

* * *

To the extent not otherwise identified above, plaintiff may also rely on individuals identified in the documents or data described in Attachment B to Plaintiff's Rule 26(a) Initial Discovery Disclosures.

IV. MOTIONS TO COMPEL PRODUCTION OF DOCUMENTS

Not surprisingly, Mr. Cuban was not satisfied with the production of documents provided to him by the SEC. He asserted that he was entitled to several key categories of documents that the Commission refused to provide. With respect to Mr. Cuban's production to the SEC, the Commission contended that Mr. Cuban should be ordered to provide a "privilege log" for materials withheld from the SEC from December 31, 2006 through March 10, 2011. *In the following "Memorandum Opinion and Order", Judge Fitzwater ruled on the parties' motions.*

MEMORANDUM OPINION AND ORDER

The September 28, 2011 amended second motion to compel production of documents of defendant Mark Cuban ("Cuban") is granted in part and denied in part. The November 22, 2011 motion to compel production of documents of plaintiff Securities and Exchange Commission ("SEC") is granted.

I

A

Cuban moves under Fed. R. Civ. P. 37(a) to compel the SEC to produce the following four categories of documents: (1) all nonprivileged portions of its investigative file for the SEC's investigation into Mamma.com; (2) all documents pertaining to the relationship between the Mamma.com investigation and the investigation into

Cuban; (3) all documents relating to the involvement of Irving ... Kott [a reputed securities violator] with Mamma.com; and (4) all factual portions of the SEC's notes and interview summaries from the witness interviews conducted in the course of its investigation of Cuban. Cuban also moves the court to require the SEC to produce a privilege log identifying all documents withheld as privileged from its productions in merits discovery in this action, specifying for each withheld document the specific basis for asserting privilege, and that all future SEC productions include a similar privilege log if documents are withheld as privileged.

B

The court considers the first two categories together. Cuban has at least shown that the nonprivileged portions of the SEC's investigative file for the investigation of Mamma.com, and documents pertaining to the relationship between the Mamma.com investigation and the investigation of Cuban, are relevant to the credibility of Mamma.com witnesses, including CEO Guy Fauré ("Fauré"), and are therefore within the scope of Rule 26(b)(1). Cuban has established that he is doing more than engaging in a fishing expedition in seeking this discovery.

The SEC has failed to demonstrate sufficient grounds to deny such production. To the extent it objects on the grounds of overbreadth and burden, the court notes that Cuban is requesting only nonprivileged parts of the investigative file. And although the SEC complains that it has already answered interrogatories regarding the Mamma.com investigation, this is insufficient under the circumstances to deny Cuban the ability to examine the documents at issue. Finally, to the extent the SEC is relying on privileges or the work product doctrine, it can withhold production on these grounds where a privilege or the work product doctrine applies.

The court therefore grants Cuban's motion as to these two categories.

C

Cuban also moves to compel the SEC to produce all documents relating to the involvement of Irving, Ian, or Michael Kott (collectively, "the Kotts") with Mamma.com.

Cuban has not satisfied his burden of demonstrating that these documents are discoverable. To the extent he maintains the documents bear on whether he acted with *scienter*—i.e., relate to his contention that he sold his Mamma.com stock partly due to concern for the Kotts' involvement in the company—he has not made a sufficient preliminary showing that these documents would pertain to what *he knew* at the time. For example, there is no suggestion that, when he decided to sell his Mamma.com stock, he was aware of such documents or of what they showed about the Kotts. Nor has he shown how these documents would relate to issues about Fauré's credibility.

Concluding that Cuban has not demonstrated the relevance of these requested documents, the court denies his request for the production of documents regarding the Kotts's involvement in Mamma.com.

D

Cuban moves to compel the SEC to produce all factual portions of the SEC's notes and interview summaries from the witness interviews conducted in the course of its investigation of Cuban. The SEC opposes this category based on the work product doctrine.

Even assuming that the materials requested are merely ordinary, not opinion, work product,[1] Cuban has failed to demonstrate undue hardship. Cuban contends that he is unable to acquire the information found in the SEC's interview notes and summaries because it reflects the *initial* statements of Fauré and other interviewees. But Cuban has access to notes taken by Mamma.com personnel of SEC interviews, and transcripts of sworn, investigative testimony of such witnesses; he has taken his own unsworn, transcribed statements from several witnesses; and he has had the opportunity to depose these witnesses. His failure to demonstrate undue hardship is alone an adequate basis to deny his motion to compel in this respect. *See, e.g., SEC v. Brady*, 238 F.R.D. 429, 443 (N.D. Tex. 2006) (Ramirez, J.) (holding that "party seeking the materials [must] demonstrate[] a substantial need for the information *and* an inability to obtain the substantial equivalent without undue hardship" (emphasis added)). The court therefore denies Cuban's motion as to this category.

II

The court considers together Cuban's final request in his motion to compel and the SEC's motion to compel. Cuban moves to require the SEC to produce a privilege log identifying all documents withheld as privileged from its productions in merits discovery, specifying for each withheld document the specific basis for asserting privilege. He also seeks an order directing that all future SEC productions include a similar privilege log, if documents are withheld as privileged. The SEC moves under Rule 37(a)(1) to compel Cuban to produce a privilege log identifying documents he has withheld based on privilege for the period after December 31, 2006 and through March 10, 2011.

A

In response to Cuban's request, the SEC maintains that the requested documents are irrelevant, substantially overlap with the SEC's privilege log [previously] produced ... or are plainly privileged and therefore burdensome to log.

[1.] Ordinary work product includes materials "prepared in anticipation of litigation or for trial by or for another party or its representative." See [FRCP] Rule 26(b)(3)(A). The party seeking discovery must "show[] that it has substantial need for the materials to prepare its case and cannot, without undue hardship, obtain their substantial equivalent by other means." *See id.* at Rule 26(b)(3)(A)(ii). Opinion work product includes "mental impressions, conclusions, opinions, or legal theories of a party's attorney or other representative concerning the litigation." *See id.* at 26(b)(3)(B). The party seeking discovery must demonstrate "a compelling need for the information." ... Because Cuban has failed to meet his burden under the lower, ordinary work product standard, the court need not conduct *in camera* review of the notes and summaries, as Cuban requests, to determine whether the requested materials are ordinary or opinion work product.

The court grants Cuban's motion in this respect and directs the SEC to produce a privilege log for all materials withheld on the basis of privilege.... The SEC must produce a privilege log for any documents withheld as privileged. The SEC has failed to show sufficient overlap to excuse this requirement. And it has not established that this requirement should be excused as burdensome.... The court therefore grants Cuban's motion in this respect.

B

Cuban opposes the SEC's request for a privilege log for materials withheld for the period after December 31, 2006 and through March 10, 2011. He contends that the requested log encompasses a temporal scope that is not reasonably related to the complaint, suggesting that the requested documents lack relevance to the case. The court concludes, however, that this period is relevant. The SEC's investigation began in early December 2006, so documents created in and after 2007 would, for example, shed light on Cuban's interaction with several potential fact witnesses. Cuban also objects based on overbreadth and undue burden. But largely for the reasons addressed above concerning the SEC's similar objections, the court rejects Cuban's objection. The SEC's motion is granted in this respect.

* * *

The court grants in part and denies in part Cuban's September 28, 2011 amended second motion to compel, and it grants the SEC's November 22, 2011 motion to compel. Despite the disagreements reflected in these motions, the parties appear to have worked cooperatively during this litigation.[2] For this reason, and because the parties are presently engaged in discovery under the court's January 13, 2012 scheduling order that may affect the optimal timing for compliance with these rulings, the court directs them to attempt to reach agreement concerning the timing for compliance. If they cannot do so within 14 days of the date this memorandum opinion and order is filed, they must advise the court by letter and set out their respective positions, and the court will establish the schedule.

SO ORDERED.

February 10, 2012.

[Signed]
SIDNEY A. FITZWATER
CHIEF JUDGE

[2.] For example, this litigation has _not_ been marked by the kind of ongoing discovery disputes that the court sometimes observes in similar cases.

V. THE SEC'S MOTION TO COMPEL MR. CUBAN'S DEPOSITION

That this litigation at times had significant contentious aspects is illustrated by the disagreement that occurred between the parties regarding the scheduling of Mr. Cuban's deposition. *The following Declaration was authored by Mr. Stephen A. Best who served as legal counsel for Mr. Cuban. The SEC's reply follows Mr. Best's Declaration. Thereafter, Judge Fitzwater's Order resolved this dispute.*

I, Stephen A. Best, declare as follows:

1. I am over 18 years old and am employed as a shareholder at Brownstein Hyatt Farber Schreck LLP. I represent Mark Cuban, the defendant in the above-captioned matter. I am a member in good standing of the bars of the District of Columbia and Virginia. I am admitted to practice before this Court.

2. I make this Declaration in Support of Defendant Mark Cuban's Opposition to Plaintiff Securities and Exchange Commission's Motion to Compel.

3. I have personal knowledge of the facts attested and documents attached to this Declaration.

4. Prior to the Court's November 1, 2011 Order that amended the discovery schedule, discovery was scheduled to close on November 30, 2011. Under this schedule, the parties agreed for Mr. Cuban to be deposed on November 18, 2011. The SEC never expressed any concerns about this schedule, despite Mr. Cuban's deposition being 12 days before the close of discovery (and with the Thanksgiving holiday in the interim).

5. In October 2011, the SEC came to counsel for Mr. Cuban and asked for an extension to the discovery schedule. SEC counsel Duane Thompson stated that he had another matter in November that would keep him occupied, and that there were still a number of witnesses that the SEC planned to notice for deposition that would be difficult to schedule in the time remaining. We obliged the SEC's request and agreed to stipulate to a joint motion to extend the discovery schedule into February 2012. Although it was a joint motion, the impetus for pushing out the schedule was solely the SEC. As part of the agreement regarding an extension, we requested that Mr. Cuban's deposition be moved to what was then a convenient date for Mr. Cuban and his counsel, December 16, 2011.

6. The parties filed a joint motion, and on November 1, 2011 the Court extended the close of discovery to February 17, 2012.

7. On November 1, 2011, SEC counsel Duane Thompson emailed me and counsel for certain Merriman Curhan & Ford ("MCF") witnesses and stated that the SEC was postponing the depositions of Arnold Owen and Christopher Aguilar that were scheduled for November 10 and 11, 2011. I objected to the continuance of Messrs. Aguilar and Owen's depositions as they were set on the SEC's schedule and the depositions were the following week. In response, Mr. Thompson stated that they were moving the dates of those depositions despite my objections....

8. On November 15, 2011, I informed SEC attorney Kevin O'Rourke via email that Mr. Cuban was no longer available for his deposition on December 16, 2011. I proposed that we look for mutually convenient dates in February....

9. Later that day, Mr. O'Rourke replied that the SEC intended to proceed with the deposition on December 16, 2011, but would consider alternate dates that were earlier in the week of December 16 or more than 30 days before the close of discovery.... With discovery set to close on February 17, 2012, the import of the message was that the SEC would not consider any February date or any date after the depositions of Messrs. Owen and Aguilar....

10. Later that day, I again told Mr. O'Rourke via email that Mr. Cuban had availability in February 2012 and stated that "[i]f you wish to propose dates in February when I know Mr. Cuban has availability, we will be happy to lock something in." ...

11. On November 18, 2011, Mr. O'Rourke replied to my email and stated that the SEC will only consider alternative dates that are more than 30 days before the close of discovery....

12. The SEC never proposed any dates for Mr. Cuban's deposition in February 2012. Because the SEC never proposed any dates, we selected a date in February that was convenient for Mr. Cuban's schedule.

13. On December 8, 2011, we proposed February 16, 2012 as the date for Mr. Cuban's deposition. To accommodate the SEC's concern regarding needing sufficient time to engage in any necessary discovery-related motions practice that might arise as a result of the deposition, we stated that we would be willing to agree to a reasonable extension of discovery if that proves necessary....

14. In response, the SEC again insisted that we propose a date for Mr. Cuban's deposition at least 30 days before the close of discovery....

15. On December 12, 2011, the parties met and conferred by telephone concerning the date of Mr. Cuban's deposition. I stated that we would agree to extend the discovery schedule for 30 days if the SEC wanted 30 days following Mr. Cuban's deposition for additional discovery. I offered for Mr. Cuban's counsel to be the party to move the Court for the extension. The SEC declined.

16. During the meet and confer, Mr. O'Rourke proposed two dates for Mr. Cuban's deposition in January 2012, January 20 and January 21 (a Saturday). Monday of that week (January 16) is a national holiday (Martin Luther King Day). Moreover, two depositions are already scheduled for that week on January 18 and 19. Mr. O'Rourke did not propose any dates in February 2012, nor did he propose any dates after the depositions of Messrs. Owen and Aguilar....

17. According to the SEC, during the meet and confer I "reiterated that [I] would not agree to any deposition date for Mr. Cuban other than February 16, 2012 and [I] would not even consult with [Mr.] Cuban on his availability for earlier dates." ... This is a mischaracterization of Mr. Cuban's position. As explained above, I previously told the SEC that Mr. Cuban was available in February 2012 and asked them to propose a date. The SEC refused and made it abundantly clear that they would not accept any date that was not at least 30 days prior to the close of discovery.

Then, in the meet and confer, the SEC only proposed January 20 and 21 as alternative dates. What I conveyed in the meet and confer was that I was not prepared to discuss a date within the unreasonable scope of what the SEC was insisting.

18. On December 16, 2011, the SEC proposed that expert depositions be conducted from February 6-13.... Further, on December 20, 2011 counsel for Mr. Cuban and the SEC discussed expert deposition dates from February 2-13. This indicates the SEC's availability for Mr. Cuban's deposition during this time....

Pursuant to 28 U.S.C. § 1746, I, Stephen A. Best, declare under penalty of perjury that the foregoing is true and correct.

Executed on December 21, 2011

*[Signed]*_____

Stephen A. Best

PLAINTIFF SECURITIES AND EXCHANGE COMMISSION'S REPLY IN SUPPORT OF ITS MOTION TO COMPEL DEFENDANT MARK CUBAN TO APPEAR FOR DEPOSITION

Cuban's Opposition to the SEC'S Motion to Compel Defendant Mark Cuban to Appear for Deposition is based on a number of fundamental errors. First, Cuban misinterprets Rule 37 of the Federal Rules of Civil Procedure. Second, Cuban provides an inaccurate account of the relevant facts. Finally, Cuban attempts to distract from the actual issue that necessitated the filing of the SEC's motion—namely, that Cuban has refused to appear at his agreed-upon and noticed deposition and rebuffed the Commission's efforts to reach a reasonable resolution.

ARGUMENT

First, Cuban incorrectly argues that Rule 37 [is] inapplicable to his refusal to appear at his noticed December 16, 2011 deposition, arguing that he has not refused to be deposed, just refused to be deposed on the date to which he previously agreed and for which he was noticed. Rule 37(a) of the Federal Rules of Civil Procedure clearly applies in this situation. The Rule specifically provides that a motion may be filed compelling discovery, and the applicability of Rule 37 to a noticed deposition is made clear by Rule 37(d), which provides an array of remedies for a party's failure to attend his noticed deposition. In particular, Rule 37(d)(2) specifically provides that a party's failure to attend his own deposition "is not excused on the ground that the discovery sought was objectionable, unless the party failing to act has a pending motion for protective order under Rule 26(c)." As Cuban points out, he had a month before the deposition date to reach an agreement or seek relief from the Court through a motion for a protective order. Cuban's failure to so move should be dispositive of the issue; the various explanations offered in his Opposition for his failure to appear or move for a protective order are irrelevant to the Commission's right to relief under Rule 37.

Second, Cuban's derivative argument—that the SEC is not actually seeking relief under Rule 37 (which it plainly is), but, instead, is seeking to modify the Court's discovery order—is nonsensical. In fact, the SEC moved to compel Cuban to attend his agreed-upon and noticed deposition expressly to avoid further amendment of the scheduling order. The SEC is seeking to complete Cuban's deposition a reasonable time before the close of discovery in order to allow for any necessary follow-up discovery as well as any necessary motions practice arising from his deposition. The SEC reasonably believes such additional discovery might be necessary. More than four and a half years ago, Mr. Cuban was questioned for less than an hour and a half by SEC investigative staff relying on the investigative record developed at that time. During the intervening years, the parties have obtained hundreds of thousands of pages of documents in discovery related to this matter. For example, in September 2009, following Cuban's financing of the acquisition of the assets of Mamma. com, Inc. ("Mamma"), additional documents were produced to the SEC that Mamma had previously withheld as privileged. Questioning concerning these documents, the thousands of documents produced by other third parties, or the documents produced by Cuban himself since his investigative testimony could all lead to a need for follow-up discovery.

Third, Cuban's suggestions that the movement of Cuban's deposition from the previously-agreed date of November 18 to the noticed date of December 16 was independent of the parties' agreement jointly to seek an extension of discovery is inaccurate. Indeed, the agreement to move Cuban's deposition to December 16, as well as Cuban's desire for additional time for expert discovery, was specifically included in the discussions to seek a joint extension of the discovery order. Cuban's related claim that the Commission refused to "reciprocate" his accommodation in extending the discovery schedule is just not true. At Cuban's request, the Commission moved his deposition from the previously-agreed date of November 18 to the agreed-and-noticed date, December 16. Moreover, when Cuban first refused to appear on the date of his noticed deposition, the Commission conferred with Cuban in efforts to identify a reasonable date that would allow the SEC adequate time for any required follow-up discovery. In return, Cuban, without articulating any detailed reason why he could not appear earlier, insisted on the final day before the close of discovery.

Finally, Cuban makes much of the scheduling of other depositions. While, as described above, the timing of the depositions of other, non-party witnesses is irrelevant to Cuban's obligation, as a party, to appear for his noticed depositions, Cuban's arguments about other depositions are without merit for several additional reasons. For example, it is unsurprising that the SEC has noticed and taken the vast majority of the depositions; the SEC bears the burden of proof in this action and must collect and organize the facts needed to prove its case. Similarly, Cuban's implication that the number of depositions the SEC has taken or scheduled is somehow improper misses the mark. The date and witness for each deposition was discussed in advance with Cuban's counsel, and each deposition occurred on an agreed-upon date in an agreed-upon location. Cuban's argument that there are several depositions already scheduled for January 2012 also misses the mark. Many of those dates were scheduled only after Cuban had made clear that he would not agree to a deposition in January. Finally, Cuban's argument that other depositions are scheduled for February 2012 is also unpersuasive. With the exception of a deposition on February 3, all depositions scheduled in February are of expert witnesses.

It is clear that the animating factor behind Cuban's insistence on a late February deposition is that he be the final deponent and thus have the benefit of all other witness's testimony. Cuban's desire for this tactical advantage has no basis in the Federal Rules. More importantly, acceding to Cuban's intractable insistence to being deposed last would deprive the SEC of any meaningful opportunity to conduct any necessary follow-up discovery or motions practice arising from his deposition absent a further extension of discovery that the SEC does not believe is advisable or should be necessary. Instead, the SEC respectfully asks that the Court order Cuban's deposition so as to provide adequate time for the SEC to conduct any required additional discovery consistent with the current discovery schedule....

ORDER

Plaintiff Securities and Exchange Commission's ("SEC's") December 15, 2011 motion to compel defendant Mark Cuban to appear for deposition is granted as follows. Defendant Mark Cuban ("Cuban") shall appear for his deposition on a date between February 1 and 16, 2012 that is mutually agreeable to the parties. If a party unreasonably fails to agree to a particular date during this period, the party will be subject to sanctions. The parties must agree on the deposition date no later than January 13, 2012 and must promptly submit a proposed order for the court's consideration. The order must provide that Cuban will appear for his deposition on the specific date agreed upon and at a specific time and location. Once the order is filed, the deposition must take place as scheduled unless the court orders otherwise.

The SEC contends that [it] is entitled to take Cuban's deposition sufficiently in advance of the close of discovery to allow for any follow up discovery that may be required based on his testimony. If as a result of this order the SEC has cause to extend the February 17, 2012 discovery cutoff, it may seek this relief by agreement of the parties (subject to incorporation into a court order) or by motion.

Additionally, it is the court's intention that, if the SEC so requests, the sequence of discovery replicate the one in place when Cuban's deposition was scheduled to be conducted on November 18, 2011. If as a result of taking Cuban's deposition in February 2012 it is necessary to delay depositions that would otherwise have been conducted after Cuban testified on November 18, 2011 but are now scheduled to take place before Cuban's deposition, these depositions may be delayed at the SEC's request, provided the discovery cutoff is enlarged to accommodate the dates of these depositions.

The SEC's motion is granted as set forth in this order.

SO ORDERED.

VI. DEPOSITION TESTIMONY

Due to length limitations of the book and that key witnesses who gave their depositions also testified at trial, this Section will highlight the deposition testimony as excerpted of Mr. Cuban and Mr. Fauré. Interestingly, Mr. Fauré did not testify at trial. Therefore, his deposition testimony was introduced by the SEC at trial and will be covered more extensively in Chapter 7. It is significant to point out (for our purposes at this point) that Mr. Fauré's deposition testimony appears to be less favorable to the Commission's case than was his investigative testimony referred to in Chapters 1 and 3 of this book. *The questioning of Mr. Fauré was by Mr. Christopher Clark who was representing Mr. Cuban. The excerpt of Mr. Fauré's deposition testimony follows.*

[Mr. Clarke]: We spoke earlier about you were telling Mr. Cuban in words or substance: "I have confidential information for you."

[Mr. Fauré]: Right.

[Mr. Clarke]: Do you recall anything Mr. Cuban said in response ... to that statement by you?

[Mr. Fauré]: No, I do not.

[Mr. Clarke]: ... Do you recall discussing with Mr. Cuban whether more detailed information about the PIPE transaction might be made available to him?

[Mr. Fauré]: On the call, not specifically.

[Mr. Clarke]: ... Do you recall discussing with [Mr. Cuban] having him speak to Mr. Owen at MCF about the PIPE transaction?

[Mr. Fauré]: Well, I did send him an e-mail after the conversation to that effect.

[Mr. Clarke]: I understand that. My question to you is ... do you right now remember it on the call or are you saying ... I know I sent him an e-mail, but I do not remember talking about [it] on the phone call?

[Mr. Fauré]: I do not specifically remember.[3]

In his deposition testimony, Mr. Cuban asserted his law-compliant conduct and expressed his distrust of the SEC. The questioning of Mr. Cuban was by SEC attorney Mr. Kevin O'Rourke. *Excerpts from Mr. Cuban's deposition testimony follow:*

[Mr. O'Rourke]: [A]fter you purchased your position in Mamma, did you communicate frequently with the CEO of Mamma, Guy Fauré, about things related to the company?

[Mr. Cuban]: No sir.

[3.] Deposition Testimony of Guy Fauré at pages 49-50 (June 6, 2012).

[Mr. O'Rourke]: Did you from time to time after you obtained your [stock ownership] position in Mamma communicate with the CEO of the company, Mr. Guy Fauré?

[Mr. Cuban]: Yes, sir.

[Mr. O'Rourke]: And it was about things related to the company?

[Mr. Cuban]: In one way or another, yes sir.

[Mr. O'Rourke]: ... [C]ould you tell us generally what you would communicate with Mr. Guy Fauré over time?

[Mr. Cuban]: I mean, I guess on two levels. One, just to help him promotionally. And the second, just acting as a normal shareholder or analyst, just asking for general information. And I guess a third would be if I could offer any strategic value.

[Mr. O'Rourke]: Well, if you could, explain what you mean by help him promotionally.

[Mr. Cuban]: I think in one of the e-mails—and I'd have to refer back to it, so don't hold me verbatim—I said I'd wear a T-shirt or a hat because I'm on TV a fair amount and that would be a promotional value.

And you might have seen my Skechers commercial. I ... would have worn my Skechers [shoes] today if I was allowed to. And no, I don't own any stock in Skechers, but the promotional value. And I was willing to offer that....

[Mr. O'Rourke]: [D]id you ... take plus 5 percent [stock] positions in companies so you could get access to the CEO?

[Mr. Cuban]: Two different things.

[Mr. O'Rourke]: How so?

[Mr. Cuban]: Getting access, yeah, they'll pick up the phone and take my call or respond to my e-mail. I certainly never was considering asking for anything beyond general information, and—and again, I was just asking like any ... other shareholder would ask.

[Mr. O'Rourke]: Well, weren't you expecting the information because you had a plus 5 percent [stock ownership] position in the company? Wasn't that part of your strategy?

[Mr. Cuban]: Wasn't what part of my strategy?

[Mr. O'Rourke]: Expecting to get information because you were a plus 5 percent investor in the company?

[Mr. Cuban]: Absolutely not.

[Mr. O'Rourke]: And what was the type of information generally that you were expecting to get, hoping to get?

[Mr. Cuban]: ... [I]f I'm a Disney shareholder, I'll go to Disney, you know. And I expected to act just like a shareholder, but my expectation was that they'd answer my call more readily and where I can provide strategic value.... I didn't expect anything beyond what you would treat a normal shareholder....

[Mr. O'Rourke]: And this activity of yours, providing strategic value, helping them develop the business, is this something you just did for Mamma or have you done it for other companies that you've invested in over time?

[Mr. Cuban]: Other companies as well.

[Mr. O'Rourke]: Okay. And is that ... something that you do?

[Mr. Best—Mr. Cuban's attorney]: Objection, form.

[Mr. Cuban]: Actually, not recently, no. Ever since this happened, I'm just going to be brutally honest, I don't trust the SEC. And so now any communications I have with anybody from another company, I make sure my lawyer is on the communications and I only do it through e-mail. I won't take any phone calls from anybody that I have ... an investment in because I don't trust you guys....

[Mr. O'Rourke]: Do you still undertake to do the same activity now except that you do it by e-mail?

[Mr. Cuban]: No. I will not do the same activities at all. I curtail any communications I have. And ... I've told CEOs who have come up to me at conferences, I've said do not call me, do not e-mail me. *And why? Because I don't trust the SEC as far as I can throw them....* [emphasis supplied]

[Mr. O'Rourke]: So it was when the SEC decided to sue you that you developed ... that attitude?

[Mr. Cuban]: Yeah. If the government came after you, wouldn't you? ...

[Mr. O'Rourke]: Have ... officers of ... a [publicly-traded] company [previously] offer[ed] to provide you with confidential information?

[Mr. Best]: Objection, form.

[Mr. Cuban]: ... I have no idea. If they're an officer of the company, it's up to them to know whether it's confidential or not and to tell me whether or not it's confidential. And I wouldn't do it unless there was an ironclad agreement that we both knew it was confidential and I agreed to accept the information.

[Mr. O'Rourke]: ... [S]etting aside Mamma, have you ever been approached with an offer of confidential information before?

[Mr. Best]: At any time? Objection, form of the question.

[Mr. O'Rourke]: Yes, at any time.

[Mr. Cuban]: No one's ever specified to me that I am giving you confidential information, and at no time have I ever said that I would accept him or her giving me confidential information. And I can't imagine what the circumstances would be that I would agree to take confidential information without it first being in writing....

[Mr. O'Rourke]: And is it your testimony today after all this hunkering down and reading all the things you've read and everything, that you still don't recall a thing that was said in the [telephone] conversation [with Mamma.com's CEO Guy Fauré]?

[Mr. Cuban]: I don't recall the details, no sir.

[Mr. O'Rourke]: ... [Y]ou can't recall a single statement made by you or question ... raised by you in the call?

[Mr. Cuban]: I don't recall the details, no sir.

[Mr. O'Rourke]: And you don't recall anything, a single item stated by Mr. Fauré or question asked by him?

[Mr. Cuban]: That's correct, sir.

[Mr. O'Rourke]: And do you recall anything about the call? [From your previous testimony], did you say [you were] mad and upset?

[Mr. Cuban]: Yes, sir.

[Mr. O'Rourke]: And did you express or articulate that you were mad and upset in the [telephone] call?

[Mr. Cuban]: I'm presuming that I did, but I don't recall specifically. . . .

[Mr. O'Rourke]: But the only thing that's been jogged after all this has been that you recall that you were mad and upset during the call?

[Mr. Cuban]: That's correct.

[Mr. O'Rourke]: And so hence my question, how is it you after all this work and jogging of memory that you now recall you were mad and upset but you can't think of a single thing that was said in the call [with Mr. Fauré]?

[Mr. Best]: Objection, form of the question.

[Mr. Cuban]: You know, I'll give some context because context is very important.

[Mr. O'Rourke]: I would like an answer to my question.

[Mr. Best]: Objection, form of the question.

[Mr. Cuban]: I'll give you that. Okay. On that day, that morning I got to spend with Michael Jordan and I got to ride around [on the golf cart at a charitable golf event] with Michael Jordan and talk basketball for the first time. That was pretty damn cool.

[Mr. O'Rourke]: And he probably thought the same thing about you.

[Mr. Cuban]: No, trust me, he didn't. Buddy, buddy, buddy, this and buddy that . . . .[4]

VII. EXPERT WITNESS TESTIMONY

Both the SEC and Mr. Cuban retained expert witnesses. Given the significant issues at stake, such retention was customary. Mr. Cuban retained two expert witnesses—(1) Dr. Erik R. Sirri and (2) Professor Marc I. Steinberg, the author of this book. Dr. Sirri, a highly respected economist, used an event study to opine that the information relating to the Mamma.com PIPE transaction was both publicly available and did not have a significant price impact on the price of Mamma.com stock, thereby signifying that this information was neither confidential nor material. In his deposition testimony, Dr. Sirri stated:

> I would note that all of those decisions I make [with respect to the event study] are conservative. That is, had I not made those decisions and used a longer event window, the event study would have found an even less significant . . . price movement on that day.
>
> . . . . I made a reasonable economic judgment. It was based on a tradeoff between the natural desire of an econometrician to get as much data as possible with the balance to have data be as meaningful as possible. Because

---

[4.] Deposition Testimony of Mark Cuban at pages 33-43, 196-199 (Feb. 10, 2012).

things like volume, volatility, price had risen in the period that we're talking about, I made the judgment to use the number of days that I used.[5]

In his expert witness report and deposition testimony, Professor Steinberg opined that "[u]nder custom and practice, Mamma.com had no reasonable expectation of confidentiality with respect to communications made to Mr. Cuban by the Company's CEO Mr. Guy Fauré and by Mr. Arnie Owen, a sales representative of Merriman Curhan Ford & Co. (MCF or Merriman) regarding the PIPE transaction."[6] Professor Steinberg provided several reasons to support this opinion, including that: (1) Mamma.com "represented that all information contained in the SPA [Securities Purchase Agreement] (including, of course, the existence of the forthcoming PIPE transaction) was neither material nor nonpublic and that Purchasers were entitled to rely on that representation;" (2) Mamma.com insiders themselves were selling their Company stock during this time period, signifying that the information relating to the PIPE transaction was either not material or had been adequately disseminated to the securities marketplace; (3) "by allegedly communicating the information related to the PIPE transaction to Mr. Cuban verbally without procuring the execution of a written non-disclosure agreement, this conduct was not in accordance with better practices;" (4) Mr. Owen of MCF did not communicate to Mr. Cuban that the information regarding the PIPE transaction was confidential and that, accordingly, "[u]nder custom and practice, the failure by a principal's agent [namely, Mamma.com's agent] to seek to preserve the confidentiality of the information provided to a third party (here Mr. Cuban) evidences that the principal (here Mamma.com) did not have a reasonable expectation of confidentiality;" and (5) Mamma.com or its agent MCF disclosed to prospective investors (other than Mr. Cuban) the forthcoming PIPE transaction without procuring a non-disclosure agreement from such investors or taking other adequate measures to safeguard the confidentiality of the information conveyed, thereby again signifying that Mamma.com did not have a reasonable expectation of confidentiality.[7]

The SEC's retained experts were Dr. Clemens Sialm and Professor Thomas Lee Hazen. Contrary to Dr. Sirri, Dr. Sialm opined under his event study that information relating to the Mamma.com PIPE transaction had significant price impact. Dr. Sialm testified in his deposition that pursuant to his event study that there were a "much higher number of significantly negative reactions if you match the characteristics of the Mamma PIPE with other PIPEs, and statistical tests ... indicate that those are important events."[8] Dr.

[5.] Deposition Testimony of Erik R. Sirri at page 247 (March 1, 2012).

[6.] Expert Report of Marc I. Steinberg at pages 3-4 (Sept. 30, 2011).

[7.] *Id.* at pages 4-16. See Deposition Testimony of Marc I. Steinberg at pages 72-87, 115-186, 196-230 (Feb. 13, 2012).

[8.] Deposition Testimony of Clemens Sialm at pages 75-76 (Feb. 22, 2012).

Sialm also addressed the stock price of Mamma.com after the formal public announcement of the PIPE transaction testifying:

> I have looked at the stock price patterns, I have read the reports of Dr. Sirri, and, therefore, I'm familiar with what happened to the [Mamma.com] stock price. The stock price dropped on the announcement [of the PIPE transaction] my recollection by 8.5 percent. In the two-day window around the announcement, it dropped by 12.9 percent ....[9]

Professor Thomas Lee Hazen was the SEC's rebuttal expert witness to respond to Professor Steinberg's opinions. Professor Hazen opined:

> I unequivocally disagree with Professor Steinberg ... that Mamma "did not have a reasonable expectation of confidentiality." Steinberg Report at 3-4. Contrary to Professor Steinberg's conclusion, Mamma reasonably believed that information concerning the imminent PIPE offering was material, non-public information when it contacted Mr. Cuban ... to invite him to participate in the PIPE. The telephone conversation that day between Mamma's CEO [Guy Fauré] and Defendant Cuban created a duty of confidentiality about the PIPE offering and its imminent closing. Pursuant to the confidentiality obligation, the CEO then directed Cuban to Merriman Curhan Ford & Co. (Merriman), the company's agent from whom Defendant Cuban learned additional details about the PIPE transaction. Not only did Mamma have a reasonable expectation of confidentiality, Defendant Cuban had a legally binding obligation to keep information about the upcoming PIPE transaction confidential and an attendant obligation not to trade on the basis of this nonpublic, material information.[10]

As typically occurs, each party seeks to exclude the expert testimony that is sought to be admitted by its opponent(s) at trial. Such was the situation in the SEC enforcement action against Mr. Cuban. Both the SEC and Mr. Cuban respectively filed motions to exclude the other side's experts. In the Memorandum and Order that follows, Judge Fitzwater ruled on these motions.

MEMORANDUM OPINION AND ORDER

In this civil enforcement action brought by plaintiff Securities and Exchange Commission ("SEC") against defendant Mark Cuban ("Cuban") under the misappropriation theory of insider trading, each party moves to exclude the testimony and

---

[9.] *Id.* at page 76.

[10.] Expert Report of Thomas Lee Hazen at page 4 (Nov. 20, 2012). In his report, Professor Hazen expands to specify further reasons why he disagreed with Professor Steinberg's expert opinion. *Id.* at pages 4-11. See Deposition Testimony of Thomas Lee Hazen (Feb. 27, 2012).

reports of the other party's experts. For the reasons explained, the court grants in part and denies in part the motion addressed to one expert, denies the motion as to another expert, and denies as moot the motions addressed to the remaining two experts.

I

Stated summarily, the SEC alleges that Cuban violated § 17(a) of the Securities Act of 1933, § 10(b) of the Securities Exchange Act of 1934, and Rule 10b-5 promulgated thereunder by selling shares of stock in Mamma.com Inc. ("Mamma. com") after learning material, nonpublic information concerning a planned private investment in public equity ("PIPE") offering by the company. According to the SEC, Cuban deceived Mamma.com by agreeing to maintain the confidentiality of material, nonpublic information concerning the PIPE and not to trade on the information, and then selling his stock in the company without first disclosing to Mamma.com that he intended to trade on the information, thereby avoiding substantial losses when the stock price declined after the PIPE offering was publicly announced. Cuban denies the SEC's allegations.

The SEC moves to exclude the testimony and reports of the two expert witnesses Cuban has designated: Professor Marc I. Steinberg ("Prof. Steinberg") and Dr. Erik R. Sirri ("Dr. Sirri"). Cuban moves to exclude the reports and testimony of the SEC's two expert witnesses: Professor Thomas Lee Hazen ("Prof. Hazen") and Dr. Clemens Sialm ("Dr. Sialm").

II

The court decides these motions in its role as gatekeeper under Fed. R. Evid. 702. "The court may admit proffered expert testimony only if the proponent, who bears the burden of proof, demonstrates that (1) the expert is qualified, (2) the evidence is relevant to the suit, and (3) the evidence is reliable." Neither party challenges an expert's qualifications; each is knowledgeable and experienced in his field and in the subjects on which he opines. The parties instead challenge the opinions on grounds of unreliability or irrelevance.

To be relevant, "expert testimony [must] 'assist the trier of fact to understand the evidence or to determine a fact in issue.'" *[See] Daubert v. Merrell Dow Pharm., Inc.*, 509 U.S. 579, 589 (1993). "Relevance depends upon 'whether [the expert's] reasoning or methodology properly can be applied to the facts in issue.'" ... *[S]ee also* Fed. R. Evid. 702(d) (requiring that "expert has reliably applied the principles and methods to the facts of the case").

"Reliability is determined by assessing 'whether the reasoning or methodology underlying the testimony is scientifically valid.'" Expert testimony "must constitute 'more than subjective belief or unsupported speculation.'" The court reviews the expert's methodology, not the conclusions generated by it. This review is usually conducted by considering the five nonexclusive *Daubert* factors.[11] But these factors

---

[11.] The five nonexclusive *Daubert* factors are: (1) whether the expert's technique can be or has been tested; (2) whether the method has been subjected to peer review and publication;

"'may or may not be pertinent in assessing reliability, depending on the nature of the issue, the expert's particular expertise, and the subject of the testimony.'"

The burden is on the proponent of the expert testimony to establish its admissibility by a preponderance of the evidence. If expert testimony can withstand a *Daubert* challenge, then criticism of it "affects the weight to be assigned to that opinion and should be left for the jury's consideration."

III

The motions to exclude Prof. Steinberg and rebuttal expert Prof. Hazen are both moot. The SEC's motion to exclude Prof. Steinberg's testimony was filed before the court decided Cuban's summary judgment motion. In his opposition to the SEC's motion to exclude, Cuban maintains that

> Professor Steinberg's opinions will be relevant *if and only if*: (i) the Court were to reject the foregoing and deny the summary judgment motion, (ii) the Court's summary judgment ruling were to indicate that Mr. Cuban could be deemed to have assumed a duty to keep the PIPE information confidential even if he did not do so by "agreement," so long as Mamma.com could still be shown to have had a reasonable expectation of confidentiality, and (iii) as such, the jury would be asked to determine whether any expectation of confidentiality that Mamma.com had was *reasonable* even if no legally binding confidentiality agreement was formed. In these circumstances, Professor Steinberg's principal opinion, and also his other, related opinion, would be germane to whether Mamma.com's expectation of confidentiality (if any) was reasonable.

In the summary judgment ruling, the court adhered to its prior decision that, "to establish liability under the misappropriation theory of insider trading in the absence of another legal duty to refrain from trading on or otherwise using material, nonpublic information for personal benefit (such as a duty arising from a fiduciary relationship), the SEC could rely on an express or implied agreement." The court did not "indicate that Mr. Cuban could be deemed to have assumed a duty to keep the PIPE information confidential even if he did not do so by 'agreement,' so long as Mamma.com could still be shown to have had a reasonable expectation of confidentiality." The SEC does not allege that Cuban and Mamma.com had a fiduciary relationship or that another duty—apart from an agreement—supports its misappropriation theory claim. Professor Steinberg's opinions are therefore irrelevant, and the SEC's motion to strike is moot.

Cuban's motion to exclude the opinions, testimony, and report of Prof. Hazen is also moot. The SEC states in response to Cuban's motion that '[i]f the [SEC's]

---

(3) the known or potential rate of error of a technique or theory when applied; (4) the existence and maintenance of standards and controls; and (5) the degree to which the technique or theory has been generally accepted in the scientific community. *Daubert*, 509 U.S. at 593-94.

motion to exclude Steinberg's testimony is granted, Cuban's motion to exclude Hazen's rebuttal testimony will be moot." Because Cuban will not be offering Professor Steinberg's opinion testimony at trial, his motion to exclude the opinions, testimony, and report of Prof. Hazen is denied as moot.

IV

Cuban moves to exclude the opinions of Dr. Sialm, the SEC's expert, regarding materiality.

A

For Cuban to be liable for insider trading, the SEC must show that he traded on material, nonpublic information. As the court explained in [a previous decision in this case:]

> to fulfill the materiality requirement there must be a substantial likelihood that the ... fact would have been viewed by the reasonable investor as having significantly altered the total mix of information made available. A fact is material if there is a substantial likelihood that, under all the circumstances, the ... fact would have assumed actual significance in the deliberations of the reasonable investor.

B

Cuban objects on the grounds of reliability and relevance to Dr. Sialm's primary opinion: that a reasonable investor would consider important for [his or her] investment decision information about Mamma.com's PIPE offering because its characteristics of warrants, discounts, and hedge fund investors would be expected to result in a stock price decline when the offering was announced.

1

Dr. Sialm conducted a study of the announcement effect that PIPE offerings had on the price of the issuer's common stock. He started with a sample of 355 common stock PIPE transactions that occurred between January 2003 and May 2004. For all 355 PIPE offerings, he measured the effect that announcing the offering had on the issuer's stock price. He used an event study to measure this effect, which is a well-established methodology that Cuban's expert, Dr. Sirri, also uses. Dr. Sialm then narrowed the sample to the PIPE offerings that had characteristics he considered important to investors based on his review of the literature: PIPE offerings that included warrants and discounts, and whether the investors were hedge funds. For each of three subsamples—warrants only, warrants and discounts, and warrants, discounts, and hedge fund investors—Dr. Sialm calculated the mean and median announcement effects. The results show that each subsample had a negative announcement effect, and with each additional characteristic, a greater average price decline. Dr. Sialm thus opines that, because Mamma.com's PIPE offering had warrants, discounts, and hedge fund investors, a reasonable investor would have expected a negative announcement effect and therefore would have considered information about the PIPE offering "important for investment decisions."

The results of Dr. Sialm's study provide circumstantial evidence that the involvement of warrants, discounts, and hedge fund investors result in a negative announcement effect because the results show a correlation between the two. Based on evidence that investors consider such characteristics important—shown by the decline in stock price that follows the announcement of PIPE offerings with such characteristics—Dr. Sialm opines that information about Mamma.com's PIPE offering would be important to a reasonable investor. His opinion is based on the importance to investors of different characteristics of Mamma.com's PIPE offering. Dr. Sirri, Cuban's expert, takes a different, *ex post* approach. He determines whether a reasonable investor would have considered the information important by analyzing Mamma.com's stock price following the PIPE offering announcement.

2

Cuban maintains that Dr. Sialm errs in considering only three characteristics to form his opinion about materiality. He posits that Dr. Sialm should account for the total mix of information available to the investor because, otherwise, there is no way to tell whether the PIPE offering information substantially alters the total mix of information available about Mamma.com. Cuban asserts that no peer-reviewed literature supports Dr. Sialm's methodology of considering information that is less encompassing than the total mix of information.

Cuban does not challenge Dr. Sialm's calculations in the event study of the 355 PIPE offerings or in determining the mean and median announcement effects of offerings in the sample that had warrants, discounts, and hedge fund investors. He instead attacks Dr. Sialm's opinion that, because the results show that certain characteristics are important, and Mamma.com's PIPE offering had these characteristics, the PIPE offering information would be important to a reasonable investor. Cuban maintains that the opinion misleadingly assumes that these three characteristics alone are all a reasonable investor would need to know. He posits that, if Dr. Sialm had also limited his sample by Mamma.com's industry, there would have been no statistically significant announcement effect.

The court declines to exclude Dr. Sialm's opinion on this basis. The opinion relates to the significance of the information—a component of the materiality inquiry—not to the materiality inquiry in all its dimensions. As the SEC recognizes, the opinion "is one aspect of the total mix of information for the jury to consider in making a determination." "Cuban is free to identify other relevant facts for the jury, if any, that he believes should be considered when assessing any alteration of the total mix of information." Cuban's objection therefore goes to the weight, not the admissibility, of the evidence.

The SEC has demonstrated by a preponderance of the evidence that Dr. Sialm's opinion is reliable and relevant. His calculations are not challenged, and

Cuban has not pointed to any authority that supports barring an expert from opining about the importance of particular information that can assist the jury in determining materiality.

3

Cuban maintains that Dr. Sialm's opinion is irrelevant because investors did not have access to his study to conclude that certain features of PIPE offerings were important or caused a negative announcement effect, and there is no evidence that investors intuitively knew this to be true based on experience. Cuban essentially argues that Dr. Sialm's opinion is so novel that a reasonable investor would not have known it beforehand. The court disagrees. Dr. Sialm's study is a reflection of investor behavior. The theory behind announcement-effect studies (which both Dr. Sialm and Dr. Sirri use) is that the importance to investors of a particular PIPE offering can be determined by analyzing its announcement effect. Accordingly, by following essentially the same logic employed by Dr. Sirri, Dr. Sialm's study shows a negative announcement effect for PIPE offerings with certain characteristics, and is thus circumstantial evidence that investors considered the characteristics important.

Cuban also maintains that, because Dr. Sirri's analysis of Dr. Sialm's study showed that only 35 of the total sample of 355 PIPE offerings resulted in a statistically significant effect on price, Dr. Sialm lacks a basis to opine that a reasonable investor would have expected a negative announcement effect. This argument goes to the weight of Dr. Sialm's opinion.

C

Cuban objects to other parts of Dr. Sialm's report and rebuttal report.

1

Cuban seeks to exclude Dr. Sialm's opinions about Cuban's understanding and opinion about PIPE offerings. In the "Background" section of his expert report, Dr. Sialm quotes public statements Cuban made about PIPE offerings. He concludes that "[t]hese statements by [Cuban] indicate that he understood that PIPE transactions with warrants and discounts have a dilutive effect to existing shareholders and an expected negative price effect." Dr. Sialm refers to these public statements as further support for his opinion that a reasonable investor would consider the Mamma.com PIPE offering information important.

Cuban objects that Dr. Sialm is improperly opining about Cuban's state of mind. He maintains that his public statements do not support Dr. Sialm's opinion because materiality is an objective inquiry about the "reasonable investor," and he knew additional, nonpublic information (e.g., an investigation into Mamma.com's connection with a known stock swindler).

The SEC contends that Dr. Sialm's discussion about Cuban's public statements is appropriate. It posits that Dr. Sialm was not opining about Cuban's understanding but was noting the statements as corroboration for Dr. Sialm's expert analysis. The SEC refers to Cuban's statements as admissions of fact that provide Dr. Sialm with additional evidentiary support for the conclusion that warrants and discounts are important characteristics of PIPE offerings. The SEC maintains that Cuban's objection can be cured by adjusting Dr. Sialm's testimony to omit mention of what Cuban "understood" and instead simply to state the fact that Cuban made these statements. Cuban agrees with this approach, provided that Dr. Sialm does not opine about Cuban's state of mind or knowledge.

The court declines to exclude Dr. Sialm's opinion and testimony regarding Cuban's public statements about PIPE offerings, provided they are modified in the manner Cuban proposes and to which the SEC appears to agree.

2

Cuban moves to exclude Dr. Sialm's rebuttal opinion that Dr. Sirri's study is "unreliable," contending that it is based on an *ex post* perspective. Dr. Sialm opines that Dr. Sirri's event study is in part flawed and unreliable because analyzing the actual announcement effect does not capture what a reasonable investor would have expected. Cuban posits that Dr. Sialm fails to cite any authority to support this opinion.

The SEC retreats from Dr. Sialm's characterization that Dr. Sirri's report is "unreliable"; it maintains that Dr. Sialm was merely making the point that, because the price reaction to Mamma.com's announcement of the PIPE offering is not an *ex ante* analysis, it does not capture the price effect that a reasonable investor would have expected.

As refined, Dr. Sialm's opinion is a relevant and reliable criticism of Dr. Sirri's study. Cuban's motion is therefore denied.

3

Cuban moves to exclude Dr. Sialm's rebuttal opinion that the change in Mamma.com's stock price after the PIPE offering announcement was "economically significant." Dr. Sialm opines that, even if Dr. Sirri did not consider the 9.7% decline in stock price to be statistically significant, the test of statistical significance has limited power here because Mamma.com's stock had a volatile price. Dr. Sialm opines that the decline in stock price is "economically meaningful or highly important to a reasonable investor." He also opines that Cuban's avoided loss of $714,000 is economically meaningful.

Cuban maintains that "economic significance" has no scientific meaning and that such a characterization cannot be tested. The SEC acknowledges that "economic significance" is not an empirical test, but it asserts that it is a term commonly used by economists.

Dr. Sialm uses the terms "economically significant" and "economically meaningful" in the section of his rebuttal report that criticizes Dr. Sirri for opining only about the statistical significance of the announcement effect on Mamma.com stock. Cuban objects specifically to the terms "economically significant' or "economically meaningful," and not to Dr. Sialm's critique of the narrowness of Dr. Sirri's opinion.

This objection relates to the weight to be given Dr. Sialm's opinion. And because Cuban's other objections relate to the weight to be given Dr. Sialm's rebuttal opinion, the court denies Cuban's motion.

V

The SEC moves to exclude the testimony and reports of Cuban's expert, Dr. Sirri. Dr. Sirri opines that the PIPE offering information Cuban received was immaterial and had become public by the time he sold his shares.

A

1

Regarding whether the information on which Cuban allegedly traded was nonpublic, Dr. Sirri opines that the information Cuban possessed "was likely already incorporated into the price of the [Mamma.com stock]" by the time Cuban sold his shares on the eve of the PIPE's announcement. As the court held in [a prior decision in this case:]

> [i]nformation becomes public when disclosed to achieve a broad dissemination to the investing public generally and without favoring any special person or group, or when, although known only by a few persons, their trading on it has caused the information to be fully impounded into the price of the particular stock.

Dr. Sirri provides four reasons to support his opinion. First, he relies on the Form 20-F that Mamma.com publicly filed [with the SEC] in May 2004 and that states that Mamma.com retained Merriman Curhan Ford & Co. ("Merriman") to "provide investment banking services to [Mamma.com] which may include" a PIPE, another type of capital raising transaction, an acquisition of Mamma.com, or acquisitions by Mamma.com. Dr. Sirri opines that the Form "conveyed information about the upcoming PIPE offering to the marketplace."

Second, Dr. Sirri opines that the PIPE offering information likely seeped into the market and was reflected in the stock price because the hedge funds informed about Mamma.com's PIPE likely discussed the information with other traders and investors. As support, Dr. Sirri cites evidence that hedge funds received information about Mamma.com's PIPE offering approximately three months before it was announced, they were not asked to keep the information confidential, and they did not consider the information to be nonpublic or confidential. Dr. Sirri also points out that one hedge fund learned of the PIPE offering from another hedge fund instead of from Merriman or Mamma.com.

Third, Dr. Sirri opines that certain activity by the hedge funds who knew of the PIPE offering indicated to certain market participants information about the upcoming offering. In the months leading up to the offering, a few of the hedge funds that invested in Mamma.com's PIPE offering engaged in pre-borrowing arrangements, which are essentially reservations of shares so that, when an investor wants to sell short, there will be available shares. Pre-borrowing arrangements reduce the number of shares available for other market participants to sell short, and therefore other market participants can infer that some investors are planning to sell short. Dr. Sirri cites one example of an investor's noticing the reduction in the Mamma.com shares available for short selling. Dr. Sirri opines that, in conjunction with Mamma.com's Form 20-F, the pre-borrowing arrangements "served to further incorporate the information of the upcoming PIPE offering into the price of the [stock]."

Fourth, Dr. Sirri opines that there was a statistically significant increase in the volume of short sales on the day before the PIPE offering was announced. He states that this abnormal increase in volume of short selling is consistent with an awareness by market participants (other than the hedge funds participating in the PIPE offering) of the impending PIPE offering, and because selling short is a strategy to profit based on this information. He thus concludes that the PIPE offering information was already incorporated into the price of Mamma.com's stock when the short sales were made.

The SEC maintains that Dr. Sirri's ultimate opinion that the PIPE offering information was incorporated into the price before Cuban sold his shares lacks sufficient basis because the four grounds on which he relies are flawed or provide only speculation in support of his opinion.

2

Generally, challenges "to the bases and sources of an expert's opinion affect the weight to be assigned that opinion rather than its admissibility and should be left for the jury's consideration." This rule does not apply when the bases are "'of such little weight that the jury should not be permitted to receive that opinion,'" which occurs when "'that testimony would not actually assist the jury in arriving at an intelligent and sound verdict.'" Even a credentialed expert like Dr. Sirri must have reliable support for his opinions; a bare, subjective opinion is inadmissible.

The court declines to exclude Dr. Sirri's ultimate opinion that the PIPE offering information was likely incorporated into Mamma.com's stock price, because his second ground provides sufficient support. The second ground—that hedge funds likely discussed the PIPE offering information with market participants beyond those informed by Merriman or Mamma.com—has an evidentiary basis and is within his expertise concerning equity markets. Dr. Sirri is a professor of finance and has held positions with the SEC, such as Chief Economist and Director of the Division of Trading and Markets. The SEC does not challenge his asserted expertise in topics such as equity markets and insider trading. Combined with this experience and specialty knowledge, Dr. Sirri relies on evidence showing that the hedge funds whom Merriman informed of the PIPE offering were not given confidentiality agreements, and that one hedge fund told another hedge fund about the offering. Evidence that the PIPE offering information was discussed with market participants not covered by confidentiality agreements is reliable support for Dr. Sirri, with his experience, to opine that the information was likely incorporated into the stock price.

The court also declines to exclude Dr. Sirri's testimony regarding the first and third bases, even though they do not of themselves provide sufficient support for his ultimate opinion. Dr. Sirri avers that his ultimate opinion is based on all four reasons "[t]aken together," and the first and third reasons have reliable sources and do provide some support. Form 20-F neither specifies that a PIPE offering will occur nor identifies when, but it does publicly disclose the possibility of a PIPE offering. Similarly, Dr. Sirri does not explain how the reduction in shares caused by pre-borrowing arrangements indicates specifically that a PIPE offering is about to occur, but it does indicate that investors are preparing to engage in short selling, which could be motivated by an impending PIPE offering. These bases, while not specific indications of an impending PIPE offering, are based in fact and offer some support for Dr. Sirri's ultimate opinion.

The court grants the SEC's motion to exclude, however, as to Dr. Sirri's fourth ground: the increased volume of short sales the day before the PIPE offering was announced. Citing Dr. Sialm's rebuttal report, the SEC contends that the increase in volume of short sales is not statistically significant because the entire volume of sales increased on June 28, 2004, resulting in roughly the same proportion of short sales to total sales. In response to this argument, Dr. Sirri testified at his deposition that the fact that the proportion of short sales to total sales remained roughly the same did not alter his conclusion, because he knew of no basis to expect that, when total volume rose, short sale volume would also rise. Dr. Sirri maintained that the increase in volume of short sales "speaks for itself," and that the increase in total sales is also consistent with the PIPE offering information's coming into the marketplace.

Cuban has failed to meet his burden of demonstrating that Dr. Sirri's opinion is reliable in this respect. Dr. Sirri is opining about behavior: that the increase in short sales shows that the PIPE offering information was available to market participants other than the participating hedge funds. He reasons that, because there was no new information that would have caused this increase in short sale volume, the increase is consistent with an awareness of the impending PIPE offering by market participants seeking to profit by short selling before the announcement. But Dr. Sirri's ability to interpret the meaning of the increase in short sale volume is undermined because the volume of total sales also rose, and the proportion remained roughly the same. Dr. Sirri maintains that he knows of no literature holding that proportionality between the volume of short sales and total shares should naturally remain the same when the volume of total sales changes, and thus does not agree that the increase in volume of total sales undermines his conclusion. But the proponent of an expert opinion bears the burden of proving reliability, and Cuban has failed to provide support to justify Dr. Sirri's interpretation of the increased volume of short sales in light of the alternative view that the volume rose simply because the volume of total sales increased. It is insufficient for Dr. Sirri to make the *ipse dixit* assertion that a statistically significant increase in volume of short sales "speaks for itself" when the proportion of short sales remains roughly the same.

Dr. Sirri's opinion is also flawed in that he fails to identify who engaged in short selling on June 28, 2004. He relies on the increased volume to opine that market participants other than the hedge funds participating in PIPE offering were aware of the impending offering and engaged in short selling. But he fails to specify that the increased short selling was not by the participating hedge funds. There is therefore no evidence that other market participants engaged in short selling, which is Dr. Sirri's basis for opining that market participants were aware of the impending PIPE offering.

Because Cuban has failed to meet his burden to prove the reliability of Dr. Sirri's fourth basis for his ultimate opinion that the PIPE offering information was incorporated into Mamma.com's stock price when Cuban sold his shares, the court grants the SEC's motion to exclude in this respect.

B

The SEC also moves to exclude Dr. Sirri's opinion regarding materiality. Dr. Sirri conducted a study to determine whether Mamma.com's announcement of its PIPE offering had an effect on the price of its stock. He opines that there was not a statistically significant price reaction, and that, "[b]ased on this statistical analysis, the information Cuban was given concerning the PIPE was not material at the time of the public announcement."

1

The SEC contends that Fifth Circuit case law precludes the use of *ex post* price reaction analysis as evidence of materiality. The SEC relies on cases describing materiality as "what a reasonable investor *would have expected* when information becomes known by the market, i.e., the likely potential effect of the information. Although this description is essentially correct, it does not follow that an *ex post* study cannot be probative of whether a reasonable investor would have viewed particular information as significantly altering the total mix of available information. And the Fifth Circuit has not rejected the probative value of *ex post* studies. In fact, it recently noted that "price impact evidence ... is probative of materiality," and that "evidence that a stock's price was unaffected by a misrepresentation is convincing evidence that a misrepresentation was not material. . . .

2

The SEC also maintains that Dr. Sirri's opinion is an improper legal conclusion that would inappropriately instruct the jury to accept Cuban's position that the PIPE offering information was immaterial unless a statistically significant announcement effect is proved. Cuban responds that Dr. Sirri does not generally opine about materiality; instead, he qualifies his opinion by introducing it with "*[b]ased on this statistical analysis*, the information Cuban was given concerning the PIPE was not material at the time of the public announcement." Despite this qualification, the SEC objects to Dr. Sirri's use of the term "material."

The court concludes that any jury confusion arising from Dr. Sirri's qualified use of the term "material" can be addressed at trial, such as through cross-examination or an appropriate instruction.

3

The SEC also objects to Dr. Sirri's characterization of the results of his study. The study concluded that the price reaction to Mamma.com's announcement was not statistically significant. Based on this analysis, Dr. Sirri opines that the PIPE offering information Cuban received was not material, and "not different from movements due to normal stock-specific fluctuations." The SEC maintains that these characterizations are scientifically inaccurate because Dr. Sirri's study only proves that the price reaction was not statistically significant, but does not prove that the information was not material or that there was no price reaction or no difference from normal price fluctuations.

At bottom, the SEC seeks to limit Dr. Sirri to testifying only about the precise result of his statistical analysis. The court declines to exclude Dr. Sirri's characterizations of his results because they have a reliable basis in his statistical analysis and any imprecision in his testimony can be addressed by objection or on cross-examination.

Accordingly, except as stated above, the court declines to exclude Dr. Sirri's opinions regarding the materiality or public nature of the PIPE offering information Cuban received.

* * *

For the reasons explained, the court denies as moot the motions to exclude the opinions and reports of Prof. Steinberg and Prof. Hazen, denies the motion to exclude the opinions and reports of Dr. Sialm, and grants in part and denies in part the motion to exclude the opinions and reports of Dr. Sirri.[12]

SO ORDERED.
July 23, 2013.

[Signed]
SIDNEY A. FITZWATER
CHIEF JUDGE

VIII. ONWARD TO PRE-TRIAL MATTERS

With the production of documents, witness testimony, and other fact discovery conducted as well as various motions being made by the parties and ruled upon by the federal district court, the discovery stage of the litigation came to a conclusion. The time had come for Mr. Cuban to seek victory by means of summary judgment. The motion for summary judgment and the court's denial of that motion are covered in the book's next chapter along with other pre-trial matters of significance.

[12.] Many citations in this opinion have been omitted.

CHAPTER 6

Prelude to Trial

This chapter focuses on three events prior to the commencement of trial: Mr. Cuban's motion for summary judgment, Mr. Cuban's motion *in limine*, and the issuance of the pretrial order. The chapter commences with the motion for summary judgment.

I. MR. CUBAN'S MOTION FOR SUMMARY JUDGMENT

As expected, at the appropriate juncture, Mr. Cuban filed his motion for summary judgment. In its reply, the SEC vigorously contested the motion. Oral argument before Judge Fitzwater subsequently was held. *Excerpts of the oral argument with respect to the motion for summary judgment follow.*

[A] The Oral Argument

THE COURT: Good afternoon, counsel.

At this time the court will hear argument on the pending motion for summary judgment in Securities and Exchange Commission versus Cuban, beginning first with Mr. Best [who represents Mr. Cuban].

MR. BEST: Thank you, Your Honor. May I approach the lectern?

THE COURT: You may proceed.

MR. BEST: May it please the court....

The SEC can only avoid summary judgment by showing specific facts in the record which a reasonable jury could find in the SEC's favor on each and every element of the SEC's claim.

Specifically, taking facts as we must in the light most favorable to the SEC at this point, for summary judgment, there is no evidence which a reasonable jury can conclude, one, that Mr. Cuban did not disclose his intent to sell his Mamma.com shares to Mr. Arnold Owen, the Merriman Curhan Ford representative and Mamma's placement agent with whom Mr. Cuban spoke on June 28, 2004.

Second, that on June 28, 2004, when Mr. Fauré called Mr. Cuban that any of the information relayed to Mr. Cuban that day was confidential information.

Three, that on their June 28, 2004 call that Mr. Cuban entered into any agreement whatsoever with Mr. Fauré, specifically, that Mr. Cuban entered into an agreement of confidentiality on the call with Mr. Fauré, and that Mr. Cuban entered into an agreement not to trade on that call with Mr. Fauré.

Finally, fourth, that is June 28th, 2004, the information about the PIPE offering that was conveyed to Mr. Cuban was material information.

Your Honor, I'll be addressing all the arguments today, save the materiality piece, with which my colleague, Mr. [Lyle] Roberts, will be addressing....

MR. O'ROURKE [representing the SEC]

MR. O'ROURKE: With all due respect to my adversaries, each point they raised in their motion ... [w]e have fully answered their arguments in the briefing and showed genuine issues for trial.

And I would say ... nothing other than [what] they have raised before and we have come forward with sufficient evidence to dispute and establish that there are triable issues, each point they have raised....

... I turn ... briefly to materiality. The fact—the fact of the matter is, Your Honor, we fully briefed materiality—and established that there's evidence of materiality, at least enough to get to the jury, but in fact much more than that, ten ways to Sunday. Without question ... with all due respect, we've established enough evidence to have a triable issue as to materiality.

And an indicia of materiality does stand out, and that is Mr. Cuban's own immediate dumping of his stock. He sold one minute after his call to Merriman's Arnie Owen.... Immediate dumping of his stock. He dumped everything. His instructions were something to the effect sell as much as you can tonight and the rest tomorrow. So he was selling it before the public announcement.... And so it's for the jury to decide the materiality issue. But also it indicates the importance of materiality to him.

But the immediacy ... he placed the order to sell one minute, the immediacy shows that he knows ... that it's material to reasonable investors. That's why he needed to sell immediately, because once the public announcement is made the reasonable investors ... [may] sell the stock and affect the price. So the immediacy of his sale doesn't just indicate the heightened importance to him, but it also is a strong indication of materiality to him and his knowledge of the materiality to reasonable investors, Your Honor.

It's also highly aberrational trading on his part. This is the first time that he ever, ever sold his position in a company where he had taken a greater than 5 percent position. So the first time ever he's done that he does it immediately. It's highly aberrational, which itself is an indication of the materiality, certainly enough to get to the jury by itself....

THE COURT: What I would like you to focus on, ... the importance of oral argument is to give you a chance, take me through the evidence that would allow a reasonable jury to find an agreement not to trade.

Because we have a June 28 phone call. We have Mr. Fauré saying I've got confidential information for you. We've got some words spoken in response. It's an eight minute telephone conversation. We have the statement, "Well, I'm screwed, I can't sell." ... Mr. Cuban ... [is] ... not a lawyer, he's thinking I've been given confidential information, that means I can't trade? ...

... [T]ake me through the evidence that would allow a jury to find that reasonably.

MR. O'ROURKE: Well, ... we'll focus on [June] 28th, but before doing that can I at least refer, Your Honor, and mention the prehistory?

THE COURT: Certainly.

MR. O'ROURKE: And that's the communications between Mr. Cuban and Mr. Fauré that took place before the 28th .... There [were] numerous and multitude of communications between the two gentlemen. And there's sufficient evidence to show that through that that Cuban had achieved his goal of establishing a line of communication with the CEO, sufficient evidence to show that Cuban had obtained the attention of the CEO .... And these communications show the context that led up to the phone call on the 28th.

And there's two emails in April, an April 6th and an April 23 email. April [6th] email Fauré expressed a willingness to trust Cuban with Mamma's confidential information and expressed the matter by telephone, "I would rather you call me, this is under confidentiality," indicating he would discuss confidential information by phone.

And the April 23 [email] which Cuban ... offered his help on acquisitions Mamma was considering and emphasized that "Obviously, what you tell me is confidential."

He goes on to say, "It's not anything I can act on either."

So you have that as the predicate.

And then you have the phone call on [June] 28th, Mr. Fauré placing the phone call—sending an email for him to call and Mr. Cuban immediately calls back. I submit we're entitled to an inference that he was expecting confidential information on the phone call back.

And then they proceeded with the ... phone call on the 28th.

And ... Mr. Cuban doesn't deny what went on on that phone call because he claims that he doesn't recall what went on, itself a credibility question.

But Mr. Fauré, as Your Honor knows, said, "I have confidential information," in words or in substance. Mr. Cuban does not dispute that.

In words or in substance Mr. Cuban told him to go ahead and provide it. And then Mr. Cuban doesn't recall what he said there.

And then [Mr. Fauré] provided the information to [Mr. Cuban]. They discussed PIPEs and his dislike of PIPEs because they dilute shareholders. And then he said—and it's undisputed, Mr. Cuban has never disputed, nor can he because he says he doesn't recall the phone call, "Well, now I'm screwed, because I can't sell." Now you have that evidence.

And the Fifth Circuit indicated in the context of a motion to dismiss [decision contained in Chapter 2 of this book] that that was a plausible basis—provides more that a plausible basis to find that the understanding between Mr. Fauré and Cuban was that he was not to trade. So that was sufficient there, Your Honor. And no evidence to the contrary. . . .

. . . Your Honor appeared in your earlier opinion to say that . . . the issue was: Was there an agreement. Mr. Cuban has briefed . . . that it has to be a formal contract with all the formalities of a contract. And it doesn't appear to us that that's what Your Honor was referring to in your numerous references to agreement, nor do we think it would be right to limit it.

As the [U.S. Supreme] Court said in *O'Hagan* [521 U.S. 642 (1997)], the key to misappropriation is deception. And the formalities of a contract don't add to the deception. The question is was their acknowledgement of a duty, was there a mutual consent, was their promissory estoppel, . . . was the source of the information induced to provide the information. It's concepts like that that relate to deception, not whether or not there was a formal contract that we would have to litigate, not just in this case but in any insider trading case, whether or not there was a formal contract. . . .

I believe the other points that they have raised we've answered in our brief, Your Honor, so . . . I submit based on what we have said in our brief and my attempt to respond to your questions here today.

THE COURT: All right. Thank you, counsel.

MR. O'ROURKE: Thank you, Your Honor.

MR. BEST: Your Honor, may I approach?

THE COURT: You may.

MR. BEST: Thank you.

THE CLERK: You have 9 minutes and 40 seconds.

MR. BEST [Counsel for Mr. Cuban]: Thank you, Your Honor.

Let me address first the going back to the nondisclosure or disclosure issue and the SEC's failure to meet their burden.

The statute by which Mr. Cuban is charged is under 10(b)—10(b) fraud. They have alleged a fraud by Mr. Cuban. That fraud by and through the misappropriation theory is a deceptive act. The deceptive act is . . . in this case, as alleged, is the agreeing to do something and then not disclosing it.

So there is . . . no statement that you have to qualify your disclosure in any way. If you state to the source of the information—and I submit to Your Honor that *O'Hagan* stands for the proposition that the source of the information in *O'Hagan* . . . was two sources. It was the law firm as well as the client. Here the source of the information is Mamma.com by and through its agents. You can't talk to a—a building. You can only talk to the building's representatives. And the building's representatives in this case was Guy Fauré and/or Arnie Owen.

So if you tell Arnie Owen that you are going to sell, Arnie Owen, the agent of Mamma.com, the source of the information, you have absolved yourself of 10(b) liability for fraud. . . .

THE COURT: Let me ask you this.

Do we have to get into the law of agency in dealing with Mr. Owen?

Do we have to know whether he was a general agent or whether he had powers that allowed him to receive that kind of disclosure?

MR. BEST: Here's the easiest explanation. The SEC wants to have its cake and eat it, too. The SEC wants to predicate liability in this case, Your Honor, based upon the details of the PIPE that were transferred to Mr. Cuban by and through Arnie Owen. If they don't have Arnie Owen's conversation they are dead in the water here. They can't say on one hand they can predicate liability based upon the conversation by and between Mr. Owen and Mr. Cuban and then say, oh, but then you have to run back to somebody else. It's an—it's an all or nothing proposition.

... [W]ith all due respect to Mr. O'Rourke, he's just wrong. Mr. Cuban stated at his investigative testimony, first, when asked, without seeing a document by the SEC: "Did you tell Mr. Owen that you're going to sell?"

And his response was: "I don't remember. I don't believe so."

But within a couple of minutes, if not an hour of that, he was shown the document, which refreshed his memory, and stated: "I sent an email saying that I told the guy I was going to sell, so I just didn't remember as I was being asked."

That's the investigative testimony from 2006, Your Honor. It's not that he said he wasn't going to sell and then changed his testimony. It's a far cry from that.

Indeed, what's important here is that the SEC is dead in the water if they don't rely upon Mark Cuban's recollection of the conversation with Arnie Owen. They hold on to Mr. Cuban's legs firmly and say, ah, Mr. Cuban, you said that Mr. Owen told you the price of the offering, ah, Mr. Cuban, you said that Mr. Owen told you that there was warrant coverage, you got the details of the PIPE from Mr. Owen....

They accept and embrace every part of the conversation that Mr. Cuban says about his—his call with Mr. Owen, except one sentence, and that is Cuban's ... statement to Mr. Owen, I'm going to sell my shares. So you can't—again, you can't have your cake and eat it, too. You can't embrace everything that Mark Cuban said and then on one point said oh, I just—I don't believe that.

THE CLERK: Five minutes.

MR. BEST: But I don't want to get away from the fact that this is the SEC's burden to show that there was nondisclosure, not our burden to show disclosure.

Now, let me turn to Your Honor's discussion about agreement not to trade. Let me turn to the testimonial record.

There was no prior confidences ever exchanged by and between Guy Fauré and Mr. Cuban. There was no prior confidential exchanges between anybody at Mamma.com and Mr. Cuban.

I specifically asked Mr. Fauré that question in his deposition.

"Had you ever exchanged confidential information [with Mr. Cuban] prior to June 28th, 2004?"

His response: "I don't believe so, no."

I said "Did you have a master confidentiality in place with Mr. Cuban prior to June 28th, 2004?"

"No."

I said: "Indeed, if you had a master confidentiality with Mr. Cuban you probably wouldn't have had to preface your conversation at the outset that you had confidential information to share, correct?"

And you know ... what his response was?

"Correct."

Interestingly, the SEC wants to bring up two emails from April as being relevant. What they don't tell you is that in neither of those circumstances was confidential information actually exchanged. There was a banter about it, but it never happened. That's the uncontradicted record from Guy Fauré, not a he said/she said. The facts are not in dispute.

I also want to go bring up Your Honor's specific question about … where is it in the record that speaks to a separate agreement not to trade.

This is from the deposition of Guy Fauré.

My question: "Mr. Fauré, when Mr. Cuban had some sort of acknowledgement at the beginning of the call, that also meant that since Mr. Cuban was going to hold this information in confidence he was also not able to sell the stock until the public announcement of this confidential information, correct?"

Mr. Fauré's response: "Correct."

Mr. Fauré, himself, acknowledges that there was no separate and distinct agreement to not use this information.

Mr. Fauré, himself, states that any obligation or agreement to not trade was embedded in the first conversation at the outset of the call where there was simply an acknowledgement that information was confidential.

Specifically, Mr. Fauré does not import any—any legal obligation to the words "I'm screwed, I can't sell." And with all due respect to Mr. O'Rourke and the entire SEC, they just misread the record as regards … reliance by Mamma.com on the "I'm screwed, I can't sell," statement, because the uncontradicted record here is they did not rely on that statement.

In fact, Mr. Fauré says, "We were just sitting around and Mr. Goldman told me to send an email to Mr. Cuban saying if he wants any more information to just contact Arnie Owen," that there was no reliance upon that statement whatsoever.

So, indeed, when the Fifth Circuit found their import to that and when Your Honor spoke to it just now, the record is crystal clear there was no reliance on that statement, whatsoever. . . .

MR. ROBERTS [Counsel for Mr. Cuban]: Your Honor, I'll be very brief.

The SEC, as perhaps predicted, wants to rely on Mr. Cuban's own actions and trades as evidence of materiality. That's not appropriate. That's not where the law is. And I thought I should point out to Your Honor … that the SEC has made the following statement to the Supreme Court in the Amgen case [131 S.Ct. 1184 (2013)] …: "The materiality standard is an objective one that focuses on the significance of an admitted or misrepresented fact [to] a reasonable investor, not to any particular investor." That's the state of the law. They shouldn't come into this court and say something different.

THE COURT: Thank you. . . .

The motion is submitted at this time.[1]

[1.] Transcript of Oral Argument on Motion for Summary Judgment (Jan. 18, 2013).

[B] The District Court's Denial of the Motion

After hearing oral argument, Judge Fitzwater denied Mr. Cuban's motion for summary judgment. *Excerpts of Judge Fitzwater's ruling follow.*

MEMORANDUM OPINION AND ORDER

In this civil enforcement action brought by plaintiff Securities and Exchange Commission ("SEC") against defendant Mark Cuban ("Cuban") under the misappropriation theory of insider trading, Cuban moves for summary judgment. Although the question whether Cuban is entitled to summary judgment is in some respects a close one, the court concludes that the SEC is entitled to present its case to a jury. The court therefore denies Cuban's motion.

I

The background facts and procedural history of this case are set out in the court's prior decision addressing Cuban's motion to dismiss ... and the Fifth Circuit's opinion on appeal [which is contained in Chapter 2 of this book]....

Following the [Fifth Circuit's] remand of the case and additional discovery, Cuban now moves for summary judgment .... He contends that the SEC has failed to show that he agreed to keep the PIPE transaction information confidential; that he agreed not to trade on the information; that he did not disclose his intention to sell his Mamma.com stock; and that the PIPE information was material and nonpublic. The SEC opposes the motion.

II

When a party moves for summary judgment on a claim for which the opposing party will bear the burden of proof at trial, the party can meet its summary judgment obligation by pointing the court to the absence of admissible evidence to support the opposing party's claim. Once the party does so, the opposing party must go beyond its pleadings and designate specific facts showing that there is a genuine issue for trial. An issue is genuine if the evidence is such that a reasonable jury could return a verdict in the opposing party's favor. The opposing party's failure to produce proof as to any essential element of a claim renders all other facts immaterial. Summary judgment is mandatory if the opposing party fails to meet this burden.

III

Cuban contends that no reasonable jury could find that he agreed to keep information about the Mamma.com PIPE confidential or that he agreed not to trade on this information.

A

As a threshold issue, the court considers Cuban's contention that the SEC cannot meet its burden of proving that Mamma.com and Cuban entered into an agreement without establishing a "valid offer and acceptance plus a meeting of the minds supported by consideration." [Defendant's Brief] 23 ("It is black-letter contract law that there can be no agreement between two parties in the absence of valid offer and acceptance plus a meeting of the minds supported by consideration. These elements have not been, and cannot be, satisfied by the record in this case."

In [an earlier decision in this case,] the court explained that ... :

> in concluding ... that an agreement with the proper components can establish the duty necessary to support liability under the misappropriation theory, the court is not creating federal general common law. Because all states recognize and enforce duties created by agreement, the court is essentially relying on the state law of contracts to supply the requisite duty.

.... The court neither adopted the contract law of any particular state nor suggested that the requirement of an agreement could only be satisfied by an express contract. The court referred several times to the sufficiency of an implied agreement to maintain the confidentiality of material, nonpublic information and not to trade on or otherwise use it.... These references to an implied agreement were intentional because, under general contract principles, an agreement can be manifested implicitly....

The court therefore rejects Cuban's contention that the SEC must prove a "valid offer and acceptance plus a meeting of the minds supported by consideration." What the SEC must establish at trial is that Cuban agreed, at least implicitly, to maintain the confidentiality of Mamma.com's material, nonpublic information and not to trade on or otherwise use it. And the existence of such an agreement can be implied from the parties' conduct and the surrounding circumstances.

B

The court now considers whether a reasonable jury could find that Cuban agreed to keep the PIPE information confidential.

"When the court denies rather than grants summary judgment, it typically does not set out in detail the evidence that creates a genuine issue of material fact." ... Here and throughout this memorandum opinion and order the court will summarize or provide examples of evidence that presents genuine and material fact issues that require a trial.

There is evidence in the summary judgment record that, on June 28, 2004, on the eve of the PIPE offering, Mamma.com's CEO, Guy Fauré ("Fauré"), emailed Cuban asking to speak with him as soon as possible. Cuban telephoned within five minutes. When Fauré answered the call, he told Cuban, "I've got confidential information." Cuban responded, "Um hum, go ahead," or "Okay, uh huh, go ahead," or something to that effect. Fauré then informed Cuban of the planned PIPE offering. Cuban reacted angrily to this news, and near the end of the conversation said something like, "Now I'm screwed. I can't sell."

Cuban's "I can't sell" statement, made in the context of a telephone call in which Mamma.com's CEO led off by telling Cuban that he was disclosing confidential information, would enable a reasonable jury to find that Cuban at least implicitly agreed to keep the information confidential. This is because the jury could at least reasonably infer that Cuban would not have considered himself foreclosed from trading unless he believed he had agreed to treat the information as confidential.

Cuban is therefore not entitled to summary judgment on this basis.

C

Cuban maintains that no reasonable jury could find that he agreed not to trade on the PIPE information.

... Although summary judgment is governed by a higher standard than the one that applies when determining the plausibility of a claim at the Rule 12(b)(6) [motion to dismiss] stage, the SEC has adduced sufficient summary judgment evidence to enable a reasonable jury to find in its favor....

After Cuban and Fauré spoke, Cuban contacted Arnold Owen ("Owen"), head of the private placement group at Merriman Curhan Ford & Co. ("Merriman"), the investment bankers who were handling the planned PIPE. Cuban had already acknowledged to Fauré that, having received the information about the PIPE, he could not sell his shares in the company. According to an email that Mamma.com's Chairman of the Board, David Goldman ("Goldman"), sent to the Board of Directors summarizing what Fauré related to him about the Cuban conversation,

> [t]oday, after much discussion, [Fauré] spoke to Mark Cuban about this equity raise and whether or not he would be interested in participating. As anticipated he initially "flew off the handle" and said he would sell his shares *(recognizing that he was not able to do anything until we announce the equity)* but then asked to see the terms and conditions which we have arranged for him to receive from one of the participating investor groups with which he has dealt in the past.

(emphasis added). If Cuban told Fauré, "I can't sell," if he recognized that he was not able to do anything until Mamma.com announced the PIPE, and he requested more information from Mamma.com about the PIPE, the jury could reasonably infer that he and Mamma.com implicitly agreed that Mamma.com would only provide him information about the terms and conditions of the PIPE "for the purpose of evaluating whether he would participate in the offering, and that Cuban could not use the information for his own personal benefit." Viewing the summary judgment evidence in the light most favorable to the SEC as the summary judgment nonmovant, there is a genuine issue of fact whether Cuban agreed at least implicitly to refrain from trading on or otherwise using for his own benefit the nonpublic PIPE information.

In reaching this conclusion, the court emphasizes the closeness of this call. As should be apparent from the court's reasoning in denying summary judgment, evidence concerning the contents of Cuban's telephone conversation with Fauré and of the conduct of Mamma.com that followed that conversation is critical. It is based on this proof that the court is able to say that a reasonable jury could find that Cuban recognized that he could not sell his shares until the PIPE was announced, that he requested more information about the PIPE, that he at least implicitly agreed that Mamma.com would only provide him this information so that he could evaluate whether he wanted to participate in the PIPE, and that, because of his implied agreement, he could not use the information for his personal benefit. Yet the summary judgment evidence portrays a relatively brief telephone conversation between Fauré and Cuban of approximately eight minutes, about which Fauré has a spotty memory in crucial respects, and sometimes only recalls Cuban's using ambiguous forms of non-verbal communication (e.g., "um hum" and "uh huh"). Even the statement Fauré does remember Cuban's making—"Now I'm screwed. I can't sell"—requires supporting context, because in isolation it "can plausibly be read to express Cuban's view that learning the confidences regarding the PIPE forbade his selling his stock before the offering *but to express no agreement not to do so.*" (emphasis added) And as for whether Cuban requested more information about the PIPE—implicitly agreeing in exchange for such information that he would not trade on it—there is substantial record evidence that Cuban did *not* ask to see the terms and conditions of the transaction but that Fauré *invited* Cuban to contact Owen at Goldman's suggestion.... This evidence would undercut the theory that Mamma.com only provided the terms and conditions of the PIPE offering after Cuban implicitly agreed that he could not use the information for his personal benefit.

Despite the closeness of this question, there is evidence—summarized above—that would enable a reasonable jury to find that Cuban agreed at least implicitly not to trade on the PIPE information. The court must therefore deny his motion for summary judgment to the extent based on this ground.

IV

Cuban also contends that he is entitled to summary judgment because there is no evidence that he failed to disclose his intention to trade on the PIPE information.

A

United States v. O'Hagan, 521 U.S. 642 (1997), "states unmistakably that '[d]eception through nondisclosure is central to [this] theory[.]'" [Under *O'Hagan*:]

> [F]ull disclosure forecloses liability under the misappropriation theory: Because the deception essential to the misappropriation theory involves feigning fidelity to the source of information, if the fiduciary discloses to the source that he plans to trade on the nonpublic information, there is no "deceptive device" and thus no § 10(b) violation[.]

.... This "disclosure obligation runs to the source of information." It is therefore necessary for the SEC to prove that Cuban did not disclose to Mamma.com his intention to trade on the nonpublic PIPE information. If he did fully disclose this intention and thereby avoid deceiving Mamma.com, there is no liability under the misappropriation theory of insider trading.

B

Cuban maintains that there is uncontroverted evidence that he made full disclosure of his intention to trade. He cites his deposition testimony that, when he discussed the PIPE with Owen (the head of Merriman's private placement group), he informed him that he was not going to participate in the PIPE and that he would sell his shares.

The court holds that a reasonable jury could find from the evidence in the summary judgment record that Cuban merely disclosed that he "was going to sell," not that he specified that he would sell *before* Mamma.com announced the PIPE....

Accordingly, Cuban is not entitled to summary judgment on this basis.

V

Cuban moves for summary judgment on the ground that the SEC cannot prove that the PIPE information was confidential.

A

Cuban contends that the summary judgment evidence shows that the PIPE information he received was not confidential because information about the Mamma.com PIPE was widely distributed to prospective investors, without confidentiality restrictions, Mamma.com had itself disclosed a possible PIPE and Mamma.com disclaimed that the PIPE information was confidential. He posits that, under *O'Hagan*, only confidential information can serve as a basis for misappropriation theory liability. Cuban also contends that, because the PIPE information that Fauré provided him was not confidential, any agreement he made to keep the information confidential would be invalid under the contract doctrine of mutual mistake of fact. Cuban maintains that a reasonable jury could only find that the information was not confidential and therefore could not have formed the basis of a valid agreement to maintain its confidentiality.

In reply to the SEC's response brief—which focuses on whether the PIPE information was nonpublic—Cuban maintains that the SEC has failed to address his arguments that the information was not *confidential*. He differentiates in his reply brief between the use of the term *confidential* in relation to whether a confidentiality agreement was formed between himself and Mamma.com, and the use of the term *nonpublic* when referring to a standard element of a § 10(b) claim....

B

Because Cuban states that his argument regarding confidentiality does not challenge whether the SEC can establish the nonpublic information element of its insider trading claim, he is necessarily contending that there is a distinction between confidential information and *nonpublic* information, and that the SEC must prove that the PIPE information qualifies as both. For support he cites an instance in *O'Hagan* where the Court used the term *confidential* information instead of *nonpublic* information in describing the misappropriation theory. *See* [Defendant's Brief] at 35 (interpreting *O'Hagan* as holding that "only '[a] company's *confidential* information ... qualifies as property to which the company has a right of exclusive use' and can serve as the basis for misappropriation theory liability" ....) Cuban's argument fails because, in the context of the misappropriation theory of insider trading, the terms *confidential* information and *nonpublic* information essentially have the same meaning. Therefore, the SEC's evidence that the PIPE information was *nonpublic* is sufficient to defeat the summary judgment argument that the information was not *confidential*....

C

Nor does the court agree that Cuban can rely on the contract doctrine of mutual mistake of fact to undermine the validity of the confidentiality agreement. In order for a duty to be sufficient to support liability under the misappropriation theory, it must at least have attributes that correspond to the ones recognized in *O'Hagan*.... Paraphrasing and applying here what this court wrote in [an earlier decision in this case], "investors likely would hesitate to venture their capital if they knew that ... a corporate outsider ... who had actually agreed with the source not to trade on such information ... *could* do so [by successfully raising a contract defense to his agreement not to trade]."

The court therefore concludes that Cuban cannot defeat an agreement that is otherwise sufficient to create misappropriation theory liability by relying on a contract defense such as mutual mistake.

D

The court holds that a reasonable jury could find that the PIPE information that Cuban received was nonpublic and therefore confidential.

A jury could reasonably find that information about the Mamma.com PIPE had not been "effectively disclosed in a manner sufficient to insure its availability to the *investing public*." [As stated by the Second Circuit:]

> Information becomes public when disclosed to achieve a broad dissemination to the investing public generally and without favoring any special person or group, or when, although known only by a few persons, their trading on it has caused the information to be fully impounded into the price of the particular stock.

SEC v. Mayhew, 121 F.2d 44, 59 (2d Cir. 1997).... The summary judgment evidence would permit the finding that information concerning the PIPE had been provided to a limited number of prospective investors, had not been disclosed to Mamma.com shareholders (except board members and officers who were restricted from trading before the PIPE was announced), and had not been disclosed to the investing public. Cuban, who was Mamma.com's largest shareholder, does not dispute that he was unaware of the PIPE until June 28, 2004, on the eve of the public announcement of the offering....

Cuban is not entitled to summary judgment on this basis.

VI

Cuban contends that he is entitled to summary judgment on the ground that the information about the Mamma.com PIPE that he possessed when he sold his shares was not material information.

A

To establish that Cuban is liable for insider trading, the SEC must show that he traded on nonpublic information of Mamma.com that was material.... "A fact is material if there is a substantial likelihood that, under all the circumstances, the ... fact would have assumed actual significance in the deliberations of the reasonable [investor]." ... Materiality is a mixed question of law and fact. *Mayhew*, 121 F.3d at 51.

Although a court can determine that nonpublic information is immaterial as a matter of law, "[b]ecause materiality is a mixed question of law and fact, it is usually left for the jury." ... The materiality determination is appropriate for the trier of fact because it "requires delicate assessments of the inferences a reasonable [investor] would draw from a given set of facts and the significance of those inferences to him." ...

B

Cuban points to the absence of evidence that would enable a reasonable jury to find that the PIPE information that he possessed when he traded was material, specifically challenging the opinion testimony of the SEC's expert, Clemens Sialm, Ph.D. ("Dr. Sialm"). He also relies on affirmative evidence in the form of an event study prepared by his expert witness, Erik Sirri, PhD. ("Dr. Sirri"), which examined how the market reacted to the Mamma.com PIPE announcement. Dr. Sirri opines that the price reaction of Mamma.com stock to the PIPE announcement was not statistically significant, and therefore the information Cuban was given concerning the PIPE was not material at the time of the public announcement. Cuban contends that, although the Fifth Circuit has not squarely decided this question, other courts consider an event study to be the best evidence of whether a reasonable investor would have viewed the information as significant. Cuban also cites instances in which the

SEC has itself relied on event studies as evidence of materiality in civil enforcement actions.

The SEC responds that, as a mixed question of law and fact, materiality is a question for the jury. It maintains that there is substantial evidence—including proof of Cuban's actions, PIPE participants' conduct, the immediate drop in Mamma.com's stock price after the PIPE announcement, the amount of the loss that Cuban was able to avoid, an assessment of Mamma.com's financial statements, and Dr. Sialm's expert analysis—that would enable a reasonable jury to find that the PIPE information was material.

C

The SEC has produced sufficient evidence for a reasonable jury to find that the PIPE information disclosed to Cuban was material. For example, the SEC's expert, Dr. Sialm, opines that the Mamma.com PIPE information was material because a reasonable investor would expect that a PIPE with such incentives to investors would have the result of diluting shareholder value. Also, the amount Mamma.com sought to raise via the PIPE offering significantly exceeded the funds it had received from its past four years of operations and stock issuance combined. This and other evidence in the record would enable a reasonable jury to find that the PIPE information that Cuban possessed would have been viewed by a reasonable investor as having significantly altered the total mix of information made available about Mamma.com.

* * *

Accordingly, for the reasons explained, the court denies Cuban's motion for summary judgment.[2]

SO ORDERED.

March 5, 2013.

*[Signed]*_____
SIDNEY A. FITZWATER
CHIEF JUDGE

II. MR. CUBAN'S MOTION *IN LIMINE*

Prior to trial, Mr. Cuban made a motion *in limine*. Generally, a motion *in limine* is a pretrial motion seeking a court order that specified inadmissible evidence may not be referred to or introduced at trial. Ordinarily, "a party makes this motion when it believes that mere mention of the evidence during

---

[2.] Memorandum and Order, 2013 WL 791405 (March 5, 2013). Many citations in the ruling have been omitted.

trial would be highly prejudicial and could not be remedied by an instruction to disregard."[3] *Applied to this case, excerpts from Mr. Cuban's motion in limine, the SEC's response, and the district court's advisory to counsel follow.*

[A] Mr. Cuban's Motion

Defendant Mark Cuban respectfully makes this motion *in limine to preclude the SEC from referring in the jury's presence to, or introducing evidence of, the following:*[4]

(i)   Emails written by David Goldman (Chairman of the Board of Directors of Mamma.com) that purport to paraphrase Mamma.com CEO Guy Fauré's paraphrase of Mr. Cuban's alleged statements during the June 28, 2004 telephone call between Mr. Fauré and Mr. Cuban, containing, inter alia, multiple levels of hearsay;

(ii) Provocative and prejudicial extrinsic evidence concerning tax liens and an unrelated SEC administrative order, ostensibly to impeach [two prospective witnesses];

(iii) Emails from April 2004 between Mr. Cuban and Mr. Fauré that do not refer to the Mamma.com PIPE, and that precede by two months the alleged formation on June 28, 2004 of a confidentiality and non-use agreement regarding information about the PIPE;

(iv) Statements made by Mr. Fauré, Mr. Goldman, and Merriman Curhan Ford (Mamma.com's private-placement agent) ("Merriman") reflecting their individual, subjective views of the alleged "materiality" of information about the Mamma.com PIPE; and, separately, a statement made by Merriman that did not mention the Mamma.com PIPE at all, but merely indicated that the SEC *might* consider information about PIPEs generally to be material; and

(v)   Excerpts from the two "Wells submissions" that Mr. Cuban provided to the SEC, in June 2007 and September 2007 respectively, in which he attempted to achieve a negotiated resolution of the SEC's insider trading claims.

For the reasons set forth below, the foregoing matters are not admissible for any purpose and have no bearing on the issues in this case. Even assuming, *arguendo*, that it could be shown that any of these matters may be relevant to a fact of consequence in this case, any probative value is far outweighed by the unfair prejudice and confusion caused by their admission into evidence. Permitting questioning of witnesses, comments to jurors or prospective jurors, or offers of evidence about these matters would be unfairly prejudicial. Once referred to in front of the venire or

---

3. *Black's Law Dictionary* 1171 (10th ed. 2014).

[4.] Emphasis supplied.

the trial jury, the unfair prejudice could not be adequately addressed by objection of Mr. Cuban's counsel, nor cured by Court instruction. Sustaining objections to such questions, statements, or evidence would not prevent the unfair prejudice, but would rather reinforce the development of questionable and inadmissible evidence.

Mr. Cuban respectfully requests that, prior to the commencement of the Court's voir dire, the Court order the SEC, its counsel, or any witnesses to refrain from any reference to these matters directly or indirectly, in any manner whatsoever, unless and until the SEC first obtains, outside the jury's hearing or presence, a ruling of the Court on the admissibility of the matters addressed....[5]

[B] The SEC's Response

Plaintiff U.S. Securities and Exchange Commission ("SEC") respectfully responds to Defendant Mark Cuban's omnibus motion *in limine. For the reasons stated below, the Court should deny Cuban's motion in its entirety.*[6]

PRELIMINARY STATEMENT

The case is about insider trading by Mark Cuban in connection with a Private Investment in Public Equity ("PIPE") transaction planned by Mamma.com ("Mamma"), at a time when Cuban was the largest individual investor in the company. The SEC alleges that Cuban received confidential information from Mamma Chief Executive Officer ("CEO") Guy Fauré in advance of the PIPE offering, that he agreed to keep this information confidential and not to trade based on the information, but that he sold his entire stake in Mamma in advance of the public announcement of the PIPE transaction and avoided a $750,000 loss on his investment in the company.

STANDARD OF REVIEW

The Court's Trial Setting Order prescribes that motions *in limine* should raise issues that cannot adequately be raised by trial objection without prejudice to the moving party and cannot be cured by an instruction from the Court. The Fifth Circuit has recognized that the purpose of a pre-trial motion *in limine* is to "'prohibit[] opposing counsel from mentioning the existence of, alluding to, or offering evidence on matters so highly prejudicial to the moving party that a timely motion to strike or an instruction by the court to the jury to disregard the offending matter cannot overcome its prejudicial influence on the jurors' minds.'"

. . . .

[5.] Motion *in Limine* of Defendant Mark Cuban at pages 1-2 (Sept. 20, 2013) (citations omitted).

[6.] Emphasis supplied.

ARGUMENT

I. THE EMAIL REPORTS TO THE BOARD REFLECTING FAURÉ'S DISCUSSIONS WITH CUBAN ARE ADMISSIBLE

Cuban requests that the Court exclude two contemporaneous emails to the Mamma Board of Directors ("Board"), and related testimony, relaying Fauré's June 28, 2004 conversation with Cuban about the PIPE. Fauré had the conversation with Cuban at the request of the Board.

In moving to preclude the admission of these documents at trial, Cuban does not argue that his own statements contained in the emails and the testimony about his statements constitute inadmissible hearsay. Nor could he. Cuban's words contained in the emails are non-hearsay statements of a party opponent. They are statements by Cuban offered by the SEC against Cuban and, therefore, are admissible. Federal Rules of Evidence ("FRE") 801(d)(2)(A). Rather, Cuban claims that the emails are themselves hearsay offered for the truth of the matters asserted in them and do not fall within any exceptions to the hearsay rule. Cuban is wrong.

First, Cuban intends to challenge Fauré's credibility by suggesting he either fabricated testimony about the call with Cuban as the result of improper influence or motive—Cuban's baseless quid pro quo allegation—or that he cannot recall his conversation with Cuban. These attacks on Fauré's credibility render Fauré's contemporaneous prior consistent statements to the Board as reflected in the emails non-hearsay by definition. FRE 801(d)(1)(B).

Second, Goldman's and Fauré's emails are admissible for the truth of the matters asserted as they possess the necessary indicia of reliability and truthfulness to satisfy the residual exception to the hearsay rule.

Third, in the alternative, the statements may be offered to show that the Board received notice from Goldman and Fauré about Fauré's conversation with Cuban. Fauré discussed the confidential PIPE with Cuban, Mamma's largest shareholder, at the Board's direction.

Because the Goldman and Fauré emails to the Mamma Board are admissible either pursuant to the residual exception to the hearsay rule or as non-hearsay notice to the Board, Cuban's motion *in limine* on this issue should be denied....

II. CUBAN'S APRIL 2004 EMAILS WITH FAURÉ ARE RELEVANT "SURROUNDING CIRCUMSTANCES" EVIDENCE TO THE IMPLICIT CONFIDENTIALITY AND NON-TRADE AGREEMENT

Cuban asks the Court to preclude the SEC from introducing certain April 2004 emails between Cuban and Fauré and testimony concerning those emails. In his motion Cuban admits that the April 2004 emails contain acknowledgements that an exchange of information about the business of Mamma would be kept confidential. Cuban claims that the emails and related testimony are irrelevant to whether Cuban agreed on June 28, 2004, implicitly or otherwise, to keep information confidential and not trade on it and will confuse and mislead the jury. Cuban's arguments, unsupported by any case law, are without merit....

Whether an agreement of confidentiality, express or implied, existed between Cuban and Fauré relating to Mamma's material nonpublic information about the PIPE is the primary issue in this case. Prior discussions between Cuban and Fauré related to company business, some of which may have been confidential, are actions of the parties and constitute surrounding circumstances that are probative of the existence of an implied agreement. Clearly the discussions about company business ... are relevant to show that Cuban and Fauré had a business relationship stemming from Cuban's position as the company's largest shareholder that gave rise to their conversations about the business of Mamma. These communications provide context for the June 28, 2004 conversation between Fauré and Cuban related to the PIPE. Indeed, Fauré testified that he and Cuban communicated about business matters at Mamma and further explained that Cuban was interested in helping the company grow and asked if "there was anything [he] could do." ...

Cuban's April 2004 email communications with Fauré are not unduly prejudicial or confusing. The content of the emails is unambiguous, they were exchanged close in time to the June 28, 2004 call, they occurred between the same parties to the June 28, 2004 call—Cuban and Fauré—were about Mamma's business, referred to certain Mamma business information as confidential, and were shown to Cuban and Fauré during discovery. Both Cuban and Fauré answered questions about the communications and provided explanations as to their meanings. Moreover, Cuban will be a witness at trial and will have an opportunity to testify again regarding these communications should he be asked. In these circumstances, any possibility of alleged jury confusion is remote at best. Accordingly, the Court should reject Cuban's efforts to prevent the SEC from presenting Cuban's April 2004 communications with Fauré and deny his motion *in limine* in this respect.

III. EVIDENCE THAT INSIDERS CONSIDERED THE PLANNED PIPE TRANSACTION TO BE MATERIAL IS ADMISSIBLE

Evidence that Fauré, Goldman, and Merriman Curran Ford & Co. ("Merriman") considered Mamma's planned PIPE transaction to be material—and that they kept it confidential precisely because it was material—is highly probative and admissible evidence of materiality. In attempting to exclude testimony from Fauré, Goldman, and the Merriman representatives, as well as a contemporaneous document created by Merriman, Cuban misapplies the evidentiary standard for determining materiality. When the proper standard is applied, Cuban' motion fails.

....

Here, the "circumstances" that shed light on the significance of the planned PIPE transaction include the views held at the time by insiders such as Fauré and Goldman, as well as others knowledgeable of the PIPE at Merriman (the PIPE placement agent). Testimony and documentary evidence from witnesses with unique, contemporaneous insight provide the context surrounding the transaction, and can only help the jury in assessing the importance of a particular fact to the "total mix" of information available. Several courts have recognized "the importance attached to the [information] by those who knew about it is a 'major factor' in assessing materiality." ... Here, Fauré, Goldman, and the representatives at Merriman were among "those who knew about" the PIPE and all easily concluded that the information was material. The views of such witnesses—"the only truly objective evidence of materiality"—should not be excluded....

Further, the evidence Cuban seeks to exclude is probative not only of whether Fauré, Goldman, and the Merriman representatives thought the PIPE was material; it is inextricably intertwined with their efforts to keep the PIPE information confidential and nonpublic. Indeed, the witnesses testified that the reason they strove to keep the PIPE confidential was because it was material information. Similarly, the Merriman PIPE Acknowledgement Letter Cuban seeks to exclude states that Merriman "has always treated knowledge of a potential private placement as material non-public information...." Fauré, Goldman, and the Merriman representatives are percipient witnesses with regard to the PIPE and, as such, should clearly be permitted to testify concerning whether the PIPE was confidential and non-public. Because their testimony concerning materiality is integral to their testimony concerning confidentiality—indeed, the materiality was the reason for the confidentiality—they should be permitted to testify concerning materiality as well.

Accordingly, Cuban's motion to exclude materiality testimony from Fauré, Goldman, and the Merriman representatives, as well as the written statement of Merriman, should be denied.

. . . .

CONCLUSION

For the reasons stated above, the Court should deny Cuban's Omnibus Motion *in Limine*.[7]

[C] The District Court's Advisory

ADVISORY TO COUNSEL

At the September 25, 2013 pretrial conference, the court granted in part and denied in part the motions *in limine* of plaintiff Securities and Exchange Commission ("SEC") and defendant Mark Cuban ("Cuban"). A ruling on a motion *in limine* "is subject to change when the case unfolds .... Indeed even if nothing unexpected happens at trial, the district judge is free ... to alter a previous *in limine* ruling." ...

The court has located authorities (1) that arguably support Cuban's position that Fed. R. Evid. 806, not Rule 613(b), governs whether the extrinsic evidence of [prospective witness] Michael Storck can be offered to impeach Guy Fauré ("Fauré"), and (2) that arguably support the SEC's position that a written statement adopted by Fauré, even if drafted by David Goldman, can qualify under Rule 801(d)(1)(B) as a

---

[7.] SEC's Response to Cuban's Omnibus Motion *in Limine* (Sept. 23, 2013) (citations omitted).

prior consistent statement. Accordingly, although the court has granted the motions *in limine* in these (and other) respects, it advises counsel that, when a party seeks a ruling outside the jury's presence concerning evidence that is subject to one of the court's orders *in limine*, the court may not follow its interlocutory ruling. At that time, the court will determine in the context of the trial and based on authorities that govern or guide its interpretation of the Rules of Evidence whether the evidence is admissible.

September 26, 2013.

_[Signed]_____

SIDNEY A. FITZWATER
CHIEF JUDGE

III. THE PRE-TRIAL ORDER

Pursuant to Rule 16 of the Federal Rules of Civil Procedure, a pre-trial order is issued. Such an order frequently addresses the claims and defenses to be adjudicated, the stipulations of fact, the contested issues of fact, and procedural matters (including with respect to the admission of evidence). *The Pre-Trial Order in this litigation follows.*

PRETRIAL ORDER

Plaintiff, Securities and Exchange Commission (SEC or Commission), and defendant, Mark Cuban (Cuban), respectfully submit this Revised Joint Pretrial Order ....

I. CLAIMS AND DEFENSES

SEC's Statement of Its Claims

This is a civil enforcement action brought by the U.S. Securities and Exchange Commission against Defendant Mark Cuban under the federal securities laws that prohibit insider trading. The SEC alleges that Cuban sold 600,000 shares of Mamma. com (Mamma) stock while in possession of material, nonpublic information that he agreed to keep confidential and on which he agreed not to trade. In March 2004, Cuban became the single largest shareholder in Mamma, and obtained access to the chief executive officer (CEO) of the company, Guy Fauré. In April 2004, Cuban offered to use his fame to promote Mamma and assist the company with, among other things, possible acquisitions they may be considering. At that time, Cuban told Fauré that "obviously what you tell me is confidential."

In June 2004, Mamma made the decision to raise cash through a type of stock offering called a private investment in public equity (PIPE). The Mamma board of directors decided to offer Cuban, the largest shareholder in the company, the opportunity to invest in the PIPE so that he could maintain his 6.3% ownership stake in the company. On June 28, 2004, Fauré told Cuban in a telephone conversation that he had confidential information for him. Cuban acknowledged that Fauré had confidential information and said "uh-huh, go ahead," or words to that effect. Fauré then told Cuban about the PIPE and offered him the opportunity to invest in the PIPE. Cuban's reaction was very negative. He did not agree with Mamma's decision to raise cash through a PIPE and expressed his views to Fauré. Towards the end of the conversation, Cuban told Fauré, "now I'm screwed, I can't sell."

That same day, Fauré, believing that Cuban had agreed to keep information about the PIPE confidential and not trade on it, gave Cuban the name and contact information for the sales agent for the PIPE, Arnold Owen, to allow Cuban to obtain more information about the PIPE to evaluate whether he would participate in the offering. Within two hours, knowing that Mamma provided him access because of his agreement of confidentiality, Cuban called Owen and asked for the details of the PIPE. One minute after hanging up the phone with Owen, Cuban called his broker and told him to sell all 600,000 shares of his stock in Mamma. Cuban did not tell Mamma that he would sell his shares prior to the public announcement of the PIPE.

Cuban's broker sold all 600,000 shares by 4:00 p.m. Eastern on June 29, 2004. Mamma announced the PIPE to the public at 6:00 p.m. Eastern on June 29, 2004. When the market opened on June 30, 2004, Mamma's stock price fell to $11.89 per share. Cuban avoided approximately $750,000 in losses by selling prior to the public announcement of the PIPE. Cuban's sale violated his agreements and deceived Mamma.

By selling his shares before the public announcement, Cuban violated Section 17(a) of the Securities Act of 1933 (Securities Act) and Section 10(b) of the Securities Exchange Act of 1934 (Exchange Act), and Rule 10b-5 thereunder. This is a civil case and the SEC is not seeking criminal penalties. Rather, the Commission seeks: (i) a permanent injunction prohibiting Cuban from further violations of the relevant provisions of the Exchange Act; (ii) disgorgement of all ill-gotten gains, plus prejudgment interest; and (iii) the imposition of civil monetary penalties against Cuban. Plaintiff incorporates by reference all allegations contained in the Complaint.

Cuban's Statement of His Defenses

To succeed on its securities fraud claims against Cuban, the SEC must prove by a preponderance of the evidence that Cuban knowingly or with severe recklessness misappropriated and then traded upon material, non-public information concerning the Mamma.com PIPE transaction he received from Mamma.com on June 28, 2004 in breach of a duty owed to Mamma.com. The SEC cannot meet this burden of proof.

First, the SEC's claims fail because it cannot prove that a confidentiality agreement was formed between Cuban and Mamma.com pursuant to which Cuban was to maintain in confidence any information relating to the Mamma.com PIPE ("PIPE information") that Cuban received from Mamma.com.

Second, the SEC's claims fail because it cannot prove that an agreement was formed between Cuban and Mamma.com pursuant to which Cuban was not to trade on any PIPE information that Cuban received from Mamma.com.

Third, the SEC's claims fail because it cannot prove that Cuban knew, or was severely reckless in not knowing, that (a) his sale of Mamma.com stock breached a duty to Mamma.com, (b) the PIPE information he received was material, and (c) the PIPE information he received was non-public. Moreover, Cuban acted in good faith in his interactions with Mamma.com concerning the PIPE information.

Fourth, the SEC's claims fail because it cannot prove that Cuban did not disclose to Mamma.com that he would sell his shares of Mamma.com stock. Given this absence of proof, the SEC cannot establish that Mamma.com was deceived by Cuban's conduct.

Fifth, the SEC's claims fail because it cannot prove that Cuban used, as defined under the law, any PIPE information he received to buy or sell Mamma.com stock.

Sixth, the SEC's claims fail because it cannot prove that any PIPE information Cuban received was material.

Finally, the SEC's claims fail because it cannot prove that any PIPE information Cuban received was non-public.

II. Stipulations of Fact[8]

1) Mark Cuban is a resident of Dallas, Texas. He owns the NBA's Dallas Mavericks, HDNet, a national high-definition television network, and Landmark Theaters.

2) Mamma.com was a Canadian corporation located in Montreal, Canada that operated an Internet search engine. Mamma.com's common stock was registered with the Commission pursuant to Section 12(b) of the Exchange Act and traded on the NASDAQ, a national security exchange, under the symbol MAMA. The company no longer exists.

3) Mamma.com stock is a security for purposes of Section 10(b) of the Securities Exchange Act of 1934 ("Exchange Act") and Rule 10b-5.

4) Mark Cuban purchased 600,000 shares of Mamma.com stock in March 2004. On March 15, 2004 Mark Cuban filed a Form 13G with the Securities and Exchange Commission reflecting this purchase.

5) From March 2004-June 29, 2004, Mark Cuban owned 600,000 of the total 9,538,011 outstanding shares of Mamma.com stock.

6) From March 2004-June 29, 2004, Mark Cuban was the largest single shareholder of Mamma.com stock and owned 6.3% of the company.

[8.] That the parties have stipulated to certain facts does not preclude either party from eliciting brief testimony about those facts at trial in order to present a complete record for the jury. The parties are relieved, however, of any obligation to lay a foundation when introducing such facts at trial.

7) On June 28, 2004 at 12:56 p.m. Eastern, Mark Cuban received an email from Guy Fauré in which Guy Fauré asked Mark Cuban to call him.

8) On June 28, 2004 at 3:51 p.m. Eastern, Mark Cuban received an email from Guy Fauré containing the Merriman sales representative's name, Arnold Owen, and his phone number.

9) Mark Cuban used the telephone in connection with his sale of 600,000 shares of Mamma.com stock on June 28 and 29, 2004.

10) During the 2004 calendar year, Mark Cuban maintained a cellular telephone with the number XXX-XXX-XXXX.[9]

11) Plaintiff's Trial Exhibit 60 ("PX-60") is a true and accurate copy of Mark Cuban's Sprint PCS (now Sprint Nextel) June 2004 cellular phone records for the number XXX-XXX-XXXX.

12) PX-60 is admissible at trial as a business record of Sprint PCS.

13) During the 2004 calendar year, Guy Fauré maintained a cellular telephone with the number XXX-XXX-XXXX.

14) Plaintiff's Trial Exhibit 59 ("PX-59") is a true and accurate copy of Guy Fauré's Bell Mobility Cellular Inc. June 28, 2004 phone records for the number XXX-XXX-XXXX.

15) PX-59 is admissible at trial as a business record of Bell Mobility Cellular, Inc.

16) Plaintiff's Trial Exhibit 55 ("PX 55") is a true and accurate copy of telephone records for the American Airlines Center located at 2500 Victory Avenue, Dallas, Texas for June 28, 2004.

17) P-55 is admissible at trial as a business record of AT&T Southwest.

18) On June 28, 2004, the telephone number of the office of Mark Cuban's broker at UBS Financial Services, Inc. was XXX-XXX-XXXX.

19) As reflected in PX-60, on June 28, 2004 at 4:32 p.m. Central time (5:32 p.m. Eastern), Mark Cuban called Arnold Owen. This call between Cuban and Owen lasted approximately eight minutes.

20) As reflected in PX-60, on June 28, 2004 at 4:41 p.m. Central time (5:41 p.m. Eastern), Mark Cuban called his financial advisor at UBS Financial Services, Inc. This call between Cuban and his financial advisor lasted approximately two minutes.

21) Exhibit C of Plaintiff's Trial Exhibit 61 ("PX-61") is a true and accurate copy of the March 2004 brokerage statement for an account of Mark Cuban at UBS Financial Services, Inc.

22) Exhibit D of PX-61 is a true and accurate copy of the June 2004 brokerage statement for an account of Mark Cuban at UBS Financial Services, Inc.

23) Exhibits A and B of PX-61 are true and accurate copies of UBS Financial Services, Inc. trade confirmations reflecting transactions in Mamma.com stock for and on behalf of Mark Cuban.

[9.] The actual phone numbers of Messrs. Cuban and Fauré have been redacted for purposes of this publicly filed Joint Pretrial Order. The parties agree, however, that the actual numbers may be used during trial and the jury will be provided with the actual numbers during deliberations.

24) PX-61 and all attached exhibits are admissible at trial as a business record of UBS Financial Services, Inc.

III. Contested Issues of Fact

SEC's Statement of Contested Issues of Fact

As the largest shareholder of Mamma stock, Cuban has developed a business relationship with the chief executive officer (CEO) of Mamma, Guy Fauré. In April 2004, Cuban offered to promote Mamma and assist the company with, among other things, possible acquisitions they may be considering. In the context of that relationship, Cuban assured Fauré that he understood that what Fauré told him was confidential and that he could not sell stock or act on such information.

In June 2004, Mamma made the decision to raise cash through a private investment in public equity (PIPE). The PIPE was offered to investors at a discount and with warrants. That Mamma was raising cash through a PIPE and that the PIPE had discounts and warrants was material, nonpublic information. Mamma's board of directors decided to offer Cuban the opportunity to invest in the PIPE, as he was the largest shareholder in the company. Mamma wanted to allow Cuban an opportunity to purchase more shares and maintain his 6.3% ownership in the company.

On June 28, 2004, Fauré told Cuban in a telephone conversation that he had confidential information for him. Cuban acknowledged that Fauré had confidential information and said "uh-huh, go ahead," or words to that effect. Fauré then informed Cuban about the PIPE and offered him the opportunity to invest in the PIPE. Cuban's reaction was very negative. Cuban believed the PIPE would dilute his ownership in the company and cause the Mamma share price to fall. He then told Fauré, "now I'm screwed, I can't sell." Cuban knew and acknowledged that he was foreclosed from selling his Mamma shares until after the PIPE became public because he had agreed to treat the information as confidential and not use it for his own benefit or trade on it.

That same day, Fauré, believing that Cuban had agreed to keep the information about the PIPE confidential and not trade on it, gave Cuban the name and contact information for the sales agent for the PIPE, Arnold Owen. Within two hours, Cuban called Owen to find out the details of the PIPE, namely whether it was being offered with discounts and warrants. Cuban and Owen spoke for eight minutes. One minute after hanging up the phone with Owen, Cuban called his broker and told him to sell all 600,000 shares of his stock in Mamma on the basis of the material, nonpublic information Cuban had learned from Fauré and Owen about the PIPE. Cuban did not tell Mamma that he would sell his shares prior to the public announcement of the PIPE.

Cuban's broker sold all 600,000 shares by 4:00 p.m. Eastern on June 29, 2004. Mamma announced the PIPE to the public at 6:00 p.m. Eastern on June 29, 2004. By selling before the public announcement, Cuban avoided approximately $750,000 in losses. Cuban's sale violated his agreements and deceived Mamma.

Cuban's Statement of Contested Issues of Fact

Cuban views the following as contested issues of fact for determination at trial:

1. As to any PIPE information that Cuban received from Mamma.com,
   a. Whether an agreement was formed between Cuban and Mamma.com that Cuban was to keep the PIPE information confidential;
   b. Whether an agreement was formed between Cuban and Mamma.com that Cuban was not to trade on the PIPE information;
   c. Whether Cuban (i) traded on the PIPE information, (ii) with the requisite scienter;
   d. Whether Cuban failed to disclose to Fauré and/or Owen that he would sell his shares of Mamma.com stock;
   e. Whether Cuban told Fauré and/or Owen that he would not sell his shares of Mamma.com stock until after the public announcement of the Mamma.com PIPE transaction;
   f. Whether Fauré and/or Owen reasonably believed that Cuban would not sell his shares of Mamma.com stock until after the public announcement of the Mamma.com PIPE transaction;
   g. Whether the PIPE information was material at the time Cuban's shares of Mamma.com stock were sold;
   h. Whether the PIPE information was non-public at the time Cuban's shares of Mamma.com stock were sold.
2. Whether Mamma.com received legal advice prior to contacting Cuban on June 28, 2004 that it should require Cuban to enter into a written agreement to hold information about the PIPE confidential and not trade on it; and whether Mamma.com failed to follow that advice.
3. Whether, in May 2004, Mamma.com publicly disclosed that it may engage in a PIPE transaction.
4. Whether Mamma.com and Merriman disclosed information about the Mamma.com PIPE transaction to prospective PIPE investors and investment firms without obtaining, or seeking to obtain from those investors and firms, confidentiality agreements or agreements not to use the information.
5. Whether, prior to the public announcement of the Mamma.com PIPE transaction, investors used information about the PIPE that they had obtained, directly or indirectly, from Mamma.com or Merriman, for their own benefit in the marketplace.
6. Cuban also considers all questions of fact that the SEC lists herein as contested, to be contested facts.
7. In addition, Cuban considers any facts that are not listed by the SEC or Cuban herein as contested facts but that may be raised at trial and are not stipulated by the parties, to be contested facts.

IV. Contested Issues of Law

SEC's Statement of Contested Issues of Law

1. Whether Section 10(b) of the Exchange Act and Rule 10b-5, in particular the misappropriation theory of insider trading, requires the SEC to prove that Cuban agreed to keep the information about the Mamma PIPE confidential and not to trade on it or otherwise use it for his benefit.
2. Whether Cuban agreed to keep the information about the Mamma PIPE confidential and not to trade on it or otherwise use it for his benefit.
3. Whether the information about the Mamma PIPE, including that it was offered with discounts and warrants, was material nonpublic information.
4. Whether Cuban violated Section 17(a) of the Securities Act, Section 10(b) of the Exchange Act and Rule 10b-5 thereunder by selling all of the stock that he owned in Mamma while in possession of material non-public information.
5. Whether the SEC is required to prove that Cuban did not tell Mamma that he would sell his shares prior to the public announcement of the PIPE.
6. In the event the jury returns a verdict of liability, whether the Court should enter an order permanently enjoining defendant from future violations of the federal securities laws and separately, the amount of money the Court should order defendant to pay as disgorgement, prejudgment interest and civil monetary penalties.

Cuban's Statement of Contested Issues of Law

1. Whether the SEC has met its burden to establish by a preponderance of the evidence that Cuban, directly or indirectly, in connection with the purchase or sale of a security, by the use of means or instrumentalities of interstate commerce, of the mails, or of the facilities of a national securities exchange, and with scienter:
    (a) Employed devices, schemes, or artifices to defraud;
    (b) Made untrue statements of a material fact or omitted to state a material fact necessary in order to make the statements made, in the light of the circumstances under which they were made, not misleading; or
    (c) Engaged in acts, practices, or courses of business which operated or would operate as a fraud or deceit upon other persons, in violation of Section 10(b) of the Exchange Act, 15 U.S.C. § 78j(b), and Rule 10b-5 thereunder, 17 C.F.R. § 240.10b-5.
2. Whether the SEC has met its burden to establish by a preponderance of the evidence that Cuban, directly or indirectly, in connection with the purchase or sale of a security, by the use of means or instrumentalities of interstate commerce, of the mails, or of the facilities of a national securities exchange, and with scienter:

(a) employed devices, schemes, or artifices to defraud;

(b) obtained money or property by means of untrue statements of material fact or omissions to state material facts necessary in order to make the statements made, in light of the circumstances under which they were made, not misleading; or

(c) engaged in acts, practices, or courses of business which operated or would operate as a fraud or deceit upon the purchasers of the securities offered and sold by Cuban, in violation of Section 17(a) of the Securities Act, 15 U.S.C. § 77q(a).

3. Whether the SEC is entitled to the following relief:

(a) a finding that Cuban violated the antifraud provisions of the above federal securities laws;

(b) a permanent injunction enjoining Cuban against violations of the above provisions;

(c) an order that Cuban disgorge the ill-gotten gains he received as a result of the above violations, the appropriate amount of disgorgement, and whether he should be ordered to pay prejudgment interest on the disgorgement and the amount of any such prejudgment interest;

(d) an order that Cuban pay a civil penalty for his violations under Section 21(d)(3) of the Exchange Act, 15 U.S.C. § 78u(d)(3), and the amount of any such penalty; and

(e) a grant of such other relief as the Court may deem just and proper.

4. Whether Cuban is entitled to be awarded his costs and expenses.

V. Estimated Length of Trial

The parties estimate that the trial will last 8-10 days.

. . . .

SO ORDERED.

September 25, 2013.

[Signed] _____

SIDNEY A. FITZWATER

CHIEF JUDGE

IV. THE ROAD TO TRIAL

After several years of conducting extensive investigation, discovery, motion practice, and pre-trial maneuvering, the SEC's case against Mark Cuban proceeded to trial. In the next chapter of the book, we arrive at this critical juncture—*The SEC versus Mark Cuban—A Trial of Insider Trading*.

CHAPTER 7

The Trial— *The SEC vs. Mark Cuban*

With discovery completed and Mr. Cuban's motion for summary judgment denied, the parties proceeded to trial. This chapter focuses on court orders, jury selection, the conducting of the trial (including opening and closing statements as well as witness testimony), the jury charge, and the verdict.

I. PREPARING FOR TRIAL

We first look at *three pre-trial documents* that were integrally connected to the conducting of the trial: (1) The parties' joint estimate of trial length and status report; (2) the district court's Order setting the trial date; and (3) Mr. Cuban's Trial Exhibit List and his Objections to specified documents set forth in the SEC's Trial Exhibit List. These documents provide a flavor of the type of orders and filings that are made in the time period immediately prior to the commencement of trial.

[A] Parties' Filing Regarding Status and Estimated Trial Duration

We commence with the parties' submission of the following Report regarding case status and estimated trial length.

JOINT ESTIMATE OF TRIAL LENGTH AND STATUS REPORT

Plaintiff Securities and Exchange Commission and Defendant Mark Cuban respectfully submit this Joint Estimate of Trial Length and Status Report.

I. TRIAL LENGTH

The parties estimate that trial of this matter would require eight to ten days.

II. STATUS REPORT

The parties have engaged in settlement discussions, but have been unable to reach a mutually agreeable resolution. The parties do not believe additional discussions would be fruitful.[1]

[B] The District Court's Order Setting the Trial Date

Judge Fitzwater's Order setting the trial date and addressing certain other matters follows.

ORDER

In response to the court's April 1, 2013 order, the parties have advised the court of their availability for trial beginning on September 30, 2013. Accordingly, the trial of this case is set for Monday, September 30, 2013 at 9:00 a.m. As set out in the court's April 1, 2013 order, the court will conduct the pretrial conference during the week of September 23-27, 2013, at a date and time to be set later.

For scheduling purposes, the parties are advised that court will not be in session on Thursday, October 10, 2013, and that the jury will not be permitted to deliberate on Friday, October 11, 2013 (normally, trials are not held on Fridays, but juries that have begun deliberations are permitted to deliberate on Fridays). Monday, October 13, 2013 is a federal holiday.

SO ORDERED

April 22, 2013

_[Signed]_____

SIDNEY A. FITZWATER

CHIEF JUDGE

[C] The Parties' Trial Exhibit Lists and Objections Thereto

Prior to trial, each party submits its Trial Exhibit List and files its Objections to specified documents contained in an adverse party's Trial Exhibit

---

[1.] Joint Estimate of Trial Length and Status Report (June 7, 2012).

List. For samples of these documents, *excerpts of Mr. Cuban's Trial Exhibit List and his Objections to specified documents contained in the SEC's Trial Exhibit List follow.*

DEFENDANT MARK CUBAN'S TRIAL EXHIBIT LIST[2]

Defendant Mark Cuban reserves the right to offer any documents which may be designated or offered by Plaintiff Securities and Exchange Commission. Cuban, in his sole discretion, additionally reserves the right to offer any exhibits as may be necessary for rebuttal and/or impeachment. Cuban further reserves the right to request that the Court take judicial notice of any pleadings and other documents filed in this case.

Cuban further reserves the right to supplement this list with any documents that have not yet been produced by the Securities and Exchange Commission.

No.	Description
1.	Mamma.com's Annual Report Form 20-F, filed May 27, 2004
2.	Engagement letter between Merriman Curhan Ford & Co. and Mamma.com, dated March 16, 2004
[3.-48.]	....
49.	Mamma.com, Inc.'s Schedule 13G, filed by Mark Cuban on March 15, 2004
[50.-61.]	....
62.	Email from Cuban to Fauré re: insider sales, dated May 4, 2004
[63-185.]	....
186.	SEC report of investigation, dated August 22, 2011
[187.-196.]	....
197.	Transcript of Deposition of Arnold Owen, dated January 27, 2012
[198.]	....
199.	Declaration of Mark Cuban with exhibits, dated May 25, 2012
[200.-281.]	....
282.	Fax from Prosser to Bertand re: Copernic Selling Securityholder Questionnaire, dated July 3, 2007

[2.] Listing of a document as an exhibit does not constitute an admission of its admissibility (including without limitation its authenticity). Defendant Mark Cuban reserves all rights to object to any listed exhibit on any ground.

DEFENDANT MARK CUBAN'S OBJECTIONS TO PLAINTIFF'S TRIAL EXHIBITS

SEC No.	Date	Description	Bates Range (per SEC)	Objections
1	03/16/04	Merriman Engagement Letter	MammaPro001 73 - 83	Lack of foundation
2	03/18/04	Emails between Mark Cuban and Guy Fauré, subject: "Thank You"	SEC-MC0002136 – 38	Hearsay
3	03/19/04	Email from Guy Fauré to Mark Cuban, subject: "Board seat"	MCSEC00002 60	Hearsay
[4-9]	....	....	....	....
10	05/10/04	Mark Cuban's BlogMaverick post, Why do people fall in love with stocks?		Duplicative of No. 11; Hearsay, relevance, prejudice.
[11-15]	....	....	....	....
16	06/14/04	Merriman Private Placement Transaction Acknowledgement letter	HBK 2-0003519A – 19B	MIL [Motion *in Limine*]; Hearsay, relevance, prejudice.
[17-18]	....	....	....	....
19	06/23/04	Email from Goldman to Owen, forwarding May 13, 2004 email from Fauré to Goldman RE: FW: Mark Cuban	MCF_37218_0 001	Hearsay
[20-22]	....	....	....	....
23	06/28/04	Email from Michael Storck to David Goldman RE: Note to Directors	DG0000885	Hearsay; authentication/ foundation/ Unreliable
[24-310]	....	....	....	....

SEC No.	Date	Description	Bates Range (per SEC)	Objections
311	10/17/07	Arnold Owen's October 17, 2007 Investigative Testimony Transcript [FOR IDENTIFICATION PURPOSES ONLY]		None
[312-314]	....	....	....	....
315		Mamma.com Price/ Volume Chart		None
316		Demonstratives		None
[317-318]	....	....	....	....
319	03/30/07	Background Questionnaire of Mark Cuban		None

II. JURY SELECTION

Of course, the composition of the members of the jury is a critical component in trying a case. In this proceeding, Mr. Cuban sought (1) approval for the use of a written jury questionnaire; and (2) permission that the SEC and he each conduct 30 minutes of attorney *voir dire*. If such a written questionnaire were not permitted, then Mr. Cuban sought 60 minutes per side of attorney *voir dire*.[3] Judge Fitzwater denied Mr. Cuban's motion. *The district court's ruling follows.*

Defendant Mark Cuban's ("Cuban's") August 12, 2013 motion for use of jury questionnaire and additional attorney voir dire is denied.

Based on "the high-profile nature of this case, the prior local and national media coverage of this litigation and the public nature of the parties ..." [Defendant's Motion at pp. 2-3], Cuban requests that the court permit a brief written jury questionnaire and permit both parties' attorneys to conduct 30 minutes of voir dire. Alternatively, absent a jury questionnaire, he requests 60 minutes of attorney voir dire per side. Cuban maintains in his reply that "there is a substantial risk that the prospective venire will come to the jury-selection process with preconceived beliefs, judgments

---

3. The term *voir dire* refers to"[a] preliminary examination of a prospective juror by a judge or a lawyer to decide whether the prospect is qualified and suitable to serve on a jury." *Black's Law Dictionary* 1805 (10th ed. 2014).

and opinions ... certainly more so than the venire in an average case." ...[4] Plaintiff Securities and Exchange Commission ("SEC") opposes the motion ....

In a civil case, the court usually conducts voir dire in three general phases. First, it poses questions to the entire venire based on questions submitted in advance by the parties and questions that it considers appropriate for the case on trial. Second, it permits one attorney per side to ask follow up questions of the entire venire (a time limit of ten minutes is usually imposed). Third, the court questions individual veni-remembers outside the presence of other veniremembers regarding hardship excuses and answers given during the questioning of the entire panel that suggest a basis for individual questioning. Before the third phase begins, each party is permitted to request at a bench conference that one or more veniremembers be questioned further. During the third phase, counsel are permitted to directly question these veniremem-bers. This questioning process is untimed and is not charged against counsels' ten minutes. Counsel can use this phase to develop grounds to challenge a potential juror for cause or to oppose a cause-based challenge.

"The district court has great latitude to conduct voir dire, including the form and scope of questioning." ... The Supreme Court has held that it is "not an abuse of discretion for the district court to question potential jurors unilaterally rather than permitting the lawyers to pose questions." [*Skilling v. United States*, 130 S. Ct. 2896, 2918, 2923 (2010)] .... Fed. R. Civ. P. 47(a) explicitly provides:

> [t]he court may permit the parties or their attorneys to examine pro-
> spective jurors or may itself do so. If the court examines the jurors, it
> must permit the parties or their attorneys to make any further inquiry
> it considers proper, or must itself ask any of their additional ques-
> tions it considers proper....

The court concludes that its usual three-phase process will be sufficient to address the concerns raised in Cuban's motion. In the first and third phases, the court can "ask[] probing questions to ferret out possible bias." ... During the second phase, counsel can make further, proper inquiries of the entire venire. See Rule 47(a). And during the third phase, counsel can question veniremembers directly, without preset time constraints, to ensure that the veniremembers who remain (and who are subject to peremptory strikes) can be fair and impartial.

Accordingly, Cuban's August 12, 2013 motion for use of jury questionnaire and additional attorney voir dire is denied.

SO ORDERED.
September 10, 2013.

_[Signed]_____
SIDNEY A. FITZWATER
CHIEF JUDGE

[4.] The meaning of "venire" is a panel of individuals chosen for jury duty. The jurors for the case are selected from this panel. *See Black's Law Dictionary* 1789 (10th ed. 2014).

III. THE TRIAL

We now turn to the trial: the opening statements to the jury, witness examination, court rulings, closing arguments, and the jury verdict. *We commence with the opening statements by the respective parties.*

[A] The Opening Statements

After Judge Fitzwater welcomed the members of the jury, the SEC presented its Opening Statement.

[1] The SEC's Opening Statement

THE COURT: .... Good morning counsel, and litigants and members of the jury....

Members of the jury, in a moment the attorneys are going to be presenting the opening statements. I anticipate that you'll first hear from counsel for the plaintiff, the SEC, and depending on how much of its time it takes, we may have a short restroom break after that and before you hear from counsel for the defendant, Mr. Cuban.

And then once the opening statements are completed, we'll begin with the testimony in the case.

I want to remind you of an instruction I gave you yesterday. The statements of counsel are not evidence, and what the attorneys say during opening statements is not evidence. It represents the contentions of the parties or what they believe the evidence will or will not show in the case.

So if during the trial of the case you do not hear evidence that supports an assertion that's made during opening statements, then, of course, you must base your verdict upon the evidence that's admitted during the trial.

Who's going to make the opening statement for the SEC?

MS. FOLENA [Attorney for the SEC]: I will, Your Honor.

THE COURT: And what time indications would you like?

MS. FOLENA: One hour, please.

THE COURT: Do you want a warning before that?

MS. FOLENA: Yes, please, if you would. At 55 minutes.

THE COURT: All right. That's fine.

MS. FOLENA: Thank you. May I proceed?

THE COURT: You may proceed.

MS. FOLENA: May it please the court, counsel, ladies and gentlemen of the jury, good morning.

"Now I'm screwed. I can't sell." [emphasis supplied]

The evidence in this case will show that those are the words of Mark Cuban, the defendant in this case.

We will prove that Mark Cuban made that statement just hours before he started to sell 600,000 shares of a stock in a company he owned called Mamma.com, armed with information that he agreed to keep confidential and on which he agreed not to trade.

The evidence will show that he [committed] insider trading. Mark Cuban violated the law. And he knew better.

Ladies and gentlemen, … my name is Jan Folena. I represent the Securities and Exchange Commission. And along with my colleagues at counsel table we will present the evidence on behalf of the SEC to you over the next couple of weeks.

As the judge indicated, who are we? The Securities and Exchange Commission. Sometimes we're called the SEC.

What is the SEC?

We are a Commission charged by Congress to protect investors. We make sure that everybody that buys and sells securities in our markets does so on a level playing field.

We make sure that nobody has an unfair advantage.

We make sure that nobody cheats.

The SEC has charged Mark Cuban with insider trading. Insider trading is buying or selling stock based on information that you agreed to keep confidential and on which you agreed not to trade.

But it's more. Insider trading is a form of cheating. It's like being the only person in the class that has the answers to the test before you take it. It's like having the other team's playbook before you play the game. It's like knowing the winner of the national championship game before you place your bet.

And just like those examples, the SEC will show in this case that Mark Cuban had information about Mamma.com that the public did not. Information that he believed would make the value of his stock fall. Information that he agreed to keep confidential and on which he agreed not to trade.

But the evidence will show Mark Cuban sold all of his stock in Mamma.com before the public knew the information, before the stock price fell, and before he lost one dime.

Insider trading causes investors to lose faith in our markets, a critical component of the United States economy, the place where hard-working people put their money to save for retirement, for their children's college educations, or even just for a rainy day.

Would you want to buy stock in a market where someone else can get out of an investment about to go bust but you couldn't?

If people lose confidence in the United States stock markets, they won't work. They won't work for any of us.

But insider trading is something else. Insider trading is deception. When an insider trader buys or sells stock in a company while in possession of information that he or she agreed to keep confidential, he or she deceives the company. They deceive the source of that information. They deceive the company that gave it to them.

And companies, as you'll hear in this case, are often required to disclose confidential information outside of the company in order to conduct the business that they do every day. Companies make business decisions about how to raise money, how to grow the company, and part of those business decisions sometimes involve sharing confidential information. Those that receive the information and agree to keep it confidential betray the trust when they use that information to benefit themselves. And that's what this case is about.

Now, make no mistake, ladies and gentlemen, Mark Cuban is a smart and successful investor and businessman. He's the owner of a nationwide theatre chain, a high-definition television network, and the Dallas Mavericks. This trial will show, however, that that same determination, that drive to win, that competitive edge that makes him successful is exactly what caused him to break the law in this case. And the evidence will show it's that competitive edge that refuses to allow him to admit what he did was wrong.

You see, ... Mr. Cuban's success as an investor and businessman in this community is admirable, but success must only come within the bounds of the law. Mr. Cuban's success in some cases is the American dream. It's what people strive to achieve. But that's the thing about America. Our laws apply to everyone. Our laws apply to the rich, the poor, the famous, and the unknown.

The United States securities laws and their rules of fair play apply to every single investor in our markets. They also apply to Mark Cuban.

So while success is to be commended, it must be fair and it must be legal. Now, this case is going to focus on Mark Cuban's ownership of 600,000 shares of a company called Mamma.com, an investment he made in 2004. But the evidence will show this was not Mark Cuban's first stock purchase. Mamma.com was not his first experience in the stock market.

You see, in 2004 Mark Cuban had an investment philosophy. He was investing in companies in his areas of expertise—technology. He would buy enough of the company's stock to become the largest shareholder and get the ear of the company's management. He did this to help the business succeed, to make the stock price go up and to make a good investment for himself.

And as he admits, in a blog that Mark Cuban writes, on May 10th of 2004 he says in his blog exactly what I've just told you, that he invests, he buys stocks only in several circumstances.

First, is the company strategic to his other companies, the technology sector?

Second, can I buy enough to get the ear of the CEO, the chief executive officer of the company?

Third, can I get enough stock where I consider myself to be a true owner of the company and can work with them to create win-win situations?

Can he help them?

[If] he help[s] them increase the stock price, the company benefits, Mark Cuban benefits, it's win-win.

Of the companies he has taken a 5 percent or greater position in, "I have yet to sell a share of any of them. Ever." Those are the words of Mark Cuban. That was his investment philosophy. He sticks with these companies to see if they're going to pay off.

You see, Mr. Cuban puts himself in a position that most investors cannot obtain, being the largest single shareholder in a company, getting the ear of the CEO. That position is one most investors will never have.

Mr. Cuban is in the investment game just like every game he's in, he's in to win. And in March of 2004, Mark Cuban discovered a new player for his investment portfolio. And that player was Mamma.com. In 2004, Mamma.com was a small search engine, in that time kind of like Google. It was located in Canada. It was a start-up company.... It had the potential to grow, the potential to succeed, the potential to become a good investment.

So with that information Mark Cuban buys 600,000 shares of Mamma.com, at a cost to him of a little over seven million dollars. And with that purchase, consistent with his philosophy, he becomes the largest single shareholder in Mamma.com. He owns 6.3 percent of the company....

Now, consistent with his philosophy, Mr. Cuban does get the ear of the chief executive officer of Mamma.com, a man by the name of Guy Fauré. Mr. Cuban develops a business relationship with Mr. Fauré based upon the fact that Mr. Cuban is the company's largest shareholder. Mr. Fauré has already testified. He was under oath. He swore to tell the truth. He answered all of the questions presented to him by the Securities and Exchange Commission and by Mr. Cuban's own lawyers. That testimony will be presented here, in a day or two, on videotape. And as the judge will explain, you are to consider Mr. Fauré's videotape testimony the same as you would as if he sat live on that witness stand.

In that testimony, listen to Mr. Fauré. He will confirm that, yes, Mr. Cuban became the largest shareholder in his company, and, yes, they were in contact about the business of Mamma.com.

Mr. Fauré and Mr. Cuban hadn't known each other before this. They weren't friends. They weren't golf buddies. Their relationship was strictly business.

You'll hear testimony that Mr. Cuban offered his help to Mamma.com because Mamma.com was a technology company. It was Mr. Cuban's area of knowledge.

You'll hear testimony from Mr. Fauré that he and Mr. Cuban discussed the business of Mamma.com on the telephone and by email.

One piece of evidence that you may see in this trial is this. It's an April 23rd, 2004 email message from Mr. Cuban to Mr. Fauré.

And what does it say?

Mr. Cuban says, "Where would you like me to help out? Happy to do it where I can if you have a specific idea. Is there a specific biz area you want promoted? Mamma.com traffic or building the network?"

He's reaching out to Mr. Fauré to offer his help.

He then says, "As you know I think blogs are hot" ... He writes his own. "... [I]f you have a product that supports blogs, I can add blogmaverick." ...

Then he says this.

"What other acquisitions are you looking at? They may be companies I can help with," companies in the technology area.

Then he says ... and this is the piece of evidence ... "And obviously, what you tell me is confidential." That's an important word, and it will be a very important word in this case.

"Obviously, what you tell me is confidential."

Technology is an area where Mr. Cuban is knowledgeable, but business is also an area in which he's knowledgeable. He's acknowledging that if he gets confidential information from Mr. Fauré he will keep it confidential. Information about mergers and acquisitions.

Now, fast-forward two months. This email is sent in April 2004. June 28th, 2004, Mr. Fauré sends Mr. Cuban an email and he says, "Mark, I would like to speak with you, please call me."

Remember, their relationship is strictly business. It began soon after Mr. Cuban became the largest shareholder in Mr. Fauré's company.

Mr. Fauré was contacting Mr. Cuban to tell him about a business decision that Mamma.com had made. Mamma.com was going to try to raise cash for the company to build the business through a transaction called a private financing.

The evidence will show that Mamma.com was raising that money to support its mergers and acquisition strategy, exactly what is discussed in this email.

Now, let's talk about the business transaction for a minute.

The business transaction is called a private financing. And it's also called a PIPE [Private Investment in Public Equity]. It may be referred to as a PIPE-type transaction.

Okay. What is that?

A PIPE is a private investment in public equity. And what that means is Mamma.com is a public company so it's traded on the stock exchange here in the United States.... What Mamma.com is going to do is reach out to a small group of private investors and ask them to invest in the company....

.... [S]ome investors, including Mark Cuban, believed that that causes dilution. And you'll hear the term "dilution" "dilute" "dilute the shareholder base" "dilute the shareholders." ...

So what does the company do?

Mr. Fauré is calling Mark Cuban because he wants to allow him to increase [his] shares [and thereby] ... the dilution to [Mr. Cuban] is avoided. And that's what Mr. Fauré is doing. He knows Mark Cuban is the largest shareholder in his company.... He's trying to get him back to his original ownership percentage in the company.

Now, the PIPE might also cause initially the price of the shares to fall. But remember, this is a business decision of the company. The company is raising money for the long term, to help the company grow. The thinking is that it will pay off, but it's going to pay off later. So while the shares might fall in price now, the hope is they will come back later. Now, it's not a guarantee, because in business nothing is. It's a business decision that the company is hoping will pay off.

Now, there's two very important components to this PIPE that you will hear in this case. They're called discounts and they're called warrants.

Now, what are they?

The new shares that are offered to this group of investors might be offered to them at a price that's lower than what the stock is trading on the exchange.

So say the Mamma.com stock is trading at $12 on [the] exchange, these investors might have an opportunity to purchase it at $10 per share, so they're getting it at a ... two dollar discount. And that's important. It's an incentive. It's to get them to invest.

The other component is called a warrant.

Now, what's a warrant?

A warrant [is] ... a certificate that goes to the small group of investors and it says to them you're coming in, you're buying the shares at $10, we're going to give you this, warrant, it allows you to continue to buy shares in our company at $10 for a set amount of time. So say five years. It's another incentive.

Now, representatives of Mamma.com will testify in this trial, [1] Mr. Guy Fauré, the CEO, and [2] the chairman of the company, Mr. David Goldman. And they will testify that the fact that Mamma.com was raising money through a PIPE transaction and the characteristics of the transaction, the discounts and the warrants, was confidential.

And what does that mean?

It means that it was not public. The public didn't know about it. It was shared, as it had to be, only with the small group of private investors. One of those prospective investors was Mark Cuban.

Now, that makes sense, right? Because if you're going to try to get people to invest in the company you have to tell them you're doing a PIPE. And that's what happened here.

Now, the crux of this case unfolds in two days in June of 2004. June 28th and June 29th.

And let's look now at what actually happened.

It's June 28, 2004. I've already explained that Mr. Fauré sends an email to Mr. Cuban saying call me.

That email is sent at 12:56 p.m. Eastern time. I've converted all of these times to Eastern time. On June 28th Mr. Fauré is in Eastern time, Mr. Cuban is in Central time.

Now, what happens after that?

Four minutes later Mr. Cuban calls back Mr. Fauré. It's a conversation that lasts for eight minutes, from 1:00 p.m. Eastern time to 1:08 p.m.

And what happens on that phone call?

Listen to Mr. Fauré's testimony. The first—one of the first things out of Mr. Fauré's mouth is, "Mark, I've got confidential information." You see, there's that word again, "confidential," a word they've used before.

Now, Mr. Cuban does not recall the words of that conversation. The only witness that will tell you what happened on that conversation and in that call is Mr. Fauré.

One of the things Mr. Fauré says to Mr. Cuban is the company is going to do a private financing, or a PIPE, would you like to invest.

Mr. Cuban says, uh-huh, go ahead.

As soon as Mr. Fauré says, Mark, I've got confidential information, Mr. Cuban's response is uh-huh, go ahead, tell me the information. Mr. Fauré tells him we're going to do a PIPE.

The evidence will show that Mr. Cuban's reaction to that was very negative. Mr. Fauré will testify Mr. Cuban was yelling at him. The evidence will show ... Mr. Cuban is not happy. Because he doesn't like PIPEs. He doesn't like private financings. He doesn't like PIPE type transactions. Because of the dilution that I explained. But he also doesn't like discounts and he doesn't like warrants.

And Mr. Cuban has more than $7 million invested in this company.

So towards the end of the yelling at Mr. Fauré, Mr. Cuban says this, "Now I'm screwed. I can't sell."

When you hear that testimony ask yourselves can that really mean anything other than what common sense tells you that means?

Mr. Cuban agreed to keep the information confidential. He just learned information that's going to make his investment fall, the value of his investment fall, and now he can't sell. That's why he's screwed.

Now, what happens next?

It's more than just common sense here. It's more than what just that statement on its face must mean.

The testimony of Mr. Fauré, he will say that he knew Mr. Cuban agreed to keep the information confidential, not share it with any outside parties, and not trade on it until it was public.

The whole reason Mr. Fauré is calling Mr. Cuban is to invite him to invest in the PIPE.

So what happens next?

Mr. Fauré sends another email to Mr. Cuban at 3:51 p.m. Eastern time. And this one tells Mr. Cuban the name and telephone number of a man named Arnold Owen. Arnold Owen will testify here probably today.

Who is Arnold Owen?

He is an individual in San Francisco, California, at this time. And he works for a company called Merriman.

Mamma.com hired Merriman to put together the PIPE. So Arnold Owen is the sales rep. He's the man out selling the PIPE. He's contacting a small group of investors. He knows what the PIPE is about. He's helping Mamma.com sell it, get the investors, get the cash into the company.

Mr. Fauré is giving Mr. Cuban Mr. Owen's name and telephone number, so that he can call him to find out about the PIPE.

Mr. Owen will testify in this case about what happened.

At 5:32 p.m. Mr. Cuban calls Arnold Owen. It's another conversation ... that lasts, ironically, eight minutes.

Mr. Owen will testify that the two men discussed the PIPE. And the one thing Mr. Owen remembers about that conversation is the tone, the tone of Mr. Cuban. He was not happy.

You see, Mr. Cuban learned on that phone call that the PIPE had discounts and the PIPE had warrants. That's what he wanted to know.

He was so furious about what he had heard that one minute later, without any hesitation, without any other consideration in his mind, he called his broker at

5:41, and he said sell every single share I own in this company. He wanted out. And he wanted out now.

... [L]adies and gentlemen, the evidence will show this is insider trading. It's deception. It's learning the company has confidential information. It's ... using that information to benefit yourself, to get out.

What happens next, that same day?

It's 5:41 p.m. when Mr. Cuban calls his broker. The markets are closed. But you can trade outside sometimes ... but you can't trade a lot.

So Mr. Cuban's broker does this: He starts to sell in after-hours trading on June 28th. And he manages to sell 10,000 of Mr. Cuban's 600,000 shares and he does it at a price of $13.49, an average sales price. That's on June 28th.

The next day the markets open and Mr. Cuban's broker continues to unload his entire ownership in the company. He sells the remaining 590,000 shares of Mamma. com between 9:30 a.m. and 4:00 p.m. Eastern time at an average price of $13.29.

By 4:00 p.m. in the afternoon Mr. Cuban owns nothing, not one share of Mamma.com.

Now, what happens next?

6:00 p.m. Mamma.com tells the [public] they're doing a PIPE. It is now public information. It's in the hands of all of the shareholders. It's in the hands of anyone who reads about it.

What happens next?

Exactly what Mr. Cuban predicted. The stock price falls.

On June 30th that stock price goes to $11.99 a share. Mr. Cuban sold the shares at 13.29 and 13.50.

The stock price is now 11.99.

Mr. Cuban avoided approximately $750,000 in losses by selling his shares before the public knew about the PIPE.

Mr. Cuban was faced with a business decision at Mamma.com to raise cash to grow the company that he didn't agree with. A decision that he wouldn't have made. A decision that he believed would decrease the value of his investment. He was going to lose. So he sold his shares before it was announced, before he lost. That's insider trading. And the evidence will show Mr. Cuban knew better.

You'll hear from Mr. Cuban's trial team in this case. And you'll hear from Mr. Cuban himself. And you may hear many reasons about why the SEC has it all wrong, why we can't prove our case, and why he really didn't insider trade....

Mr. Cuban will claim he made no agreement not to keep this PIPE confidential. No way. He will claim that because he didn't agree to keep it confidential in writing that that means he didn't agree to keep it confidential.

Judge Fitzwater will explain to you that this type of agreement in an insider trading case does not have to be in writing. It could be oral. It could be express. It could be implied from the circumstances of the parties.

It does not have to be a formal contract.

And use your common sense here. Has someone ever asked you in your lives to keep something confidential?

Did they ask you to sign an agreement?

Did you nonetheless keep it confidential?

Did the fact that you didn't sign a piece of paper change how you viewed that information and what you should do with it?

Do you often agree to things in your everyday lives, very important things, that you don't keep in writing? ....

The other thing you'll hear is Mr. Cuban claim that his words "Uh-huh, okay, go ahead" is not an agreement.

Again, let's use your common sense here.

Do you always use formal language when you agree to something?

If someone asks for you to do something, do you always use a full and complete grammatically correct sentence?

Yes. "Absolutely I will do that, you have my agreement?"

No. Sometimes we just say, sure, "Yeah. Okay. No problem."

That's how we speak. That's the English language. That's how Mark Cuban speaks....

Because that's how we all speak. We don't always use full and complete sentences. Sometimes we just make an acknowledgement with, yeah, okay, uh-huh.

Mr. Cuban's trial team will try to take the words of Mr. Fauré's and Mr. Cuban's eight-minute conversation and pull the phrases apart and separate them into words and phrases that are totally disconnected and when viewed separately seem innocent. But we all know that's not how conversations work.

Conversations are a back and forth between two people. And the evidence in this case will show that the conversation between Mr. Fauré and Mr. Cuban lasted eight minutes. It was about a business decision at Mamma.com, a business decision communicated about what the company was going to do to raise money.

But it's more than just that phone call. The agreement may be found based on the facts and the circumstances in this case, in the conduct of the parties. So when you hear the evidence, view it as a whole....

Finally, Mr. Cuban may try to make this case about everybody else's actions but his own, the actions of Mr. Fauré, the actions of Mr. Owen, maybe even the actions of the SEC. Mr. Cuban's team may argue that Mr. Fauré is a liar, his testimony is false, because he was somehow trying to curry favor with the SEC. There will be no evidence in this case that supports that argument.

At the end of this case, my colleagues and I will show you just how baseless that allegation about Mr. Fauré really is. Because when you listen to the evidence keep this in mind: Who in this courtroom is charged with insider trading?

Mark Cuban.

Of all the witnesses you're going to hear, who really has [the] motivation to lie?

You also might hear that Mamma.com and Mr. Fauré were somehow unfair to Mr. Cuban by telling him about the PIPE. Somehow he gets stuck now with a bad decision of the company. But all Mr. Cuban had to do was wait one more day until the public knew about the PIPE. Then he could have sold all of his shares. Then he would have had the same information that all the ordinary investors had. Then he could have legally dumped his shares.

But the evidence will show Mark Cuban couldn't do that, because in his mind that's losing, and Mark Cuban is a winner.

The Cuban team may also try to blame the PIPE investors, okay, the other small group of investors that actually did invest the money in the PIPE. You might hear they weren't asked to sign confidentiality agreements, they weren't told explicitly to keep it confidential.

But here's what you won't hear.

You won't hear any evidence that the PIPE investors told the public about the PIPE, and you won't hear any evidence that any of the PIPE investors went into the market and bought or sold shares before that PIPE was public. The only prospective investor that did that ... was Mark Cuban.

So whatever it is that Mr. Cuban and his defense team say about Mr. Fauré, Mr. Owen, the SEC, or even the PIPE investors, they will not be able to hide from the evidence. They won't be able to hide from that timeline, because the evidence doesn't lie.

The evidence will show in this case that the only person responsible for selling more than $7 million in Mamma.com stock before the public announcement was Mr. Cuban.

It was Mr. Cuban that agreed to keep the information confidential. And the evidence will show that nobody but Mr. Cuban said "Now I'm screwed, I can't sell." And it's important. The evidence will show that it is Mr. Cuban who was responsible for putting his own desire to win in this investment above his agreement to the company and above his responsibility to all the other investors in the market....

And as Judge Fitzwater said, this is not a criminal case. We will not come back here at the end of the evidence and ask you to convict Mark Cuban of a crime. We won't ask you to send him to jail. Nor will any of those things happen to him in this case, because this is a civil case. It's about the rights and responsibilities of all investors in our markets, the right of every investor to trade in a market that's fair, and the responsibility of every investor, including Mark Cuban, to play fair.

We will ask you at the end of this trial to hold Mr. Cuban responsible, responsible as an investor, because the evidence will show he didn't play fair. He cheated. And ... out of all investors Mark Cuban knew better.

Thank you.

After the Opening Statement by the SEC, Judge Fitzwater gave the jurors the following instructions.

[2] The District Judge's Instructions to the Jury

Before we take our restroom break, I want to remind you of the important instructions you must follow during the recess.

As you already know, this trial has received coverage in the media and over the Internet, and I anticipate that this coverage will continue throughout the course of the trial. During the break, you will have access to telephones and perhaps media sources. Those of you who have cell phones, smartphones, and similar devices, may be able to access the Internet and other tools of technology. It is extremely important that during this recess you not talk about the case with anyone or allow anyone to talk with you about the case or the trial. This includes communications with family members, personal friends, coworkers, and business associates.

It is also extremely important that you not try to do any research about the case, the parties, or the trial by talking to anyone, reading or listening to any media source, or using the Internet. This includes through use of cell phones, smartphones, such as iPhones, Androids, BlackBerries, and Galaxy phones, and electronic tablet devices such as iPads, Microsoft Surfaces, and Kindles.

Do not communicate through email, text messaging, Twitter, a blog, Facebook, LinkedIn, YouTube, MySpace, Google+ or the many other means of technology and social media that our world makes available. You must decide this case based only on the evidence presented here in court within the four walls of this courtroom and not something that you read about, hear about, or see from another source.

Members of the jury, I thank you very much for following these instructions. It's important that you do so, so that the trial is fair to both sides.

After recess was taken, legal counsel for Mr. Cuban presented the Opening Statement on his client's behalf.

[3] Mr. Cuban's Opening Statement

THE COURT: . . . Mr. Melsheimer, are you making the opening statement for the defendant?

MR. MELSHEIMER [Attorney for Mr. Cuban]: I am, Your Honor. . . .

THE COURT: All right.

MR. MELSHEIMER: . . .

Over the next three weeks you will see what happened over nine years ago in 2004. And it is a very, very different story than I think the one the government told you.

The truth in this case is not complicated. The truth is very straightforward. And the truth is that Mr. Cuban has done nothing wrong.

Good morning. I'm Tom Melsheimer. I along with my colleagues, Mr. Best and Mr. Clark, will be presenting Mr. Cuban's defense to you in this case.

And that evidence will prove three things. It will prove first that the information that the government claims is nonpublic or confidential information related to Mamma.com's use of a special kind of stock offering called a PIPE, was known by the investing public well before June 28, 2004, well before Mr. Cuban sold his stock. In other words, it was known in the marketplace.

On June 28th, the day the PIPE was originally supposed to close, [the amount of] trading in the stock spiked by 2000 percent. You will see that in the evidence.

And when that happens that means information is in the marketplace and the information was this PIPE transaction.

Number 2. The evidence will show that Mr. Cuban never made any agreement, express or implied, with Guy Fauré. You will hear him say that. Never made any agreement to keep any information confidential. Never made an agreement to refrain from selling stock. Did not happen.

In fact, the uncontradicted evidence that you'll hear is just the opposite. Mr. Cuban told the CEO of Mamma.com, and Arnie Owen [of Merriman], that he was going to sell his stock in the company. And that's exactly what he did.

The lack of any agreement is very, very important in this case. And we're going to talk more about it later.

This is not the kind of insider trading case that you may have heard about before you came to court. Here the law says, and Judge Fitzwater will tell you, that the government must prove that Mr. Cuban made an agreement with Guy Fauré.

It is not enough that Mr. Fauré told Mr. Cuban some information. It is not enough that Mr. Fauré may have used the word "confidential."

The government must prove to you that Mr. Cuban clearly agreed to keep information ... confidential, and they must prove to you that he also agreed not to sell his stock.

Under the law they have to prove both elements to you and they won't even be able to prove either one.

Let's be clear about this, and you heard it strong from the government: The government accuses Mr. Cuban of committing a fraud, but fraud requires deception or trickery, and Mr. Cuban didn't deceive Mamma.com. He didn't deceive anyone. He did exactly what he told the company he was going to do. He did exactly what he told Arnie Owen he was going to do, and you will hear from Mr. Owen later in this trial. [Mr. Cuban] sold his stock.

Third point. Mr. Cuban's actions back in 2004 are totally, totally inconsistent with someone who has done something wrong or has something to hide....

What will the evidence show?

The evidence will show that long before Mr. Cuban sold his stock he raised concerns with the executives at Mamma about Mamma.com's possible association with a known criminal, a man named Irving Kott. The company assured Mr. Cuban that, no, the company has no involvement with Mr. Kott. Now, you're going to hear it turns out the SEC had the exact same concerns about the company....

The very trades that the government claims in this courtroom are a fraud and a cheat he emailed to the government shortly after these trades took place.

Voluntarily sharing information is not the behavior of someone who is trying to deceive anyone. It's not the kind of behavior you would expect from someone who had something to hide. And I'm surprised the government didn't preview you that evidence in their opening.

These facts and others you will hear are why Mr. Cuban is in court today, to stand up to the government and refute these allegations.

We are committed to bringing you the truth of what happened and letting you decide what happened, to have you decide who was right and who was wrong. That is what juries in this country have been doing for over 200 years. And we know and trust that you'll do the same.

Let me give you some background on the case:

Although some of the financial terms you may hear during this trial may seem unfamiliar to you, the evidence in this case I promise you is not complex.

Most of the important events occur on a single day, June 28th, 2004, in two phone calls.

Now, you've heard about Mamma. It was an Internet search engine based in Canada.

In the first quarter of 2004 the company had shown some promise in its business and Mr. Cuban's investment advisors brought it to his attention and he decided to make an investment.

Mamma was the kind of business that Mr. Cuban knew and understood, Internet technology. It also appeared to have the kind of characteristics that he liked in a company. It was focused on growing its business in the right way, that is to say, by growing organically, having more customers, developing more business.

So he made an investment in the company of about 600,000 shares.

Now, this made him a 6 percent owner of the company. Under the law when someone buys more than 5 percent of the stock of a company they have to file a document with the SEC to identify yourself as having more than 5 percent of the company. Mr. Cuban filed that public form in March of 2004.

... [O]nce everyone knew that Mr. Cuban was an investor in the company, the stock price went up. And you'll hear him explain that that happens a lot, when he makes investments people say, well, Mark Cuban is buying [stock in] that company, maybe it's a good investment, I should buy it [too].

Now, Mr. Cuban will also explain to you that when he buys stock in a company like Mamma, the first thing he does is he offers to help with the company's business, to help the business grow.

He reached out to the president of the company, Mr. Fauré, back in March and April and said, hey, do you have some company hats or a T-shirt, maybe I can wear it during a Mavericks game, maybe I can wear something while I'm on television....

Over time this is what happened: People began to send [Mr. Cuban] emails and questions about the company.

Now, some of you may know that Mr. Cuban's email is public. Anyone can email him. And he's going to tell you, many people do.

At first he received unsolicited emails about Mamma.com ... from people, people that wanted to know about the company, people that may have been investors, people that wanted to know why he invested, random people off the Internet, some people from the press contacted him.

But eventually you will hear an FBI agent contacted him. An FBI agent contacted him and told him to be careful about dealing with Mamma, because this agent told him that Mamma was associated with a known stock swindler or may be associated with a known stock swindler named Irving Kott.

Now, as you might expect, this caused Mr. Cuban some concern. And you will see in this email that he sent to Mr. Fauré in April 2004, "Mr. Kott is still getting investigated by the FBI. My getting a call from the FBI asking me about this is more than a little unsettling."

Now, Mr. Fauré assured him that Mr. Kott had no involvement with the company.

[Mr. Cuban] then ... asked another board member of the company to answer some questions about Mr. Kott. And that [person] said, no, no, Irving Kott, this convicted felon, he's not involved with our company.

So Mr. Cuban had some concerns, but not enough to cause him to sell the stock at the end of April.

In late June, however, something happened that caused Mr. Cuban to realize that his earlier concerns were well founded. He wanted to sell his stock. He wanted out of this investment.

What happened?

Well, on June 28th Mr. Cuban gets an email from Guy Fauré. The email asked Mr. Cuban to call him. But, no, it doesn't say why. It doesn't say what he's calling about or what he needs to call about.

On June 28th you will hear that Mr. Cuban was at a charity golf tournament benefitting the Make A Wish Foundation. He sees Mr. Fauré's email when he returns to the Mavericks' offices.

So Mr. Cuban calls Mr. Fauré, and learns to his great surprise that the company was going to raise money through this private placement, or PIPE, where certain people can buy stock at a lower price than everybody else.

You'll hear a lot more about Mr. Cuban's thoughts about private placements during the trial, but during that call there's no dispute he became very angry. Mr. Cuban didn't like what he was hearing about Mamma.com, because it was inconsistent with what the president told him was the goal of their company, to grow organically.

Mr. Cuban told Mr. Fauré he was going to sell his stock, which he did later that day, and the very next day.

He filed the required form with the government announcing that on June 29th he had sold all of his stock in Mamma.com. ...

Now, folks, that should have been the end of it.

Mr. Cuban held an investment for about four months, one that was about one-half of 1 percent of his total stock investments, developed concerns about the company over time, and then when he learned that the company had lied to him or not shot straight with him about what their business plans truly were, [he] got out. ...

So why are we here today?

We're here today for one reason: This fellow, Guy Fauré.

We're here today because Mr. Fauré's testimony that Mr. Cuban said during the phone call he had with Mr. Fauré something like, something like: Uh-huh, go ahead. And later said, according to Mr. Fauré, something like: Now I'm screwed, I can't sell it. ...

The only source of that evidence or claimed evidence to that effect is uttered from Mr. Fauré.

Mr. Cuban, he will take the stand and tell you he never made such a promise, never made such a statement to Mr. Fauré. And he will explain to you why he would never have done so.

Nonetheless, the reason we're here today is this man, Guy Fauré, the story that the government pulled out of him over time is why we're here.

What is his story? What is Guy Fauré's story?

To understand it you need to go back a few months.

What ... Mr. Cuban didn't know when he got that email on June 28th, that mysterious email that said call me but didn't say why, is the company had been planning to do a PIPE transaction, for many months....

And it turns out when they called Mr. Cuban on June 28th they had been talking to investors for months and the deal was supposed to close that day. The day they sent the email. The ASAP email is the day the PIPE was supposed to close.

So why in the world would you call Mr. Cuban on June 28th? ....

Because on June 28th the evidence will show you that the company didn't believe Mr. Cuban was going to be interested in the PIPE. Other investors had already committed to fully participate, and it was fully subscribed. It was sold out....

And they also knew, and you'll see this in a bit, that he didn't like PIPES because he thought they were a sign of scam.

So why call him just a few short hours before the deal was supposed to close?

Let's focus on what's going on from Mr. Fauré's perspective.

I'm going to be using a timeline to aid our discussion.

If you had been in downtown Montreal, Canada, on June 28th on Saint Jacques Street around lunchtime you might have seen a man coming off an elevator hurriedly to get to lunch.

That man was Guy Fauré. At about 1:00 o'clock he received a call from Mark Cuban in Dallas, who he asked to call him but he hadn't said why.

Now, Mr. Fauré knew good and well why he wanted to talk to Mr. Cuban. He wanted to talk to Mr. Cuban about the PIPE transaction, one that he knew that Mr. Cuban wouldn't like and one that he knew would dilute Mr. Cuban's investment.

Now, Mr. Fauré must have been a little nervous when he made this call, because back in May he had discussed internally with Mr. Goldman [Mamma.com's executive board chairman], who's going to be the government's first witness, that Mr. Cuban doesn't like PIPES....

In any event, Mr. Fauré certainly feared that Mr. Cuban would sell his shares, because he knew he didn't like PIPES. And he knew that would be bad for Mamma, because Mr. Cuban was the highest profile investor in the company.

He also knew that Mr. Cuban had raised concerns about this Irving Kott fellow and this call he got from the FBI. So maybe from Mr. Fauré's perspective that the news he had for Mr. Cuban was going to be the last straw.

The call didn't go well.

After about 30 seconds ... take a look at this. This is something else you didn't see from the government.

The international cell phone connection was lost. Here's the cell phone records of the actual call.

There's two calls. First call is for about 30 seconds, next call's for about eight minutes.

Mr. Fauré must have gotten even more nervous when Mr. Cuban called him right back, and told him about the proposed transaction and then Mr. Cuban became angry and suspicious.

Mr. Fauré does not remember any of the exact words that Mr. Cuban said. That's not in dispute.

I'll say that again. He doesn't remember any of the exact words.

According to Mr. Fauré, he told Mr. Cuban he had some confidential information to give him. But you're also going to hear him say, and you'll hear this from every Mamma.com witness, that no one, no one told Mr. Fauré to get an agreement from Mr. Cuban to hold the information confidential. No one told him to do that. And he didn't do that. And you'll see that in the evidence. He never got such an agreement from Mr. Cuban....

Think about this: Mr. Fauré gave out this supposedly confidential information on his cell phone, in the lobby of a public building, where anyone could overhear him.

That may sound careless or even reckless, but it turns out Mr. Fauré didn't really have anything to worry about. That's because the PIPE was already known. It was known in the marketplace, known by potential investors, known by others, none of whom had any obligation to keep it secret....

As I said earlier, the evidence will show that the PIPE information that the government claims was nonpublic was in fact known by the investing public.

You're going to hear from the former economist [Dr. Eric Sirri] of the SEC, the fellow that was charged with doing all their economic analysis. And he's going to show you that the information was in the market on June 28th, before Mr. Cuban sold a single share of stock....

The truth is, is that this information was out there. This supposedly nonpublic information was known. And it was known well before Mr. Cuban picked up the phone, called his broker and sold his stock.

Let's get back to the June 28th phone call.

Mr. Fauré doesn't remember how the call ended.

We do know that it only lasted about eight minutes. Two calls.

We do know this though, there's not an email from Mr. Fauré to Mr. Cuban confirming their conversation.

There's no email from Mr. Cuban to Mr. Fauré agreeing to anything that Mr. Fauré said.

What we do know is that three hours later Mr. Fauré sent an email to Mr. Cuban suggesting that if he had any questions he should contact this fellow Arnie Owen. Arnie Owen was the outside broker drumming up interest in this PIPE with investors. He was a salesman for the PIPE to potential investors. He was Mamma's agent.

Let me say that again. He was Mamma's agent.

Mr. Fauré admits that Mr. Cuban didn't ask for this email. And he didn't ask for any contact information for Mr. Owen.

Note that Mr. Fauré in this email doesn't say a word about any agreement of confidentiality or an agreement not to trade. That's because no such agreement existed.

Now, Mr. Owen will testify and you will hear from him soon, that he did not consider anything he told Mr. Cuban to be confidential. There was no agreement between Mr. Fauré and Mr. Cuban and there was no agreement between Mr. Owen and Mr. Cuban either.

What you'll hear is that it was Mr. Owen's job to sell the idea of the PIPE to potential investors, including the specifics of the investment, these so-called discounts and warranties. He never had an agreement with anyone to keep that information confidential or to not trade on the basis of that information.

So there can't be any way that the information that Mamma's agent told Mr. Cuban can magically become confidential.

Mr. Owen's conversation with Mr. Cuban was not a confidential information conversation. It was not an agreement not to trade.

Indeed, you're going to hear Mr. Owen say it was just a courtesy call. It was a courtesy call. It's certainly not the basis for a claim that Mark Cuban tricked, deceived or defrauded anyone.

Now, the evidence will show you that Mr. Cuban told Mr. Owen, just like he told Mr. Fauré, that he was going to sell his shares in the company....

So at the end of the day on June 28th, what do we know?

We know that Mark Cuban has told the president of Mamma and its agent that he's selling his shares in the company. We know he's told both men that he thinks PIPEs are a bad idea. And we know that neither man has put anything in writing contradicting any of this, telling him in any way that he was limited, prevented, or restricted in any way from selling his stock....

Now, think about it. One of the great things in our jury system ... is that it requires you to use your common sense....

Does it make any sense at all that Mark Cuban, if he knowingly engaged in a deceptive scheme to sell his shares of Mamma to avoid losses, that he would openly and freely talk to an SEC lawyer, alone, without any lawyer present, and then voluntarily send the government all kinds of documents about all his contacts with Mamma?

Does that sound like a person that has done something wrong?

Does that sound like a person who is a guilty man fleeing under the cover of darkness?

Or does that sound like an innocent man who ... knows that he has nothing to hide....

We will show you the evidence of how Mr. Fauré has changed his story. And you'll also hear some of the reasons, some of the motivations for Mr. Fauré to have changed his story....

Mr. Fauré and Mr. Cuban had never even met. They haven't met to this day in person.

You heard the government say this was a business relationship.

Let's talk about the evidence you're going to see in the case.

The SEC will go first with the evidence, just like they did with the opening statement, because that's the way this trial is set up. They get to go first because they have the burden of proof. They have to prove every single fact to you. And they have the burden of proof on every element of their claims. That's why they go first.

I'm going to ask you to be patient and listen to the evidence that we're going to bring, because it's going to give you the complete picture.

Lots of things were left out of their opening.... That's going to happen day after day in this case....

Now, again, the claim that the SEC has made, a claim of fraud by insider trading, requires proof of a deception or trick by Mr. Cuban. And there will be no evidence of anything like that.

The government can get up here and call Mr. Cuban a liar and call him a cheat, which is what they did in their opening, but that's not evidence. And they're not going to be able to prove a lick of that.

Under the law it is not simply buying or selling stock with information about a company that's illegal. There must be proof that Mr. Cuban agreed to keep the information confidential and agreed not to trade on it and went ahead and did so anyway, all the while not telling Mamma that he was going to sell the stock.

So the SEC's theory is really this: Mr. Cuban made an agreement to keep the information confidential, made an agreement to not sell the stock, and then hiding his true intentions went ahead and sold his stock anyway.

The evidence that you'll hear, the truth that you'll hear, is just the opposite. Never agreed to keep it confidential. Never agreed not to trade. Never broke any promise. Did exactly what he said he was going to do. Did not deceive Mamma....

Now, the final issue I want to address is this statement that you saw over and over again that Mr. Cuban supposedly said to Mr. Fauré, according to Mr. Fauré only, something to the effect of, "Now I'm screwed, I can't sell."

Now not only will the evidence show that Mr. Fauré is not believable, all the other evidence that you'll hear will show just the opposite of what Mr. Fauré claims happened on that call.

The evidence will show, first, that well before June 28th the folks at Mamma believed Mr. Cuban would sell his shares if he found out about the PIPE.

Think that's why they waited until the day it was supposed to close to tell him about it in a rushed eight minute phone call?

That's going to be up to you to decide.

The evidence will show that Mr. Cuban told Arnie Owen [of Merriman] that he was going to sell his stock on June 28th.

After Mr. Cuban told Mr. Owen that, one minute later he did just that. He called his broker.

And, finally, the evidence will show that when Mr. Cuban visited with the SEC on June 30th he told the SEC the exact testimony he's going to provide you on the witness stand, which is, "I told them I was going to sell my stock and I did sell my stock after talking to Mr. Fauré and Mr. Owen."

It certainly corroborates, corroborates quite clearly Mr. Cuban's testimony and his recollection ....

All of this evidence ... flatly contradicts the words that Mr. Fauré has placed into Mr. Cuban's mouth of "Now I'm screwed. I can't sell." Flatly contradicts that. And he will tell you that as well.

As I said at the outset, the plain truth in this case will become apparent in the evidence. The information about the PIPE was not confidential. It was not nonpublic.

Mr. Cuban made no agreement of any kind on June 28th with Guy Fauré to do anything.

And Mr. Cuban acted like a person who had nothing to hide, because he had and has nothing to hide.

We're here in court today because Mr. Cuban has insisted and demanded that he stand up to the government. And he's going to stand up to them when they call him a liar and he's going to stand up to them when they call him a cheater, because he knows the truth and the truth is in the evidence, and the truth will prove that Mr. Cuban has done nothing wrong.

At the end of the case, when all the evidence is in, I predict that you, all of you, are going to share our deep, deep disappointment that the government has ever sought to bring this case.

Thank you for your time.

[B] Trial Testimony

We now proceed to trial testimony. With the SEC bearing the burden of proof (by a preponderance of the evidence), the government presented its case first. Because of the length of the trial and the number of witnesses called by each side, excerpts of the trial testimony of each witness are necessary. *We now begin with the SEC's presentation of its case.*

[1] The SEC Presents Its Case

At trial, the SEC was compelled to use the video deposition of a number of witnesses due apparently to those witnesses' refusal to appear at trial and their not being subject to a court order requiring them to be present—as such individuals are Canadian citizens. *The first witness called by the SEC was Mamma.com executive chairman of its board of directors, Mr. David Goldman.*

Mr. Goldman testified at trial by means of video deposition. Prior to the commencement of his testimony, Judge Fitzwater gave the following instructions to the jury.

THE COURT: I'm going to give you an instruction before this witness is called by video deposition. I anticipate that a similar instruction will be included in the court's charge, which is the written document each of you will receive at the end of the case.

A deposition is the sworn recorded answers to questions asked of a witness in advance of the trial. Before this trial attorneys representing the parties in this case questioned the witness under oath. A court reporter was present and recorded the testimony. This deposition testimony is entitled to the same consideration and is to be judged by you as to credibility and weighed and otherwise considered by you insofar as possible in the same way as if the witness had been present and had testified from the witness stand.

I will also instruct you, in this case it comes up later during the trial, that deposition testimony can also be introduced for the purpose of impeaching or discrediting a witness. If in the deposition the witness made any statements in conflict with testimony the witness gave in court, you may consider such conflicts and any explanation therefore in determining the witness' credibility....

All right. Counsel, you may proceed.

---

[a] Testimony of Mr. David Goldman

The testimony of Mr. Goldman follows.

DIRECT EXAMINATION BY VIDEO DEPOSITION
[By Mr. O'Rourke, Attorney for the SEC]

Q. Good morning, Mr. Goldman. Could you state your full name for the record, please.

A. David Goldman.

Q. And what is your age or date of birth, please?

A. February 17, 1943.

Q. Where do you reside?

A. Toronto, Ontario.

Q. And are you a Canadian citizen?

A. Yes....

Q. Do you recall your position [with Mamma.com] in 2004?

A. I was executive chairman, and Guy Fauré ... became the president over the new Mamma.com....

Q. And what was the working relationship between you and Mr. Guy Fauré?

A. We were very close. We exchanged information openly. We worked closely together. Our offices were next to each other. It was a very small company with only three officers....

Q. Now, sir, do you know the investment banking firm of Merriman Curhan Ford?

A. Yes.

Q. Did there come a point in time at which Mamma.com entered into an investment banking agreement with Merriman Curhan Ford?

A. Yes, we did. We ... engaged them sometime early in 2004 as our financial advisors to assist us in mapping where we would be going in the future, whether it would be capital raised for acquisition or merging with somebody or being acquired.

Q. By the way, if I refer to Merriman, you'll understand I'm referring to Merriman Curhan & Ford?

A. Yes.

Q. And if I perhaps refer to it or you refer to it as MCF, it means the same thing?

A. Yes....

Q. Now, sir, did there come a point in time on June 29th, 2004, in which Mamma announced a PIPE transaction?

A. Yes....

Q. Now, sir, as you started the process and continued the process in June of considering the possibility of this PIPE, how did the company view the concept of a PIPE in terms of confidentiality?

A. From ... our perspective, and we had discussions with U.S. counsel, the officers and directors of the company felt that this was to be regarded as confidential information and that we would be restricted from taking any market-related actions until this was concluded one way or the other.

Q. Okay. And was it ... in terms of taking market-related actions, would it have been ...

A. Trading in securities at Mamma.com.

Q. And what about beyond that, was it treated confidentially at the company?

A. Yes.

Q. And how is that?

A. The only people who were aware of it were those with absolute need to know, and we did not discuss this with anybody outside the company, except MCF, and ... with potential investors....

Q. Okay. Why was that?

A. Because we believed it was material information.

Q. And did you understand that ... [Mr. Cuban] was ... the largest shareholder of Mamma?

A. Yes.

Q. And did you ever speak to Mr. Mark Cuban concerning matters related to Mamma?

A. No. I never communicated directly, although I did have some email communications with him.

Q. And, again, I'm not talking about the PIPE right now, but did anyone else from [Mamma.com], to your understanding, have communications with Mr. Mark Cuban after such time as he became the largest shareholder of Mamma?

A. Yeah. I believe Guy [Fauré] had several conversations.

Q. Do you recall generally what some or any of those were about?

A. I think they were general in nature ... discussed general principles of the company and where it was going and how ... the company could be grown in a general sense.

But those were conversations held prior to anything to do with the private placement.

Q. And as part of those general conversations, was an offer made to Mr. Cuban to join the board, as you understood it?

A. I believe I sent him an email offering that, and he declined. ...

Q. Okay. [Regarding the PIPE transaction,] what about with Mr. Guy Fauré?

A. I believe we concluded [that] Guy would contact Mark Cuban, ask him if he was interested, and following discussion with directors, Guy was reminded that he would stipulate to Mr. Cuban that he was in receipt of confidential information [regarding the PIPE transaction].

Q. And why was it that Guy Fauré was to make that contact [regarding the PIPE transaction]?

A. Because he was the only officer up until that time who had any direct communications with Mark Cuban.

Q. And what do you mean when you say was to stipulate about the confidentiality of [the information?]

A. He was just to advise Mark Cuban that he was receiving confidential information.

Q. The information about the PIPE?

A. About the PIPE.

Q. And did you so advise him?

A. I believe so.

Q. All right. ... And was that pursuant to the discussions with the board and with Mr. Fauré?

A. Yes.

Q. And was it your understanding that Mr. Cuban was expected to act in accordance with that stipulation?

A. The reason we asked Guy to tell Mr. Cuban that it was confidential was because we believed that ... this was a transfer of information not generally available to others.

Q. What did that mean to you?

A. It meant that ... he should recognize that he's receiving ... confidential information not available to anybody else.

Q. And did you come to understand that Mr. Fauré made that phone call to Mr. Mark Cuban?

A. Yes.

Q. And how did you understand that?

A. Guy, I believe, on the 28th reviewed the context of the phone call with Mr. Cuban and ... I believe because many things were happening in clearing the PIPE, in my communications with the board with respect to the PIPE, I included a summary of the context of his conversation with Mr. Cuban.

Q. ... What did you mean by that?

A. Guy summarized his conversation with Mr. Cuban for me and I summarized it on an email which Guy read and concurred with the summary ... as representing the nature of the discussions that he had with Mr. Cuban....

Q. And ... what did [Mr. Fauré] tell you Mr. Cuban said?

A. That Mr. Cuban recognized that he had received this information and ... according to Guy recognized that that imposed some restrictions on him....

Q. And did Mr. Fauré to your recollection ever propose any edits to [your email's] summary of [Mr. Fauré's] conversation with Mr. Cuban?

A. I don't recollect, but if he had they would have been reflected in the final email.

Q. The final email being the one sent to the [Mamma.com] board members?

A. Yes.

Q. The statement included in the summary and the attachment, "As anticipated, he" referring to Mark Cuban, "initially flew off the handle and said that he would sell his shares (recognizing that he was not able to do anything until we announced the equity) but then asked to see the terms and conditions which we have arranged for him to receive from one of the participating investor groups which he has dealt with in the past."
    Do you see that?

A. Yes.

Q. Now, the reference to Mr. Cuban initially having ... flew ... off the handle, what did you understand that to mean?

A. It was just the tone of Guy's relaying information to me that upset Mr. Cuban and [Mr. Cuban] ... was [verbally] upset by the information which [Mr. Fauré] had relayed to him....

Q. And then recognizing that he was not able to do anything until we announced the equity, ... what did you understand that to mean?

A. Again, I am only relaying the information Guy relayed to me from his conversation and the substance of that information was that ... Guy saying that that comment that Mr. Cuban made ... indicated that he recognized that he would not ... sell his shares or could not sell his shares until after the PIPE had been announced.

Q. ... Did Cuban in any way tell you, or anyone from Mamma, that he had in fact sold before the public announcement of the Mamma PIPE?

A. No.

Q. And did he ever tell you that?

A. I never spoke to Mr. Cuban.

Q. Well, did he ever communicate that to Mamma, that he had sold before the announcement?

A. Not to my knowledge....

Q. ... [W]hat was your reaction when you learned that ... Mr. Mark Cuban had sold prior to the public announcement?

A. It was in the past. It was a done deal. That was it.... I don't even know if I had any disappointment or anything or any feelings of that nature. It was just a fact that I had to deal with.

Q. Was it something you expected though?

A.   I had not anticipated that he would sell before the release of the information.

Q.   Do you recall exactly what you said to Mr. Fauré as to how to approach Mr. Cuban?

A.   Only the substance of it, that … it was a concurrence of the board that he was to ask him whether he had any interest of participating in the PIPE to the extent of retaining his equity interest, and that he had to be sure to mention to him that this would be receipt of confidential information.

Q.   Okay. And did you inform Mr. Fauré as to when in the sequence of the conversation to advise Mr. Cuban that there would be confidential information being shared?

A.   No. Guy was president/CEO. He had capabilities of his own, I was only reiterating the discussions of the board with respect to relaying the information and its confidential nature. It was not for me to give him an ABC primer of how to go about that.

Q.   What do you recall the specific words that Mr. Cuban told Mr. Fauré who then in turn told you?

A.   As I recollect, Guy had given me some pretty strong words about Mr. Cuban's reaction to him being advised of the PIPE and that it was confidential. And my summary of it.… when it's strong words, I tend to rephrase it and then forget the exact words, was that he recognized that we had put a collar around him in terms of his ability to sell the shares until such time as the PIPE was announced. But the words that Guy used were much stronger than that.

Q.   Okay. Do you recall today sitting here what those words were?

A.   I don't recall exactly. I remember some swear words involved, but I don't remember exactly.…

Q.   … Did you infer from what Mr. Fauré told you that Mr. Cuban was constrained and that he was not able to sell his shares until after the announcement of the PIPE?

A.   I didn't infer. Guy's summary was that he understood that he could not sell. He understood. He recognized.

[The cross examination of Mr. Goldman then proceeded.]

CROSS EXAMINATION BY DEPOSITION
[By Mr. Clark, Attorney for Mr. Cuban]

Q.   Good morning, Mr. Goldman.

Did you at any point after Mr. Cuban acquired his position in Mamma.com stock believe that he was an insider at the company?

A.   No.

Q.   Indeed, [counsel for the SEC] Mr. O'Rourke mentioned Mr. Cuban was invited to join the board of Mamma.com at least once, I think actually twice; is that correct?

A. Yes.

Q. All right. Did he ever accept ... any of those invitations?

A. No.

Q. Did ... Mr. Cuban ever attend management meetings of the company?

A. Absolutely not.

Q. Prior to June 28, 2004, did you ever share financial information with Mr. Cuban in advance of public release?

A. No.

Q. Do you know of anybody at the company that did that?

A. No.

Q. Let me turn our attention now to June 28th, 2004. Where were you when you advised Mr. Fauré on how to approach Mr. Cuban?

A. I think I was in my office.

Q. Okay. And do you recall what time of day this was?

A. No.

Q. Do you recall the specific words you used with Mr. Fauré as to how to inform Mr. Cuban that there would be information shared on the teleconference that was confidential?

A. No.

Q. Did you when speaking to Mr. Fauré ever suggest to Mr. Fauré that he secure an agreement from Mr. Cuban to hold this information in confidence?

A. No.

Q. Did you suggest to Mr. Fauré that he secure from Mr. Cuban a commitment or guarantee or words to that effect from Mr. Cuban to hold the information in confidence?

A. No.

Q. How confident are you that you did not advise Mr. Fauré to secure an agreement of confidence from Mr. Cuban?

A. I'm fairly confident that I did not mention that.

Q. Okay. At some point later that day Mr. Fauré advised you of his conversation with Mr. Cuban?

A. Yes....

Q. ... [D]id Mr. Fauré ever report back to you what specifically he told Mr. Cuban about the financial terms of the PIPE transaction?

A. No.

Q. All right. Indeed, did Mr. Fauré ever say that Mr. Cuban agreed, committed, or promised to hold the information in confidence?

A. No.

Q. As of June 28, 2004, Mamma.com had standardized confidentiality agreements available to use, correct?

A. Yes.

Q. And why did the company not consider using a standard confidentiality agreement with Mr. Cuban?

A. That confidentiality agreement is used primarily for commercial purposes and also ... had been used when discussing with another company acquisition or merger or something where proprietary information and financial information could be disclosed.

... [I]n the case of Mr. Fauré's communication with Mr. Cuban, I didn't think about it as being required, and I don't think Guy in the context would have thought that before discussing he would ask him to sign that non-disclosure agreement [NDA] which generally has reference to disclosure of financial information and proprietary commercial information, none of which was part of it except for the details of the PIPE.

Q. Okay. So I'm clear: It was never considered ... to approach Mr. Cuban with a written confidentiality agreement....?

A. No.

Q. So past June 28th, on June 29th, 2004, did you have conversations with Mr. Fauré that day?

A. Yes.

Q. Okay. Did Mr. Fauré ever tell you on June 29th, 2004, that Mr. Cuban had told him that he agree[d] to hold the information on the June 28th teleconference with Mr. Fauré in confidence?

A. Not in that context, no.

Q. Okay. When Guy Fauré reported the conversation with Mr. Cuban to you, did he tell you how long the conversation was?

A. No.

Q. Did he tell you that Mr. Cuban announced that he would sell his shares?

A. Yes.

Q. Do you recall Mr. Fauré specifically telling you though in this conversation, I know it's long ago, but do you specifically recall Mr. Fauré saying that Mr. Cuban told him he would sell his shares?

A. Yes....

Q. Did Mr. Fauré ever say to you that at any point, whether you were speaking about it or not, did Mr. Fauré ever bring up the subject of Mr. Cuban had agreed to hold the information on the June 28th, 2004 telephone conference in confidence?

A. No.

Q. Did you speak ... to Mr. Fauré in 2006 when the SEC initiated their investigation involving Mr. Cuban's trade of Mamma.com stock?

A. Yes.

Q. Did Mr. Fauré ever tell you then that Mr. Cuban had agreed, committed, promised, guaranteed to hold the information on the June 28th, 2004 telephone conference in confidence?

A. No.

Q. Up to today, ... did Mr. Fauré ever tell you that Mr. Cuban told him on the June 28th, 2004 telephone conference that he agreed, committed, promised, guaranteed to hold the information that was relayed to him on ... that telephone call in confidence?

A. No....

Q. I want to go back to your conversation with Guy Fauré on June 28th as to how to approach Mr. Cuban.

Q. Did you ever advise Mr. Fauré to secure an agreement of any type from Mr. Cuban?

A. No.

Q. Did you advise Mr. Fauré to secure an agreement to restrict trading from Mr. Cuban?

A. No.

Q. ... Did you ever ask Merriman Curhan Ford whether they, in fact, obtained non-disclosure agreements for any of the prospective investors?

A. No. That was their obligation. I didn't ask them....

Q. Referencing now back to the June 28th call with Mark Cuban, did you ask or advise Guy Fauré to get a nondisclosure agreement from Mark Cuban?

A. No.

Q. Did Mr. Fauré ever tell you at any point that he secured a nondisclosure agreement from Mr. Cuban on his June 28th, 2004 call?

A. No.

Q. ... You did not participate in the call with Mark Cuban?

A. No....

Q. Mr. Goldman, I'm showing you what's marked as Defendant's [Exhibit] 3, which is the SEC's complaint against Mark Cuban in this matter that you're a witness to. And I'm going to ask you if you can to turn to paragraph 14 of the SEC's complaint. Do you see paragraph 14?

A. Yes.

Q. Okay.... And this is the SEC's allegations. And I'm going to read to you the following two sentences in paragraph 14.

"Do you see the first line ... on page 14 which says, "The CEO prefaced the call [with] Cuban that he had confidential information to convey to him, and Cuban agreed that he would keep whatever information the CEO intended to share with him confidential."

Do you see this?

A. Yes.

Q. Okay. Did Mr. Fauré ever tell you the following, "Cuban agreed that he would keep whatever information the CEO intended to share with him confidential?"

A. I'm not aware of that.

Q. Did you ever ask Mr. Fauré "to get Mr. Cuban to agree to keep whatever information the CEO would share with him confidential"?

A. No.

Q. Mr. Goldman, I want to refer you back to Defendant's Exhibit 3, which is the SEC [Complaint] ... And turn your attention back to paragraph 14, please.

And do you see the second sentence which says "'The CEO'" ... who we all know to be Guy Fauré ... "in reliance on Cuban's agreement to keep the information confidential proceeded to tell Cuban about the PIPE offering."?

Do you see that?

A. Yes.

Q. Do your recall Mr. Fauré ever telling you that he relied on Mr. Cuban's agreement to keep the information confidential before he proceeded to tell Mr. Cuban about anything regarding the PIPE?

A. No.

Q. ... Let me turn your attention to SEC Exhibit 41.... Now, I want to go through the text of this email ... referencing Mark Cuban....

"Today after much discussion, Guy spoke with Mark Cuban about this equity raise and whether or not he would be interested in participating."

Now, do your recall if Guy Fauré had ever told you what particulars he informed Mark Cuban about regarding this equity raise?

A. About the PIPE.

Q. Okay. Other than Guy Fauré informing Mark Cuban ... that the company was engaging in a PIPE transaction, do you recall if Guy Fauré ever told you any of the particulars regarding the PIPE that he informed Mr. Cuban about?

A. No. He just said ... I spoke to Mark Cuban about the PIPE transaction.

Q. Okay. Do you recall if Guy Fauré ever told you that he informed Mark Cuban as to the discount of the price for the PIPE offering?

A. Terms and conditions, no, ... he didn't discuss that with me.

Q. Okay. The next sentence says, "As anticipated, he initially flew off the handle." end quote?

A. Yes.

Q. Okay. Let's start with "as anticipated." What was anticipated?

A. Guy and I both had expected that Mark Cuban would not be very positively inclined to the idea of a PIPE, that he would react negatively to it....

Q. Okay. And it says he initially, quote, "Flew off the handle." end quote. Now, can you describe for me ... what you meant by that?

A. That was a summary of Guy saying that some colorful exchanges had occurred between him and Mark Cuban.

Q. Okay. Do you remember what those colorful exchanges were?

A. Not specifically....

Q. Did Mr. Fauré ever inform you as to when Mr. Cuban announced ... that he felt some constraint about selling his shares vis-à-vis his statement he was going to sell?

A. ... I don't know the sequence.

Q. Okay. When did Mr. Cuban's statement that he felt constrained about his ability to sell his shares take place in his conversation with Mr. Fauré?

A. I can't answer that question because I wasn't there....

[b] Testimony of Mr. Arnold Owen

The trial testimony of Mr. Arnold Owen of Merriman Curhan Ford (MCF or Merriman) follows.

DIRECT EXAMINATION
[By Mr. Thompson, Attorney for the SEC]

Q. Good afternoon, Mr. Owen....
    Could you please state your full name for the record.
A. Arnold Owen....
Q. And, Mr. Owen, when did you learn that you had become a witness in this trial?
A. When I got subpoenaed.
Q. And who subpoenaed you?
A. Both the SEC and Mr. Cuban's lawyers.
Q. Before coming here today did you make yourself available to counsel for both parties?
A. Yes, I did.
Q. And did you meet with Mr. Cuban's counsel?
A. Yes, I did.
Q. Do you recall how many times you met with Mr. Cuban's counsel?
A. Three times.
Q. What was the most recent time that you met with Mr. Cuban's counsel?
A. Last night.
Q. And did you discuss with them your testimony here today, sir?
A. Part of it.
Q. Mr. Owen, do you have any financial interest in the outcome of this case?
A. None.
Q. You have no dog in this fight?
A. None at all....
Q. In the past were you ever employed with a firm named Merriman Curhan Ford?
A. Yes, I was.
Q. What were your approximate beginning and end dates of employment with Merriman?
A. I think I started at Merriman in May of 2003 and ended in December of 2006.
Q. What was Merriman's line of business when you worked there?
A. They were also a broker dealer, investment banker, research, and trading....
Q. Did you give a deposition in this case, sir?
A. Yes, I did.
Q. And did that deposition largely [concern] your tenure at Merriman?
A. Yes, it did.
Q. And were you represented by counsel for Merriman during that deposition?
A. Yes, I was.
Q. Are you represented by counsel here today?
A. No, I'm not.
Q. Mr. Owen, for the remaining questions I'm going to ask you not to disclose in answer to my questions anything that you may have discussed with Merriman's counsel or anything that you may have told Merriman's counsel, because as I understand it, Merriman does assert attorney/client privilege, so I'd like to respect that privilege.
    Can you do that, sir?

A. Yes.
Q. Now, with that out of the way, let me get back to my questions:
Referring now to the year 2004, in what part of the country was the Merriman office in which you worked located?
A. In San Francisco, California.
Q. And still referring to 2004, what was your title at Merriman at that time?
A. ... [M]anaging director....
Q. Now, Mr. Owen, during your tenure at Merriman were you familiar with the term "material nonpublic information"?
A. Am I familiar with that term? Yes.
Q. And what was your understanding of what "material nonpublic information" [means][?]
A. "Material nonpublic information" is material, affects the company. "Nonpublic" means it's not in the public domain....
Q. Mr. Owen, what type or types of investors did you approach about potentially investing in PIPE offerings?
A. I dealt with institutional investors on the PIPE offerings. They were all professional money managers. And that was basically the cadre or the core of my institutional investment group.
Q. When you say "cadre or core," were these investors with whom you had ongoing relations?
A. Yes.
Q. So you didn't make cold calls to investors about PIPEs?
A. No, I didn't....
Q. During your time at Merriman was Mamma ever one of Merriman's clients?
A. Yes, they were.
Q. And did you have any involvement with Mamma in 2004?
A. Yes, I did.
Q. What involvement did you have, Mr. Owen?
A. I helped run the transaction to raise Mamma money.
Q. And when you refer to "the transaction," what type of transaction was that?
A. We did a PIPE....
Q. Do you have a recollection as to whether you followed your usual practice about how you went about approaching potential investors about the Mamma PIPE?
A. Well, my protocol was to just call them up and tell them that I had a transaction, would they like to hear about it....
Q. And, as I heard you, you indicated that you had a conversation with each of those investors with respect to telling them that the SEC may consider PIPE information to constitute material nonpublic information.
Do I have that correct?
A. Yes.
Q. And so my question is, sir: If you recall of the investors you contacted in 2004 about the Mamma PIPE, were they all investors with which you had had such a conversation at some point in the past?
A. Yes....

Q. Do you recall having had any discussion with Mr. Goldman about the possibility of Mr. Cuban participating in the Mamma PIPE?

A. Not really. No.

Q. Mr. Owen, have you ever had a telephone conversation with Mark Cuban?

A. Yes, I did.

Q. And what was the subject matter, generally, of that ... call?
We're going to get into it in some detail, but what was the subject matter?

A. The Mamma PIPE.

Q. And, Mr. Owen, the parties have stipulated that Mr. Cuban telephoned you on June 28th, 2004 ... and the parties have also stipulated that that phone call lasted approximately eight minutes.
Now, before we talk about the call itself, let me ask this
Had you ever spoken with Mr. Cuban before?

A. No....

Q. And since that phone call have you ever spoken with Mr. Cuban again?

A. No, I have not.

Q. And do you recall having communicated with anyone about Mr. Cuban calling you about the Mamma PIPE?

A. Not that I can remember.

Q. When you spoke with Mr. Cuban on June 28th, 2004, did you know whether he had spoken with anyone at Mamma about the PIPE?

A. No[t] that I can recall.

Q. And before we get to the substance of the call, to the extent you remember, Mr. Owen, could you just tell the jury whether you recall where you were when you took the call?

A. I was in my office at Merriman Curhan Ford.

Q. And that was in San Francisco, California ....

A. That's in San Francisco, yes.

Q. Did you take any notes of the call?

A. No, I did not.

Q. And did you make any notes about the call afterwards?

A. No, I did not....

Q. Can you please tell the jury what you remember about the substance of the call with Mr. Cuban on June 28, 2004?

A. This is a very long time ago, and I remember more the ten[or] of the call than the specific wording or the substance of the call.

Q. And what was the ten[or] of the call?

A. Mr. Cuban seemed upset.

Q. All right. You say Mr. Cuban seemed upset.... [D]id he raise his voice during the call?

A. I can't remember specifically.

Q. Did you have a reaction to Mr. Cuban being upset?

A. Yes. I didn't really want to be on the phone very long.

Q. And why was that?

A. Because ... it was Mark Cuban.

Q. What do you mean by that, sir?

A. He's ... a very famous, very powerful kind of a person, and I'm anything but that.

Q. You were uncomfortable on the call?

A. Yes, I was.

Q. Now, Mr. Owen, based on your practices at the time you believe that you told Mr. Cuban about the terms of the Mamma PIPE during that phone call?

A. I would imagine that based on my practice at the time, if he had asked me, I would have told him the terms.

Q. And certainly if Mr. Cuban wanted to know the terms and asked you, you would have told him?

A. Yes....

Q. ... What I'm asking is whether you recall telling Mr. Cuban that there was going to be a press release [regarding the Mamma.com PIPE transaction] issued the following day.

A. I don't recall.

Q. You don't have a specific recollection of that?

A. No. No.

Q. And do you have a general recollection on that subject?

MR. CLARK [Attorney for Mr. Cuban]: Object, Your Honor, asked and answered.

THE COURT: Overruled.

THE WITNESS: Could you repeat the question?

BY MR. THOMPSON:

Q. Do you have a general recollection of whether you informed Mr. Cuban that the Mamma PIPE would be announced in the press tomorrow, the following day?

A. I don't recall.

Q. Do you recall that you gave testimony to the staff of the Securities and Exchange Commission back in 2007?

A. Yes, I do.

Q. And was that October 2007, if you recall?

A. I think so.

Q. And just like you've been subpoenaed here today, were you subpoenaed by the SEC to provide your testimony?

A. Yes, I was.

Q. And were you represented by counsel during that testimony?

A. Yes, I was.

Q. And was there a stenographer present, taking down everything you said?

A. Yes.

Q. And did you swear to tell the truth?

A. Yes.

Q. And did you do your best to provide accurate testimony?

A. Yes.

MR. THOMPSON: Judge Fitzwater, may I approach the witness to provide him with a copy of his testimony to determine whether it refreshes his recollection?

THE COURT: You may.

. . . .

Q. Mr. Owen, what you've been provided is a copy of the transcript of investigative testimony that you provided to the Securities and Exchange Commission back in October of 2007.

A. Okay.

Q. I'm going to ask you to refer to a couple of sections of that testimony and read them silently to yourself, because what I want to see is whether after you've read the testimony you have a refreshed recollection and are able to recall whether or not you told Mr. Cuban about the timing of the press release.

A. Okay. . . .

Q. And my question, sir, is . . . after reading that excerpt, does that refresh your recollection such that you now sitting here today actually have a recollection of whether or not you told Mr. Cuban about the timing of the PIPE on the phone call that you had with him on June 28, 2004?

A. Do I remember now . . .

Q. Yes, sir.

A. . . . what I said then?

Q. Yes, sir.

A. No, I don't.

Q. Mr. Owen do you have any reason to believe that the stenographer's transcription of the testimony that you just read is not an accurate record of what you said back in October of 2007?

        MR. CLARK: Objection, Your Honor, relevance.

        THE COURT: Overruled.

BY MR. THOMPSON:

Q. Do you need the question again, Mr. Owen?

A. Yes, please.

Q. Do you have any reason to believe that the court reporter's transcription of your testimony that you just read from back in October of 2007 isn't accurate in any way?

A. I have no reason to believe that.

Q. And at the time that you gave that testimony, did you ever refresh your recollection of whether you told Mr. Cuban that the press release on the Mamma PIPE would be announced the following day, which was June 29, 2004?

A. I was closer to the transaction.

Q. Well, based on the testimony that you read to yourself a moment ago, is it fair to say that you had sufficient recollection at that time to answer the questions that were asked of you?

A. Yes.

        MR. THOMPSON: Your Honor, at this time, pursuant to Rule 803.5 of the federal rules of evidence, which deals with recorded recollection . . . , I would like permission to read from page 58, line 19, to page 59, line 3, of Mr. Owen's investigative testimony.

MR. CLARK: Objection, Your Honor. It's not a proper recorded recollection, and it's improper impeachment.

THE COURT: Okay. I'll overrule the objection.

MR. THOMPSON: Thank you, Your Honor.

Ladies and gentlemen of the jury, I am now going to read to you a couple of lines from Mr. Owen's investigative testimony on the subject of his conversation with Mr. Cuban.

"Q. Mr. Owen you have a specific recollection of telling Mr. Cuban that the transaction was going to hit the tape the next morning?

"A. I would use words that are similar to those words. I have no idea what my actual wording or phrasing was.

"Q. Do you have a specific recollection of conveying to Mr. Cuban, even if you don't remember the exact words you used, that the transaction was going to hit the tape the next morning?

"A. That's the intent of the call."

Thank you, Your Honor.

BY MR. THOMPSON:

Q. Mr. Owen, I'd like to stay on the subject of your phone call with Mr. Cuban.

Did Mr. Cuban tell you during that phone call that he had had a phone call with Mr. Guy Fauré that same day?

A. I don't recall.

Q. Did you otherwise know what agreements, if any, Mr. Cuban had with the company regarding the PIPE information?

A. I have no idea.

Q. Mr. Owen, let's stay on the subject of the call with Mr. Cuban on June 28, 2004.

What, if anything, did Mr. Cuban tell you about selling his stock in Mamma. com?

A. I don't recall.

Q. You have no recollection on that subject?

A. No, I don't.

Q. Do you remember whether Mr. Cuban said he was going to sell his stock as soon as he got off the phone with you?

A. I don't remember that.

Q. Did there come a time when you learned that Mr. Cuban had sold his Mamma stock before the public announcement that you had told him about according to your investigative testimony?

A. Yes.

Q. And when did you learn that, Mr. Owen?

A. I don't remember. I just know I learned it.

Q. Was it some period after June 28, 2004?

A. Yes....

Q. Mr. Owen, in the investigative testimony that I read to the jury from what you said back in 2007 regarding whether you told Mr. Cuban that the transaction was going to be announced the next day, I believe you used the term "hit the tape" in that testimony.

Can you explain what "hit the tape" means in your industry?

A. Yes. "Hit the tape" was jargon, meaning that a transaction was going to be announced, that the news services were going to put out the press release and that the information would be out on a news service....

MR. THOMPSON: Thank you, sir.

I have no further questions at this ... at this time.

THE COURT: Cross-examination?

MR. CLARK: May I inquire, Your Honor?

THE COURT: You may.

CROSS EXAMINATION
[By Mr. Clark, Attorney for Mr. Cuban]

Q. Good afternoon, Mr. Owen.

A. Good afternoon.

Q. ... I think Mr. Thompson asked you whether you met me before.

A. Yes.

Q. And you answered you had. It that correct?

A. Yes.

Q. You've met with the SEC a number of times in this case too; is that correct?

A. Yes.

Q. How many times have you met with them?

A. Not counting depositions?

Q. Yeah. Just to prepare for your testimony today.

A. Three times.

Q. Did you meet with them today?

A. Not today.

Q. No?

Last night?

A. Yes....

Q. Based on these years of experience in various aspects of the securities industry, do you feel like you're familiar with stock markets, stock offerings, and those sorts of things?

A. Yes....

Q. ... Did you understand as a placement agent that you acted as a representative of the company that was issuing the PIPE?

A. Yes.

Q. Did you understand as a placement agent you were authorized to provide information about the PIPE to PIPE investors?

A. Yes.

Q. And as a placement agent, did you ... you understand you were authorized to receive information about the PIPE from investors?

A. Yes.

Q. In fact, you were the company's authorized representative for PIPEs; is that correct?

A. That's correct....

Q. ... Did Merriman Curhan ever require you to get a written confidentiality agreement about PIPE information from potential PIPE investors?

A. No.

Q. And did Merriman Curhan ever require you to get an oral confidentiality agreement from potential PIPE investors about PIPE information.

A. No.

Q. You never at any of the places you worked that issued PIPEs [through the years] had to ask any of your clients to keep PIPE information confidential, did you?

A. That's correct....

Q. Your investors communicating with other investors about PIPE transactions was a good thing for you, right?

A. Yes.

Q. And why was that?

A. It could help fill out a book. If there was somebody I missed they would call me up.

Q. ... [T]hey could find other potential investors for you, right?

A. Yes.

Q. And did that happen?

A. Yes....

Q. When you were at Merriman were you ever asked to have potential PIPE investors agree to restrict their trading based on PIPE information?

A. No.

Q. Were you ever asked to have them agree orally?

A. No.

Q. Were you ever asked to have them agree in writing?

A. No.

Q. I want to switch a little bit now ... to the specificity of the Mamma.com deal, if that's okay.

A. Okay.

Q. Do you know a gentleman named Eldad Gal?

A. Yes.

Q. Can you just tell us a little about your background with him and how you know him?

A. Eldad was at a firm called Sage Capital and he was one of my best clients and very often a lead investor on a lot of my transactions....

Q. Can you tell us what a lead investor is in a PIPE transaction[?]

A. They are the investor that comes forward with a term sheet, usually is the largest investor in the transaction, and negotiates the terms of the transaction with the company....

Q. Do you recall when you first spoke with Mr. Gal about Mamma.com?

A. I actually took Mamma to go see him at his offices in New York before there was even the potential of a transaction or not that I knew of....

Q. Before introducing Mr. Gal to Mamma.com, did you ask Mr. Gal to enter into any kind of a confidentiality agreement about Mamma.com?

A. No.

Q. Did Mamma.com ask Mr. Gal to enter into any kind of a confidentiality agreement?

A. No.

Q. Did you or Mamma.com ask Mr. Gal to enter into any kind of an agreement about restricting his trading in Mamma.com stock?

A. No....

Q. ... [A]t some point ... Mr. Gal was recognized as the lead investor in the PIPE; is that correct?

A. That's correct.

Q. And there wasn't any change at that time in his status as not having any confidentiality agreement with Mamma.com, correct?

A. Would you explain that again?

Q. When [Mr. Gal on behalf of his firm Sage Capital] became lead investor in the PIPE did anyone ask him at that point to enter into a confidentiality agreement with Mamma.com?

A. No.

Q. And did anybody ask him at that point to enter into an agreement to restrict his trading in Mamma.com?

A. No.

Q. Was part of his role as lead investor to go speak to other investors?

A. I don't know if you would say that was part of his role but that's pretty common in the industry.

Q. And, indeed, that's what he did; is that fair to say?

A. Yes....

Q. And so it certainly was no surprise to you that he went and spoke to other investors about it?

A. No, it wasn't.

Q. And he wasn't barred from doing that, because he had no confidentiality agreement, correct?

A. That's correct....

Q. Does this document [the Form 20-F filed by Mamma.com with the SEC] say that Merriman Curhan Ford will provide investment banking services to the company which may include representing the company in its efforts to obtain financing in the form of a private placement in either, A, public equity, or B, convertible debt or equity, a "PIPE" or "Capital raising transaction"?

A. Yes, it does.

Q. Do you understand that to say that Mamma.com is hiring Merriman Curhan Ford to do a PIPE?

A. Yes.

Q. Have you ever seen the fact that you had been hired to do a PIPE publicly disclosed in a company's SEC filings in all your experience?

A. At times, yes.

Q. And at that point, did you consider the information about the PIPE to be public?

A. Yes....

Q. Now, if we could go to Defendant's Exhibit 105. Thank you, Mr. Owen....
    MR. CLARK: Your Honor, I'd offer Defendant's Exhibit 105.
    MR. THOMPSON: No objection.
    THE COURT: Defendant's Exhibit 105 is admitted in evidence.

BY MR. CLARK:

Q. Mr. Owen, you're not on this email; is that correct?
A. That's correct.
Q. But you're discussed in it; is that right?
A. Yes, I am.
Q. And it says ... Mr. Cuban from Mr. Fauré, "If you want more details about the private placement, please contact (I guess you or your financial advisors) Arnie Owen," and it gives your phone number. Is that correct?
A. That's correct.
Q. Does this document anywhere relate to a confidentiality agreement that would govern a call between Mr. Cuban and you?
    MR. THOMPSON: Objection, Your Honor, calls for speculation, lack of foundation.
    THE COURT: Overruled as to "relate to."
    THE WITNESS: Could you repeat the question, please?

BY MR. CLARK:

Q. Does this document relate to a confidentiality agreement that would govern a call between Mr. Cuban and you?
A. No.
Q. Did you understand that there was any agreement of confidentiality between Mr. Fauré and Mr. Cuban relating to a call between Mr. Cuban and you?
A. No.
Q. Did you understand that there was any agreement whatsoever between Mr. Fauré and Mr. Cuban relating to a call between Mr. Cuban and you?
A. I would have no knowledge of that....
Q. If Mr. Cuban's financial advisors had called you wanting information about the PIPE, would you have discussed it with them?
    MR. THOMPSON: Speculation, Your Honor.
    THE COURT: Overruled.
    THE WITNESS: Yes, I would have.

BY MR. CLARK:

Q. Would you have asked them for a confidentiality agreement?
A. No.
Q. Would you have asked them for an agreement to restrict trading?
A. No.
Q. So I'd like to now move on to your discussion with Mr. Cuban, the call....
    Okay. Do you remember having a telephone call with Mr. Cuban[?]
A. Yes, I do.
Q. And did that call take place as best as you recall on June 28th, 2004?
A. Yes.

Q.   Do you recall why you spoke to Mr. Cuban that day?

A.   It was in regards to the Mamma PIPE.

Q.   And do you remember whether it was your idea or someone else's idea or Mr. Cuban called you out of the blue?

A.   I think the way I remembered it was David Goldman had asked me to speak to Mark Cuban regarding the PIPE.

Q.   And in connection with Mr. Goldman asking you to speak to Mr. Cuban, did he say to you, "Arnie, we have a confidentiality agreement with Mark Cuban concerning your call"?

A.   No, he did not.

Q.   Did he say to you, "Arnie, we have an agreement that Mark Cuban won't trade his stock concerning your call"?

A.   No, he did not.

Q.   Did he tell you any agreement whatsoever that governed your call with Mr. Cuban?

A.   No, he did not. . . .

Q.   At the time that you spoke to Mr. Cuban you were Mamma.com's agent; is that fair to say?

A.   That's fair to say.

Q.   And so you weren't having a call about Merriman business, except insofar as they were Mamma's agent for the PIPE; is that right?

A.   That's correct.

Q.   And at that time you were Mamma's representative on the call.

A.   Yes.

Q.   You were authorized to provide and receive information on behalf of Mamma. com?

A.   That's correct.

Q.   Now, the call with Mr. Cuban took place after trading closed on June 28th, 2004, . . . as best you recall; is that right?

A.   That's correct.

Q.   And you believed that the Mamma PIPE deal was going to [close] on June 28th, 2004; is that your recollection?

A.   Close and be announced the next morning.

Q.   When you got on the phone with Mr. Cuban you didn't believe the purpose of the call was to convey confidential information . . . to him, did you?

A.   No.

Q.   You understood your call with Mr. Cuban to just be a courtesy call; is that correct?

A.   That's correct.

Q.   And what do you mean when you say a courtesy call?

A.   Courtesy is a practice . . . just to give them the heads up the next morning that there was going to be an announcement of a transaction, and I would rather have it come from me the night before than have them find out and call me up and yell.

Q.   You said that you've been yelled at a number of times because of that?

A.   Sure.

Q. Do you ever get yelled at on these courtesy calls too by people who aren't happy about the news of the PIPE?

A. Sure.

Q. You testified ... that Mr. Cuban yelled at you about the PIPE.

A. Yes.

Q. Was that anything out of the ordinary for one of these deals?

A. No, it's always uncomfortable.

Q. Well, is there anything that Mr. Cuban did that made you feel especially uncomfortable or was this just the normal back and forth of one of these courtesy calls?

A. It was pretty much a normal back and forth of a courtesy call.

Q. And you don't have any dealing that Mr. Cuban tried to intimidate you on that call in any way; is that correct?

A. That's correct.

Q. And you don't have any hard feelings about Mr. Cuban at all, do you?

A. None at all.

Q. So you explained that you do these courtesy calls because you don't want large investors to find out about it somewhere else; is that right?

A. That's correct. Or they will read it on the tape.

Q. But in doing that you're not communicating confidential information?

A. That's correct.

Q. At any time from the very beginning of your talking to Mr. Cuban to the end, did you ever ask him to agree to keep the information you were telling him confidential?

A. No, I did not.

Q. Did he ever volunteer that he would keep it confidential?

A. No, he did not.

Q. At any time during that call did you ask Mr. Cuban to agree not to trade on the information you were giving him?

A. No, I did not.

Q. Did he ever volunteer not to trade on the information you gave him?

A. No, he did not.

Q. Did you ask him to agree to anything on that call?

A. No, I did not.

Q. ... I understand that you've testified you don't remember the substance of the words of that call otherwise; is that right?

A. That's pretty well right.

Q. Other than what you've testified to so far in court.

A. Correct.

Q. You can't testify that Mr. Cuban didn't say, "I'm going to sell my shares."
    Is that right?

A. Say that again.

Q. Do you have a recollection that Mr. Cuban didn't say, "I'm going to sell my shares"?

A. No.

Q. So it's perfectly possible he did say "I'm going to sell my shares."

A. It's possible.

Q. And you do recall him being upset?

A. Yes....

Q. Did you on the call with Mr. Cuban provide him with additional confidential details about the PIPE?

A. Confidential?

Q. Yeah.

A. No.

Q. Because you didn't provide him any confidential information; is that right?

A. That's correct....

Q. I'd like to finish up by simply reviewing with you the investors and stockholders you contacted in connection with the Mamma PIPE.

And we have a chart we'd like to track the information on, Your Honor.

It's a summary. May we publish it to the jury?

THE COURT: Has opposing counsel seen it?

MR. CLARK: They have, Your Honor.

THE COURT: Any objection? ... There being no objection, you may proceed....

So that the jury understands, is this being used as a demonstrative aid?

MR. CLARK: That's right, Your Honor.

THE COURT: As opposed to a trial exhibit?

MR. CLARK: That's correct, Your Honor.

THE COURT: So the jury understands, when a demonstrative aid is used during the trial, that means it is not being admitted in evidence.... It is used to assist you in understanding what the party contends is the evidence.

You may proceed.

MR. CLARK: Thank you, Your Honor.

BY MR. CLARK:

Q. On the top here, Mr. Owen, it says Arnold Owen's contact with Mamma PIPE investors and shareholders. I think we've established we don't [know] exactly how many people you contacted about the Mamma.com PIPE?

A. That's correct.

Q. But we do know who ultimately invested?

A. That's correct.

Q. And we also know you spoke to Mr. Cuban?

A. Yes.

Q. So did you contact Enable Growth about the Mamma.com PIPE?

A. Either I contacted them or they contacted me.

Q. But you spoke to them?

A. Yes.

Q. ... Did you ask them or did you get any agreement to keep the PIPE information confidential from Enable Growth?

A. No.

Q. Did you ask Enable Growth or did they agree to restrict their trading in any way?

A. No.

Q. Did you speak to HBK Investments about the Mamma.com PIPE?
A. Yes.
Q. Did HBK agree in any way to keep the information about the PIPE confidential?
A. No.
Q. Did HBK Investments agree not to trade in any way?
A. No.
Q. Did you speak to Amaranth Growth investors?
A. Somebody else in my firm spoke to Amaranth.
Q. Mr. Fineberg?
A. Yes. I made the courtesy call to them after my call with Mr. Cuban.
Q. Okay. Are you aware of any agreement with them to keep the information about the PIPE confidential?
A. No.
Q. And was there any policy at Merriman that there needed to be such an agreement?
A. No.
Q. And are you aware of any agreement by Amaranth not to trade on the PIPE information?
A. No.
Q. Sage Growth was the lead investor?
A. That's correct.
Q. And you already explained to us there was no agreement with them to keep the PIPE information confidential at any time; is that correct?
A. That's correct.
Q. And there was no agreement by them not to trade on the PIPE information; is that right?
A. That's correct.
Q. Was Highbridge Capital an investor in the Mamma.com PIPE?
A. Yes, they were.
Q. Did they enter into any agreement to keep the PIPE information confidential?
A. No.
Q. Did they enter into any agreement not to trade based on the PIPE information?
A. No, they did not.
Q. And finally you spoke to Cranshire Capital is that right?
A. That's correct.
Q. Did they have any agreement to keep the information confidential?
A. No, they did not.
Q. And did they have any agreement not to trade?
A. No.
Q. Now, for Mamma.com shareholders, you spoke with Mr. Cuban; is that correct?
A. That's correct.
Q. Did Mr. Cuban have any agreement to keep the information confidential?
A. No, he did not.
Q. And did he have any agreement not to trade on the information?
A. No, he did not.

MR. CLARK: Your Honor, I have no further questions.

THE COURT: Redirect? ....

REDIRECT EXAMINATION
[By Mr. Thompson, Attorney for the SEC]

Q. Mr. Owen, good morning.

A. Good morning.

Q. Mr. Owen, I'd like to ask you a few questions about the [Mamma.com Form] 20-F report [filed with the SEC]. Do you remember discussing that a few minutes ago?

A. Yes....

Q. I'm going to take you to page 294 of the exhibit, and you recall that is the engagement letter [which was contained in the Form 20-F].

　　Do you have that, sir?

A. Yes.

Q. I'm going to ask you a question about the first paragraph of the letter.

　　Does it not state that "Merriman Curhan Ford is pleased to act as financial advisor to Mamma.com, a company who will provide investment banking services to the company which may include" ... do you see the word "may"?

A. Yes.

Q. And then does it list a number of possibilities?

A. Yes.

Q. And those possibilities include a PIPE or capital raising transaction. That's one option. Do you see that?

A. Yes.

Q. And it also goes on to talk about assisting the company with ... evaluating, prioritizing, negotiating proposals to purchase the company. Do you see that?

A. Yes.

Q. And it also talks about assisting the company in acquiring various potential acquisition targets, correct?

A. Yes.

Q. So this engagement was not limited to a potential PIPE transaction, was it?

A. That's correct.

Q. And a PIPE was just one of the options that was being considered?

A. That's correct.

Q. And at the time of the engagement, it's dated March 16, 2004, were there any terms of a PIPE in place?

A. No.

Q. Was there even a deal in place?

A. No....

Q. Now, Mr. Owen, let's take a look at the press release that was issued on June 29th, 2004, to announce the Mamma PIPE.

A. Where would I find that?

Q. That is ... Plaintiff's Exhibit 36.

MR. THOMPSON: One moment, Your Honor, we will provide the witness a copy of ... that exhibit. ...

Q. ... Now, this is the actual press release and yesterday you testified that this was the document that made the PIPE and its details public, correct?

A. ... I don't remember if those were my words yesterday but this is what memorialized the PIPE as a transaction that was completed.

Q. And in announcing the PIPE to the public there is specific detail. There's no indication that the company may be doing a transaction or may be doing other types of transactions. They're actually announcing a completed deal. Is that correct?

A. That's correct.

Q. And they announce specific details about the PIPE, including the 10 percent discount. Do you see that?

A. Yes.

Q. And there are warrants also announced?

A. Yes.

Q. So what I'd like you to do, Mr. Owen, is look at the engagement letter that was included in the 20-F report [that Mamma.com filed with the SEC] and the press release side by side.

And we're going to put those on the screen together. ...

Now, the bottom portion is the engagement letter and the top portion is the actual press release.

You would agree, would you not, sir, that where the engagement letter indicates that Mamma may be doing a transaction that could include a PIPE, that that is not the same thing as a press release announcing that a specific transaction has been put together, has been subscribed, that terms have been agreed and that investors have been found?

You would ... acknowledge that, would you not, sir?

A. Yes, I would. ...

Q. And the information about the PIPE is not made available to the general public until a press release is issued; is that correct?

A. That's correct. ...

Q. Mr. Owen, were you aware that in June of 2004 your company, Merriman, sent letters to PIPE investors regarding whether PIPE information was considered material nonpublic information?

A. We were starting the process in June of 2004, yes.

Q. And you were familiar with those letters that went out, correct?

A. That's correct.

Q. Let me direct your attention to a portion of the letter that's highlighted on the screen, where it states, "Merriman Curhan Ford has always treated knowledge of a potential private placement as material nonpublic information."

You wouldn't disagree with that, would you, sir?

A. That would be something that I think in my knowledge you would have to speak to the general counsel about, because this is an ongoing process. Prior to that nobody at Merriman ever said we have this policy to me.

Q. Mr. Owen, I'm asking whether you would disagree with the statement that was sent out to PIPE investors in Merriman's cadre of investors where it states,

"Merriman Curhan Ford & Company has always treated knowledge of a potential private placement as material nonpublic information."

Would you disagree with that, sir?

A. Would I disagree with that?

Q. Yes.

A. I guess not. . . .

Q. And, in fact, you were not aware of any of your clients ever buying or selling stocks of a company in which you had approached them to invest in a PIPE. You weren't aware of them buying or selling stocks in that company before public announcement, were you?

A. That's correct.

MR. THOMPSON: I'm going to ask if Mr. Cuban's team could please put up on the screen the demonstrative that they used with Mr. Owen.

BY MR. THOMPSON:

Q. Do you recall being asked questions about this exhibit in your cross-examination, Mr. Owen?

A. Yes.

Q. Now, do you know whether Mamma.com had any discussions with any of the investors listed there about the confidentiality of the PIPE information?

A. No, I don't. . . .

Q. You don't know what, if any, understanding Mamma and the PIPE investors may have had as between themselves, correct?

A. Correct.

Q. Likewise, were you ever made aware of the content of a discussion between Mr. Guy Fauré and Mark Cuban on June 28th, 2004, regarding the Mamma PIPE?

A. Was I made aware of that . . . I saw an email.

Q. Other than the email that defense counsel showed you, do you have any personal knowledge of that, sir?

A. I don't remember that.

Q. You don't remember ever having any personal knowledge of that, correct?

A. That's correct.

Q. So you don't know whether there's an agreement reached between Mr. Fauré and Mr. Cuban before you spoke with Mr. Cuban, do you?

A. That's correct.

Q. And you don't know what, if anything, was said in that conversation about the confidential nature of the information Mr. Cuban was receiving from Mr. Fauré, do you?

A. No, I don't.

Q. And you don't know whether anything was said about the confidential nature of the information that you might provide to Mr. Cuban in your call with him, do you?

A. No, I don't.

Q. And you don't know whether Mr. Cuban in that conversation said, "Now I'm screwed. I can't sell," do you?

A. No.

MR. CLARK: Objection, Your Honor.

THE COURT: What's the legal basis?

MR. CLARK: Leading question. It's the fifth leading question in [a] row about something no one is saying Mr. Owen has any knowledge of.

THE COURT: Okay. I'll overrule the objection. But unless you have basis I will sustain objections to leading questions.

BY MR. THOMPSON:

Q.   Let's talk about your phone call with Mr. Cuban....

Now, ... you indicated, I believe, that you thought Mr. Cuban was upset on the call and that you were uncomfortable; is that right?

A.   That's correct.

Q.   And you indicated that you were uncomfortable because he was a very powerful man and you were not; is that right?

A.   That's correct.

Q.   Now, Mr. Owen, you knew at the time he spoke with Mr. Cuban he was a greater than 5 percent shareholder of Mamma.com, correct?

A.   I knew he was a very large shareholder.

Q.   And you knew he was an important shareholder?

A.   Yes.

Q.   And I believe you were asked questions to the extent on cross-examination as to whether you were absolutely sure that Mr. Cuban did not tell you anything about selling his shares. But, Mr. Owen, if a large shareholder, a powerful man like Mr. Cuban, had said something like that to you, don't you think that's something you would have remembered?

MR. CLARK: Objection, Your Honor, leading.

THE COURT: I'll allow him to impeach in light of the cross-examination. Overruled.

THE WITNESS: Could you repeat the question, please?

MR. THOMPSON: Sure.

BY MR. THOMPSON:

Q.   You're on the call with Mr. Cuban. You are uncomfortable because he's a powerful man and you're not. You know he's a large shareholder in the company. You feel an obligation to report the call to your clients, correct?

A.   Correct.

Q.   Wouldn't ..., Mr. Owen, you have remembered if Mr. Cuban said that he was going to sell his shares one minute after getting off the phone with you before the press release was issued the following day?

A.   I would have thought so.

MR. CLARK: Objection, Your Honor. Calls for speculation. I ask that the answer be stricken.

THE COURT: Overruled....

BY MR. THOMPSON:

Q.   Mr. Owen, again on the subject of the phone call that you did have with Mr. Cuban, as you sit here today do you specifically recall what you said to Mr. Cuban in that phone call?

A. Not specifically, no.

Q. But you do recall ... or at least you believe that had Mr. Cuban said anything to you to the effect of there's a stock swindler involved in the Mamma PIPE you would remember that, wouldn't you?

A. ... [T]hat would impugn my reputation, and I think that would be something ... I would remember.

Q. And therefore, you're fairly certain that there was no such discussion in the phone call?

A. Not that I'm aware of....

Q. Mr. Owen, one final question.

If Mr. David Goldman, the chairman of Mamma, testified that Mamma considered the PIPE information to be material nonpublic information prior to the public announcement on June 29, 2004, do you have any basis to dispute Mr. Goldman's testimony?

A. No, I don't.

Q. Not at all?

A. Not at all.

MR. THOMPSON: Thank you, Mr. Owen.

I have nothing further at this time, Your Honor.

THE COURT: Recross?

MR. CLARK (Attorney for Mr. Cuban): Thank you, Your Honor.

RECROSS EXAMINATION
[By Mr. Clark, Attorney for Mr. Cuban]

Q. .... Was it your understanding in June of 2004 that ... there was no law that said that PIPE information was material nonpublic information?

MR. THOMPSON: Objection, Your Honor. This witness is not here as a legal expert.

THE COURT: Okay. If you're simply asking his understanding, I'll overrule the objection.

MR. CLARK: I am, Your Honor.

THE COURT: Members of the jury, the witness is being asked his understanding of the law. That's different from his being asked to give you an opinion on the law.

The law of the case will come from the court. He's being asked a fact question, which is what was his understanding at the time.

THE WITNESS: Could you do me a favor and repeat the question?

MR. CLARK: I understand. Absolutely.

BY MR. CLARK:

Q. Was it your understanding in June of 2004 ... that there was no law that said that PIPE information was material nonpublic information?

A. That was my understanding....

Q. And the question is, Mr. Owen, do you recall Mr. Cuban on the phone call with you telling [you] he would sell his [Mamma.com] shares?

A.   I don't recall that....

Q.   Mr. Thompson asked you earlier whether or not you knew whether there was an agreement between Mr. Cuban and Mr. Fauré on a phone call in June 2008; is that correct?

A.   That's correct.

Q.   In this document, Mr. Fauré is referring Mr. Cuban to you; is that correct?

A.   Yes, he is.

Q.   Is there any agreement referenced on this document at all?

A.   No.

Q.   Did you have any understanding that there was an agreement between Mr. Cuban and Mr. Fauré that governed the telephone call you had with Mr. Cuban?

A.   No.

Q.   Not a confidentiality agreement?

A.   No.

Q.   Not an agreement not to sell his shares?

A.   No.

Q.   Finally I just want to ask: And at the end of that call did you have any doubt in your mind that Mr. Cuban, if he wanted to, would have been free to sell his shares?

A.   I had no doubt.

      MR. CLARK: Thank you, Your Honor.

      No further questions.

      MR. THOMPSON: Not from the plaintiff, Your Honor.

      MR. CLARK: None, Your Honor.

      THE COURT: All right. Thank you, sir....

---

[c] Testimony of Mr. Guy Fauré

As with Mr. Goldman's testimony, the SEC was compelled to use Mr. Fauré's video deposition testimony at trial. As discussed previously in this chapter, the SEC lacked the power to require that Mr. Fauré testify in court because he was outside of the United States—namely, in Canada. This absence was disadvantageous for the SEC. As one commentator pointed out: *"You don't want your star witness on videotape. The jury is deprived of getting to assess his credibility."*[5] *The testimony of Mr. Fauré follows.*

---

5. Erin Fuchs, *Why the SEC Lost Its Big Case Against Mark Cuban*, Business Insider (Oct. 17, 2013), *available at* https//www.businessinsider.com/how-mark-cuban-defeated-the-sec-2013-10 (statement by defense attorney Stuart Slotnick) (emphasis supplied).

DIRECT EXAMINATION BY DEPOSITION
[By Ms. Riewe, Attorney for the SEC]

Q. Could you state your full name for the record, please.

A. My name is Guy Fauré....

Q. And, sir, where do you reside?

A. I reside in Saint Des Lacs, which is north of Montreal, Quebec, Canada.

Q. Did there come a point in time in which you were employed at a company called Mamma.com?

A. Yes.

Q. And you worked at Mamma.com until when?

A. Until the end of January 2007....

Q. ... [D]id you remain [as President and CEO] until such time as you left the employ of Mamma?

A. Yes.

Q. And who did you report to as president and CEO of Mamma.com once it became the public company?

A. To the board.

Q. And ... were you familiar with a man named David Goldman?

A. Yes.

Q. And what was his position?

A. He was the executive chairman of the board.

Q. And did you work for him for some or all the period that you were at Mamma?

A. All the period. Pretty much all the period, yes.

Q. Did there come a time in which you, yourself, joined the board of Mamma.com?

A. Yes. I believe in 2003 when Mamma became the public company.

Q. And did you remain as a member for the entire time that you were at Mamma, a member of the board?

A. Yes....

Q. Now, did you have occasion to communicate with Mr. Cuban from time to time about operation or business matters? And I'm not asking about the PIPE for this purpose.

A. Yes.

Q. Could you explain that to us?

A. Through mostly, if not exclusively, email correspondence, ... Mr. Cuban and I have ... exchanged correspondence where he was asking about the business and can I help you. You know, he was genuinely interested in helping Mamma grow. So he would ask is there anything I can do....

(Outside the presence of the jury.)

THE COURT: ... The court reporter advised me that there might be a matter that someone wished to take up regarding the testimony of Mr. Fauré this afternoon. I thought perhaps we could cover it now and save cutting into the afternoon break.

MR. MELSHEIMER [Attorney for Mr. Cuban]: Yes. May it please the court? May I approach?

THE COURT: You may.

MR. MELSHEIMER: Briefly, Your Honor, at the conclusion of Mr. Fauré's testimony by videotape deposition it would be my intent to offer evidence and publish that evidence to the jury in the nature of impeachment of Mr. Fauré at that time. Seems like that would be the logical time to do it. If he were here live, that's when we would do it. And the evidence that we would offer would be in the nature of impeachment. There are ... five different pieces of impeachment evidence ... that I've provided to the court and I've provided to counsel, and I could go through them quickly ... and tell you what I would intend to do with them, both in terms of offering them and also publishing them to the jury at the conclusion of Mr. Fauré's testimony....

So ... what I would propose is for all these documents to be admitted for impeachment purposes and that I be allowed to present them to the jury at the conclusion of the offer from both sides of Mr. Fauré's testimony by videotape deposition.

THE COURT: All right. So that I understand, Mr. Melsheimer, after both sides have offered their portions of the deposition of Mr. Fauré, you would then ask for leave to essentially publish these five documents ...

MR. MELSHEIMER: Correct.

THE COURT: ... All right. Who wishes to be heard by the plaintiff?

MS. FOLENA [Counsel for the SEC]: I do, Your Honor.

THE COURT: All right.

MS. FOLENA: I can't emphasize enough that we object to all of this.

We have been working with defense counsel for days to work through the deposition designations of Mr. Fauré and work through the exhibits that we'd both be using. And this was never raised with us once. Not once in the hours and hours of meeting and conferring we did.

And here's why. Because this is an obvious attempt to come in and present evidence that they forgot to present when they deposed Mr. Fauré. They had every opportunity to present these documents. They had these documents for years before he was deposed in 2011. They didn't ask the questions because they didn't want to know the answers.

And now they want to mislead the jury into believing that these things actually impeach Mr. Fauré, when he has no opportunity to respond. That is incredibly prejudicial to the government. He is the key witness. It's his word versus ... Mark Cuban's. And fortunately, Mr. Cuban is in trial and he's here, but Mr. Fauré simply isn't. And we cannot get him here. If we could, we would. This is incredibly unfair what's ... going on here....

THE COURT: Okay. So do I understand your ... objection is a Rule 613(b) objection? [With certain exceptions, Rule 613(b) of the Federal Rules of Evidence provides:

"Extrinsic evidence of a witness's prior inconsistent statement is admissible only if the witness is given an opportunity to explain or deny the statement and an adverse party is given an opportunity to examine the witness about it, or if justice so requires...."]

MS. FOLENA: Absolutely. It was not presented at the time....

THE COURT: I want to make sure I understand what the grounds are for the objection. If it's 613(b), this is an issue that came up and I'm prepared to rule on it.

In other words, are there objections to foundation? Are there ... other objections....

MS. FOLENA: Well, Your Honor, I mean, I just got these right this minute. Can I have an opportunity to review them over lunch?

I'm sure I made a ton of objections to these on the actual exhibit itself, but I was not given an opportunity to address how they could be presented as impeachment of Mr. Fauré.

Right now, yes, I think it's impeachment by extrinsic evidence that was never shown to him.

But if I could just please have an opportunity to read the documents over the lunch break.

THE COURT: I was not aware that you didn't have an opportunity to read them....

MS. FOLENA: I've seen them, okay, because I am familiar with the case, but we were never asked if we agreed to this. I was not handed this binder until you got it.

THE COURT: Okay.

MR. MELSHEIMER: May I briefly be heard on that, Your Honor, or do you want to not hear?

THE COURT: You may.

MR. MELSHEIMER: I don't know ... there's ramping up here of the anxiety. This was not part of the give and take with Mr. Fauré's deposition, so there was no attempt to sandbag on that. These are documents that are exhibits, have been on ... our exhibit list for a long time.

So I acknowledge I just handed her the binder. I acknowledge that. But, I mean, there's no real suggestions these are any kind of hidden exhibit[s]....

THE COURT: Let me make some rulings on certain issues before we break, and then you'll have the lunch hour ... to consider other objections.

It seems to me what I've heard thus far breaks into three areas. One is whether this evidence can be presented at the particular time that Mr. Melsheimer has in mind. I have the authority under Rule 611(a) [of the Federal Rules of Evidence] to control reasonably the mode and the order of examining witnesses and the presentation of evidence to make the procedures effective for the determination of the truth. Given that this is a deposition witness, I see less concern about allowing this presentation to be made after the witness is passed, because we're not talking about a live witness where this could potentially affect the testimony in some way.

And so preliminarily, I'm of the view to the extent this is admissible there's not a problem with presenting it after the deposition is concluded.

Number 2, as far as the need for a sponsoring witness or not, there is no need for a sponsoring witness for self-authenticating documents. There's no need for a sponsoring witness where in response to the Rule 26(a)(3) disclosures there's no objection to foundation, those exhibits come in and can be offered and published.

Typically, publication takes the form of showing it to a jury or reading verbatim what's on a document to bring it to their attention. [emphasis supplied]

Third, as far as 613(b) does, counsel knows what my observations were at the pretrial conference. They also know from my advisory to counsel that after the pretrial conference I found authority that caused me to question whether that rule applied to Mr. Fauré....

    So there may be other objections, and I'll take those up....

[Testimony Continues Before the Jury]

BY MS. RIEWE:

Q.   Now, [Mr. Fauré], calling your attention to the PIPE transaction ... of Mamma. com that was publicly announced on June 29th, 2004.

    As that PIPE or proposed PIPE was evolving through the month of June, 2004, how did the company treat information concerning the possible PIPE?

A.   Could you clarify in your question? What do you mean by ...

Q.   Was it treated confidentially?

A.   I believe so, yes.

Q.   And why was that?

A.   Because this PIPE transaction ... was a material transaction, was a significant investment in a public company; therefore, it had to be treated as confidential information.

Q.   Now, did there come a point in time in June of 2004 in which someone raised the idea of approaching Mark Cuban, concerning possible participation in the Mamma.com PIPE?

A.   Yes.

Q.   And how did that come to be?

A.   I don't specifically recall who, but I remember in late June that the board members had a discussion where they said should we invite Mr. Cuban, who is an important shareholder in the company, to participate in this PIPE transaction....

Q.   What was said about whether Mr. Cuban should be offered a chance to participate? ....

A.   Well, I recall that there were some discussions that Mr. Cuban, being a significant shareholder, supported the company, but then not necessarily supportive of PIPE transactions, should we or should we not be inviting him to participate in this PIPE transaction. And the conclusion was that we should.

Q.   And for what reason?

A.   Again, I don't specifically recall the words, but, you know, if we don't invite him and he doesn't like PIPEs he'll feel offended. At least if we invite him that he likes the company enough that he might want to participate.

    But the conclusion was ... weighing the pros and cons was to basically invite him....

Q.   ... [W]as anything said about how that invitation would be extended?

A.   Yes.

    The board asked me to contact Mr. Cuban, because I had been in contact with him. And the board specifically asked me to convey that I had confidential information for Mr. Cuban and then invite him to participate in the PIPE....

Q.   And you ... referred to, "Tell him that it was confidential information," what did you understand by that?

A.   My understanding is that the board proceeded to ask me to invite Mr. Cuban, and just make sure that ... you know, "Make sure you tell him that you have confidential information, and then invite him to participate," because this PIPE was a confidential matter....

Q. And then did you contact Mr. Cuban as you were instructed to do?

A. Yes.

Q. And how did you proceed with that?

A. I recall after the meeting sending an email to Mr. Cuban ... asking him to call me, and that I had something to tell him or discuss.

Q. Did you receive a return call from him?

A. Yes, I did.

Q. What was the timing of the return call compared to when you sent the email out?

A. I recall it was very quick, a matter of minutes, I believe....

Q. Let me show you a one-page phone bill, which I will ask the court reporter to mark as Exhibit 67.

    Note for the record ... that Exhibit 67 bears the Bates Number SEC MC 2992, also Investigative Exhibit Number 3.

    And the entity at the top ... could you pronounce it for us?

A. Well, it's Bell Mobilite. And in French it's Bell Mobilite.

Q. Thank you.

    ... [D]oes this exhibit reflect calls on your cell phone made or received on June 28th, 2004?

A. Yes.

Q. And can you tell by review of this exhibit what time you received the call from Mr. Cuban?

A. It would be the 1:00 o'clock call. 13 hours ... where it says "13 hours." ....

Q. And the time indicated there is eight minutes and 35 seconds, correct?

A. Correct....

Q. Mr. Fauré, when Mr. Cuban called you in response to your email, the phone call that you received at 1:00 o'clock on June 28th, ... what was said in the phone call?

A. Well, Mr. Cuban called me. I answered the phone, and I said, "Mark, I've got confidential information."

    He somewhat acknowledged that I had confidential information. Yes. I don't remember any specific words, but he said, "Um-hum, go ahead," something to that effect.

    And I proceeded to mention to him that we were close to concluding a PIPE transaction, and that the board wanted to invite him to participate in this PIPE transaction.

Q. Okay. Now, when you said that you had confidential information, was that the first thing that you said to him about the PIPE?

A. I believe so, yes.

Q. Was that at the beginning of the call?

A. Yes.

Q. ... Did he acknowledge that, what you said to him?

A. I believe so, yes.

Q. And just so we're clear, how did he acknowledge that?

A. Again, I don't remember the specific words, but it was "Okay, uh-huh, go ahead," which ... in my mind certainly said, "Okay, I understand, you've got confidential information. Go ahead."

Q. And was it after that that you proceeded to say something else?

A. Yes.

Q. And what was the something else that you said?

A. ... [W]e're concluding a PIPE transaction. The board would like to invite you. Are you ... interested in participating in this ... PIPE?

Q. And then what was his response?

A. His response was ... very negative. He said, "No. No way. I'm against PIPE[s]. It dilutes shareholders ... it dilutes shareholder base. You know, you should be growing organically. You don't need any financing."

And the conversation went back and forth where I said, "Well, I think it is the right time for us to do this type of investment. The stock price is well priced right now. It's a good moment to do this type of transaction."

But he ... disagreed, and did not want to participate. And then I guess at the end of the call he did mention to me, "Well, now I'm ..." Something like, "Now I'm screwed. I can't sell."

That was pretty much the conversation, the gist of the conversation.

Q. What was the tone of the conversation after you mentioned that the company was proceeding with the PIPE?

A. Well, Mr. Cuban was not impolitely yelling at me. It was, I would say somewhat ... you know, it was okay, courteous, but it was emotional. He ... was not happy, obviously not happy about us making this type of transaction.

Q. Now, you mentioned a back and forth discussion. Did I hear you correctly?

A. Yes.

Q. Was that back and forth discussion before he made the comment, "Well, now I'm screwed. I can't sell"?

A. Mostly, yes. ...

Q. I mean the language that was used, did ... you have a reaction to the language that he used?

A. Well, I was not personally offended and not necessarily surprised because the tone of the conversation was ... obviously there were some emotions, and Mr. Cuban was obviously displeased with the situation.

Q. Now, when you told him that you had confidential information to provide, did Mr. Cuban say anything to indicate that he did not want to receive such information?

A. No.

Q. After the discussion, the back and forth discussion and the statement by Mr. Cuban, "Well, now I'm screwed. I can't sell," did you understand that he would not sell until after the public announcement?

A. Yes.

Q. After the phone call with Mr. Cuban was concluded, what did you do?

A. I don't specifically recall if I went out for a quick sandwich for 15, 20 minutes, 30 minutes, but I certainly came back to the office fairly quickly after, and I recall basically informing Mr. Goldman of the gist of the conversation.

Q. Did you have ... further communication with Mr. Cuban concerning the PIPE?

A. I recall later on that day sending Mr. Cuban an email basically telling him that if you want more information about the PIPE contact ... Arnie Owen [at Merriman] and gave him the coordinates.

Q. And by "coordinates" you mean the phone number to call him at ... or email?

A. Phone number or email, yes....

Q. And why were you ... sending him to Mr. Owen for more details?

A. I vaguely recall that after informing Mr. Goldman about my phone conversation ... [Mr. Goldman] asked me "Why don't you at least send Arnie's coordinates that if he wants more information about the PIPE he can contact him directly."

Q. Did Mr. Arnie Owen have more information about the PIPE, the details of it, than you had?

A. ... Yes.

Q. ... [W]ould Mr. Arnold Owen have known the terms of the deal at that point in time?

A. Yes.

Q. Or if you knew the terms at that point in time?

A. Yes, I knew some of the broader terms, but Mr. Owen was the expert in those types of transactions. That's ... what he was doing.

Q. And by sending Mr. Cuban to Mr. Arnie Owen if he wanted those additional details, ... did you understand that Mr. Arnie Owen could provide them to Mr. Cuban?

A. Yes....

Q. And what did you tell Mr. Goldman about the phone call and the communication with Mr. Cuban?

A. Well, I don't remember the specific words, but the essence of the conversation was that Mr. Cuban was not happy about the PIPE transaction, he will not participate in the PIPE transaction, and he will most probably sell his shares and get out of the company, because ... he's not happy with this transaction.

Q. Did you ... tell Mr. Goldman ... in substance about the back and forth that you had with Mr. Cuban?

A. Yes.

Q. And did you in words tell Mr. Goldman about Mr. Cuban's statement, "Well, now I'm screwed. I can't sell"?

A. Most probably, yes.

Q. Is that your best recollection?

A. Yes. Well, I'm sure I mentioned that phrase because it's not a standard response....

Q. And did ... Mr. Goldman proceed to do anything with the report that you had ... provided to him?

A. I believe he eventually informed the board. I don't remember exactly when, but he did inform the board of my conversation with Mr. Cuban, that Mr. Cuban would not participate in the PIPE, and that probably, in fact, he will not be a shareholder for very long....

Q. Let me show you, sir, what was marked previously as Plaintiff's Exhibit Number 49, a two-page exhibit. Ask you to review that. After you have reviewed that if you could tell us what it is.

A. Yes. This is the press announcement, the public announcement of the completed private equity financing. . . .

Q. And was this the first time that the PIPE was publicly announced?

A. Yes.

Q. And the press release announces the amount of the PIPE, the amount of money being raised by the PIPE, does it not?

A. Yes.

Q. What was the amount of money being raised, sir?

A. It was in the order of $16 million plus.

Q. And . . . did it also announce the discount to market price that was a term of the PIPE?

A. Yes.

Q. And what was that?

A. 10 percent.

Q. And did it also announce whether or not warrants were a part of the PIPE?

A. Yes. . . .

Q. And . . . was it also your understanding that as of the June 28th, 2004 call that since you told Mr. Cuban that the information was confidential and he gave some sort of acknowledgement, that he was . . . prevented from trading Mamma.com securities based upon that information?

A. Yes. And that was confirmed with, "Well, now I'm screwed. I can't sell." . . . When he said "Now I'm screwed. I can't sell," that sort of confirms to me that he understands that he cannot sell, he cannot trade stock right now.

Q. But importantly at the beginning of the call when he gave some sort of acknowledgement . . .

A. Yes.

Q. . . . to your statement that you have confidential information, you also believe that acknowledge[ment] inferred that he was restricted from trading in the securities of Mamma.com?

A. Well, . . . that he understands he's about to get confidential information and he accepts it.

Q. And part of accepting it is that he can't share it with others, correct? Others outside of the company, correct?

A. That's my understanding, yeah.

Q. And another part of your understanding was that he cannot trade Mamma.com based upon his receipt of confidential information.

A. Up until this information becomes public information. . . .

Q. At some point towards the end of the call, you say Mr. Cuban uttered words to the effect of "I'm screwed. I can't sell"?

A. Correct.

Q. This was at the end of the conversation, towards the end of the conversation?

A. Towards the end, yes.

Q. Okay. And do you recall any conversation that took place after those words were uttered?

A. Not specifically, no.

Q. Okay. Now, do you recall Mr. Cuban saying "I can't sell" or "I wouldn't sell"?

A. I believe he used the words "I can't sell."

Q. And do you recall Mr. Cuban saying "I will not sell"?

A. No. Again, I believe he said "I can't sell. I'm screwed. I can't sell." ...

CROSS EXAMINATION BY DEPOSITION
[By Mr. Best, Attorney for Mr. Cuban]

(Video playing.)

....

Q. ... Did anybody on the Mamma.com board, including Mr. Goldman, specifically tell you to get an agreement of confidentiality ... from Mark Cuban, prior to inviting him to participate in the [PIPE] equity offer?

A. No.

Q. ... Did anyone from the Mamma.com board, including David Goldman ..., ever inform you to get Mr. Cuban to agree to restrict his ability to trade prior to informing him about the private placement opportunity?

A. No....

Q. ... Now, let's look at your email to Mr. Cuban on June 28th.

... you say, "Hi, Mark. I would like to speak to you ASAP. Can you please call me?"

Do you see that?

A. Yes.

Q. Did you indicate in this email that you wanted to speak to him about Mamma.com information?

A. No.

Q. Did you indicate to Mr. Cuban that you wanted to speak to him about ... an investment opportunity?

A. No.

Q. Did you put any context whatsoever as to why you wanted to speak to Mr. Cuban?

A. No.

Q. Did you consider putting in an email to Mr. Cuban that you'd like to speak to Mr. Cuban about confidential information concerning Mamma.com?

A. Did I consider it?

Q. Yes.

A. No.

Q. Why not?

A. Because I would convey that through the telephone conversation.

Q. Okay. And so because you were going to convey it on a telephone call [to] him, if he indeed called you, you felt you didn't need to put it on an email?

A. I didn't think about it. This was like a last minute thing. We were having to close the PIPE. So call me.

Q. ... [D]id you ever consider putting in an email that "Before I speak to you, you're going to have to agree to hold information confidential prior to me discussing it with you"?

A. No.

Q. Did you ever consider putting in this email that Mr. Cuban would have to agree to restrict trading in Mamma securities prior to having a telephone discussion with him?

A. No....

Q. And at the time you called Mr. Cuban, the transaction had not closed, correct?

A. Correct....

Q. There were deal terms still being negotiated on the afternoon of June 28, 2004, correct?

A. Well, I don't remember all the points, but we have seen emails today here that talk about a few of the points that were still in limbo, yeah, or not resolved.

Q. So there were unresolved deal terms as of the time you called Mr. Cuban?

A. Correct.

Q. Was it a certainty that the PIPE transaction was going to close when you called Mr. Cuban?

A. My impression was at that time I believed it was pretty certain, correct.

Q. Well, pretty certain is different than a certainty, correct?

A. Correct.

Q. Was it a certainty that this PIPE transaction was going to close? Nothing is ever certain ...

A. It's never over until the fat lady sings.

Q. That's right. Or the ink is on the paper?

A. That's right.

Q. Now, you said that Mr. Cuban called you sometime shortly after you sent the email to him, correct?

A. Correct.

Q. When you said you had confidential information or words to that effect, you don't recall the exact words you used to express that you had confidential information?

A. I probably used that term, "I have confidential information for you."

Q. Okay. You didn't tell Mr. Cuban that the information related to Mamma.com.

A. I don't recall that.

Q. Okay. You didn't tell Mr. Cuban that the confidential information related to an investment opportunity.

A. Not when I said I've got confidential information, right.

Q. And you didn't tell Mr. Cuban that the confidential information was information that the company considered [was] also material information?

A. No.

Q. Okay. And did you tell Mr. Cuban that the information may be material information?

A. No, I don't recall saying that.

Q. Did you put any context whatsoever to the statement you have confidential information?

A. No.

Q. The point is that at the time you informed Mr. Cuban that you had confidential information to share, you hadn't given him any context whatsoever to understand that it surrounded a private placement opportunity with Mamma.com, correct?

A. That's correct.

Q. At ... the time you called Mr. Cuban on June 28, 2004, had you ever given him confidential information prior to that date?

A. I don't recall, no.

Q. Okay. Do you recall that you ever gave Mr. Cuban confidential information?

A. Not specifically, no. . . .

Q. Mr. Fauré, did you consider Mr. Cuban at any point to be management, part of management of Mamma.com?

A. I don't believe so.

Q. Did ... Mr. Cuban participate in any board meetings prior to June 28th, 2004?

A. Not to my knowledge, no. . . .

Q. ... [D]o you recall whether or not Mr. Cuban said he will sell his shares in Mamma.com?

A. No. . . .

> MR. MELSHEIMER: That concludes our offer, Your Honor.
> THE COURT: Do you have redirect?
> MS. BRANDT [Counsel for the SEC]: We do, Your Honor.
> THE COURT: You may proceed.

REDIRECT EXAMINATION BY DEPOSITION
[By Ms. Riewe, Attorney for the SEC]

(Video playing.)

. . . .

Q. Mr. Best [attorney for Mr. Cuban] asked you about the email to Mr. Cuban asking him to call you. Do you recall that?
    It was Exhibit 66, the, "I would like to speak to you ASAP."

A. Yes.

Q. And he asked you if there was anywhere in your email where you advised Mr. Cuban that the thing you wanted to talk to him about was this Mamma business; do you recall that?

A. Yes.

Q. Was there anything else you would have contacted Mr. Cuban about at that time, other than Mamma.com business?

A. I don't believe so.

Q. In your discussions and communications ... by email with Mr. Cuban once he became an investor, did it always concern Mamma.com business?

A. I believe so, yes. . . .

Q. Your understanding of what Mr. Cuban said was that he wanted to sell?

A. That he wanted out. Not only did he not want to participate in the PIPE, but he wanted out.

Q. Okay. He did not say those words, but is that what you understood his words to mean? Is that a fair characterization?

A. "Um-hum. I'm screwed. I can't sell." It sounds pretty obvious, yes....

Q. You were asked questions about a written nondisclosure agreement. Mr. Best [attorney for Mr. Cuban] spent some time with you.

Did you believe it was necessary for you to have a written nondisclosure agreement?

A. Not at this point in time.

Q. Now, when Mr. Cuban said to you in your phone conversation with him on June 28th, 2004, "... Well, now I'm screwed. I can't sell," did you feel that you needed to ask him what he meant by that?

A. No, not necessarily.

Q. Now, you told us today, and you told both sides previously, that Mr. Cuban said in that call "Now I'm screwed. I can't sell." Now, as you sit here today, is there any doubt in your mind that those were his words to you?

A. No. I have repeated [those words] fairly consistently.

Q. When he gave some sort of acknowledgement to you, that meant to you that he agreed that he would hold the information in confidence, correct?

A. Correct.

Q. And that meant by holding it in confidence that he wouldn't share it with any outside party, correct?

A. Correct.

Q. And that when he said some sort of acknowledgement at the beginning of the call, that also meant that since he was going to hold this information in confidence he would also not be able to sell the stock until the public announcement of this confidential information, correct?

A. Correct....

MS. BRANDT: No further questions right now, Your Honor....

RECROSS EXAMINATION BY DEPOSITION
[By Mr. Best, Attorney for Mr. Cuban]

(Video playing.)

....

Q. Sitting here today have you ever told anyone that Mark Cuban specifically told you he agreed to ... hold the information in confidence?

A. In those words?

Q. Yes.

A. No.

Q. Have you ever told anybody sitting here today that Mr. Cuban specifically agreed to restrict his trading in ... Mamma.com securities prior to learning about the equity raise? In those words?

A. No.

MR. MELSHEIMER [Attorney for Mr. Cuban]: That concludes the cross-examination, Your Honor.

Your Honor, at this time we have an offer of impeachment. [emphasis supplied]

THE COURT: You may proceed.

MR. MELSHEIMER: Your Honor, we'd like to offer the following documents into evidence as impeachment of Mr. Fauré, starting with Defendant's Exhibit 53.

MS. FOLENA: Objection, Your Honor. Just to preserve it.

THE COURT: Yes. All ... prior objections are preserved and don't have to be repeated.

So if there are any additional objections, you can state those.

MS. FOLENA: Yes. I object to all of the documents.

THE COURT: All right. And are there any additional grounds, other than those already stated?

MS. FOLENA: I've already stated them.

THE COURT: All right. Fine.

MS. FOLENA: I mean, in addition to hearsay for a number of 'em that are not necessarily obvious.

THE COURT: Okay. If ... there's a hearsay objection, what I'll do is ask Mr. Melsheimer to state the limited purpose or the exception....

MR. MELSHEIMER: Your Honor, our next offer for identification purposes is Defendant's Exhibit 162, which is the examination of Guy Fauré on September 7th, 2007, conducted by counsel for Mr. Cuban, including Mr. Clark and Mr. Best.

The statement that we're offering is a question on page 92.

"Q. We spoke earlier about you were telling Mr. Cuban, in words or substance 'I have confidential information for you.'

"A. Right.

"Q. Do you recall anything Mr. Cuban said in response or replied to that statement by you?

"A. No, I do not." ....

Your Honor, that concludes our impeachment as to the bias and motivations of Mr. Guy Fauré.

THE COURT: For the record, Mr. Melsheimer, were you offering as exhibits in evidence, for example, the SEC letters and then just publishing the testimony?

MR. MELSHEIMER: Yes, Your Honor....

THE COURT: ... Any additional objections? ....

MS. FOLENA: ... I just request an instruction on how to consider the evidence.

THE COURT: All right ...

Mr. Melsheimer, do you have any objection to my instructing the jury that this is offered for impeachment?

MR. MELSHEIMER: That ... it's evidence for impeachment of Mr. Guy Fauré?

THE COURT: Correct.

MR. MELSHEIMER: Yes, Your Honor. I have no objection.

THE COURT: I understand.

Members of the jury, the proffer or the statements that Mr. Melsheimer just made in relation to the documents and the excerpts are offered for purposes of impeachment, which is a legal term that we use to mean to discredit a witness, and ... the offer is being made by the defendant to discredit or impeach the testimony of Mr. Fauré. And that is the limited purpose for which the evidence is being offered.

All right. You may call your next witness. . . .

---

[d] Testimony of Mr. Mark Cuban

As part of the Government's direct case, the SEC called Mr. Cuban to testify. This strategy is fairly common in both private litigation and civil government enforcement actions. Proponents of this approach believe that calling the defendant in the plaintiff's direct case prevents such defendant from revising his or her testimony and defenses as the case unfolds. It also lessens the defendant's ability to harmonize his or her testimony with that of other witnesses who have not yet testified and whose deposition testimony may be ambiguous. Following this strategy, it is asserted, also enables the plaintiff to more effectively illustrate to the jury issues relating to the defendant's lack of credibility by means of the testimony of subsequent witnesses. Moreover, leading questions may be asked of an adverse witness on direct examination.[6]

From the defense perspective, many attorneys believe that it is best to have the defendant testify as the last or near last witness in the case. Proponents assert that this strategy permits the defendant to comment on the testimony given by other witnesses and harmonize as much as practicable slightly conflicting testimony. It also better enables the defendant to testify with respect to flaws in the adverse party's case.[7]

Of course, the plaintiff may disrupt this strategy by calling the defendant as an adverse witness in its case-in-chief. This strategy was implemented by the SEC in this case—and may well have been the correct decision. *Mr. Cuban was the last witness called by the SEC in presenting its case. The testimony of Mr. Cuban follows.*

---

6. See Rule 611(c) of the Federal Rules of Evidence; CYC. FED. PROC. § 26:201 (3d ed. 2018); 2 Lane Goldstein, TRIAL TECHNIQUE § 11:81 (3d ed. 2017); Gregory Forman, *Making the Defendant Testify in the Plaintiff's Case-in-Chief*, Internet Post (Feb. 12, 2011); Paul N. Levera, *The Attitude of a Trial Lawyer, Calling the Defendant in Your Case & Neuroscience*, Internet Post (July 17, 2010).

7. See Forman, note 6 *supra*.

MARK CUBAN
DIRECT EXAMINATION
[By Ms. Folena, Attorney for the SEC]

Q. Mr. Cuban, good morning.

A. Good morning.

Q. As you know, my name is Jan Folena, and I represent the Securities and Exchange Commission.

    As you can well imagine, I have some questions for you....

    ... So, Mr. Cuban, in March of 2004, sir, you bought 600,000 shares of Mamma.com stock, correct?

A. Yes, ma'am.

Q. And those shares cost you approximately 7.5 million dollars; is that right?

A. I don't remember the exact amount, but that sounds right.

Q. Okay. The parties have stipulated before this trial, Mr. Cuban, to your trading records, and we've agreed that those are admissible in this case as a business record....

    ... Now, at that time, March of 2004, you also filed with the SEC ... what's called a Form 13-G. Is that right, sir?

A. Yes, ma'am.

Q. Okay. And you had to do that because of the amount of shares you purchased in Mamma.com; is that right?

A. That's correct....

Q. All right. Now, on this form it indicates that you were at this time a 6.5 percent owner in the company. Is that right?

A. I believe it's 6.3 percent.

Q. I'm sorry. You are correct, sir. 6.3 percent owner.

A. Yes, ma'am.

Q. Okay. And that's a fact that you disclose in this form, correct?

A. Yes, ma'am.

Q. Okay. And this form is available to the public; is that right, sir?

A. Yes, ma'am....

Q. Now, on March 15th, 2004, Mr. Cuban, you knew you were the largest shareholder in Mamma.com, correct?

A. As of which date, ma'am?

Q. March 15th, 2004.

A. I'm not sure of ... which date I knew, but, yes, I knew at some point right around then that I was the largest shareholder....

Q. And you wouldn't disagree with me that in 2004 that ... one of your investment philosophies [was] to become the largest shareholder in the company; is that right?

A. In 2004 that was one of my investment philosophies, that's correct.

Q. All right. Now, Mr. Cuban you keep what's called a blog on the Internet. Is that right, sir?

A. Yes, ma'am. I write a blog.

Q.   And you write it yourself?

A.   Yes, ma'am.

Q.   And the blog is called blogmaverick; is that right?

A.   Blogmaverick.com. I actually didn't come up with the name, but I will take it.

Q.   That's what people call you?

A.   I own the Dallas Mavericks.

Q.   But blogmaverick refers to you, right?

A.   It's my blog, yes....

Q.   ... My question ... [is] if you post an opinion or idea on there, that's an opinion or an idea that you honestly hold; isn't that right, sir?

A.   Not a hundred percent of the time, no. Again, a lot of times I'm trying to get people's response to something.

Q.   Okay. So it's possible then, sir, that what you're tell[ing] me is you post ideas and opinions on blogmaverick that are not true?

A.   I wouldn't characterize it as not true. I might talk about the Lakers. I might talk about a family thing. You know, again, it's not about [being] true. It's just about trying, you know, to send a message or get a point across or get feedback. That's what blogs are for.

Q.   I understand that. I'm not saying you ever have, but this is an example. If you post on your blog that you think the Lakers are going to stink in 2013, okay, you're not telling this jury that that's an opinion that you don't honestly hold, right?

A.   This year?

(Laughter)

Q.   I'm saying as an example, if you said that.

A.   Well, no. In 2004 I wouldn't say it. They had Shaq, they had Kobe, they actually went to the finals.... To answer your, question, if I said in 2004 that they stink, I didn't believe it.

Q.   You didn't believe it?

A.   No.

Q.   Okay.... [W]hat I'm saying to you, sir, is that if you post an opinion on your blog what I hear you saying is it's not always your opinion. You might be actually posting opinions that are not actually yours because you're trying to get a response.

A.   Yeah. In general. Yeah. I've written a blog for ten years. So over the course of ten years, I try different things.

Q.   Okay. So when we read your blog, then we don't know what opinions you honestly hold and what ones you don't, right?

A.   That's why there's opinions and follow-ups, and that's why there's a blog. That's why I post updates. That's why I can post more than one time in the day. That's why I can post day after day after day. It's a blog. It's not a newspaper that's limited in any way. It's just a blog.

Q.   Okay. Let me make sure I understand this. What I hear you saying is ... what you put in the blog is hyperbole?

A.   Yeah. Something like Lakers stink. Yeah.

Q. Hyperbole means exaggeration?

A. Yes, ma'am.

Q. Okay. Mr. Cuban, if I take my shoes off, I stand five foot three in this courtroom. Would you agree with that, if I told you?

A. I guess.

Q. If I applied tomorrow for a Texas driver's license, and I put down that I'm six feet tall that would be an exaggeration, wouldn't it, sir?

A. Yes, ma'am.

Q. It would also be false, wouldn't it?

A. Yes, ma'am.

Q. So some of the exaggerations in your blog are actually false statements; is that right?

A. Yeah. Literally speaking ... they would be false. If I said that I like the Lakers, that would be false.

Q. And you do that on purpose when you write your blog, correct?

A. Over the course of ten years, yes, I've done things to engender a response.

Q. Okay. And to engender a response, sometimes you make false statements, correct?

A. Again, ... I wouldn't want to characterize it that way, but, yes, there's times when I'm going to have hyperbole, give an opinion. That's what opinion is about, just saying something to get a response....

Q. If we look at the last line of [your May 10, 2004 blog] it says, "Of the companies I have taken a 5 percent or greater position in, I have yet to sell a share of any of them. Ever."

    Do you see that statement?

A. Yes, ma'am.

Q. Was that a true statement when you made it in May of 2004?

A. Yes, it was....

Q. ... You are not selling these shares ... you're keeping all [the shares in] the companies you own 5 percent greater interest in, because you want to see if your investment paid off over the long haul, right?

A. I mean ... yes.

Q. Now, would you agree with me in 2004 one of the things you were attempting to do is purchase shares in companies in which you had knowledge of that area? Is that right?

A. I invest in companies and purchase shares where I understand the industry, if that's what you're asking.

Q. Yes. That is what I'm asking.

A. Yes, ma'am.

Q. And technology is an industry that you have a significant amount of understanding, would you agree?

A. It's all relative, but, yes, I feel more confident in technology than other industries.

Q. Okay. By technology, that's a broad term. What I mean is the Internet, search engines, computers, that type of thing.

A. Yeah. Different types of technologies.

Q. And that's where you got your start, right, selling computer software, correct, sir?

A. Yes, ma'am.

Q. All right. And from there you launched into an expertise in the computer, technology, internet area, correct?

A. Yes, ma'am.

Q. Okay. All right. And in fact, Broadcast.net was a company you founded on the idea that people should be able to see college basketball anywhere they are in the country, right?

A. Actually it was Broadcast.com, and I went to school at Indiana University ["Hoosiers"], and so my partner, Todd Wagner and I, wanted to create the opportunity for people to listen to sports, Indiana University basketball in this case, anywhere in the world. So that's where the whole streaming business was born.

Q. Okay. But that whole Internet streaming, being able to watch things through the Internet, that's your area, correct, Mr. Cuban?

A. Yes, ma'am.

Q. All right. And Mamma.com was a search engine at the time you bought it, right?

A. Yes, ma'am.

Q. All right. And that's an area you're also familiar with and were familiar with in 2004, right?

A. Yes, ma'am.

Q. And one of the things you hoped to do with a company like Mamma.com is provide what you would describe as strategic value to that company; is that right?

A. Yes, ma'am.

Q. All right. And strategic value means your, Mark Cuban's, insights, correct?

A. It depends on what they ask. But, yeah, if I'm asked for it. Wherever I can help. It could be any number of things.

Q. Right. Your insights, your ideas?

A. Potentially.

Q. And your ideas you would consider strategic value in some cases to a company, correct?

A. Not everybody always agrees, but I ... would hope so.

Q. Okay. Now, let me make sure I just understand this.

   If you actually could provide strategic value to the company and they agreed with what you ... presented to them, you could help that company succeed, correct?

A. Hypothetically speaking, that's true.

Q. Okay. And if the company does well and you own over 6 percent of the company, you're going to do well. Does that make sense?

A. That's the American way.

Q. That's how it works, right, Mr. Cuban?

A. Yeah. Like I said, yes.

Q. At least that's how it worked for you in 2004?

A. Hey, that's the beauty of this country. We all have an opportunity....

Q. ... [I]n 2004 your practice was to correspond with people by email. Correct?

A.   As much as I could, yes, ma'am.

Q.   As much as you could.

A.   Right.

Q.   Because in 2004, as today, there's no question you're a busy man. Right, Mr. Cuban?

A.   That's correct....

Q.   ... Before you made that first stock purchase you did not know the CEO of that company, Guy Fauré, did you?

A.   That's correct....

Q.   ... You ultimately did become acquainted with Mr. Fauré, correct?

A.   We exchanged emails.

Q.   Okay. And that was after you owned stock in his company, right?

A.   Yes, ma'am.

Q.   Now, after you purchased your 600,000 shares in Mamma.com you had email correspondence, or you engaged in email correspondence with Mr. Fauré, correct?

A.   About once or twice a month.

Q.   Okay. Had you ever spoken to him on the telephone?

A.   At which point in time?

Q.   In March, April, May, June of 2004.

A.   I mean, I know now that I did speak to him on the telephone.

Q.   Okay. Take away the June 28th, okay, just put that out of your mind.

  Did you speak to ... Mr. Fauré on the telephone?

A.   I believe I spoke to him one time other than June 28th.

Q.   Okay. Fair enough. That was my question. Do [you] remember if you called him or he called you?

A.   I don't recall....

Q.   Mr. Cuban, you can turn to your binder and look at Plaintiff's Exhibit 8. It's ... email correspondence between you and the CEO of Mamma.com, Guy Fauré.

  And it's dated April 22nd, 2004.

  Do you see that, sir?

A.   Yes, ma'am....

Q.   [In that April 22nd email] you say, "And obviously, what you tell me is confidential," and then it goes on from there.

  Do you see that, sir?

A.   Yes, I do.

Q.   All right, Mr. Cuban, when you wrote that statement, "Obviously, what you tell me is confidential," what you meant was you were willing to have a confidential exchange via email that if there's something confidential we could agree that it's confidential and go from there. Is that right, sir?

A.   I know that's what I said ....

  I was referring to here is that he said he's looking at specific acquisitions, and then I said in relationship to those acquisitions if he wanted to have a discussion with them then, yes, obviously I would keep that confidential....

Q. ... I'm going to ask you to turn your attention now if you would to June 28th, 2004.

I want you to turn in your binder to Plaintiff's Exhibit 166. It's an email to you on that date from Mr. Fauré.

Do you see that, sir?

A. Yes, ma'am.

Q. Okay. Do you recognize that email?

A. Yes, ma'am.

Q. All right.

MS. FOLENA: Move to admit Plaintiff's Exhibit 166.

MR. MELSHEIMER: No objection, Your Honor.

THE COURT: Plaintiff's Exhibit 166 is admitted in evidence.

MS. FOLENA: Okay. Let's pull that up on the screen so everybody can see it.

BY MS. FOLENA:

Q. Okay, Mr. Cuban, if we look at the top of Plaintiff's Exhibit 166, it's an email to you from Guy Fauré on Monday, June 28th, at 11:56 a.m.

Do you see that, sir?

A. Yes, I do.

Q. Okay. And on June 29th, 2004, Mr. Fauré is in Canada, correct?

A. Yes, ma'am.

Q. And you're in Dallas, correct?

A. Yes, ma'am.

Q. All right. And you're in Dallas that entire day, June 28th, correct?

A. Yes, ma'am.

Q. All right ... I think we heard your counsel say you were at a charity golf tournament that day?

A. Yeah. I was doing a deal with Michael Jordan and [Dallas Maverick's star] Michael Finley for Make-A-Wish.

Q. Okay. In this email, ... the subject is "call me please." Do you see that?

A. Yes, ma'am.

Q. And you know what that meant, that meant he wanted you to call him?

A. Yes, ma'am.

Q. And he says, "Hi Mark. I would like to speak with you ASAP. Can you call me please."

And then he gives you his cell phone and his office phone. Do you see that?

A. Yes, I do....

Q. Now, in response to receiving this email, Mr. Cuban, you called Guy Fauré. Correct?

A. Yes, I did....

Q. I want you to look at it in your binder, Mr. Cuban.

Okay. Do you recognize Plaintiff's Exhibit 55 as the telephone records from the American Airlines Arena here in Dallas?

A. Yes. It's the first time I've ever looked at one. We've got a hell of a phone bill....

MS. FOLENA: Your Honor, may I approach ... the witness, so he can get to the ... right page [of the Exhibit]?

THE COURT: You may.

MS. FOLENA: Thank you.

BY MS. FOLENA:

Q. Mr. Cuban, let me help you out here. Sorry about that.

A. You're so nice. Thank you. . . .

Q. All right. Mr. Cuban, I'm showing you a page from the American Airlines Arena phone bill. And what I want to direct your attention on that page [to] two telephone calls on June 28th, 2004, to Montreal, Canada.

Do you see those?

A. Yes, ma'am.

Q. Okay. Do you see the first one to Montreal, it lasts about a minute?

A. Yes, ma'am.

Q. Okay. I want to focus your attention on the second one. That's your telephone call to Guy Fauré, correct?

A. Both were.

Q. Both were. Okay.

And you'll agree that the second telephone call lasts approximately eight and a half minutes, sir?

A. Yes, ma'am.

Q. All right.

Mr. Cuban, you do not have a recollection of the words exchanged between you and Mr. Fauré on June 28th, 2004, on the phone call at 1:00 p.m. Eastern Standard Time, do you?

A. Both calls? The first one and the second? Or just the second?

Q. The second.

A. No, I do not.

Q. Just so it's clear, you don't know what you said to Mr. Fauré on that eight and a half minute phone call, correct?

A. That's correct.

Q. And you don't know what Mr. Fauré said to you on that eight and a half minute phone call, correct?

A. That's correct.

Q. The only thing you recall about that phone call, sir, correct, is that you were angry?

A. Yes, ma'am.

Q. So when Mr. Fauré testified in court yesterday, I think he said that you were yelling at him, you wouldn't disagree that that's what was going on. Right?

A. I think he said I was yelling politely or something like that.

Q. Yeah. You remember that?

A. Yeah. I was upset.

Q. Right. You were upset?

A. Yes, I was upset.

Q. Okay. So you don't disagree with him when he said that?

A. No, not at all.

Q. Now, Mr. Cuban, after your conversation with Mr. Fauré, the eight and a half minute telephone call, you didn't send him an email about that call, did you?

A. No, ma'am.

Q. He didn't send you an email about that call, did he?

A. No, ma'am.

Q. Mr. Cuban, turn in your binder to Plaintiff's Exhibit 165.

It's an email dated June 28th, 2004, to you from Mr. Fauré.

Do you recognize that, sir?

A. Yes, ma'am.

MS. FOLENA: Okay. Move to admit Plaintiff's Exhibit 165.

MR. MELSHEIMER: No objection.

THE COURT: Plaintiff's Exhibit 165 is admitted in evidence.

BY MS. FOLENA:

. . . .

Q. Okay. [Exhibit] 165 is an email sent to you, Mr. Cuban, from Guy Fauré, dated June 28th, 2004, 2:51 p.m.

Do you see that?

A. Yes, ma'am.

Q. And it says, "Hi Mark. If you want more details about the private placement please contact (I guess you or your financial advisors) Arnie Owen at 415-248-5613. Arnie is with Merriman Curhan Ford & Company. Regards, Guy Fauré."

Do you see that?

A. Yes, ma'am.

Q. ... [W]hen you received this email you didn't know Arnie Owen, correct?

A. No idea who he was....

Q. You heard him yesterday when he was testifying indicate that you were powerful and he was not. Did you hear that?

A. Yes.

Q. You agree with that, right?

A. No....

Q. ... Now, you called Mr. Owen on June 28th, 2004, correct?

A. Yes, I did....

Q. Now, when you called Mr. Arnie Owen he seemed to be expecting your call; is that right, Mr. Cuban?

A. I don't recall.

Q. You don't recall?

Do you recall that you testified in a deposition with the SEC on February 10th, 2012?

A. That I did testify?

Q. Yes.

A. Yes, I do.

Q. Okay. Do you have any reason to dispute that on February 10th, 2012, in that deposition, you told the SEC that you understood Mr. Owen was expecting your call?

A. I have no reason to dispute it.

Q.   Okay. So if you said that, then at that time that was your recollection . . . .

A.   Correct.

Q.   . . . and as far as you know that's correct.

A.   Correct.

Q.   Mr. Owen was expecting your call?

A.   He was expecting my call then.

Q.   Okay. Now, when you called Mr. Owen you asked him whether the Mamma private placement was being offered with discounts and warrants, correct, sir?

A.   I don't know if I said it that way, but I asked those questions. . . .

Q.   All right. And there's no question that you talked to Arnie Owen about the Mamma.com private placement, or PIPE, correct?

A.   Again, I don't want to say that I said those words, but whatever that financial instrument was, I asked him about warrants and pricing. . . .

THE COURT: Counsel, we would normally break about now, are you close to a break point . . . ?

MS. FOLENA: Yes. Actually, I can . . .

THE COURT: All right.

MS. FOLENA: Thank you.

THE COURT: Members of the jury, in a moment we're going to be recessing for our morning break until 10:45.

It's extremely important that you remember the instructions of the court not to talk with anyone about the case, including one another, not to read or listen to any media coverage of the case or try to do any research about the case. . . .

BY MS. FOLENA:

Q.   Mr. Cuban, before we broke, we were talking about your conversation with Arnie Owen on June 28th, 2004, just to get us back there.

Okay. Do you recall that?

A.   Yes, ma'am.

Q.   Okay. Now, in that telephone conversation you learned that the Mamma private financing gave the investors a discount and it was offered with warrants, correct?

A.   That's correct.

Q.   And a discount means that the private investors were able to buy the new shares at less than the market price, correct?

A.   Yes, ma'am.

Q.   And warrants meant that they can continue to buy shares at a set price for a set amount of time, correct?

A.   That's correct.

Q.   All right. And you understood that those two things were incentives to get the private investors to invest, right?

A.   Yes, ma'am.

Q.   During that telephone conversation, Arnie Owen invited you to be one of those private investors; is that right?

A.   He invited me to be an investor, yes.

Q.   Now, after you hung up that phone call with Mr. Owen, you didn't send him an email following up on the call, did you, sir?

A. No, ma'am.
Q. And Mr. Owen didn't send you an email following up on the call, did he?
A. No, ma'am. . . .
Q. All right. You see [on the Exhibit] the call underneath . . . at 4:41?
A. I do.
Q. And that's a call to Dallas, Texas?
A. Yes, it is.
Q. That's the call to your broker at UBS, isn't it, sir?
A. Yes, it was.
Q. And on that call you told your broker to sell all 600,000 shares that you owned in Mamma.com?
A. I told him to sell at market price and sell everything.
Q. Yeah. You told him to get out, right?
A. At market price, yes.
Q. Mr. Cuban, you didn't follow that telephone call with an email, did you, sir?
A. No, ma'am.
Q. And he didn't follow-up that telephone call with you with an email, did he?
A. No, ma'am.
Q. Mr. Cuban, before you called your broker one minute after you hung up with Arnie Owen, you didn't conduct any research into whether or not the Mamma private financing was public, did you?
A. I didn't need to.
Q. I'm not asking you if you needed to. I'm asking you whether you did.
A. No, there's no reason to.
Q. I'm not asking if there's a reason. You did not conduct any research.
A. No, I did not conduct any research.
Q. Before selling your shares, correct, sir?
A. That's correct.
Q. And by research, I mean research into whether or not the Mamma financing was public, correct?
A. That's correct.
Q. Now, after the call to your broker one minute after you hung up with Mr. Owen, UBS began to sell some of your 600,000 shares in Mamma.com on June 28th, 2004, correct?
A. I presume so.
Q. Do you have any reason to doubt that they began to sell those shares on that date?
A. No. I gave them a market order, so no.
Q. Okay. And UBS sold 10,000 of your 600,000 shares in after-hours trading on June 28th, 2004. Correct?
A. Yes, ma'am.
Q. And they sold those shares at an average price of $13.50, correct?
A. I don't remember specifically, but, yes, I presume so.
Q. Okay. You don't have any reason to disagree?
A. No, I do not.

Q. Your broker sold the remaining 590,000 shares of your Mamma.com stock the next day, on June 29th, 2004, correct?

A. Yes, he did....

Q. And he sold those 590,000 shares on June 29th at an average share price of $13.29, correct?

A. Yes, ma'am.

Q. So as of 4:00 p.m. on June 29th, 2004, you owned no shares of Mamma.com; is that correct?

A. Yes, ma'am. That is correct.

Q. And you sold those shares, Mr. Cuban, for 7.9 million dollars; is that correct?

A. Whatever it comes out to. I'll accept that, yes, ma'am....

Q. ... Now, the first you ever heard Mamma.com was going to do a private financing or a PIPE was on June 28th, 2004, correct?

A. Yes, ma'am....

Q. Mr. Cuban, do you remember in [your attorney] Mr. Melsheimer's opening statement he showed the jury a slide ... that was a Yahoo! message board. Do you remember that, sir?

A. Yes, ma'am.

Q. And do you remember that he told the jury that that Yahoo! message board meant that the PIPE was public. Do you remember that?

A. Yes, ma'am.

Q. Mr. Cuban, you never saw that Yahoo! message board in 2004, did you?

A. I personally did not, no....

Q. You'll agree with me that this slide says nothing about discounts ... right?

A. No, it doesn't.

Q. It doesn't say anything about warrants, does it?

A. No, it doesn't....

Q. ... [Mr. Melsheimer] indicated to the jury that they could rely on this message board when determining whether or not the Mamma.com PIPE was public. Do you remember that?

A. Yes, ma'am.

Q. Mr. Cuban, you don't really believe that any of the information in this message board is reliable, do you?

A. That's not true.

Q. That's not true?

A. That's absolutely not true.

Q. You believe that what is said in this message board is reliable information?

A. In some cases, yes....

Q. ... Mr. Cuban, you sold your 600,000 shares in Mamma.com because of the private financing of the PIPE, right?

A. I would say that was one of the reasons, yes.

Q. Okay. But you don't deny that was why you sold your shares, because of the PIPE?

A. Again ... It was one of the reasons, not the only reason by a long shot.

Q. Okay. It was one of the reasons?

A. Yes, ma'am.

Q. Okay. So you're going to contend that there are other reasons, ... do I understand that correctly?

A. Yes.

Q. Okay. Very well.

Mr. Cuban, at the time you sold your 600,000 shares in Mamma.com you believed, sir, that ... PIPE-type transactions dilute the shareholders, correct?

A. Yes, ma'am.

Q. And in your min[d] that was not a good thing for a shareholder, correct?

A. Coming from a PIPE, that's correct.

Q. And in your words when a company does a private transaction or a PIPE-type financing, that is an automatic sale for you if you own the stock, right?

A. I have written that, but that is not literal, no. That's just one of many reasons.

Q. Okay. But you will agree you have written that?

A. Yes....

Q. [Mr. Paul Shread, the editor of the Internet Stock Report,] sends you an email on July 2nd, 2004. That's what this is, right?

A. Yes, ma'am.

Q. That's two days after you finished selling your Mamma.com stock, correct?

A. Yes, ma'am.

Q. And in that email he asked you, "Hi Mark, why'd you sell your Mamma stake? Anything change in the fundamentals or your outlook for the company?"

Do you see that?

A. Yes.

Q. And you see your response, "I hate when companies do PIPEs-type transactions to raise money. It's dilutive, and I hate being diluted ... that simple. M." That's you, right, ... sir?

A. That's me.

Q. And you made that statement on July 2nd?

A. I wrote that email, yes, ma'am.

Q. And that was a true statement on July 2nd when you made it wasn't it, sir?

A. This is a stock answer that I send out because I get so many emails. So it's part of the whole story, but it wasn't the whole story.

Q. You don't say anything in this email other than you sold because of the PIPE; is that right, sir?

A. That's correct....

Q. Now, Mr. Cuban, you not only sold your stock in Mamma.com because of the PIPE, sir, you sold your stock because the PIPE had discounts and warrants. Isn't that right?

A. They go hand in hand.

Q. Yes. Right?

A. Yes.

Q. You sold because of the discounts and the warrants, correct?

A. Again, those weren't the only reasons.... [I]f you have a PIPE transaction ... chances are it was going to have a discount, and chances are you're going to have warrants....

Q. Okay. My question was real simple.

You sold your Mamma.com stock because the Mamma.com PIPE had discounts and warrants, correct, sir?

A. Again, that's just part of the reason....

Q. [Showing Mr. Cuban a different Exhibit] ... [Y]ou will agree with me that this is a letter that's dated March 16th, 2004, correct?

A. Yes, ma'am....

Q. All right. Now, this is a letter to Guy Fauré and David Goldman at Mamma.com from Mr. Owen's company, Merriman Curhan & Ford. It that correct?

A. Yes, it is.

Q. Now, ... do you remember also that your counsel, Mr. Melsheimer, showed the jury this [letter] in opening statements, correct?

A. Yes, ma'am.

Q. And he indicated to the jury that this letter meant that the PIPE was public, correct?

A. I don't recall verbatim, but yes, ma'am.

Q. Okay. But you testified today the first you ever heard of the PIPE was June 28th, 2004, right?

A. ... [Y]es. The actual instrument itself, that's correct.

Q. In fact, you don't disagree, Mr. Cuban, that this letter ... indicates that Merriman will provide investment banking services to the company which "may" include?

Do you see that term?

A. Yes, I do.

Q. It doesn't say "will," does it?

A. No, it doesn't.

Q. Okay. And one of the options [is] representing the company in efforts to obtain financing in the form of a private investment. Correct?

A. Yes, ma'am.

Q. In either public equity or convertible debt. Correct?

A. Yes, ma'am.

Q. Would also assist the company in identifying acquirers and evaluating, prioritizing, negotiating proposals to purchase the company, in whole or in part.

Do you see that?

A. Yes, I do.

Q. And, 3, assisting the company in acquiring various potential acquisition targets in one or a series of transactions by purchase, merger, consolidation, and other business combination involving all or substantial amount of the business, securities, assets or a target, an acquisition transaction.

Do you see that, sir?

A. Yes, ma'am.

Q. You will agree there is a lot of information in [the letter]?

A. Sure is.

Q. Okay. It doesn't say in that paragraph, does it, Mr. Cuban, that this company will do a PIPE, does it?

A. It does not use those words, no.

Q. Okay. And, Mr. Cuban, you'll agree with me you didn't sell your shares in May of 2004, correct?

A. No, I did not.

Q. You didn't sell your shares until June 28th, 2004, right?

A. That would be correct....

....

Q. Didn't you answer the question earlier when I asked you, you were trying to get dirt on Mr. Fauré because he was the only one that could tell the SEC what you said on that phone call ...

A. Then I did a poor job of listening ... and I apologize, because that was an incorrect answer.

Q. So you're changing your testimony?

A. Yes, ma'am, and I apologize.

Q. Okay. Let me ask the question again, Mr. Cuban:

You wanted to get real dirt on Mr. Fauré in July of 2007 because you knew the SEC was considering suing you and you knew that the only person that could testify about what happened on that June 28th phone call was Mr. Fauré. Right?

A. No. That's incorrect.

Q. That's not correct?

A. No, ma'am....

Q. ... Mr. Cuban, in July ... 2007, you would agree you were looking to find a link between [convicted stock swindler] Irving Kott and Mamma.com; is that right?

A. Additional links, yes.

Q. And you knew at that time the SEC was considering suing you, right, sir?

A. Yes, ma'am.

Q. Mr. Cuban, you wanted to get to Mr. Fauré before he got to you, right?

A. Absolutely not....

Q. ... Now, ... you understood, Mr. Cuban, didn't you, that insider trading was illegal?

A. Yes, I did.

Q. And you knew in 2004 when you sold your shares in Mamma.com on June 28th that insider trading was illegal, right sir?

A. Yes, ma'am.

Q. Turn in your binder if you would, sir to Plaintiff's Exhibit 38.

I'm showing you what's been marked Plaintiff's Exhibit 38. This is an email to Charles McKinney, your broker at UBS, from you, Mark Cuban, dated June 30th, 2004.

Do you see that, sir?

A. Yes, ma'am....

Q. The title of this email is Mamma.

And June 30th is the day after you finished selling all of your shares in Mamma.com, correct?

A. Yes, ma'am.

Q. Let's highlight the first sentence.

"CM" that's Charles McKinney, correct?

A.   Yes, it is.

Q.   You write to him, "CM, I want to make sure I was a 100 pct" ... That's percent, right?

A.   Yes, ma'am.

Q.   "... kosher on that trade."

   Do you see that?

A.   Yes, ma'am.

Q.   By "kosher" you meant you wanted to make sure your trade was legal?

A.   Yes, ma'am.

Q.   Because you knew at this time that insider trading was not legal, right?

A.   Yes, ma'am.

Q.   At the bottom of the email, the last sentence, starting with the word "can," you say "Can you check with your folks, to make sure all is cool."

   Do you see that?

A.   Yes.

Q.   And then you say THX, M. That's thanks, Mark, right?

A.   Yes, it is.

Q.   Now, on this email, if we look at the top, you cc'd or carbon copied yourself, correct?

A.   Yes, ma'am....

Q.   ... Mr. Cuban, you never received a response back in writing from Charles McKinney or anyone else at UBS, did you, sir?

A.   In writing?

Q.   Yes.

A.   I never received something back in writing, no, ma'am....

Q.   Did you ever send an email back to UBS asking for a response in writing?

A.   No, ma'am, I never asked for a response in writing.

Q.   But you expected the folks at UBS to check, like you asked them too, correct?

A.   Absolutely.

Q.   But you didn't insist on a response in writing?

A.   No, ma'am.

Q.   Mr. McKinney at this time managed hundreds of millions of dollars of your money; is that right, sir?

A.   Yeah. More than. Yes, ma'am.

Q.   And you paid UBS a lot of money in commissions to manage your money, do you not, sir?

A.   I would presume so, yes, ma'am.

Q.   And you didn't tell them that you wanted a response to this email in writing?

A.   No.... You know, I presumed they would do their job. They're good at what they do. They have a compliance department, and it's in their best interest to make sure nothing goes haywire. Their job is to protect me. So I turned to Charley [McKinney] you know, to make sure things are good.

Q.   Okay. Let me just ask it this way. You sent an email to UBS asking them if you insider traded, correct?

A.   Of course not.

Q.   You asked them if your trade was legal, correct?

A.   That's not what I asked them, no.

Q.   When I asked you a minute ago if what you meant by "kosher" was "legal," you said yes. Are you changing that answer?

A.   No.

Q.   So you asked UBS if your trade was legal, correct?

A.   What I asked them was I wanted to make sure I was a hundred percent kosher on that trade.

Q.   You wanted to make sure you were a hundred percent legal on that at any rate, right, Mr. Cuban?

A.   Okay. That's fair. Yes.

Q.   Okay.
     But you didn't send them anything in writing when you didn't get a responsive email back, did you?

A.   Remember, they had an option of breaking the trade. So the way it works …

Q.   I'm not asking you how it works.

A.   Well, but you're asking for what the response was.

Q.   No. I'm asking you whether or not you insisted on a response from them in writing. And I understand your answer is no.
     Correct?

A.   You are right. I did not ask for it. …
     MS. FOLENA: I have no further questions for the witness at this time.
     THE COURT: Cross-examination.
     MR. MELSHEIMER: May I approach, Your Honor?
     THE COURT: You may.

CROSS EXAMINATION
[By Mr. Melsheimer, Attorney for Mr. Cuban]

Q.   Good afternoon.

A.   Good afternoon.

Q.   How you doing?

A.   I'm here.

Q.   All right. Let's take a look at … one of the last exhibits the government showed you, Mr. Cuban.
     And that is an email from you to Charlie McKinney on June 30th, 2004.
     Do you see that, sir.

A.   Yes, sir.

Q.   Now, you were asked a question about whether or not this was the day that you visited with the SEC lawyers who had reached out to make an inquiry about Irving Kott and Mamma.com.
     Do you remember that question?

A.   Yes, I do.

Q.   Was this email [to Mr. McKinney] sent before or after you visited with those lawyers?

A. Long before . . . .
Q. Long before . . . .
     Was it sent before you knew that the [SEC] lawyers were contacting you?
A. Yes, sir.
Q. This email was sent in the morning?
A. Yes it [was].
Q. When did you find out that the SEC lawyers wanted to speak with you about Mr. Kott and Mamma?
A. In the afternoon.
Q. And when did you speak with them?
A. I think it was 4:00 o'clock in the afternoon.
Q. Let's take a look at this: Now, Charlie McKinney, are we going to hear from him later?
A. Yes, ma'am . . . yes, sir.
Q. And is he a good friend of yours?
A. Yes, he is. . . .
Q. . . . And you write to him with the subject of Mamma.
     And you say, "CM, I want to make sure I was a hundred percent kosher on that trade," and that's the part that the government highlighted. Correct?
A. Correct. . . .
Q. . . . [B]ut I want to ask you: What motivated you to send this email to Mr. McKinney on June 30th, 2004, at 9:42 in the morning.
A. I'm a very conservative investor. I don't like to do anything that's not a hundred percent kosher. And so . . . at that time in 2004, I really didn't understand how private placements work. I had never done one. But they had certain features that . . . companies that I was . . . aware of that used 'em implied a negative.
     And so I sold my shares, knowing it was public information, but on the 30th, Charlie contacted me and said there was a press release that came out saying that Mamma had finished this PIPE.
Q. Now, when you . . . talked to Mr. Owen on the 28th did you know exactly when the PIPE was going to close?
A. I had no idea.
Q. So when Mr. McKinney told you it had closed on the 30th, is that what prompted this email?
A. Yeah. It caught me by surprise. . . .
Q. And the sentence [in the email to Mr. McKinney] says . . . "Can you check with your folks, to make sure all is cool." What did you mean by that?
A. When you buy and sell . . . a share of stock, . . . you . . . get a confirmation saying I sold this share of stock for $10. But because you have to have a confirmation to deal with the person on the other side who's buying it, it goes through a five day process [actually 3 day process in 2004].
     And so all of the paperwork has to be exchanged between the buyer and the seller, which is done by the brokers.
     In that five [actually in 2004 three] day process, if . . . something's not going right, could be any number of things, you could have that transaction unwound.

Q. What does that mean?

A. That means that it didn't happen. I take back all my shares of Mamma that I sold and I own them again. And any money that I would have gotten for the sale they don't have to pay me....

So it's as if it didn't happen.

Q. Did the folks from UBS, where Mr. McKinney worked, ever get back to you and tell you there was a problem?

A. No, they never did.

Q. ... [T]o your knowledge, did they get back to you and tell you everything was okay?

A. I believe so. I believe they did....

Q. Did you ever get any kind of email or anything in writing?

A. No, I never got anything in writing. But had there been a problem they would have cancelled the trade.

Q. Your relationship with Mr. McKinney had been existing for a long time?

A. Yeah. At that point, yes.

Q. Did you trust him?

A. Absolutely.

Q. Is he competent at what he does?

A. Absolutely.

Q. Is UBS one of the country's leading investment firms?

A. Yes.

Q. Now, Mr. Cuban, I want to ask you some general questions and then get into some background with you.

Now, you understand that the government here has accused you, sir, of committing fraud.

A. Yes, I do.

Q. Do you understand that the government has argued that you agreed to keep Mamma.com PIPE information confidential?

A. I understand that.

Q. Agreed not to trade on it?

A. I understand that.

Q. And then went ahead and did that anyway?

A. That's what I understand.

Q. Mr. Cuban, did you trick or deceive or defraud anyone at Mamma.com?

A. Of course not.

Q. Did you agree with Guy Fauré ... or anyone else, that you would keep information about the PIPE confidential?

A. Absolutely not.

Q. Would you have done that?

A. Absolutely not.

Q. Now, Mr. Cuban, here's the question: You don't remember exactly what was said on that call [between] Mr. Fauré [and] you; is that correct?

A. That's correct.

Q. You don't remember today?

A.   I don't.

Q.   How do you know that you didn't agree with Mr. Fauré on that call to keep information about the PIPE confidential information?

A.   First, and foremost, I would never agree to do something without knowing what I'm being asked to do.

Q.   What do you mean by that?

A.   You know, he says I have confidential information. There's no context. I'm not going to go do anything without knowing what I'm being asked to do.

Q.   Did you have any sense of why he was calling you?

A.   I just knew he was calling about Mamma.com, nothing else.

Q.   Why he was e-mailing you?
       I said calling, but I want to make it clear. He emailed you, correct?

A.   Yes, he did.

Q.   Did you have any sense of what that was about?

A.   No, I did not. Other than it was about Mamma.

Q.   Did the email say it was about anything in particular?

A.   No, it did not. . . .

Q.   . . . Now, would you have agreed not to trade on any information you may have received on June 28th?

A.   No.

Q.   How do you know that?

A.   I just wouldn't. . . . I didn't know what he was going to tell me.

Q.   Now, what about with respect to Arnie Owen?
       Did you have a communication with Arnie Owen later in the day?

A.   Yes, I did.

Q.   What did you tell him about your intentions with respect to your Mamma stock?

A.   I told him I was going to sell, and that's exactly what I did.

Q.   If you had agreed with either Mr. Fauré or anyone else not to sell your stock on June 28th, would you have done so?

A.   No. . . . [I]f I agree to do something I'm going to do . . . I'm going to stick to my word.

Q.   Have you ever made an agreement to restrict your trading in the stock of any company in an eight-minute cell phone call?

A.   Never.

Q.   Would you do that?

A.   Never.

Q.   Why not?

A.   It just makes no sense.

Q.   Do you have a pattern and practice, Mr. Cuban, when it comes to people requesting that you enter into agreements such as confidentiality or other agreements?

A.   Yeah. . . .

Q.   What is that pattern and practice?

A.   I don't do NDAs [Non-Disclosure Agreements].

Q.   What do you mean by that?

A. ... I get asked all the time, Mark, we have an investment idea, Mark we have an investment idea for you, you got to sign an NDA. And my answer is always no.

Have I made exception every now and then, like if it's a big company? Yes. But for a huge percentage, it just doesn't make sense for me to do....

Q. What [event] triggered [your tangible financial wealth]?

A. We sold the company, Broadcast.com, to Yahoo!, Inc.

Q. That's the Internet company Yahoo!?

A. Yes, it is.

Q. When did that sale take place?

A. It was announced April 1st and closed middle of ... 2000, right around July.

Q. Mr. Cuban, what did that sale of Broadcast.com to Yahoo!, what did that mean for you personally?

A. I mean, I'll be the first to tell you I'm the luckiest guy in the world, and I say it all the time.... [I]t was incredible. You can't describe it. And it changed my life and my family's life, my dad's life, my mom, and future generations. It's just incredible.

Q. Were you suddenly a billionaire?

A. Yes.

Q. Did the sale to Yahoo! create wealthy people at Broadcast.com?

A. Yes, it did.

Q. How did it do that?

A. We had 330 employees, and 300 of them became at least millionaires. 30 of them started too late to get there. But when we sold ... I wanted to make sure that everybody was able to participate. And so we had been giving stock and stock options along the way. And so when we sold, 300 people, on paper at least, became millionaires.

Q. Mr. Cuban, at some point did you purchase a basketball team?

A. Yes, I did.

Q. When was that?

A. January of 2000.

Q. The Dallas Mavericks?

A. Yes.

Q. Why did you do that?

A. Because I'm a basketball junkie.

Q. What do you mean by that?

A. I mean, I still play basketball.... I'm not saying I was good, but it's just something that I've always loved for as long as I can remember.

I play to this day. I played in the tournament last weekend. So when I'm sore you know why. It's ... just in my blood. I love the game.

Q. Were you a basketball fan of the Mavericks before you became wealthy?

A. I was a season ticket holder.

Q. Did you try to go to all the games?

A. Yes, I did.

Q. Now, I've heard you tell a story about going to the games with your girlfriend, now your wife, that prompted you to actually buy the team.

A. Right.

Q. Could you share that with the jury?

A. It was the start of the '99/2000 season. And this is a streak when the Mavs weren't that good. Up until 1999 ... they had won the award for the worst professional sports franchise of the Nineties. If you're a fan, you will remember it wasn't so good. But I was still a fan. And so I had season tickets. And it was the very first game, the opening game of 1999/2000, and we're undefeated.

You know, I was in [a] good mood. I was excited for the season to start. And I looked around and ... there was no energy.... [T]he crowd wasn't big. And I just thought to myself, you know, I can do better than this.

And ... I realized that I was financially fortunate and in a position that I actually could buy the team.

And so I reached out to Mark [Aguirre], who was a former player, who then in turn helped me make it happen. [Mr. Aguirre was the Dallas Mavericks' first overall selection in the 1981 NBA draft.]

Q. Did you try to attend all the games?

A. I can't anymore because of my kids, but I try to attend as many as I can.

Q. Does your wife go with you to the games?

A. She goes with me, yes.

Q. Does she sit with you?

A. No, not anymore.

Q. Why not?

A. We used to sit right next to each other right before I bought the team and right after I bought the team, but if you've ever seen me at a game I get ... maybe a little out of control. You know, everybody's got that one time or that one place or that one thing where they just let loose, and this is how ... they ... vent and get [out] all their anger, or whatever. Basketball's my thing. And even before I bought the team I would scream and yell, but once I bought the team it was a little bit more, and my wife couldn't stand sitting next to me ....

Q. Mr. Cuban, ... [y]ou appear on a TV reality show, right?

A. Yes.

Q. What's that show?

A. Shark Tank.

Q. For those that haven't seen it, what's the premise of that show?

A. It's kind of like American Idol for business. Entrepreneurs come and present their companies to a panel of five of us. And they give us their best pitch. And then we make a decision on whether or not to use our own money to invest in those companies.

Q. Do you actually invest your own money on that program?

A. Yes, we do.

Q. Why [are] you involved in that show?

A. You know, I think it's almost like my philanthropy in a lot of respects, in that I think we've all been hardened ... like the American dream doesn't exist anymore. Like ... if you can't go out there and work hard ... it doesn't matter, that you don't have a chance.

Shark Tank, on the other hand, proves that the American dream is alive and well. You have people from anywhere, you know, the middle of Iowa, big cities, small cities, great ideas, big ideas, little ideas … It's just a wide range of ideas. And I know from the feedback I get from people that they look to Shark Tank as inspiration. They look at it and say if this person can do it I can do it, if they can get in front of the sharks and get money, I can get in front of the sharks, I can create a business that makes it happen, I can do this as well.

And what's the most motivating part of it, Sony actually distributes the show, and they tell us that it's one of, if not the, most widely watched show[s] on television by families together. …

Kids come up to me and give me critiques about the deals I did, you paid too much, you paid too little, why did you invest in this, why did you invest in that. …

… It's like the new era lemonade stand, that instead of just setting up a lemonade stand, you can do more. You can watch Shark Tank and learn. And I get entrepreneurs. I get moms, dads, … everybody, kids, that look to the show as inspiration.

And it's a lot of work to get involved with all these different companies, but it's just amazing.

And I say this all the time: It's just a unique opportunity, and that's why I do the show.

Q. Now, in 2004, sir … and I'm not trying to get into … your personal finances, but in 2004 where did this Mamma investment rank in terms of your overall investments?

A. I mean, including all investments and my total net worth, … far less than one-half of one percent. …

Q. In your experience when people know that you've bought stock in a company, what happens to the stock?

A. It goes up.

Q. Why is that?

A. … There are certain people that trust me as an investor.

I've gone on CNBC and talked about stocks, and while I was talking about a particular stock, right on the screen you could see the stock price go up.

Q. What about when you sell a stock, what happens?

A. The exact opposite.

Q. Why is that?

A. I guess for the same reason. Some people … like what I do, and then when I get out, they get out. …

Q. Mr. Cuban, I want to return to a subject we talked about before the break about non-disclosure, or confidentiality agreements.

A. Okay.

Q. Have you ever in all your years as a businessman made an oral confidentiality agreement or non-disclosure agreement?

A. No.

Q. Would you do that?

A. No.

Q. Why not?

A. I'm a target, and I get sued like you wouldn't believe. And so I have to be careful. . . .

Q. What do you generally do with ... requests [from people who want you to invest in their company]?

A. I tell them no, usually, but every now and then, if there's something that I think is worth exploring further, I send [it] to my lawyer.

Q. Who is that?

A. Robert Hart [an alumnus of the SMU Dedman School of Law].

Q. Is this Mr. Hart sitting right there?

A. That man, yes, sir.

Q. All right. How long has he worked with you, sir?

A. 30 years, maybe, 25, 30 years.

Q. Does he actually have an office at your home here in Dallas?

A. Above my garage.

Q. Okay. It's converted from being a garage though, isn't it, sir?

A. Yes.

Q. But that's where he offices?

A. Yes, sir.

Q. And is he available to you if you need questions or issues answered about things like confidentiality agreements?

A. Yes, sir. . . .

Q. [On] ... April 1st [2004 did a] Yahoo! blog reference a rumor ... of a private placement taking place within Mamma?

A. Yes. . . .

Q. Let me ask you about ... message boards now, sir: Now, not everything on the Internet is true, right?

A. No, sir.

Q. And not everything on those message boards is true?

A. No, sir.

Q. But, of course, the Yahoo! message board on April 1st saying that ... there was going to be a private placement at Mamma was true?

A. Yes, it was.

Q. Because it ended up happening?

A. That's correct.

Q. Okay.

And you're not trying to tell the jury that everything that's on the Internet is true or on a message board is true.

A. Of course not.

Q. [Now, let's turn to] an email from you to Mr. Fauré on April 22nd, 2004. . . .

A. Yes, sir. . . .

Q. Then you say [in the April 2004 email], "Obviously, what you tell me is confidential." What did you mean by that?

A. If he gave me any names I would keep them confidential.

Q.   ... [W]ere you telling him that everything he was going to tell you from here on until the end of time was confidential, sir?

A.   Of course not.

Q.   Okay. Were you relating it to this specific exchange?

A.   Absolutely.

Q.   Was it in writing?

A.   Yes, it was.

Q.   Did you ever tell him on the phone or in an email that ... everything he told you was confidential?

A.   No, I did not.

Q.   Did he ever give you any information that was confidential in response to this email?

A.   He didn't give me any information at all....

Q.   You say [in the email], "Since I can't buy stock right now ..." now this is in April of 2004.
       What was your understanding in April of 2004 that led you to say that, sir?

A.   It was an incorrect understanding, whatever it was. I was under the impression at the time that I was not able to trade in Mamma.com stock.

Q.   Why?

A.   I'm not quite sure. I think it was because I had filed my [Form] 13G [with the SEC]. And there was some period of time after that where I [believed that I] was restricted from trading.

Q.   So you had filed your 13G saying that you were in excess of 5 percent shareholder?

A.   Correct.

Q.   And you had some understanding that there was a period of time after you filed that where you couldn't trade your stock?

A.   As best I recall, yes.

Q.   Have you since learned that was incorrect?

A.   Yes, that's true....

Q.   ... Mr. Cuban, we were talking about the concerns you had with a man named Irving Kott [a convicted stock swindler].

A.   Yes.

Q.   Do you recall the questions from the government about your concerns with Mr. Kott?

A.   For the most part, yes, sir.

Q.   And was there some suggestion [by the SEC in this case] that your concerns about Mr. Kott were somehow made up by you after you received a letter from the SEC in 2007, suggesting that they might sue you?

A.   Yes, sir.

Q.   Okay. You recall ... your blog post in March of 2005, and ... about what you posted about Mr. Kott in 2005?

A.   Yes, sir.

Q.   That was before you received the letter from the SEC?

A.   Yes, it was.

Q. Was March 2005 the first time you ever mentioned Irving Kott and his criminal activity?

A. Of course not.

Q. When was the first time you connected Mr. Kott with Mamma.com?

A. In talking to Mamma.com or just seeing it?

Q. Just the first time you ever had any connection in your mind between Irving Kott and Mamma.

A. I saw it on a message board.

Q. What do you mean by that?

A. Yahoo! ... and there's a bunch of different message boards online, and I was just doing homework, and I saw on a Yahoo! message board posting from someone that there was this convicted stock swindler involved with Mamma.com.

Q. Was that around the time you purchased your shares in March of 2004?

A. A little bit after.

Q. Did you do anything to investigate this information that you saw on the message board?

A. Of course.

Q. What did you do?

A. I asked the company about it and started looking online at other sources.

Q. Did you ask your advisors to inquire with the company?

A. Yes....

Q. Did you receive a call from an FBI agent in April of 2004?

A. Yes, I did.

Q. What was the nature of that call?

A. He left a voicemail ... saying that I ... should reach back out to him, that ... he had information about the connection between Irving Kott and Mamma.com.

Q. Did you call this agent back?

A. Yes, I did.

Q. What did he tell you?

A. He told me that Irving Kott was under investigation by the Justice Department, by whoever, and that I really needed to be careful because they believed that he was involved with Mamma.com....

Q. Were you unsettled by having gotten a call from the FBI in April of 2004?

A. Without question.

Q. Did the FBI suggest you had done anything wrong?

A. No, of course not.

Q. Let's take a look at ... Mr. Fauré's response to you on April 29th, 2004, at 9:08 a.m.

He says to you, "Hi, Mark, yesterday I forwarded your question about [Mamma.com board of director member] Mr. Raich's relationship with Mr. Kott. Please find his attached response. The board of directors of Mamma.com, Inc. has been aware of this relationship."

And [Mr. Fauré] attached a letter from [Mamma.com director] Mr. Raich ... supposedly explaining this relationship?

A. I don't recall the attachment, sir....

Q. Let's take a look at your response to Mr. Fauré on April 29th, 2004 ....
A. Yes, sir.
Q. Read for the jury that first paragraph of your response.
A. "Actually, that's not a very encouraging response. Mr. Raich told me in our conversation that he had no business relationship with Mr. Kott whatsoever. In this email he says he does."
Q. Why was that concerning?
A. Well, he lied ... he misled me.
Q. What's your next two sentences?
A. "You" ... meaning Guy Fauré ... "in our first discussion told me that you had no idea who Mr. Kott was. Are you now saying that you did know?"
Q. What do you mean by that?
A. I mean, it's obvious. I mean, when I talked to him on the phone the first time, he told me when I asked him about it he had no idea who Mr. Kott was. Now they obviously did know....
Q. What's your next sentence to Mr. Fauré?
A. "In addition he" ... Robert Raich ... "explains that he does have a business relationship as a tax advisor. Yet he doesn't say anything more about it. This is a known stock manipulator who is under investigation by the FBI and is currently negotiating a settlement for such crimes. A member of the Mamma board has an admitted business relationship with this known stock manipulator. I see that as a huge problem."
Q. What did you mean by "a huge problem"?
A. They're dealing with crooks ....
Q. Now, you raise another question with Mr. Fauré in the next paragraph. What do you ask him?
A. "I have another question for you. Has Mr. Kott or anyone or any entity which represents Mr. Kott participated in the purchase of any financial instruments of [Mamma.com] in the past five years?"
Q. Why was that a concern of yours, sir?
A. Well, because the basis of what I had been hearing on message boards, in particular, was that Irving Kott actually controlled the company.... There was no documentation saying that he was a shareholder, but there were a lot of people who felt that he actually was controlling the company itself from behind the scenes.
Q. What do you conclude in your email to Mr. Fauré?
A. "This is of significant concern to me. Any relationship with a known stock manipulator/swindler should be a situation that is not tolerated by any CEO of any company. To allow anyone, Mr. Raich or anyone else to continue on the Mamma board after such a relationship is acknowledged creates a very significant ethics problem for me."
Q. Does Mr. Fauré respond to this email on April 29th, 2004?
A. Yes, sir.
Q. Let's take a look at what he says.

A.   He says, "Hi, Mark, I will further investigate your concerns and coordinate a response to you shortly." ....

Q.   Is that well before you sold your stock?

A.   Yes, sir....

Q.   Now, getting back to May of 2004, did anything else occur in May of 2004 that informed your judgment about Mr. Kott and his possible connection with Mamma?

A.   Well, ... we got a copy of a letter I believe connecting Mr. Kott to the company.

Q.   Did you learn anything that had happened on May 4th [2004?]

A.   Oh, on May 4th, that day ... the Justice Department put out a press release, or it was in an article I read, saying that Mr. Kott had settled the accusations that ... he was a stock swindler....

Q.   ... You talked to the SEC on June 30th about Mr. Kott and Mamma?

A.   Yes, I did....

Q.   Was that two days after the calls with Mr. Fauré and Mr. Owen?

A.   Yes, sir.

Q.   Okay. Did you have an understanding of the focus of the SEC's attention on that call?

A.   Yes, I did.

Q.   What was it?

A.   They were investigating Irving Kott and Mamma.com.

Q.   Who was on the phone for the SEC?

A.   Alton Turner and Kara Brockmeyer.

Q.   Do you understand them to be SEC lawyers?

A.   Yes, I do.

Q.   Did they ask you about Irving Kott on June 30th?

A.   Yes, they did.

Q.   And from a timing perspective, sir, when was this call with the government in relation to the letter you received from [the SEC] saying they might sue you over your sale of Mamma stock?

A.   ... Years prior....

Q.   Mr. Cuban, I want to go over with you a timeline that really summarizes what we've just talked about in terms of the dates.

Now, March of 2004, is that when you first raised your concerns with Mamma about their possible connection with Mr. Kott?

A.   Yes, sir.

Q.   In April of 2004, did you get a call from the FBI?

A.   Yes, sir.

Q.   We talked about the email exchanges you had with Mr. Fauré raising your concerns with Mr. Kott. Were those in late April and early May ...

A.   Yes, sir.

Q.   ... of 2004?

A.   Yes, sir.

Q.   All right, sir. And you had a call with Mr. Raich on the board of directors of Mamma. Was that on May 4th, 2004?

A.   Yes, sir.

Q.   Then you got an email from [another source] on June 28th suggesting that he had some additional evidence?

A.   Yes, sir.

Q.   June 30th, what'd you do late afternoon June 30th?

A.   Talked to the SEC.

Q.   About?

A.   Irving Kott and Mamma.com.

Q.   All these events happened three years or more before the SEC ever threatened to sue you?

A.   That's correct.

Q.   Finally, ... March of 2005, what happened then?

A.   I wrote my blog post....

Q.   Where you mentioned a connection between Mr. Kott and the company?

A.   Yes, sir....

Q.   Do you recall the government suggesting that you were trying to dig up dirt on Mr. Fauré to, quote, get to him before he got to you?

A.   Yes, sir.

Q.   In 2007, is that why you were investigating Mr. Fauré and the company?

A.   To get dirt?

Q.   To get to him before he got to you?

A.   Oh, no. Of course not.

Q.   What were you doing in 2007 with respect to looking at information about Mr. Kott, Mr. Fauré, and others at the company?

A.   There was a lawsuit that had been filed against Mamma.com....

Q.   Was there a securities fraud lawsuit filed against Mamma in 2007? ....

A.   There was a class action lawsuit filed against Mamma accusing them of hiding the fact that Irving Kott was running the company.

Q.   Were you a potential party to that lawsuit?

A.   Yes. Because I had purchased stock I was a potential party.

Q.   So all the plaintiffs in that lawsuit were anyone that purchased stock in the company during a certain time frame?

A.   I believe so.

Q.   Did you stay a part of that lawsuit or get out of it?

A.   No. I opted-out of the lawsuit so I could look at suing them on my own.

Q.   What happened with the rest of the lawsuit that you opted out of?

A.   ... Mamma.com settled with the party that sued them, accusing them of Irving Kott running the company....

Q.   Mr. Cuban, why did you continue to see what connection this convicted felon, Mr. Kott, had with Mamma?

A.   Well, I wanted, you know, information for the potential lawsuit, and I just wanted to find the truth.

Q.   Do ... you recall the government asking you some questions ... and I'm moving to a different topic ... about your blog and whether what you say on your blog is true or untrue?

A.　Yes, sir.

Q.　Okay. What topics do you generally discuss in your blog?

A.　Everything. I mean, I've written it for 10 years, so I've talked about everything from motivational speeches and opportunities, financial stuff, sports, you name it. Anything ... I mean, that's the purpose of a blog, is to put out there anything that happens to be on your mind.

Q.　Is it an investment blog?

A.　No.

Q.　What percentage of your blog do you think relates to investment advice?

A.　In terms of original posts on investment advice over the ten years, probably fewer than 15....

Q.　Is your blog supposed to be entertaining?

A.　Yes.

Q.　Do people tell you it's entertaining?

A.　Yeah.

Q.　Do you try to be provocative?

A.　That's the most interesting part to me....

Q.　I want to transition into a discussion of your June 28th phone call with Mr. Fauré that he testified about by videotape.

A.　Yes, sir.

Q.　Mr. Cuban, do you understand that the SEC is alleging that during your June 28th phone call with Mr. Fauré that you agreed from the get-go of the call to keep everything that Mr. Fauré was telling you confidential?

A.　I understand that's what they're alleging.

Q.　Is that something you would have agreed to?

A.　Of course, not....

Q.　... Now, remind us, what are the two reasons in your mind why you would not have agreed to keep information confidential on that phone call with Mr. Fauré?

　　　MS. FOLENA: Objection, speculation.

　　　THE COURT: Overruled.

　　　THE WITNESS: One, I'm not going to agree to keep something confidential when I don't know the subject or the context.

　　　And, two, I just don't do oral confidentiality agreements....

Q.　Mr. Cuban, we've heard several times from Mr. Fauré on his videotape that he said you said towards the end of the call, "Now I'm screwed. I can't sell."

A.　Yes, sir.

Q.　Mr. Cuban, again, you don't recall what he said or you said. Right?

A.　Yes, sir.

Q.　Would you have said "Now I'm screwed. I can't sell."?

A.　No, sir.

　　　MS FOLENA: Objection, calls for speculation.

　　　THE COURT: Overruled.

BY MR. MELSHEIMER

Q.　Why wouldn't you have said something like that?

A.   Because it makes no sense....
     ... Even though I don't remember a call, there are multiple places where ... I said I was going to sell my stock, and I didn't feel like I was under any limitations whatsoever. I didn't make any agreements to not do anything. So there's no reason for me to say it.

Q.   Did you in fact tell Mr. Owen ... later that same day that you would sell your stock?

A.   Yes, I did.

Q.   Did you agree in any way with either Mr. Fauré or Mr. Owen that you would not sell your stock?

A.   No, I did not.

Q.   Have you seen documents that are consistent with your position contemporaneous with this time period, consistent with your position, that you would not and did not say "Now I'm screwed. I can't [sell]"?

A.   Yeah. I sent an email to Charles McKinney, and I told him that I told Mr. Fauré that I would sell my stock.

Q.   That's the June 30th email to Mr. McKinney?

A.   Yes, sir....

Q.   Mr. Cuban, did you receive an email from Mr. Fauré after your eight-minute phone call with him?

A.   Yes, sir.

Q.   Let's take a look at SEC Exhibit 165.
     Now, just like the other email we looked at, were you shown this email by the government on [your direct examination]?

A.   Yes, sir....

Q.   ... Now, let's talk about this email a little bit, sir.
     Does it say anything about a confidentiality agreement?

A.   No, it does not.

Q.   In fact, what's the subject?

A.   It says "Contact."

Q.   Does it say anything about an agreement between you and Mr. Fauré not to trade your stock?

A.   No, it does not.

Q.   What does it say?

A.   It says, "If you want more details about the private placement, please contact (I guess you or your financial advisors) Arnie Owen. Arnie is with Merriman Curhan & Ford." ....

Q.   Does the email say who he is in relationship to [Mamma.com]?

A.   No. This is just some guy that is with Merriman Curhan & Ford.

Q.   Had you ever set eyes on Mr. Owen before he came to court and testified?

A.   No, I had not....

Q.   ... Does this email from Mr. Fauré say that you or your financial advisors have to keep anything you discuss with Mr. Owen confidential?

A.   No, it does not.

Q. Does this email say anything about you or your advisors not selling your stock before the press release of the Mamma PIPE?

A. No, it does not....

Q. Mr. Cuban, did you have a call with Mr. Owen the afternoon of June 28th?

A. Yes, sir.

Q. During that call did Mr. Owen ever tell you that the information you were discussing was confidential?

A. No, he did not.

Q. On that call with Mr. Owen did you agree not to trade Mamma stock for any period of time?

A. No, I did not....

Q. Mr. Cuban, when you told Mr. Owen the agent of Mamma on June 28th, 2004, that you were going to sell your shares of stock ... Did you qualify it in any way?

A. Absolutely not....

Q. Okay. Now, did Mr. Owen tell you that any of the information that he was giving you in response to your questions was confidential?

A. No, he did not.

Q. Did he tell you when specifically the transaction was going to happen?

A. No. I had no idea when it would happen.

Q. Did you tell Mr. Owen a response to his offer that you, Mark Cuban, participate in the PIPE?

A. Yes.... I told him I did not want to participate in the PIPE.

Q. And you told him you would sell your stock?

A. And I told him I would sell my stock.

Q. What did you do, consistent with what you told Mr. Owen, what did you do right after that call ended?

A. I sold my stock....

Q. Now, were you here for Mr. Owen's testimony?

A. Yes, sir.

Q. Did you hear him say that he had no doubt that, if you wanted to, you would have been free to sell your shares at the end of your call with him?

A. Yes, I did....

Q. ... [T]he call that you had with the SEC lawyers on June 30th, what was your understanding of the focus of the SEC's inquiry?

A. Mamma.com and Irving Kott ... Irving Kott's relationship with Mamma.com.

Q. Did you participate in that call voluntarily?

A. Yes, I did.

Q. Did you have a lawyer present with you on that call?

A. No, I did not.

Q. Did you feel the need to do so?

A. No, sir.

Q. Why not?

A. I had done nothing wrong. I was just trying to help.

Q. Now, I want to touch on one point that was mentioned [at this trial] last week.

You sent an email to Charley McKinney on June 30th, seeking to confirm that you were 100 percent kosher on the trade in your Mamma stock.

A. Yes, sir.

Q. Did you send that email to Mr. McKinney confirming your trade before or after you learned that the SEC had called you?

A. Before.

Q. ... It was your understanding that on June 30th your trade could have been reversed?

A. Yes, sir.

Q. What does that mean?

A. What that means is that you could undo or unwind the trade so it basically never happened.

Q. ... Is there the availability of doing that within three to five days after you've made a trade?

A. Yeah. I believe I said earlier it was five days, but I've been corrected that it's three days.

Q. Okay. Either way, your email to the UBS compliance group was ... within the time that those trades could have been unwound, right?

A. Yes, they could have unwound the trades.

Q. Mr. Cuban, did you file something with the SEC saying you had sold all of your stock in Mamma?

A. Yes, I did.

Q. What is that called?

A. It's an amendment to the [Form] 13-G.

Q. Is that the ... same type of form you filed when you announced you had bought more than 5 percent?

A. Yes, sir....

Q. You talked about on Thursday this notion of giving a stock answer sometimes to reporters or even other inquirers?

A. Yes, sir.

Q. What is a stock answer?

A. It just means it's a quick and dirty response so that it sends a message and I can be done with it. There's just not enough hours in the day to go into detail ... with all the emails I get. So a short and simple answer gets the job done.

Q. Do you use stock answers in other contexts?

A. Of course.

Q. In what context?

A. It can be within the concept of basketball. I have good relationships with players, and I want to keep good relationships with players whether they stay with the Mavs or not. We might release a player, and then the media will ask me why did you release them. I'm not going to say because he can't hit a jumper or he's too slow or whatever. I'm going to say we're going in a different direction because I don't want to negatively impact that player's career....

Q. .... Mr. Cuban, let me move to a couple of final subjects with you. All right?

A.   Okay.

Q.   … Mr. Cuban, were you an insider at Mamma?

A.   Absolutely not.

Q.   Did you hear Mr. Fauré agree that you were not an insider?

A.   Yes, I did.

Q.   Did you ever attend a board meeting of Mamma?

A.   No, I did not.

Q.   You were asked twice to be on the board of the company, right?

A.   Yes, sir.

Q.   What was your response both times?

A.   I declined.

Q.   Did you ever participate in a telephone conference with members of Mamma. com's board?

A.   No, sir.

Q.   Mr. Cuban, did you ever meet Guy Fauré in person?

A.   I had no idea what he looked like until I saw his video.

Q.   Did you ever meet Mr. Goldman in person?

A.   Same. No, I have not.

Q.   Ever meet Arnie Owen in person before the trial?

A.   No, sir. …

Q.   Mr. Cuban, did you do anything to try to get Mr. Fauré to come to Dallas, Texas, to testify in person?

A.   Yes, I did.

Q.   What did you do?

A.   I, through my attorneys, had my attorneys reach out to his attorneys ….

      MS. FOLENA: Your Honor, objection.

      THE COURT: State the basis, please.

      MS. FOLENA: The witness is in Canada. He has no obligation to come. He's not within the subpoena power of the court and whatever efforts were taken are not relevant here.

      THE COURT: I'll overrule the objection at this point.

BY MR. MELSHEIMER:

Q.   Mr. Cuban, did you ask your lawyers to invite Mr. Fauré to come to Dallas, Texas?

A.   Yes, sir, I asked them …

Q.   In order to testify live?

A.   Yes. Just recently, yes, sir.

Q.   Could have come to the trial and testified in person had he wanted to?

A.   Yes. I, through my attorneys, had my attorneys reach out to his attorney and ask that Mr. Fauré come down and that I would cover all his expenses.

Q.   Right. Could have gone to the State Fair?

A.   I'm sorry?

Q.   He could have gone to the State Fair?

A.   And had fried everything.

Q.   Did you ever hear a response?

A. Yeah ... through my attorneys, yes, sir.

Q. And what did his attorney respond?

A. That he declined....

Q. ... Mr. Cuban, when did you first learn that the SEC had sued you for fraud?

A. It was ... the Mavs were playing in Charlotte. And I woke up in the morning and turned on CNBC, and I was the headline.

Q. Was this in 2008?

A. Yes, sir.

Q. How did you feel when you learned the SEC had sued you?

A. Sick to my stomach.

Q. Why?

A. I had done nothing wrong.

Q. Now, Mr. Cuban, in all the years that this case has been going on, don't you think you could have just settled it and made it go away?

A. Yes, sir.

Q. Why haven't you done that? Tell the jury.

A. Because I did nothing wrong and I refuse to be bullied. I don't care if it's the government.

Q. Is that why you're here today, because you refused to be bullied?

A. Yes, sir.

MR. MELSHEIMER: Your Honor, I have no further questions of Mr. Cuban at this time....

REDIRECT EXAMINATION
[By Ms. Folena, Attorney for the SEC]

Q. Good afternoon, Mr. Cuban.

A. Good afternoon.

Q. I have some questions to follow-up on questions Mr. Melsheimer asked you ....
... [Y]ou heard Mr. Owen testify in this case last week, correct?

A. Yes, I did.

Q. And you heard Mr. Owen say that he told you on June 28th that the press release was going to hit the tape on June 29th, 2004, correct?
Do you remember that testimony?

A. I don't recall specifically, but generally, yes.

Q. Okay. So you actually knew then, Mr. Cuban, on June 28th, 2004, that the press release was going to be announced to the public, the PIPE, on June 29th. Is that right?

A. I didn't know it. I don't recall him saying that. Yeah, I don't recall him saying that at all. So I can't say that I knew it....

Q. ... You don't recall it, but you don't have any reason to dispute that when he told the jury that he told you on the 28th the information would hit the tape on the 29th. You have no reason to say that's not accurate, correct?

A. I just ... I don't know....

Q. You heard Mr. Owen testify last week that he did not recall you saying anything about selling your stock in Mamma.com before the public announcement. Do you remember that testimony?

A. Yes, I do.

Q. And you heard Mr. Owen say when he was asked again about that testimony that if a powerful man like you said you were going to sell your stock one minute after hanging up the phone with him, that's something Mr. Owen believes he would have remembered. Do you remember that testimony?

A. Yes, I do.

Q. You don't have any reason to dispute Mr. Owen's testimony, do you, sir?

A. No, ma'am. I mean ... Well, I guess let me take that back. The facts state otherwise. All right. We know what the facts are here....

Q. ... My question is, do you have any reason to dispute Mr. Owen when he says if a powerful man like you said he was going to sell all of his shares a minute after hanging up the phone with him, that's something he would have remembered, right, sir?

A. I can't ... speak to his memory, but I know I told him that I would sell.

Q. Okay. But you're not saying he's lying, are you?

A. Maybe he's ... got it wrong. I don't know. I don't want to characterize him one way or the other.

Q. You also testified that in that conversation with Arnie Owen on June 28th, 2004, you mentioned something to him about Irving Kott. Do you remember that testimony? ....

A. Yes....

Q. Okay. Now, you also heard Arnie Owen say that he didn't recall you ever saying anything in that phone call about Irving Kott, right?

A. Yes, I do.

Q. Do you also recall his testimony ... where he said I would have remembered that because it would have impugned my reputation?
   Do you remember that?

A. Yes, I do.

Q. You don't have any reason to dispute Mr. Owen's testimony that he doesn't ever recall you saying anything about Irving Kott, right?

A. Dispute the fact that he said it or dispute the content?

Q. Dispute the content.

A. Yes, I do.

Q. And you dispute it because you ... say you told him that, correct?

A. Absolutely.

Q. And he says you didn't tell him that, right?

A. Yes. That's what he said....

Q. Mr. Cuban, you just testified a few minutes ago ... I don't know if I'll ... capture your exact words, but something to the effect of you wanted to get these guys at Mamma.com. Is that what you said?

A. I don't ... remember exactly what I said, but I probably used a little bit of hyperbole, yes.

Q. There's that exaggeration again, right?

A. Yeah.

Q. Nonetheless, what you did say just a few minutes ago is that you did want to find something on the guys at Mamma.com. Is that right, sir?

A. I wanted to find ... the facts, is what it came down to.

Q. And you were looking for those facts in July of 2007 in those emails that we looked at, correct, sir?

A. Yes, ma'am.

Q. Okay. And those emails were dated July 2007, after you had received notification that the SEC was considering suing you, right, sir?

A. I don't recall the exact timing of it, but I believe so.

Q. Mr. Cuban, isn't it true that you signed a release with Mamma.com in which you forever released, acquitted, forgave and discharged Copernic, including Mamma.com, Mr. Fauré, Mr. Goldman, Mr. Bertrand, and their agents ....?

A. Now, you know why I don't do oral agreements.
     Yes. That's correct.

Q. Okay. So you released this company from any claim you may ever have against them; is that correct, sir?

A. That's correct.

Q. And you did that in September of 2007?

A. If that's the date on there, yes, ma'am.

Q. Okay. So is it fair to say you never found any dirt on this company; is that right?

A. No, that's not fair to say at all.

Q. Okay. So you released them from all claims, even though you had dirt about them?

A. That's correct.

Q. Okay.
     Isn't it true, Mr. Cuban, that you released them from those claims because they agreed to sit down and talk to your lawyers; is that right, sir?

A. That's correct....

Q. You told the SEC in that June 30th [2004 telephone] interview that your broker was Charles McKinney, correct, sir?

A. Yes, I did....

Q. You told the SEC, Mr. Cuban, did you not, that Charles McKinney had discretionary authority over your trading account, right?

A. Yes, I did.

Q. That wasn't a true statement, was it, sir?

A. As I found out now, it's incorrect....
     I told them that he had discretionary control of the account. I was incorrect.

Q. Let me make sure I understand this.
     The SEC is calling you about a relationship between Irving Kott and Mamma. com, correct?

A. Yes, ma'am.

Q. And you knew ... you had owned stock in Mamma.com, correct?

A. That's correct.

Q. And they asked you about your broker, Charles McKinney, right?

A. Yes, they did.

Q. And you mistakenly tell them McKinney has discretionary authority over your accounts; is that what you're saying?

A. That's what I'm saying.

Q. Because Mark Cuban does not know ... whether Charles McKinney has discretion or not over his trading accounts; is that right, sir?

A. Mark Cuban doesn't know a lot of things. And that's one of them. Yes, ma'am.

Q. In all the correspondence that Mr. Melsheimer showed you between yourself and the SEC about the Mamma.com Irving Kott conversation, do you remember that?

A. Do I remember all of it?

Q. Do you remember what he showed you?

A. Generally.

Q. He didn't show you any correspondence where you told the SEC, I'm sorry, I realize [that] ... Mr. McKinney does not have discretionary authority over my account, correct?

A. That's correct.

Q. Sir, you never [to] this day corrected that misstatement, did you?

A. No, I did not.

Q. So you left the SEC with the impression that Mr. McKinney could place trades in your account without your authority; is that right?

A. Because up until you showed me these documents that's the impression I had ....

Q. Okay. Because you had no idea.

A. None.

Q. Mr. McKinney invests I think you told me last week hundreds of millions of dollars of your money; is that right, sir?

A. Yes, ma'am.

Q. The man who's investing hundreds of millions of dollars of your money you have no idea whether he has discretionary authority over your accounts; is that your testimony?

A. That is absolutely my testimony....

Q. Mr. Cuban, do you remember on April 3rd, 2007, the SEC showed you a document during [your SEC investigative] testimony and it was a subpoena?
    Do you remember that?

A. I don't recall it specifically, no, ma'am, but ... I'll take your word for it....

Q. And when you gave that testimony you were under oath?

A. Yes, I was.

Q. And you swore to tell the truth; is that right?

A. Yes, I did.

Q. Now, Ms. Riewe [attorney for the SEC] asked you at that time: "Q. Did you speak to anyone from Mamma.com about the PIPE at any point?"
    Do you remember that question?

A. I do not remember it....

MS. FOLENA: If we can pull up page 47 of this transcript, please, so Mr. Cuban can see it?

Pull it up.

Your Honor, may I approach?

THE COURT: You may.

BY MS. FOLENA:

Q. Mr. Cuban, I'm handing you the transcript from the April 3rd, 2007 interview that you had with the SEC, sir. And I want you to turn to page 47 of that, if you would.

And tell me when you get there.

A. Yes, ma'am.

Q. Okay. Now, ... this was the interview or the testimony where you were being asked about your trading in Mamma.com stock, right, sir?

A. Yes, ma'am.

Q. Okay. And ... in this testimony you were under oath, correct?

A. Yes, ma'am.

Q. And you swore to tell the truth?

A. Yes, ma'am.

Q. And Ms. Riewe asked you, on line 19:

"Q. Did you speak to anyone from Mamma.com about the PIPE at any point?"

Do you see that, sir?

A. Yes, I do.

Q. And your response was: "A. I don't remember."

Do you see that?

A. Yes, ma'am.

Q. Then you go on to say, "I saw the reference in the documents like you guys did that said I called them about the PIPE, but I don't remember that conversation about it at all or if there was a conversation."

Do you see that, sir?

A. Yes, I do.

Q. So you did not provide the SEC in 2007 any details about that conversation, correct?

A. That's correct.

Q. Your response was, "I don't remember," right?

A. Yes, ma'am.

Q. ... You listened to Mr. Fauré's testimony by videotape last week. Do you remember that?

A. Yes, ma'am.

Q. And you remember that on the videotape there was a date on there, and it was November 4th, 2011; is that correct?

A. I don't remember specifically, but yes, ma'am.

Q. Okay.... Do you have any reason to disagree with me that that was the date of the videotape?

A. No, ma'am.

Q. And that was the date [Mr. Fauré] gave that testimony, right?

A. I presume so, yes, ma'am.

Q. Now, you heard him testify on that videotape that when you called him one of the first things he said to you was, "Mark, I've got confidential information." You heard him say that, right?

A. I think he said, "I have confidential information."

Q. Okay. But you heard that, right?

A. Yes, ma'am.

Q. And then you heard him say ... I think I counted it ... at least 15 times that you said "Now I'm screwed. I can't sell."
     Do you remember that?

A. I didn't count, but, yes, I heard him say it.

Q. And you remember him testify that he told you that the company was going to do a PIPE, correct?

A. I remember him saying that, yes, ma'am.

Q. And you heard him say that there was no doubt in his mind after telling you that the company was going to do a PIPE you said "Now I'm screwed. I can't sell." Right?

A. I heard him say that. I don't agree with it, obviously.

Q. You don't agree with it?

A. No, ma'am.

Q. Let me make sure I understand it.
     You claim Mr. Fauré is lying when he said that he told you, "Mark, I have confidential information." Right?

A. No, that's not the case. I don't know if he said that or not.

Q. Okay. Are you saying that he lied 15 times when he said he heard you say, "Now I'm screwed. I can't sell"?

A. Again, I didn't count, but ... I did not say that.

Q. But you're not calling him a liar?

A. I wouldn't want to ... I don't know ... I can't speak for him, and ... you know, maybe he just made a mistake.

Q. But nonetheless, you are claiming that he's wrong about those things. Is that right?

A. The ... second statement, yes.
     The first statement, I just don't know.

Q. He's wrong about the second statement. You're sure about that, right?

A. Yes, ma'am.

Q. But you have no recollection of anything that was said on that call; is that right, sir?

A. That's correct.

Q. You just know in your heart that that's not right?

A. That's correct....

Q. Do you remember last week when you changed your testimony on the stand about tracking down Guy Fauré when I initially asked you, "Mark Cuban, You were trying to find dirt on the only man that could testify against you?" You initially told me yes. Do your remember that?

A. Yes, I do.

Q. And then you went back and you changed that testimony. Do you remember that?

A. Yes, I do.

Q. And then you explained why you changed that testimony, correct?

A. Yes, ma'am. . . .

Q. . . . [Y]ou testified this morning that you had received a call from the FBI, correct?

A. Yes, ma'am.

Q. And I think you said they were warning you about Irving Kott. Is that right?

A. Yes, ma'am.

Q. Because you were a shareholder in Mamma.com, right?

A. Yes, ma'am. He's telling me to be careful.

Q. Okay. You didn't sell any of your shares in Mamma.com after that phone call with the FBI, did you, sir?

A. No, I did not.

Q. You didn't sell those shares until June 28th, 2004, the same day you spoke to Guy Fauré, right?

A. Yes, ma'am.

Q. The same day you spoke to Arnold Owen, right?

A. That's correct, ma'am. . . .

Q. . . . [M]y question is: You spoke to Arnie Owen just hours [after] you spoke to Guy Fauré on June 28th; is that correct, sir?

A. Yes, ma'am.

Q. So you recall telling Arnie Owen that you'd sell your shares, right?

A. Yes, ma'am.

Q. But you have no recollection of anything you said to Guy Fauré just hours before that, right?

A. That's correct.

Q. And you have no recollection of what Guy Fauré said to you, correct, sir?

A. That's correct.

Q. So you can't really sit in this courtroom and tell this jury that you did not say "Now I'm screwed. I can't sell."

    Right?

    MR. MELSHEIMER: Your Honor, argumentative, asked and answered.

    THE COURT: Overruled as to argumentative, but I'll give her some leeway because it's effectively cross.

    Go ahead.

BY MS. FOLENA:

Q. So you can't sit here and tell this jury that you did not tell Guy Fauré, "Now I'm screwed. I can't sell." Right, sir?

A. That's incorrect.

Q. You have no recollection of anything you said on the call, right?

A. That's correct.

Q.   And you have no recollection of anything Mr. Fauré said on the call?

A.   That's correct.

Q.   So you can't sit here for sure and say that you didn't tell Mr. Fauré, "Now I'm screwed. I can't sell," right?

A.   That's incorrect....

Q.   Mr. Cuban, remember Mr. Melsheimer asked you about his counsel's efforts to contact Mr. Fauré and ask him to come to court?

A.   Yes, ma'am.

Q.   And they told you that they did that; is that right?

A.   Yes, ma'am.

Q.   Did anyone ever tell you, Mr. Cuban, that I spoke to Mr. Fauré personally about a month before this trial, sir?

A.   That you spoke to him personally?

     No, ... I was not aware of that.

Q.   So you're not aware that I had a conversation with Mr. Fauré and his lawyers about a month before we started this trial?

     MR. MELSHEIMER [attorney for Mr. Cuban]: I'm going to object, Your Honor.... [S]he's testifying about a conversation ...

     MS. FOLENA: I'm just asking him if he knew.

     THE COURT: Well, the question suggests testimony by counsel. So I'll sustain the objection.

     MS. FOLENA: Okay.

     THE COURT: You can ask about the topic, but just don't assert as if you're testifying.

BY MS. FOLENA:

Q.   Okay. Would you have any reason to disagree, Mr. Cuban, if I told you I had a conversation with Mr. Fauré?

     MR. MELSHEIMER: Your Honor, I think that's ... just a rose by any other name.

     THE COURT: Well, I'll sustain the objection, although I've never heard the rose-by-any-other-name objection.

     MR. MELSHEIMER: But you sustained it.

     THE COURT: Well, ... who can argue with Shakespeare.

                    (Laughter)

BY MS. FOLENA:

Q.   Mr. Cuban, do you know, sir, or have any information at all about whether or not, like your counsel asked Mr. Fauré to come to trial, whether the SEC did?

A.   I believe ... I was told that they did.

Q.   So you do know?

A.   I don't know the details. I just believe I was told.

Q.   Okay. So you were told that the SEC had asked Mr. Fauré to come to trial, correct?

A.   Yes, ma'am.

Q.   Okay. Were you told what Mr. Fauré told the SEC?

A. No.

Q. And you don't dispute, sir, that the SEC made a similar attempt to ask Mr. Fauré to come to trial, the same as your lawyers, correct?

A. I have no reason to dispute that.

Q. Okay.

MS. FOLENA: Your Honor, nothing further at this time.

RECROSS EXAMINATION
[By Mr. Melsheimer, Attorney for Mr. Cuban]

Q. Mr. Cuban, Mr. McKinney is your stockbroker?

A. Yes, he is.

Q. You were asked questions about whether he had discretionary authority over your trading accounts?

A. Yes, I was.

Q. Do you understand that to mean whether he can make decisions on investments without consulting with you?

A. Yes, I do.

Q. And he does not have such authority, does he, sir?

A. No, he does not.

Q. Mr. Cuban, have you ever told anyone in the world that Mr. McKinney is the one who made the decision to sell your Mamma stock?

A. No, sir.

Q. ... Who made that decision?

A. I did.

Q. All right. Is that what you told the SEC ... when you sat down with them on the phone ... on June 30th, 2004?

A. Yes, sir....

Q. Mr. Cuban, you were asked about whether or not you said what Mr. Fauré claims in his videotape that "Now I'm screwed. I can't sell." Do you remember him saying that?

A. Yes.

Q. And you said, absolutely not, I did not say that?

A. Correct.

Q. Why, sir, are you so confident you didn't say that if you can't remember the details of the conversation?

A. ... There's a lot of things I know I just wouldn't possibly say just in life and business in general. I'm not going to agree to keep something confidential when I don't know the content or the context. I'm not going to agree to do an oral agreement for all the reasons I mentioned before. It will come back to haunt me. It just doesn't make good business sense.

Q. What about an agreement to restrain or restrict the trading of your stock?

A   ... I told him I was going to sell. He knew I was going to sell....

MS. FOLENA: Your Honor, that concludes the government's case in chief....

THE COURT: Does the plaintiff rest at this time?

MS. FOLENA: Yes, we do. Plaintiff rests.

THE COURT: Members of the jury, the plaintiff has rested its case....

[2] Mr. Cuban Moves for a Directed Verdict

After the SEC presented its case, Mr. Cuban moved for a directed verdict pursuant to Rule 50(a) of the Federal Rules of Civil Procedure. Generally, after a party is fully heard during a jury trial, the opposing party under Rule 50(a) may make a motion for judgment in its favor as a matter of law. This motion frequently is made at the end of the plaintiff's presentation of its case as was the situation in the Cuban trial. *Representing Mr. Cuban, an excerpt of Mr. Melsheimer's argument requesting that the district court grant judgment as a matter of law follows.*

(Jury exits the courtroom.)

THE COURT: Be seated, please.

Who wishes to be heard?

Mr. Melsheimer?

MR. MELSHEIMER: Briefly, Your Honor.

May it please the court.

Defendant, Mark Cuban, makes a motion pursuant to Rule 50(a) of the Federal Rules of Civil Procedure. We are going to submit ... a brief on this issue, but I will simply summarize orally what the basis for the Rule 50(a) motion is, reflecting having been made at the close of the government's case. There are ... at least two reasons or issues that are essential to the SEC's insider trading claim here, to which no legally sufficient basis exists for a reasonable jury to find in the government's favor.

To establish its claim the government must prove by a preponderance of the evidence, among other things, that Mr. Cuban received confidential information from Mamma about its PIPE transaction that was, one, material, and two, that Mr. Cuban agreed to keep the information confidential and agreed not to trade on it. Based on the evidence adduced, no reasonable jury could find in favor of the government on these issues.

First, the SEC has presented no evidence that the information Mr. Fauré gave Mr. Cuban was material.

Second, while Mr. Cuban was given additional information by Arnold Owen, Mamma's placement agent, the SEC has presented no evidence that any of that information was the subject of any confidentiality or non-use agreement entered into by Mr. Cuban and Mamma....

Because the government's claim can be only maintained if the jury makes a finding favorable to the SEC on these issues, ... judgment in Mr. Cuban's favor is warranted, and we would request that the court enter judgment pursuant to Federal Rule of Civil Procedure 50(a).

As I said at the outset, Your Honor, we will submit a brief in writing to the court citing both the evidence, or lack of evidence, as well as the legal authorities upon which we rely.

THE COURT: Thank you, Mr. Melsheimer.

The motion is denied without prejudice to reconsideration after the verdict, if necessary. [emphasis supplied]

First, the court in ruling on a Rule 50(a) motion is to view the evidence and draw all reasonable inferences in favor of the party on whom the burden of proof has been placed, which in this case is the plaintiff, Securities and Exchange Commission. Viewing the evidence under the applicable standard, the court denies the motion.

Alternatively, it is the preferred approach in the Fifth Circuit for the court to submit the case to the jury and then re-examine the verdict after it is returned, if necessary. . . .

As Mr. Melsheimer informed the court, Mr. Cuban subsequently filed a memorandum in support of his motion for judgment as a matter of law. As summarized therein:

> In sum, none of the information provided to Mr. Cuban by Mr. Fauré and Mr. Owen can support an insider trading claim because none of that information was **both** material information **and** subject to confidentiality and no-trade agreements. Because the SEC's claim can only be maintained if the jury makes a finding favorable to the SEC on these issues . . . , judgment in Mr. Cuban's favor is warranted. Mr. Cuban respectfully requests that this Court enter judgment, pursuant to Fed. R. Civ. P. 50(a), dismissing the SEC's claim against him.[8]

The district court denied Mr. Cuban's motion.

[3] Mr. Cuban Presents His Defense

After Judge Fitzwater denied his motion for judgment as a matter of law, Mr. Cuban proceeded to present his defense. The first witness called was Mr. Cuban's stockholder who placed the Mamma.com stock sales, Mr. Charles McKinney.

[8.] Memorandum of Law of Defendant Mark Cuban In Support of His Motion for Judgment As A Matter of Law at page 2 (Oct. 7, 2013) (emphasis in original).

[a] Testimony of Mr. Charles McKinney

The testimony of Mr. Charles McKinney follows.

DIRECT EXAMINATION
[By Mr. Melsheimer, Attorney for Mr. Cuban]

Q. This is probably an obvious question, Mr. McKinney, but have you ever testified in court before?

A. Not like this, no. . . .

Q. Let's focus back in 2004, sir.

Did you get investment proposals . . . for Mr. Cuban back in 2004?

A. Yes.

Q. And were you asked to . . . get Mr. Cuban to enter into nondisclosure or confidentiality agreements?

A. Yes. All the time.

Q. Now, . . . when you have an investment opportunity . . . when you had one back in 2004, someone wanting Mr. Cuban to invest, how would you handle that?

What would you do?

Would you reach out to him?

A. Usually I would tell . . . the guy trying to raise the money that Mark doesn't sign NDAs, nondisclosure agreements.

Q. And in your experience working with Mr. Cuban, when he's asked to sign a non-disclosure or confidentiality agreement, does he have a general response or approach?

A. Very much no.

Q. That he will not sign them?

A. Yes. . . .

Q. But when you say mostly or typically he will not sign a nondisclosure agreement or confidentiality agreement, have there been circumstances and were there such circumstances in 2004 when Mr. Cuban would consider signing a nondisclosure agreement?

A. I'm sure.

Q. Let me ask you, . . . back in the 2004 time frame did Mr. Cuban have a process for reviewing those nondisclosure agreements?

A. Yeah. Mr. Robert Hart, his in-house counsel, would review them.

Q. Okay. And who is Mr. Hart again?

A. Mr. Hart is Mark's in-house counsel. I think that's what you call it.

Q. Mr. McKinney, to your knowledge, has Mr. Cuban ever entered into a nondisclosure agreement without Mr. Hart having reviewed it first, to your knowledge?

A. To my knowledge, no.

Q. To your knowledge, has Mr. Cuban ever agreed to an oral non-disclosure or confidentiality agreement?

A. Not that I know of. . . .

Q. Mr. McKinney, to your recollection did Johnny C. [Ciaramitaro] or anyone at [UBS] compliance raise any concerns with you about Mr. Cuban's sale of his Mamma stock?

A. No.

Q. Mr. McKinney, what, if anything, could have been done to remedy the situation if there had been a problem with Mr. Cuban's sale of his Mamma stock?

A. Well, say, if Johnny had come back to me and said, you know, something's wrong, we'd probably talk to one of Mark's lawyers and try to see if we could unwind the trade or something like that.

Q. What does it mean to unwind the trade?

A. Well, sometimes, trades are done when they shouldn't have been done ... [A stock trade] ... actually doesn't finalize for three days, and in that time period you can unwind the trade.

Q. When you sell a stock is it final the moment you sell it?

A. No. I mean, it's not. It's got to settle....

Q. What's "T plus 3"?

A. Trade day plus three. So by the third day the shares actually trade hands and cash trades hands. So if you make a sale today you don't get your money for three days, or the proceeds.

Q. That period of when the sale is started or executed and plus three days when you get your money, is that the period you're talking about in which a trade could in theory be unwound?

A. It ... could. Yes....

Q. On ... June 30th was ... Mr. Cuban's sale of Mamma within that window that you just described?

A. Yeah.... I think he sold on the ... if I recall, 28th or 29th....

Q. Mr. McKinney, I ... want to change subjects on you a little bit.
    You have known Mr. Cuban for 16 years?

A. That's correct.

Q. Do you know him both personally and professionally?

A. I do.

Q. Now, do you understand that the government is claiming that Mr. Cuban defrauded Mamma.com in connection with the sale of stock he owned?

A. That's my understanding....

Q. Mr. McKinney, is that allegation consistent with the opinion you have of Mr. Cuban?

        MR. THOMPSON: Objection, Your Honor.

        May we approach?

        THE COURT: You may.

        (Discussion at the bench with counsel present.)

        MR. THOMPSON [Attorney for the SEC]: Your Honor, I think I know where this line of questioning is going. It's attempting to elicit the character for the purpose of proving that Mr. Cuban acted in conformity with this character. That is strictly forbidden by Rule 404. [See Rule 404(a) of the Federal Rules of Evidence: "Evidence of a person's character or character trait is not admissible to prove that on a particular occasion the person acted in accordance with the character or trait."] There is no applicable exception. Mr. Cuban's reputation or his character for truthfulness has not been attacked in this case. The case law is clear, and I have Fifth Circuit precedent that merely challenging the defendant's veracity in the suit and what he says in that suit does not constitute an attack on his reputation or character for truthfulness or untruthfulness.

MR. MELSHEIMER: He's being sued. So they're suing him for fraud, and I think they are attacking him. This witness is entitled to offer an opinion of reputation based on his knowledge of Mr. Cuban, and that's what we intend to elicit.

THE COURT: ... If you have some [support] in a civil case I'll reconsider it, but absent that, I'm going to sustain the objection.

MR. MELSHEIMER: Okay.... As to any reputation or opinion testimony from this witness about Mr. Cuban?

I just want to make sure I don't run afoul of the court's ruling.

THE COURT: Exactly on general character type.

MR. THOMPSON: Thank you, Your Honor.

(Back in open court in the hearing of the jury.)

THE COURT: The objection is sustained.

BY MR. MELSHEIMER:

Q. Mr. McKinney, remind us how many trades you and your team have done for Mr. Cuban over the years.

A. We figured out 16 years, 260 business days a ... year, an average of ten trades a day, could be 20, but that's 40,000 trades. More than 40,000 trades.

Q. Mr. McKinney, how would you characterize Mr. Cuban's investment approach?

A. Extremely conservative.

Q. What do you mean by that?

A. ... [M]ost of his portfolio is in things like municipal bonds which finance roads and sewage and water and hospitals and ... things that have low returns, returns in the 3 to 4 percent range.... It's not high-risk I-want-to-get-rich type investments.

Q. Does Mr. Cuban always make money on the investments he's made with you or your firms?

A. No. No, he does not.

Q. I don't want to bring up bad memories, Mr. McKinney, but what are some examples of some losses that Mr. Cuban has experienced with investments you and he have worked on?

MR. THOMPSON: Objection, Your Honor. Relevance.

THE COURT: Overruled.

A. One of the worst was [when] he went with a trade with a Russell 2000, which is an index .... In that trade, he lost 26 million dollars. He's lost 12 million doing the same kind of trade in the Dow Jones, which is the 30 biggest companies.

He ... traded in Google and lost 12 million.

Last week ... yeah. Last week he closed a position with JC Penny where he lost over five million dollars....

Q. You're not suggesting Mr. Cuban needs a new stockbroker, are you?

A. No....

Q. As Mr. Cuban's financial advisor for over 16 years, have you ever seen Mr. Cuban do anything improper to avoid a loss in an investment?

MR. THOMPSON: Objection, Your Honor.

THE COURT: State the basis.

MR. THOMPSON: Rule 404.

THE COURT: Overruled as long as we don't get broader into character.

Q. ... I'll ask it again.

In the 16 years you've been Mr. Cuban's financial advisor, have you ever seen him do anything improper to avoid a loss in an investment?

A. Never.

MR. THOMPSON: Same objection.

THE COURT: All right. Overruled....

MR. MELSHEIMER: Your Honor, we tender the witness for cross-examination.

THE COURT: All right. Cross-examination.

You may proceed, counsel....

CROSS EXAMINATION
[By Mr. Thompson, Attorney for the SEC]

Q. You never actually spoke with Mr. Cuban in 2004 about possibly unwinding his trade of Mamma stock, did you?

A. I did not.

Q. And you had never unwound any securities trade for Mr. Cuban, had you?

A. In 2004 or ever?

Q. As of 2004.

A. No. No....

Q. ... Mr. Melsheimer showed you the letter by which Mamma hired Merriman Curhan Ford & Company to be its placement agent, correct?

A. Correct.

Q. And that letter was attached to the Mamma 20-F?

A. Yes.

Q. And you agreed ... with Mr. Melsheimer that once a report is filed with the SEC it becomes public, correct?

A. Correct.

Q. And you're saying that the engagement letter also becomes public, correct?

A. Yes. It was attached to the 20-F.

Q. Just so the jury is clear, Mr. McKinney, you're not saying that the terms of the Mamma PIPE, the PIPE that would later be announced on June 29th, 2004, became public by virtue of the publication of the engagement letter on May 27, 2004?

You're not saying that, are you?

A. That's correct.

Q. You're not saying that?

A. I'm not saying that.

Q. ... [T]oday I believe you indicated that as Mr. Cuban's broker you viewed it as part of your job and your team's job to try to keep abreast of news that might affect stocks that your clients hold, correct?

A. That's correct.

Q. But isn't it correct, sir, that you were not aware of the Mamma PIPE until the public announcement on June 29th ....

A. That's correct.

Q. ... 2004?

A. That's correct.

Q. So either you weren't doing your job or the information wasn't public before the press release; is that correct?

A. Well, ... I believe it was public. You could say I didn't do my job. I can give you reasons why I think that happened.

Q. You were not aware of the PIPE information until the press release was issued; is that correct, sir?

A. That's correct.

Q. And you made every effort and your team made every effort to keep abreast of developments affecting the stock that Mr. Cuban held, didn't you?

A. I can't say we made every effort.... That's an unfair claim.

Q. You made an effort. That was part of your job, right?

A. It sure was.

Q. And you were big boys; you were a major brokerage firm?

A. We were. UBS didn't have coverage of Mamma.com. So usually what happens is we rely on our research department to help us with that....

Q. In looking back at what the engagement letter [between Mamma.com and Merriman] says, in the second line ... do you see it says "We will provide investment banking services to the company which may include," and then it goes on with a whole list of options?
    Do you see that, sir?

A. Yes.

Q. So it's not saying any of those things would actually be done, is it?

A. No. It gives them the right to start working on that.

Q. .... Mr. McKinney, did you have a conversation with Mr. Cuban on June 29, 2004, about the press release being issued announcing the Mamma PIPE?

A. I don't ... know.

Q. You're ... a blank slate on that?

A. Correct.

Q. You have no recollection one way or the other?

A. Correct. That was nine years ago.

Q. Let me ask you this, sir.
    Did Mr. Cuban tell you at any time prior to the public announcement of a Mamma PIPE that he was going to sell his shares in Mamma?

A. No....

Q. I'd like to ask you a few follow-up questions.

This is the email that Mr. Cuban sent to you on June 30 regarding Mamma; is that correct?

A. Yes.

Q. And this would be after Mr. Cuban sold his shares in the company; is that also correct?

A. That is correct.

Q. And Mr. Cuban asked you in the email to make sure that all was cool with the transaction, right?

A. Yeah, he did.

Q. Mr. McKinney, you don't have any memory of ever actually discussing this email with Mr. Cuban, do you?

A. That's correct.

Q. None whatsoever.

A. That's correct.

Q. You don't even know if you ever discussed the subject matter of this email with Mr. Cuban, do you?

A. That's correct.

Q. In fact, you can't even say that you ever discussed with Mr. Cuban the Mamma PIPE, can you?

A. Well, not at this point, not at this time.

Q. Let's look at ... what Mr. Cuban said in his email to you.

First of all, is there anything in the email that refers to a conversation between you and Mr. Cuban regarding the press release on the Mamma PIPE?

A. No....

Q. Do you know why Mr. Cuban didn't start his email by saying something like "as we discussed"?

A. I have no idea.

Q. Let's look at what Mr. Cuban does say in his email.

Just to be clear, sir, you have no recollection of actually receiving the email, do you?

A. That is correct. I mean, can I add to that?

Obviously I did. We talked about this in the deposition. It's from him to me.

Q. Mr. McKinney, I'm going to ask that you just answer my questions, please.... [Mr. Cuban's attorney] Mr. Melsheimer will have an opportunity to ask you additional questions ....

A. Okay....

Q. Do you see where Mr. Cuban starts the email by saying, "CM, I want to make sure I was 100 percent kosher" or 100 pct on that trade. Do you see that?

A. Yes, I do.

Q. And you would agree that "100 Pct" means 100 percent, right?

A. Yes.

Q. And you would agree that "kosher" means legal, wouldn't you?

A. Yeah. Yeah. He ... did everything right.

Q. So Mr. Cuban was asking you whether he insider traded, correct?

A.   No. You can't say that.

Q.   Mr. Cuban was asking you whether his trade was legal, you would agree with that, wouldn't you, sir?

A.   Yeah.

Q.   Now, Mr. Cuban had never before asked you to check on the legality of one of his trades that you did for him at UBS, had he?

A.   I can't confirm that. I can say I don't remember it.

Q.   You don't remember any such event?

A.   Yeah. Correct.

Q.   Mr. Cuban goes on to talk about his conversation with the sales representative, and I'll represent to you, sir, that the sales representative that Mr. Cuban was talking about was ... Arnie Owen. Does that sound correct to you, sir?

A.   I think I've read that in some emails....

Q.   Mr. McKinney, you don't have any personal knowledge of a phone conversation between Mr. Cuban and Mr. Guy Fauré on June 28, 2004, do you?

A.   I do not.

Q.   So you have no personal knowledge of whether Mr. Fauré told Mr. Cuban that the PIPE information was confidential, correct?

A.   Correct.

Q.   And you have no personal knowledge of whether Mr. Cuban agreed to keep the PIPE information confidential, do you?

A.   That's correct.

Q.   Were you aware that Mr. Fauré has testified that Mr. Cuban said on his phone call with Mr. Cuban on June 28, 2004, "Now I'm screwed. I can't sell," or words to that effect?

         MR. MELSHEIMER: ... I'm going to object to improper comparison of testimony.

         THE COURT: Sustained.

BY MR. THOMPSON:

Q.   Mr. Cuban's email doesn't say he told the sales rep [Mr. Owen] that he would sell before the public announcement, does it?

A.   No.

Q.   And it also doesn't say that he told Guy Fauré that he would sell before the public announcement, does it?

A.   It does not.

Q.   Now, Mr. Cuban's email does express concern or indicates that he expressed concern that the PIPE might be some type of scam. Would you agree with that, sir?

A.   I would.

Q.   But just so it's clear, you don't have any recollection of ever discussing the individual named Irving Kott with Mr. Cuban; is that right, sir?

A.   That's correct. It's in the email though.

Q.   So if Mr. Cuban thought that Irving Kott was somehow behind the Mamma PIPE he didn't feel the need to discuss it with you as a broker managing hundreds of millions of dollars of his money: is that right?

A. I can't tell you what he was thinking.

Q. Sir, I'm going to now ask you to look at Plaintiff's Exhibit 193. And this is in evidence.

This is the email by which you forwarded Mr. Cuban's email to you to Johnny C. That hard to pronounce name, Mr. Ciaramitaro, correct?

Did I get that right?

A. You got it right.

Q. All right. Now, all you said in your email was "See below ... Thanks." Is that correct?

A. Yes....

Q. You didn't ask Mr. Ciaramitaro to provide any type of legal review, did you?

A   No.

Q. And was Mr. Ciaramitaro even a lawyer, sir?

A. No. He was compliance manager [at UBS]....

Q. So you didn't ask Mr. Ciaramitaro to do anything in particular; is that right?

A. No, you cannot say that.... [T]his is me, a broker, telling him to take a look at this and follow the instructions, make sure it's kosher.

Q. Well, sir, you don't know whether he did anything in particular, do you?

A. That's correct. I do not know.

Q. You didn't follow-up to see whether he did anything in particular, did you?

A. I didn't feel like I needed to.

Q. The question is you never did that, you never followed up:?

A. Correct. Correct....

Q. And you never got an email back from Mr. Ciaramitaro?

A. That is correct.

Q. Now, sir, isn't it also true that at the time you sent the email to Mr. Ciaramitaro saying "See below ... Thanks. Charley," you had no idea what procedures, if any, UBS had to respond to a client's request to make sure all is cool with a transaction? That's true, isn't it, sir?

A. Specific procedures?

Q. That's true, sir, is it not?

A. Yeah, ... that's true. You have a lot of confidence in the people you work with though.

Q. Well, sir, isn't it true any testimony on your part about what, if anything, may have been done in response to your sending an email to Mr. Ciaramitaro saying "See below ... Thanks," would be pure speculation?

A. I guess. Legally, the way y'all talk, I guess so.

Q. But you do know Mr. Cuban never before asked you to have UBS check on the legality of one of his stock trades, right?

A. Again, I said I don't remember if he did.

Q. Mr. McKinney, you know that Mr. Cuban likes to communicate by email, don't you?

A. Sure. Everyone does.

Q. But you never sent Mr. Cuban a response to the email that he sent to you about making sure all was kosher with his trade of Mamma stock before the public announcement, did you?

A. That's correct.

Q. And you weren't in the habit of simply ignoring Mr. Cuban's requests, were you?

A. No. Of course not.

Q. And if I asked you, sir, whether Mr. Cuban ever said to you with a wink and a nod, Charley, you know, I don't really expect you to get back with me on this email, it's just something I need to send to you, you wouldn't be able to say, hell, no that never happened, would you?

A. Yeah, I would.

Q. You would be able to say that?

A. That he looked at me, winked and nod[ded] and said ....

Q. Or in some manner indicated to you that you didn't need to respond to the email, you wouldn't be able to ... deny that one way or the other, would you, sir?

A. Yeah. He's never winked and nodded to me to say something like what you just said. That's ridiculous.

Q. Let's look at what you said in your deposition, sir. Do you recall you gave a deposition in this case?

A. I do.

Q. And do you recall that you raised your hand and you swore an oath to tell the truth, just like you did just now?

A. Of course, yes....

Q. Mr. McKinney, I'm going to show you videotape of that deposition at pages 108, line 19 to 109, line 9, and then I'll have some additional questions for you.

(Video playing.)

"Q. I take it you don't recall whether Mr. Cuban ever asked you to report back to him?

"A. I don't remember.

"Q. Did Mr. Cuban ever say to you, with a wink and a nod that I don't really expect you to get back to me on this?

"A. I don't remember.

"Q. I'm sorry?

"A. I don't remember."

(Video stopped.)

THE WITNESS: I have no problem with that and how I just answered that question.

BY MR. THOMPSON:

Q. That was your testimony back when you gave your deposition, wasn't it, sir?

A. Yeah.

Q. Now, Mr. McKinney, approximately how much money do you currently manage for Mr. Cuban in your capacity as his broker at Credit Suisse?

A. 695 million dollars round numbers.

Q. Rounding up to round numbers, right?

A. Pardon me. Yeah. Sometimes it's more, sometimes it's less.

Q. And Mr. Cuban pays a lot of commissions ... is that right?

A. A lot, define that. He pays market rate, yes....

Q. And did we also figure out that translated to something like two and a half to four and a half million dollars a year?

A. Yes. Round numbers.

Q. And did we also figure out that you got a sizable cut of that money, correct?

A. Yes, I do....

Q. And you've been earning a substantial amount of money as a result of your work as Mr. Cuban's broker since 1999; is that right?

A. '97....

Q. Is it fair to say, sir, that you would expect if you continue to be Mr. Cuban's broker through the end of your career you will earn a substantial amount of money as a result of commissions that he pays to your firms?

A. Yeah. Sure. Yes.

Q. Now, yesterday you also testified that you have a certain reputation for being Mr. Cuban's long-term financial advisor; is that right?

A. That's correct.

Q. And you would agree that there's a certain amount of prestige that goes along with that?

A. From I would say most people, absolutely.
I'm proud of it.

Q. And do you think, sir, that you would still be Mr. Cuban's broker tomorrow if you came in here and told the jury that he insider-traded?
    MR. MELSHEIMER: Your Honor, I'm going to object as argumentative.
    THE COURT: Overruled....
    THE WITNESS: I don't know what he would do.

BY MR. THOMPSON:

. . . .

Q. ... You don't want to put to the test whether or not if you came in here today and told this jury some facts that might indicate he insider-traded you would still be his broker tomorrow, do you, sir?

A. That is incorrect. If I thought that, I would tell the truth, without a doubt, sir....

Q. You also testified, Mr. McKinney, that you have not seen Mr. Cuban make any improper trades in his various accounts. That's your testimony, right?

A. Yes, it is.

Q. That doesn't mean that he hasn't made any improper trades, does it?

A. Not with me.

Q. You don't know everything Mr. Cuban has done, do you?

A. Of course not.

Q. You don't know whether he's made any improper trades in his lifetime, do you?

A. With me, correct. I mean, with me I know he hasn't.

Q. ... [Y]ou don't know what was said as between Mr. Cuban and Guy Fauré on June 28th, 2004, do you, sir?

A. That is correct.

Q. And you don't know with respect to trades that you have executed for Mr. Cuban what conversations he may have had with third parties, do you?

A.   I would agree with that.

Q.   So you can't sit here today and tell this jury that you can guarantee that Mr. Cuban has never made any improper trades, can you, sir?

A.   Of course not.

Q.   I want to go back to your testimony about unwinding trades. Do you remember that testimony, sir?

A.   I do.

Q.   Now, you're a broker, correct?

A.   Yes.

Q.   And you're licensed to sell securities?

A.   Yes.

Q.   And you know that insider trading is illegal, don't you, sir?

A.   Yes.

Q.   And you're not saying to this jury that reversing a trade reverses the illegality of insider trading, are you, sir?

A.   I don't know.

Q.   You're not a lawyer?

A.   No, I'm not a lawyer.

Q.   So you're not saying that?

A.   No.

Q.   I mean, you're not saying that it would be like if ... a bank robber giving back the money after the fact and saying, well, no harm, no foul. You're not telling this jury that, are you?

    MR. MELSHEIMER: Just one moment.

    I would object as argumentative.

    THE COURT: Sustained.

BY MR. THOMPSON:

Q.   Just so the record is absolutely clear, you did testify about procedures for unwinding a trade and you explained the trading window and all of that, but, sir, Mr. Cuban never asked you to unwind this trade, did he?

A.   No, he did not.

    MR. THOMPSON: I have nothing further at this time, Your Honor.

    THE COURT: Redirect?

    MR. MELSHEIMER: Briefly, Your Honor

REDIRECT EXAMINATION

[By Mr. Melsheimer, Attorney for Mr. Cuban]

Q.   You never told [Mr. Cuban] there was any reason to unwind the trade, did you, sir?

A.   No.

Q.   And no one at UBS got back to you and told you that there was any issue with the trade?

A.   That's correct.

Q. Based on your experience with compliance at UBS would it have been your expectation back in 2004 that if there had been a problem that someone would have gotten back to you?

A. Yes.

> MR. THOMPSON: Objection, Your Honor. Speculation.
> THE COURT: He's asking based on his actual experience, so I'll overrule.
> MR. THOMPSON: He's also leading.
> THE COURT: Overruled.

. . . .

BY MR. MELSHEIMER:

Q. Based . . . on your experience . . . and based on the compensation that Merriman is going to be receiving [pursuant to the Mamma.com-Merriman engagement letter], what is Merriman going to be out in the marketplace doing in March of 2004?

> MR. THOMPSON: Objection, Your Honor. There's no foundation here.
> THE COURT: Okay. Overruled.
> THE WITNESS: This is . . . an engagement letter that allows them to do a PIPE. We know they did a PIPE. . . . [T]hey're doing a PIPE. It's right here, in black and white. They're . . . getting a fee for it. It's the very first thing in capital raising that they're talking about. . . . Merriman is going to get warrants for putting this deal together. It's . . . what it is. . . .

Q. You were asked some questions about whether or not you recall whether Mr. Cuban ever mentioned Irving Kott to you?

A. Correct.

Q. Mr. McKinney, did he send you an email about Irving Kott?

A. He did.

Q. Is that Exhibit 50?

A. Yes.

Q. Can we look at it again?

A. Sure.

Q. On March 13th, 2004, Mr. Cuban emailed you and says "Also, read on a message board, which of course means this is total BS, but said the company was, and could still be related to a bucketshop crook named Irving Kott."

> So is there any doubt in your mind that Mr. Cuban mentioned Irving Kott to you way back in March of 2004?

A. There's no question. . . .

Q. . . . I think you've told us you don't actually remember this. And tell the jury why you don't remember something that happened nine years ago?

A. Well, it's nine years ago. . . .

> There are literally a million emails that I've received between then and now. You just . . . don't remember. I don't know what I had for dinner then, but I know I had dinner.

Q. Mr. McKinney, towards the end of your examination before the break did you get the sense that the government was suggesting to you that you would come in here and lie for Mr. Cuban?

A. That's what my sense was.

Q. Did that upset you?

A. Well, yeah, It's integrity.

Q. Why did it upset you, sir?

A. ... I've been in Dallas my whole life. Integrity is everything I have.

Q. Mr. McKinney, would you come in here and lie?

A. Never.

Q. Have you made yourself available to the government to be interviewed in preparation for your trial testimony?

A. I have.

Q. Did they tell you that ... they were going to call you as a witness?

A. They talked to my counsel and said that they ... wanted to meet with me.

Q. Did you make arrangements to meet with them on multiple occasions?

A. Twice.

Q. Did they ever take you up on your offer to meet with them?

A. They cancelled both times.

Q. Did they tell you why they were canceling?

A. No.

Q. Mr. McKinney, has Mr. Cuban spoken one word to you in preparation for this trial about a syllable of your testimony?

A. Zero.

Q. Mr. McKinney, the government may have some more questions of you, but I do not have any more questions.

   Thank you.

   THE COURT: Recross?

   MR. THOMPSON: Briefly, Your Honor.

RECROSS EXAMINATION
[By Mr. Thompson, Attorney for the SEC]

Q. When you talk about "confidence," do you believe that Mr. Cuban has confidence in you?

A. Most of the time, sure.

Q. And you're loyal to Mr. Cuban, aren't you?

A. I am.

Q. And you wouldn't want to do anything to harm Mr. Cuban's interest, would you, sir?

A. Of course not.

   MR. THOMPSON: I have nothing further, Your Honor.

[b] Testimony of Mr. Daniel Bertrand

Mr. Daniel Bertrand, who served as the chief financial officer (CFO) of Mamma.com was called to testify. Like other Mamma.com executives, Mr. Bertrand testified by video deposition. *Mr. Bertrand's testimony follows.*

MR. MELSHEIMER: Your Honor, at this time we're going to call by video deposition Daniel Bertrand who is the chief financial officer of Mamma....

This witness speaks [French] through a translator, a certified translator, and so there's . . . some back and forth in the deposition. I just don't know if you want to address that with the jury....

THE COURT: For my purposes of the instruction, was there any objection to the quality of the translation?

MR. MELSHEIMER: No, Your Honor.

THE COURT: All right. Members of the jury, the witness is going to be testifying through a translator, and interpreter, and there is no objection to the quality of the interpretation. So the answers given by the interpreter are certified to be the true answers of the witness....

(Video playing.)

DIRECT EXAMINATION

[By Mr. Best, Attorney for Mr. Cuban]

Q. Please state your name.

THE WITNESS (Through interpreter): Daniel Bertrand.

Q. Mr. Bertrand, are you Canadian?

THE WITNESS (Through interpreter): Yes, I am....

Q. Now, focus your attention, sir, on the year 2004, if you would. And for starters, in that year who did you report to?

THE WITNESS (Through interpreter): I reported to Guy Fauré, who was the company's CEO.

Q. And did you know a gentleman by the name of David Goldman as well?

THE WITNESS (Through interpreter): Yes, Mr. Goldman, the executive chairman of Mamma.com.

Q. And was he somebody that you regularly interfaced with as well as Mr. Fauré?

THE WITNESS (Through interpreter): Yes.

Q. Now, did you come to participate in a discussion at Mamma about the PIPE the day before the PIPE, June 28th?

THE WITNESS (Through interpreter): Yes.

Q. And could you tell us what that discussion was?

THE WITNESS (Through interpreter): During that discussion we talked about the possibility of communicating with Mr. Mark Cuban and to signify to him that the company was in the course of making a transaction....

Q. And who participated as you recall in that discussion?

THE WITNESS (Through interpreter): A few members of the board.

Q.   And did that include Mr. David Goldman?

THE WITNESS (Through interpreter): Yes.

Q.   And Mr. Guy Fauré?

THE WITNESS (Through interpreter): Yes.

Q.   And you were present for that discussion as well?

THE WITNESS (Through interpreter): Yes.

Q.   ... [Y]ou do recall that there was discussion about Mr. Mark Cuban during this in-person meeting....?

THE WITNESS (Through interpreter): Yes.

Q.   What was said about Mr. Mark Cuban?

THE WITNESS (Through interpreter): There were discussions mentioning the fact that we should communicate with Mr. Cuban and offering him the possibility of investing in the PIPE.

Q.   Was there a discussion about why the communication should be had?

THE WITNESS (Through interpreter): Well, yes, taking into account that Mr. Cuban was Mamma.com's major shareholder.

Q.   And was a decision made as to whether to contact Mr. Cuban?

THE WITNESS (Through interpreter): Yes....

Q.   And was anything decided or discussed about who should contact Mr. Cuban?

THE WITNESS (Through interpreter): Yes. It was decided that Guy Fauré, the company CEO, should communicate with Mr. Cuban.

Q.   Do you recall any discussion as to why Mr. Fauré should be the person?

THE WITNESS (Through interpreter): Considering the fact that Mr. Fauré was the CEO and the person who represented the company, and I am not sure, but I believe that Mr. Fauré ... had already had communications with Mr. Cuban in the past.

Q.   Okay. And what was Mr. Fauré told with respect to contacting Mr. Cuban?

THE WITNESS (Through interpreter): We mentioned to Mr. Fauré that he had to let Mr. Cuban know that this information was confidential, to ask him whether he was interested in participating in the PIPE project. That's it.

Q.   Prior to June 28, 2004, had the company used written non-disclosure agreements with any third parties in discussions leading up to any business opportunities?

THE WITNESS (Through interpreter): Yes, we have a standard non-disclosure form....

Q.   ... [D]id any of the members of the board of directors discuss using Mamma. com's standard non-disclosure agreement in Guy Fauré's discussions ... with Mark Cuban?

THE WITNESS (Through interpreter): No....

Q.   Let me go to the specific instructions.

Was Mr. Fauré instructed to ask Mr. Cuban to agree to maintain the confidentiality of the information?

THE WITNESS (Through interpreter): Not to my knowledge.

Q.   Was Mr. Fauré instructed to ask Mr. Cuban to restrict his trading in Mamma.com securities?

THE WITNESS (Through interpreter): Not to my knowledge.

Q. Was Mr. Fauré instructed to ask Mr. Cuban to agree to obligate himself in any way as regards the information Guy wished to share?

THE WITNESS (Through interpreter): Not to my knowledge.

Q. Let me turn now to later in the day on June 28th, 2004.

Do you recall Mr. Fauré speaking to you and Mr. Goldman about the details of his conversation with Mr. Cuban?

THE WITNESS (Through interpreter): Yes.

Q. Did Mr. Fauré say when he spoke to you on June 28th that Mr. Cuban ever stated on the phone call that he agreed to maintain the confidentiality of the information?

THE WITNESS (Through interpreter): No, I do not recall his having confirmed that.

Q. Again, going back to this conversation with Mr. Fauré that you were present for on June 28th, did Mr. Fauré say that Mr. Cuban ever stated on the call that he agreed to restrict his trading in Mamma.com securities?

THE WITNESS (Through interpreter): No, I do not recall him having said that.

Q. Indeed, you recall Mr. Fauré stating to you and to Mr. Goldman that Mark Cuban will sell his shares of Mamma.com?

THE WITNESS (Through interpreter): Yes.

Q. Do you recall Mr. Fauré stating that Mr. Cuban qualified his statement about selling his shares in any way, shape or form?

THE WITNESS (Through interpreter): No, I recall nothing about that.

MR. BEST [Attorney for Mr. Cuban]: Thank you, Your Honor. That concludes our direct examination by videotape.

MR. SCHULTZ [Attorney for the SEC]: Your Honor, the SEC has some cross-examination. . . .

CROSS EXAMINATION
[By Mr. O'Rourke for the SEC]

(Video playing.)

Q. . . . [W]hat was your understanding about how information about the PIPE was treated at Mamma.com?

THE WITNESS (Through interpreter): This information was considered as being confidential, and we treated them in that way.

Q. And did that remain true up until the PIPE was publicly announced on June 29th, 2004?

THE WITNESS (Through interpreter): Yes. To my knowledge, yes.

Q. Mr. Bertrand, I show you what previously was marked as Plaintiff's Exhibit 43, bearing the Mamma production Bates number at the time it was produced in the SEC's investigation . . . And my question to you is: Are you familiar with this email?

THE WITNESS (Through interpreter): Yes.

Q.   And is this an email that Mr. Goldman sent to you and the members of the board on June 28th, 2004?

THE WITNESS (Through interpreter): Yes....

Q.   And calling your attention to the fifth paragraph that begins: "Today, after much discussion, Guy spoke to Mark Cuban."

Do you see that paragraph?

THE WITNESS (Through interpreter): Yes.

Q.   Did you understand that to refer to the discussion with Mark Cuban that you told us about before the break?

THE WITNESS (Through interpreter): Yes....

Q.   It says: "We did speak to Mark Cuban, Guy, and subsequently our investment manager to find out if he had any interest in participating to the extent of maintaining his interest."

Do you see that?

THE WITNESS (Through interpreter): Yes.

Q.   And did I read it correctly so far?

THE WITNESS (Through interpreter): Yes.

Q.   And then it goes on to say: "His answers were: He would not invest, he does not want the company to make acquisitions. He will sell his shares, which he cannot do until after we announce."

And did I read that correctly?

THE WITNESS (Through interpreter): Yes....

Q.   Subsequently, did there come a point in time that you learned that Mr. Cuban sold his shares prior to the public announcement?

THE WITNESS (Through interpreter): Yes....

Q.   And what was your reaction?

Did you have a reaction?

THE WITNESS (Through interpreter): I was surprised.

Q.   Now, in your recollections, who instructed Guy Fauré to tell Mr. Cuban that the information was confidential?

THE WITNESS (Through interpreter): I couldn't say precisely who from the board originally made the request, but I think that David Goldman reiterated the situation.

Q.   And when ... you say "reiterated," what exactly do you recall Mr. Goldman saying to Mr. Fauré?

THE WITNESS (Through interpreter): He summarized what Mr. Fauré should say to Mr. Cuban, that the information that was going to be disclosed to Mr. Cuban was confidential.

Q.   .... [W]here were you vis-a-vis Mr. Goldman when he made that statement?

THE WITNESS (Through interpreter): To the best of my knowledge, I think that we were in the conference room.

Q.   Excuse me. Do you recall Mr. Goldman instructing Mr. Fauré to tell Mr. Cuban that the confidential information was about Mamma.com?

THE WITNESS (Through interpreter): To the best of my knowledge, yes.

MR. BEST: Your Honor, I have objection to the next question.

THE COURT: Just a moment.

MR. BEST: Can we stop the video, please? May we approach?

THE COURT: Just a moment.

MR. BEST: It's for optional completeness.

THE COURT: Do you have the optional completeness?

MR. BEST: I do, Your Honor. . . .

MR. BEST: Optional completeness is this next question, the first Q and A, [SEC attorney] Mr. O'Rourke's examination of him, which follows to my question right before. . . .

THE COURT: It's your request to read this question and answer before the next section?

MR. BEST: Yes, Your Honor.

THE COURT: Do you have any objection?

MR. SCHULTZ: They have known about this. They didn't raise this offer for completeness. We probably wouldn't have agreed to . . . .

THE COURT: I'll grant your request. Go ahead and read the question and answer aloud.

(Back in court in the hearing of the jury.)

THE COURT: The way we'll proceed is counsel will read aloud a question and answer, and then we'll resume the playing to the deposition.

MR. BEST: Thank you.

For optional completeness the question to Mr. Bertrand was:

Q. Did Mr. Fauré ever say at any time that Mr. Mark Cuban specifically stated that he agreed to maintain the confidentiality of the information on the June 28th call?

Mr. Bertrand's response: "A. No."

Optional completeness.

THE COURT: You may proceed.

(Video playing.)

Q. . . . And the offer made to Mark Cuban with respect to participating in a PIPE, was that a sincere offer by the board, as you understood it?

THE WITNESS (Through interpreter): My interpretation was that, yes, it was a sincere offer. . . .

---

[c] Testimony of Mr. Mitchell Kopin

Mr. Cuban next called Mr. Mitchell Kopin to testify by videotape deposition. Mr. Kopin, representing Cranshire Capital, was one of the investors in the Mamma.com PIPE transaction. *The testimony of Mr. Kopin follows.*

MR. BEST [Attorney for Mr. Cuban]: Your Honor, by videotape the defense calls Mitchell Kopin, . . . who represents Cranshire Capital, one of the investors in Mamma.com, and it will be by videotape.

. . . .

Q. And after your time obtaining the MBA, could you summarize your employment history for us?

A. Yes. I spent a year trading futures at the Chicago Mercantile Exchange. . . .

And at the end of '95 I started up . . . Cranshire Capital, which is . . . my own fund. . . .

Q. Do you recall that there was a PIPE offering by Mamma.com in which Cranshire participated, which PIPE offering was publicly announced on June 29, 2004?

A. Yes.

Q. And do you know the name "Arnie Owen" or "Arnold Owen," who had been at Merriman?

A. Yes, I do.

Q. And did you know him previously?

A. Yes.

Q. Do you have a belief as to whether or not he would have been the person you had communications with?

A. I mean, most likely he would have been the one at Merriman that I would have spoken with.

Q. And why do you say that?

A. He was my contact over there, and he was the person that I spoke to at Merriman.

Q. And had you been involved with previous PIPES with him?

A. I believe so. . . .

Q. You have indicated that you believed it was Merriman that would have contacted you in 2004 concerning the Mamma PIPE and informed you of it. Am I correct so far?

A. Yeah, I believe that it was Merriman that would have contacted me.

Q. And would . . . that have been in June of 2004?

A. Again, I don't recall the exact date, but it's probable that it would have been June of 2004. . . .

Q. . . . [W]hat was [Cranshire Capital's] policy?

A. The policy was when we found out about a potential transaction in a company, we would add that company to our restricted list, and we would not trade on it until after the transaction was publicly announced, or we were informed that the transaction was no longer going to happen.

Q. And that's a policy that was in effect at the time of the Mamma offering?

A. That's correct.

Q. And you followed that policy with respect to Mamma?

A. Yes, we did.

Q. And when did that policy then kick in?

I know you testified, but just so I am clear here, was it when you were told about the PIPE?

A. When we were initially called and . . . we were told that Mamma was looking to raise capital, we immediately added it to our restricted list.

Q. And can you explain . . . the basis for you having this policy or why you have this policy?

A.   We put this policy into effect because ... it had come to our attention that this was an area that the Commission was looking at, and we thought it was one of these gray areas.

We did not believe that there was anything wrong with trading; however, we decided that since we didn't want to be one of the funds that was going to be called in to be talked to by the Commission, that we would try to be as conservative as possible, and we instituted a policy where we just ... were not going to do that....

MR. SHULTZ [Attorney for the SEC]: Your Honor, we have objections on clips 32 through 35, as well as clip 39 on an improper lay opinion, relevance, going to the ultimate issue of fact to a jury as well as leading questions.

And clip 39 we believe it's additionally argumentative and overbroad.

THE COURT: Would you approach the bench, please.

(Discussion at the bench with counsel present.)

. . . .

THE COURT: Ladies and gentlemen of the jury, when you hear in a few seconds testimony from Mr. Kopin that he is expressing his opinion, it is his personal belief, and that's what we are offering it for.

All right. You may proceed.

(Video playing.)

Q.   Did you have an opinion back in 2003 and '4 whether the information that you received about a prospective PIPE offering was material information?

A.   My personal opinion and my personal feelings was that it was not.

Q.   Okay. And why is that?

A.   A couple of reasons.

Number one, every one of these companies everybody knows is going to try to raise additional capital. And because ...

Q.   When you say "everyone knows" ... I'm sorry, I'm going to let you finish.

A.   Most [of] these companies in their 10-Qs [quarterly reports filed with the SEC] have lines ... that basically say this company is going to continue to raise capital. And so normally when these deals get announced it should not be a huge surprise to the marketplace, because people know ... their company has already disclosed that they're going to be raising additional capital....

Q.   Aside from your own internal policies and procedures, did Merriman Curhan & Ford restrict your use in any way, shape, or form of the information about the Mamma.com PIPE offering?

A.   Not that I'm aware of or that I can recall.

Q.   And aside from your internal policies and procedures, did anyone at Mamma. com restrict the use of your information concerning the private investment in ... the Mamma.com offering?

A.   I have no recollection of that ever happening.

Q.   Okay. Did anyone in the free world restrict your use of the information about the Mamma.com PIPE offering except you and your own internal policies and procedures?

A. Not that I recall....

> MR. BEST: Thank you, Your Honor.
>
> That concludes our direct of Mr. Kopin by video.
>
> MR. SCHULTZ: Your Honor, the SEC has cross-examination....

CROSS-EXAMINATION

(Video playing.)

Q. ... I asked you ... if you would discuss the Mamma PIPE with anyone other than Merriman or perhaps the other investors. Just to make sure I am clear or we get the best we can get here in terms of a full record, did you ever hear of the Mamma PIPE from anyone else or any other source?

A. I did not.

Q. And did you ever read about it anywhere other than the documents received as part of the transaction?

A. You are talking before the closing?

Q. Before closing.

A. No, I did not.

Q. For instance, ... did you ever read about it in any financial press or the press?

A. I don't believe so.

Q. And did you treat the information about the PIPE as confidential after you learned about it up until the time of the announcement?

A. I mean, again, our policy is when we find out information about transactions, unless we are told by the broker who another investor is, we do not discuss it with anybody else.

Q. And that's regardless of whether anyone asked you to keep it confidential; is that right?

A. That's correct....

> MR. SCHULTZ: Your Honor, that completes the SEC's cross-examination.
>
> And, Your Honor, we had similar objections to defendant's redirect examination, as I articulated earlier. With the same representation from counsel that they will limit an offering providing Mr. Kopin's testimony in this section, we'll reserve those objections.
>
> THE COURT: All right. In other words, you'll just stand on the prior objections?
>
> MR. SCHULTZ: Yes, sir.
>
> THE COURT: And the court's ruling will be the same.
>
> And if you will make that clear.
>
> MR. BEST: Yes. And, Your Honor, we present our redirect examination of Mr. Kopin and make the following representation.
>
> This testimony you're about to hear is regarding Mr. Kopin's personal beliefs.

REDIRECT EXAMINATION

(Video playing.)

Q. ... Even with receipt of the final financial terms of the Mamma.com PIPE offering, is it your position you do not consider that information to be material information?

A. I don't believe that it is.

Q. And why is that?

A. I just believe that there is enough information in the marketplace, ... I just never personally believed it was material nonpublic information.

Q. I have no further questions.

 THE COURT: Defendant Exhibit 123 is admitted.

 ... Is there recross?

 MR. SCHULTZ: Yes.

 THE COURT: You may proceed.

RECROSS EXAMINATION

(Video playing.)

Q. Whatever your opinion, personal opinion was, as you called it, as to materiality back when you first got a call with respect to the information that you got about the PIPE ... is that something that ... you think a reasonable investor would have been interested in?

A. The answer is I don't know. I mean, I'm not sure.

Q. But it was important to you because warrants and discounts is what you were looking at in determining whether or not to invest in a PIPE?

A. I mean, look it's important to me because I need to know what the pricings are of the transaction because otherwise I wouldn't give the company my money.

Q. And you are a reasonable investor, right?

A. I believe I am....

---

[d] Testimony of Mr. Christopher Aguilar

Thereafter, Mr. Cuban called to the witness stand the former general counsel of Merriman Curhan Ford (Merriman or MCF), Mr. Christopher Aguilar.[9] Mr. Aguilar testified in person at the trial. *Excerpts of Mr. Aguilar's testimony follow.*

---

9. For a book by the author focusing on inside (or in-house) legal counsel, see Marc I. Steinberg and Stephen B. Yeager, *Inside Counsel—Practices, Strategies, and Insights* (West Academic Publishing 2015).

[By Mr. Best, Attorney for Mr. Cuban]

MR. BEST [Attorney for Mr. Cuban]: Yes, Your Honor. Mr. Cuban calls Christopher Aguilar, the former general counsel of Merriman Curhan & Ford by person.

Q.   ... [D]id Merriman Curhan Ford represent a company, an issuer client named Mamma.com in 2004 in connection with a PIPE transaction?

A.   Yes, that's correct.

Q.   Okay.... [D]id you understand Merriman to play the role as a placement agent for Mamma.com in their PIPE transaction?

A.   Yes. That's how we would be referred to, as the placement agent. We were trying to place the offering with the buy side [namely, the prospective purchasers].

Q.   Okay. And as placement agent did Merriman have the authority to speak for Mamma.com to any institutional investors?

A.   Yes, that's correct.

Q.   And as the placement agent for Mamma.com did Merriman have the authority to speak to Mark Cuban about the Mamma.com PIPE? ....

A.   Yes.

Q.   Focusing your attention on 2003 and 2004 as general counsel of Merriman Curhan Ford, were you aware of the policies and procedures at Merriman regarding employees' use of information relating to PIPE offerings?

A.   Yes.

Q.   Okay. Were there any policies or procedures at Merriman in 2003 and 2004 up through the time frame of the Mamma.com PIPE that would restrict the use of the PIPE information to any institutional investor?

A.   No.

Q.   Was Mr. Owen's private placement group required to get under these policies and procedures at Merriman any confidentiality agreements from the institutional investors before telling them about PIPE offerings?

A.   No.

Q.   Was Mr. Owen required under the policies and procedures at Merriman Curhan Ford during this ... same period of time to secure restrictions on trading from these institutional investors before telling the institutional investor clients about a PIPE offering?

   MS. FOLENA: Objection, leading.

   THE COURT: Overruled

   THE WITNESS: No.

BY MR. BEST:

Q.   Did this include the time frame regarding the Mamma.com PIPE as well?

A.   Yes, that's correct.

Q.   So under the policies and procedures at Merriman Curhan Ford was Arnie Owen or his group required to get any restrictions from any of the institutional investors prior to informing them about the Mamma.com PIPE?

A.   No, they were not required to do something like that....

Q. Did you find any non-disclosure agreements between Merriman Curhan Ford and institutional clients regarding the Mamma.com PIPE?

A. No, I did not. . . .

Q. Did you find any information recording a confidentiality agreement between Merriman Curhan Ford and Mark Cuban?

A. No, I did not.

Q. Did you find any information about a non-disclosure agreement . . . with Merriman Curhan Ford and Mark Cuban?

A. No, I did not.

Q. Did you find any information about an oral representation of a confidentiality agreement or restriction on trading by and between Merriman Curhan Ford and Mark Cuban?

> MS. FOLENA: Objection to the leading.
> THE COURT: Overruled.
> THE WITNESS: No, I did not.
> MR. BEST: Your Honor, thank you.
> I have no further questions at this time.
> THE COURT: Cross-examination?

CROSS EXAMINATION

[By Ms. Folena, Attorney for the SEC]

Q. . . . So you were the general counsel of Merriman, correct?

A. Yes.

Q. Thank you.

> And as the general counsel you are the top lawyer at that company; is that true, sir?

A. That's true.

Q. All legal decisions for the company are approved by you, right?

A. I'm involved in all the legal matters for the company. That's the nature of a general counsel. Whatever it may be involving the law.

Q. And you advise the folks at Merriman about legal issues affecting the company; is that right, sir?

A. Yes. I advise mostly the executive committee and the board of directors. That's correct. . . .

Q. . . . Now, Mr. Aguilar, in 2004, before the PIPE became public, during the time your firm was engaged on this PIPE, you, sir, never spoke to any one of [the six institutional] investors; is that correct?

A. Yeah. That's correct.

Q. So is it fair to say, sir, you had no information what any of those six PIPE investors knew about the Mamma.com PIPE, correct? Based on any conversation you had with them. Is that right, sir?

A. You know. . . . It almost sounds like you're asking me two things there.

Q. Let's go back.

A. Could you, please.

Q. You never spoke to any of the PIPE investors; is that correct?

A. That's true.

Q. All right. So you never had any personal conversation with them about any of the details that they knew about the Mamma.com PIPE, correct?

A. Well, I didn't have any conversations with them.

Q. At all.

A. Right.

Q. Okay. Mr. Aguilar, you don't know, sir, sitting here, do you, whether any of those PIPE investors bought or sold Mamma.com securities before the PIPE was public, do you?

A. No, I don't have any of that knowledge.

Q. And you don't know, sir, do you, whether any of those six PIPE investors told anybody else about the PIPE.

A. No, I don't know that....

Q. ... If any of those six PIPE investors had conversations with anyone outside of Mamma.com, outside of their firm, or outside of Merriman, you would not know about it, correct?

A. I guess if they had a conversation with someone outside of their firm I would not know about that, no.

Q. Okay.

A. I did not talk with these people....

Q. You had a policy at Merriman that your employees could not trade on PIPE information before it's public. Right?

A. Yes....

Q. Mr. Aguilar, Merriman entered into a non-disclosure agreement with ... Mamma. com related to the PIPE, correct?

A. ... I think we did, but I'm not sure....

Q. But let me just bring you back to [your] January 25th, 2012 [deposition]. You did say you believed your firm entered into a non-disclosure agreement with Mamma.com about the PIPE?

A. I don't know. Why don't you give me that transcript, and I'll look at my exact words and your exact question.

        MS. FOLENA: May I approach?

        THE COURT: You may.

BY MS. FOLENA:

Q. Your exact words are on 11. Read them to yourself....

A. ... I'm going to read this. Just a second.

        Okay. I testified [in my deposition] that I do believe we entered into an NDA [Non-disclosure agreement] ....

Q. But you don't know whether Merriman had non-disclosure agreements with the six PIPE investors, ... correct, sir?

A. That's not correct. We did not have NDAs with the PIPE investors.

Q. You did not have NDAs?

A. With the PIPE investors.

Q.   Sir, do you recall being asked on January 25th, 2012 [at your deposition], with regards to non-disclosure agreements:
     "Q. What about with investors or possible investors for the Mamma PIPE?"
     Do you remember that question?
A.   Not particularly, but I trust you.
Q.   Do you remember your answer was: "A. I don't know"?
A.   Not particularly, but that's what I'm saying.
         MS. FOLENA: May I approach, Your Honor?
         THE COURT: You may.

BY MS. FOLENA:
Q.   Sir, I want you to read the same page we were just on, page 64, January 25th, 2012, lines 15 through 17.
A.   Yes. I testified I don't know.
Q.   But you know now, sir?
A.   You got me. I don't know. If the documents existed, I know I would have produced them to the SEC, your group. And I'll bet you ... got them over there in a binder or box, if they existed. So you're right, I don't know.
Q.   But you know, Mr. Aguilar, your firm was supposed to get non-disclosure agreements from each of the six PIPE investors, correct?
A.   No. I disagree with you.
Q.   Okay. Why don't you turn to Plaintiff's Exhibit 1 in that folder....
A.   Yes....
Q.   Just so the record is clear, I'm showing it to you as Plaintiff's Exhibit 1 which has already been admitted. It's a stand-alone. It's not part of the [Form] 20-F, but I'll represent to you it is the same attachment that is in the 20-F. Okay?
         Just so we're clear....
         And if we can focus in on paragraph 1-A, capital raising....
         Do you see that, sir?
A.   I sure do.
Q.   That reads "MCF ..." that's your firm?
A.   Yes.
Q.   "... will clear any potential investors with the company, obtain non-disclosure agreements and provide them with the confidential memorandum."
         Do you see that, sir?
A.   I do.
Q.   You're not sitting here as the general counsel of Merriman and saying that you didn't get non-disclosure agreements, are you?
A.   I think that's a double negative....
Q.   Let me ask it again.
A.   Ask it again and I'll listen more carefully.
Q.   You didn't get non-disclosure agreements, sir?
A.   That's correct.
Q.   From your six PIPE investors?
A.   That's correct. I believe. I don't know.

Q.   Plaintiff's Exhibit 1 that you have in front of you, sir, that's the [Mamma.com-Merriman] March 16th engagement letter that I was just referring to.

 That agreement is signed by the president of Merriman, is it not, sir, a man, Gregory Curhan?

A.   Yes, that's right.

Q.   And it's also signed by Guy Fauré, the president and CEO of Mamma.com?

A.   Yes.

Q.   And it's also signed by David Goldman, correct, sir?

A.   Yes, it is.

Q.   Okay.

 So this letter was signed by the president of your firm and the president of Mamma.com, correct?

A.   Yes, it was.

Q.   And it says will obtain non-disclosure agreements, does it not, sir?

A.   That's what it says.

Q.   And your testimony is your firm failed to do that. Is that right?

A.   I don't know if we failed anything, but we didn't do that.... If I did have them I assure you I would have produced them to the SEC....

Q.   You didn't get non-disclosure agreements, did you, sir?

A.   I don't know, but I don't think so.

Q.   And as the general counsel that was your job, wasn't it, sir, to make sure that this letter was followed; is that right?

A.   I don't really think that's fair, but I'm not supposed to argue with you.

Q.   You're the top lawyer in that company, correct, sir?

A.   Yes, I am.

Q.   A non-disclosure agreement is a legal document, is it not?

A.   Yes. It can be a document or contained within a document. Yes, it's a legal document.

Q.   And you're sitting here saying you did nothing to make sure your firm got those with regards to the Mamma.com PIPE, right?

A.   Nope. I didn't say that. You just said that.

Q.   Do you agree with me?

A.   I don't agree with you.

Q.   You don't have them, do you, sir?

 MR. BEST [ATTORNEY FOR Mr. Cuban]: We would object to that question, Your Honor.

 THE COURT: State the basis.... I don't know what his objection is.

 MR. BEST: Asked and answered.

 THE COURT: This is cross-examination. I'll give her some latitude. Overruled.

BY MS. FOLENA:

Q.   Can you answer the question?

A.   I am not aware that there were non-disclosure agreements for these investors in the Mamma.com PIPE transaction....

Q.   As the general counsel of Merriman, sir, testifying in a case about the Mamma.
     com PIPE, you do not know whether your firm got a non-disclosure agreement,
     as was required by Plaintiff's Exhibit 1. Is that right?

A.   You got a couple of different questions in there, and I'm not just going to give
     you a yes or no to that.
          I don't know whether we have 'em.
          I don't think we did.
          And whether or not it was required depends on the whole transaction and the
     whole document. Not just you picking a few words out.

Q.   Sir, you'll agree with me that that line that's highlighted says, "MCF will," right?

A.   Yes, I do agree with you about that. Yeah.

Q.   Okay. And followed by "will" is "clear any potential investors with the com-
     pany," right?

A.   Yes.

Q.   "Comma, obtain non-disclosure agreements," correct?

A.   Yes, that's what it says.

Q.   It doesn't say "maybe obtain them," does it?

A.   No, it doesn't. . . .

Q.   . . . You will agree that that first line [of the Mamma.com-Merriman engagement
     letter] identifies your firm, Merriman. It reads, "Merriman is pleased to act as
     financial advisor to Mamma.com, the company." Do you see that?

A.   Yes.

Q.   And do you see the next line, "We will provide investment banking services to
     the company which may include." Do you see that word, sir? Do you see the
     word "may"?

A.   Yes, that's right.

Q.   That says "may," not "will," right?

A.   It says "may," not "will," that's right.

Q.   And you know there's a difference between "may" and "will." Is that right, sir?

A.   I do.

Q.   And followed that by word "may" is the word "include." Do you see that?

A.   Yes.

Q.   And then do you see a whole list of things that your firm may do for Mamma.
     com. Correct?

A.   Yes, I see them.

Q.   There is nothing in that paragraph or anywhere else in this letter that says your
     firm is absolutely going to do a PIPE transaction for Mamma.com, is there?

A.   Well, . . . should I read the whole thing?

Q.   Do you think you need to?

A.   To truly answer your question, since you said it's nowhere in the whole
     document. . . .

Q.   . . . I'm asking you whether or not the letter says that Merriman is going to abso-
     lutely do a PIPE for Mamma.com to raise 15 million dollars?
          Does it say that, sir?

A.   I don't believe this letter says that anywhere.

Q. Okay.

Does this letter say anywhere that Merriman is going to do a PIPE for Mamma.com to raise 15 million dollars with discounts provided to the PIPE investors?

A. No. We didn't ... say that here....

Q. ... Is your testimony that because this [Mamma.com-Merriman engagement] letter, Plaintiff's Exhibit 1, is contained in the Mamma.com [Form] 20-F that the information about the PIPE was no longer confidential?

Is that your testimony?

A. Yes. It was public. That's right.

Q. Sir, do you remember being asked this question in your deposition?

MS. FOLENA: May I approach, Your Honor?

THE COURT: You may.

BY MS. FOLENA:

Q. I'm showing you page 184 in the January 25th, 2012 deposition, starting with the question on line 2 and going through 9.

Read it to yourself, please.

(Pause.)

A. So I actually read the parts you highlighted. I wanted to read the context so I read a little more than you asked me to read.

Q. Okay. That's fine.

Now I have to ask a question: Mr. Aguilar, you don't know, do you, sir, that ... because this letter is in the [Form] 20-F that means ... the PIPE is no longer confidential, do you?

A. Please ask that question again. I'm sorry.

Q. You testified this morning ... or you said you testified this morning that because this letter, Plaintiff's Exhibit 1, is in the 20-F, that means the PIPE is no longer confidential. Right, sir?

A. That's my testimony.

Q. But you actually don't know that to be true, do you?

A. I disagree with you.

I know that a public filing is accessible to the public and therefore not hidden away from the public.

Q. You know that today, sir, correct?

But you didn't know that on January 25th, 2012, did you?

A. I testified I don't know.

I was surprised. That was the first time that I had ever learned that they had published our engagement letter, and I don't know how many years later that was.

What year is that? ....

Nine years later I found out that they published our engagement letter. I never knew that.

So, yeah, I didn't know that that was published.

Q. You were surprised, correct, sir?

A. Yes, I was.

Q. And you were asked [at your deposition] in January 25th, 2012, if that takes the veil of confidentiality off the letter. Correct?

A. I just read that question, correct.

Q. You were asked that. And your answer in 2012 was:
    "A. I don't know about that."
    Correct?

A. I said, "I don't know about that." And I followed it by saying . . . "Well, what I do know is that I've never seen something like this before, that someone would file our engagement letter with a publish[ed] disclosure."

Q. But we just went through what that letter actually says, correct, sir?

A. Portions of it, absolutely. We read them.

Q. And you agree with me that it doesn't say that Merriman is absolutely going to do a PIPE for Mamma.com, right, sir?

A. I agree we didn't guarantee anything or use the word "absolutely." Yes, I agree with you.

Q. Mr. Aguilar, you testified you live in San Francisco area?

A. That's right. I live in the City and County of San Francisco.

Q. So you had to travel to come here, sir?

A. Yes, I did.

Q. You were called by the defense to testify in this case; is that right?

A. Yes, I received a subpoena, actually.

Q. Who is paying for your expenses to be here today, Mr. Aguilar?

A. The defendant is. . . .

Q. If the executives at Mamma.com believed that their PIPE was material nonpublic information of their company, you would have no reason to disagree with that, would you, sir?

A. No.

Q. If the executives at Mamma.com wished to keep the information about their PIPE confidential, you would have no reason to disagree with that, would you, sir?

A. No.

Q. You're aware, Mr. Aguilar, that on June 28th, 2004, Arnie Owen of your firm had a conversation with the defendant in this case, Mark Cuban, correct?

A. Yes.

Q. You do not have any idea what Mr. Owen said to Mr. Cuban, do you?

A. No, I do not.

Q. And you don't know what Mr. Cuban said to Mr. Owen, correct?

A. No.

Q. And you must know by now, sir, that also on June 28th, 2004, at 1:00 p.m. in the afternoon the defendant, Mr. Cuban, had a conversation with the former CEO of Mamma.com, Guy Fauré.

A. I don't know that personally. I've learned it in preparing for this case, my deposition.

Q. Okay. So then you don't know what, if anything, Mr. Fauré said on that phone call, do you, sir?

A. No, I don't.

Q. And you don't know what, if anything, Mr. Cuban said on that phone call; is that correct?

A. Yes. That's correct.

Q. So you don't know sitting in court today whether Mr. Cuban agreed on that phone call on June 28th, 2004 with Mr. Fauré to keep the PIPE information confidential, right?

A. I don't know what they talked about.

Q. And you … also don't know, sir, whether on June 28th, 2004, during the phone call with Mr. Fauré if Mr. Cuban said, "Now I'm screwed. I can't sell," do you?

A. I don't know what Mr. Cuban said.

Q. And you don't know whether Mr. Cuban agreed on that phone call with Mr. Fauré not to trade before the public announcement, do you?

A. I don't know.

MS. FOLENA: I have no further questions at this time.

REDIRECT EXAMINATION
[By Mr. Best, Attorney for Mr. Cuban]

Q. Can you tell the ladies and gentlemen of the jury what restrictions Merriman Curhan as a company placed on institutional investors about PIPE information as of June 28th, 2004?

A. We didn't put any restrictions, so none.

Q. Okay. So do you know what the institutional investors who were solicited for the Mamma.com PIPE offering did with the information about the PIPE offering when they received it?

A. No, I do not.

Q. Do you know … whether or not they traded on the information?

A. No, I do not.

Q. Do you know whether or not they got on the phone and called all their buddies in the industry about the information?

A. No, I do not….

Q. Okay. Ms. Folena spoke about the call with Mr. Cuban on June 28th, 2004. If Mr. Cuban wanted to participate in the Mamma.com PIPE offering as of June 28th, 2004, would he have been able to do so at Merriman Curhan Ford immediately, without completing any paperwork?

MS. FOLENA: Objection. Foundation.

THE COURT: Overruled.

THE WITNESS: No. All participants have got, frankly, a significant amount of paperwork to complete before they can invest….

Q. Okay. Now, Ms. Folena asked you about whether or not you flew down here at the cost of Mr. Cuban. Do you remember those questions …?

A. Yes.

Q. At all times in this investigation and in this trial preparation, have you made yourself available to the SEC at … at their convenience?

A. Yeah. On every occasion….

RECROSS EXAMINATION
[By Ms. Folena, Attorney for the SEC]

Q.   ... I want you to take a look at [the private transaction acknowledgement] letter that you testified you sent to all of the PIPE investors. That last sentence
says, "Upon our receipt of your signed acknowledgement, we will continue to
approach you with new offers of private placement investment opportunities."
   Do you see that, sir?

A.   Yes.

Q.   So if PIPE investors did not sign this letter and send it back to the firm, your
firm would not give them any other information about other private placement
opportunities going forward. Is that right, sir?

A.   That's what it says....

Q.   Mr. Best asked you whether or not you had ever spoken to the SEC prior to this
trial. Do you remember that?

A.   Yes....

Q.   Mr. Aguilar, who'd you have dinner with last night?

A.   Myself.

Q.   Are you sure about that?

A.   Yeah. I'm real sure.

Q.   You didn't have dinner with Mr. Best?

A.   No, I did not.

Q.   You didn't discuss your testimony?

A.   I talked to Mr. Best yesterday ....

Q.   And did you discuss your testimony?

A.   No. He said I should try to be nicer to you and that I should try and give short
answers.

Q.   You had no further discussions with Mr. Best; is that right?

A.   That's right.

   MS. FOLENA: Your Honor, I have no further questions.

   THE COURT: Any objection to excusing the witness?

   MR. BEST: No, sir.

   MS FOLENA: No.

   THE COURT: Thank you, sir. You may step down. You're excused.

   The defendant may call his next witness.

   MR. CLARK: Your Honor, the defendant calls Alton Turner by videotape.

---

[e] Testimony of Mr. Alton Turner

   Interestingly, the next witness Mr. Cuban called was an enforcement
attorney for the SEC. Normally, one would not expect that the defendant in
a government enforcement action would call as a witness an attorney of the
SEC. In view of the complexities and twists that this litigation experienced,

perhaps this development is not all that surprising. In the inquiry stage of the SEC investigation, SEC enforcement attorney Alton Turner contacted Mr. Cuban. A generalized telephone interview of Mr. Cuban was thereafter conducted by Mr. Turner. *Excerpts of the testimony of Mr. Turner, which was by video presentation, follow.*

Q.   … Do you recall certain notes you took of the interview with Mr. Cuban?

A.   Yes.

Q.   Let's talk about the Mamma.com investigation. The Commission opened an informal investigation into trading in the securities of Mamma.com; is that correct?

A.   Correct.

Q.   Do you recall when that was approximately?

A.   Approximately 2003, 2004.

Q.   Okay. Was that matter captioned "home office-09900"?

A.   Yes.

Q.   Okay. What was your role in that 09900 matter?

A.   I was the staff attorney assigned to the case.

Q.   Can you tell us the reason that the inquiry into Mamma.com was opened?

A.   There were indications that there was possible market manipulation of the company's stock.

Q.   What … were the indicia of the potential market manipulation of the company's stock?

A.   Price swings in the company's stock in public trading.

Q.   Volume swings as well, to your recollection?

A.   Yes.

Q.   Did you ever determine whether the cause of the price and volume spikes we talked about a moment ago were actually the result of market manipulation?

A.   We didn't make a final finding of that, no.

Q.   I mean, did you make a determination … whether or not the dramatic price in volume spikes in Mamma.com stock were the result of market manipulation?

A.   Our initial assessment was that there was market manipulation. After conducting the investigation, we could not definitively tie any … manipulation to an individual.

Q.   Okay. So you didn't come to a final determination either way. Is that fair to say?

A.   We didn't have evidence to move forward with the case, no.…

Q.   Your investigation of Mamma.com didn't involve Mr. Cuban directly; am I right?

A.   Correct.

Q.   You did speak to Mr. Cuban in connection with your Mamma.com investigation though, correct?

A.   I did.

Q.   Why did you do that?

A.   It was our understanding that Mr. Cuban invested in the company.

Q.   Did you speak to every investor in Mamma.com?

A.   No.

Q.   What in particular about Mr. Cuban motivated you to speak to him?

A.   Mr. Cuban is a rather large investor, and I believe he filed at some point a 13D. I think he got at least a 5 percent stake in the company, which is what brought him in the radar.

Q.   Okay. Do you recall conducting a telephone interview with Mr. Cuban sometime in 2004?

A.   Exact date I don't recall, but I do recall speaking with Mr. Cuban on the phone.

Q.   ... [W]e established you took notes of the call, correct?

A.   I did take notes.

Q.   But you try to capture everything that you can in the notes; is that fair to say?

A.   True.

Q.   Ms. Brockmeyer [SEC enforcement attorney] was on the phone as well with Mr. Cuban. Is that your recollection?

A.   Yes.

Q.   What do you recall from your telephone conversation with Mr. Cuban?

A.   Contacting Mr. Cuban and we had a conversation about his investment in Mamma.com. ...

Q.   Do you recall what you asked him about relating to his investment in Mamma.com?

A.   My questions were primarily focused on why he invested in the company at that time and also ... most importantly, prior to investing in the company, did he know about an individual named Irving Kott, who was ... related to Mamma.com in some way, shape, or form.

Q.   What did he tell you about Mr. Kott?

A.   That he was aware of an individual named Irving Kott investing in the company at some point.

Q.   Did he say he was troubled by that?

A.   I think he said he had concerns about it. ...

Q.   What do you recall him saying to you about any ... any conversations he had with Guy Fauré?

A.   ... They had a conversation from what I recall. Mr. Cuban indicated concerns about Mr. Kott being involved with the company because Mr. Kott had a bad reputation, so to speak, in the securities world.

Q.   Do you recall Mr. Cuban expressing the basis for his understanding that Mr. Kott had a bad reputation in the securities world?

A.   I forget exactly how he came in contact with that information, but he ... did know that of Mr. Kott's reputation. ...

Q.   Do you recall asking any question that Mr. Cuban declined to answer?

A.   I don't recall that.

Q.   Okay. Was he cooperative?

A.   He answered my questions. ...

MR. CLARK: Your Honor, that concludes the deposition of Alton Turner taken on June 16th, 2013.

THE COURT: Does the government wish to offer any portions?

MS. BRANDT: We have no questions for Mr. Turner.

---

[f] Testimony of Dr. Erik Sirri

Mr. Cuban called Dr. Erik Sirri as his final witness. As you may recall from Chapter 5 of this book, Dr. Sirri was retained as an expert witness by Mr. Cuban. Interestingly, the SEC declined to rebut Dr. Sirri's testimony by calling the government's expert Dr. Clemens Sialm to testify at trial. Given the result of the trial, this apparent strategic decision can be questioned.

In his testimony at trial, Dr. Sirri presented two key opinions: *first*, that the information regarding the Mamma.com PIPE transaction was publicly known—namely, that this information was in the public arena—prior to the time that Mr. Cuban sold his shares of the company; and *second*, that a price drop of over nine percent in Mamma.com's stock price after the company publicly announced the consummation of the PIPE transaction on June 29th was not statistically significant. These issues were of fundamental importance in this litigation: In order for Mr. Cuban to be found liable for engaging in illegal insider trading, the fact-finder (i.e., the jury) was required to determine that Mr. Cuban traded while being aware that the subject information was *both material and non-public. Excerpts of the testimony of Dr. Sirri follow.*

[By Mr. Clark, Attorney for Mr. Cuban]

BY MR. CLARK [Attorney for Mr. Cuban]:

Q. Good morning, Dr. Sirri.

A. Good morning....

Q. What do you do for a living?

A. I'm a college professor at Babson College.

Q. What do you teach?

A. I'm a finance professor....

Q. In addition to teaching at Babson during the time period after you were the chief economist of the SEC, did you visit as a scholar at any other institutions?

A. Yeah. I was a visiting scholar for a year at Harvard Law School

Q. Was there a time period when the SEC again asked you whether you would take a leave of absence and come work in a managerial position there?

A. Yes, there was.

Q. Can you tell us about that?

A. In about 2006, I was approached again by the SEC to come and work there. This time it was a different position. This time ... I became eventually the director of the division of trading and markets, which is one of the divisions within the Securities and Exchange Commission.

Q.   I want to get into what you did in that job in just a minute, but can you just briefly describe to us what the division of trading and markets is and what the director does?

A.   The SEC is composed of some divisions. There's four or five big divisions. One of them is ... the division of trading and markets. I ran that division. I was the senior person in it. And this is the division that deals with exchanges, stocks, bonds, brokers, how traders behave in the market, those sorts of things....

Q.   Dr. Sirri, what subject are you providing an expert opinion on here today at trial?

A.   ... I'm offering an opinion about whether ... information about the upcoming Mamma.com PIPE was public at the time Mr. Cuban traded.

Q.   And what do you mean by "public"?

A.   When I say "public" I mean that that information was available to investors and therefore incorporated into the price of Mamma.com stock.

Q.   What do you conclude on the issue of whether the PIPE information was public at the time Mr. Cuban sold his shares?

A.   I conclude that that information was available to investors, that it was public, and that it was incorporated into the price of Mamma.com stock.

Q.   Let me ask you: When you say "public," does that mean every investor in Mamma.com or in the market knew the information at the time let's say of June 28th?

A.   No, that's not what I mean by public.

Q.   What do you mean by public?

A.   When I use the term "public," I mean that that information was impounded, that is reflected, into the price, and that people who wanted access to that information could get it....

Q.   I want to discuss the information you examined to come to your opinion.
     Did you examine data related to the common stock of Mamma.com?

A.   Yes, I did.

Q.   What sorts of data did you examine?

A.   I looked at information about stock prices.
     I looked at information about trading volume.
     I looked at information in terms of filings that were at the Securities and Exchange Commission.
     I looked at message board postings.
     I looked at testimony affirmations of people involved in the Mamma.com PIPE.
     I looked at information about pay-to-hold transactions that were associated with short selling. Those are the things that I can remember....

Q.   Aside from the documents and testimony and message boards and SEC filings that you reviewed in this case, is there anything else upon which you've based on your opinion?

A.   Well, ... I'd say I also based it upon my experience, my expertise in the financial markets, in trading, in the way information comes to be reflected in the prices, that experience I get from being a professor, from doing research, from being an active participant in the markets and from working at the Securities and Exchange Commission....

Q.   And have you done a study of whether information about the Mamma.com PIPE was public prior to Mr. Cuban's trades....?

A.   Yes, I have.

Q.   Dr. Sirri, can information come into the market through SEC filings and news articles?

A.   Yes, it can. Certainly.

Q.   Can information come into the market through rumors?

A.   Yes.

Q.   Can information come into the market through word of mouth?

A.   Sure.

Q.   You spoke earlier about information being public and being incorporated into the stock price. What do you mean by that?

A.   What I mean is that when people who trade securities, trade stocks, have a view on something, they will express their view often by trading....

Q.   With that in mind, do you have a conclusion about whether information about the Mamma.com PIPE was public before Mr. Cuban traded after this spike?

A.   Yes, I do.

Q.   What is it?

A.   My conclusion is that the information about the Mamma.com PIPE was public, was available to investors, and was incorporated into the price of Mamma.com before Mr. Cuban traded....

Q.   ... [D]oes the testimony that you've reviewed and the testimony you've reviewed in this trial, support your conclusion that there were no confidentiality agreements that restricted participants in the Mamma.com PIPE?

A.   Yes. It does.

Q.   And does that support your conclusion that the information about the Mamma.com PIPE was public before Mr. Cuban traded at the end of the day on June 28th?

A.   Yes, it does....

Q.   And what, if anything, does that tell you about what traders did with that information, the fact that they weren't bound by confidentiality agreements?

A.   Well, it leaves them free to converse amongst themselves and with others that they know, so they can talk.

It leaves them free to trade on that information, so if they chose to they could trade the shares, the equity of Mamma.com. And that would be true in an unconstrained manner. Their conversations may be amongst themselves or amongst others, other people....

Q.   Based on your experience with traders, what would traders do with information about the Mamma.com PIPE if they had no confidentiality obligation?

MR. SCHULTZ: Objection, foundation. Calls for speculation.

THE COURT: Overruled.

THE WITNESS: Traders are free to do what they wish with it. They can talk, they can trade, they can talk to whomever they like.

Q. By that mechanism would traders make the information public by discussing it with other traders?

A. That's one of the mechanisms whereby information becomes public, it disseminates out into the market, and people come to learn of that information. Not necessarily everybody in the whole world, of course, but people will come to learn of that information.

    The other thing is that if they trade on it, for the reasons we talked about earlier, it can come to be reflected in the price of Mamma.com stock.

Q. Is that your position of what happened in this case?

A. It is....

Q. Dr. Sirri, we've gone through your opinion about information that the Mamma.com PIPE was public prior to the time Mr. Cuban sold his shares; is that correct?

A. Yes.

Q. Can you summarize those for us before we move on?

A. Sure. I evaluated three types of information in coming to my opinion.

    One was information about the nature of traders, how they collect information and how they act on information. The point being that traders use whatever information is useful to them. If they're not restricted, then they will talk, they will trade, and that information that is available to them will come to be reflected in market prices. That was the first point.

    The second point in this case was the point about the pay-to-hold transactions. In that case my point was that people associated with a PIPE who are in the future going to become PIPE investors would lock up shares through these pay-to-hold arrangements facilitating their ability to sell stock short in the future.[10] Having done that, they also convey information to the market, because other traders in the market realize that the supply of shares is constrained ..., a conclusion they can come to is that a PIPE is upcoming.

    The third type of information I referred to are documents associated with Mamma.com. That also contributed support to my opinion. And in that case I talked about the Yahoo! message board filing. I talked about the [SEC Form] 20-F. And I discussed the term sheet which you just had up there. All those together are examples of information that are available that are out in the market on which traders are free to act, and so that information comes into the price....

[10.] Generally, the term *short-sale* may be defined as follows:

> Practice where an investor places an order to sell at the current market price a security which he/she does not then own. By so doing, he/she incurs an obligation to sell which is to be fulfilled by purchasing the securities at a later date, hopefully for a lower price, and thereafter delivering such securities to the purchaser. Rules promulgated by the SEC regulate short sales. Moreover, § 16(c) of the 1934 Act prohibits short sales by insiders.

Marc I. Steinberg, *Understanding Securities Law* 498 (7th ed. 2018).

CROSS EXAMINATION
[By Mr. Schultz, Attorney for the SEC]

Q. Good afternoon, Dr. Sirri.

A. Good afternoon.

Q. You testified against the SEC in court last year in the Options Express matter, correct?

A. I did.

Q. You were testifying as an expert for an individual who was accused of committing securities fraud, correct?

A. Yes.

Q. One of the principal areas of your testimony in that case was that the trader, your client, could legitimately cover his trades using a certain type of transaction called a buy-right transaction. Isn't that correct?

A. Correct.

Q. And in her opinion, Judge Murray wrote that you did not provide any support for your belief that the trader could cover the short position with a buy-right; isn't that right?

    MR. CLARK: Objection, Your Honor, relevance.

    THE COURT: Overruled.

    THE WITNESS: I did not read her opinion.

BY MR. SCHULTZ:

Q. So you've never been advised about her assessment of the testimony you provided?

A. Not ... at that detail.

Q. Were you advised that your client was found liable of securities fraud?

A. Yes.

Q. You're not testifying here that Mr. Cuban did not commit insider trading, correct? That's not an opinion you're offering today?

A. I'm not offering a legal opinion, no....

Q. About your professional experience in academia and working at the SEC, correct?

A. Correct.

Q. You've never been a professional trader, correct?

A. Correct.

Q. You've never been employed at a brokerage firm, correct?

A. That's correct.

Q. You've never been a market maker, correct?

A. That's correct.

Q. You've never been employed by a market maker, correct?

A. No, I have not.

Q. You've never been employed by a hedge fund, correct?

A. That's correct.

Q. Mr. Clark [Attorney for Mr. Cuban] started out asking you some questions about the work that you've done in this matter.

You're being paid $900 an hour; is that right?

A. That's correct.

Q. At the time of your deposition you had worked on this matter somewhere in the neighborhood of 90 to 100 hours. Is that right?

A. That's approximately right. Correct.

Q. So that's about two and a half weeks of work, if you were working full-time, correct?

A. I haven't done the math, but I'll take your word for it.

Q. I mean, if it was 90 hours, that would be two 45-hour work weeks, right?

A. Yes.

Q. And for that work Mr. Cuban paid you 80 to $90,000; is that right?

A. If that's what the math works out to. I'll take your word for it, yes.

Q. It's 2:00 o'clock in the afternoon.

A. Yes.

Q. ... You've been available since 9:00 o'clock this morning?

A. Yes.

Q. Being compensated for all that time?

A. Yes.

Q. So far we're looking at five hours, correct?

A. Yes.

Q. So for coming in and answering questions today, Mr. Cuban is going to pay you $4,500, up until right now; is that right?

A. Approximately, yes....

Q. ... You haven't seen any evidence that the people who participated in the PIPE transaction spoke with anyone about the PIPE who didn't ultimately become an investor in that PIPE; isn't that true?

A. I'm just thinking.
    I can't recall that I did. That's correct....

Q. At the time you completed your [expert] report in September of 2011, you had not identified any PIPE investors or anyone employed or connected by one of the PIPE investors who bought or sold Mamma.com stock on the NASDAQ on June 28th or June 29th, correct?

A. I believe that's correct. Yes.

Q. At the time you completed your report in September 2011, you had not identified anyone connected with Mamma.com, anyone who worked at Mamma.com or was connected or related to anyone from Mamma.com who bought or sold stock on the NASDAQ on June 28th or June 29th, correct?

A. Anyone at Mamma or anyone who was connected with Mamma who bought stock on the 29th on NASDAQ. That's correct.

Q. And at the time you completed your report in September 2011, you had not identified anyone connected in any way with Merriman, the placing agent, who bought or sold Mamma.com stock on the NASDAQ on June 28th or June 29th, correct?

A. That's correct.

Q. Are you aware that no one from Merriman has testified that they bought or sold Mamma.com stock on the NASDAQ on either of those two days?

A. No.

Q. You don't have any reason to dispute that though, do you?

A. I have no reason one way or the other....

Q. Right.... So Merriman was representing Mamma.com in connection with what ultimately became a PIPE transaction, correct?

A. That's my understanding from reading the engagement letter, correct.

Q. Mamma.com and Merriman had a confidential relationship, correct?

A. I don't know about the nature of the confidential relationship between those. I can't comment on that one way or the other.

Q. So ... you're not aware of the testimony that has been given at this trial about the confidential relationship between Mamma.com and Merriman?

A. No, I am not.

Q. That's information that hasn't been brought available to you as you prepared for your testimony today?

A. I had never heard what you're telling me until you told it to me right now....

Q. The acknowledgement letter that Mr. Aguilar [General Counsel for Merriman] sent to the PIPE investors reads, "Given the possibility for the Commission to consider knowledge of a potential private placement to be material nonpublic information ... you should not trade in a company's securities (either directly or indirectly) based upon material nonpublic information.

"Further, you should not disclose the fact of a potential private placement, until that information has been made available to the public."

Do you see that?

A. I do.

Q. And you were unaware that Mr. Aguilar sent these to the PIPE investors in June of 2004, correct?

A. That's correct.

Q. You were unaware that in this letter Merriman is advising the PIPE investors that they should not disclose the fact of a potential private placement until that information has been made available to the public, correct?

A. That appears to be the case, yes.

Q. You are unaware from Mr. Aguilar's testimony that PIPE investors had to acknowledge this before they would receive information about PIPEs after June 14th, 2004, correct? You didn't know that?

A. I did not know that....

Q. Now, the stock price of Mamma.com closed on June 30th, 2004, at $11.99, correct?

A. That's my recollection, yes.

Q. And the stock price at the close on June 29th, 2004, was $13.10 and a half cents, correct?

A. That's my recollection, yes.

Q. That's what you wrote in your [expert] report, both of those figures, correct?

A. Yes.

Q.   And after adjusting the price for market movements, the drop in the price that you attribute ... to Mamma.com specific factors was $1.19, correct?

A.   That sounds right, yes.

Q.   So the difference between 11.99 and $13.10 and a half cents is more like a dollar twelve, correct?

A.   Correct.

Q.   And then you've adjusted for market movements and said the change in that price that's due solely to Mamma.com was $1.19, it's actually bigger than that inherent dollar twelve difference, correct?

A.   Yes.

Q.   And that's approximately 9.1 percent, correct?

A.   I can't remember off ... by memory what the percentage was, but that sounds about right.

Q.   Do you want to look at your report, page 10, paragraph 26?

A.   Sure.
     The dollar nineteen is there and 9 percent, yes.

Q.   So you attribute a dollar nineteen to the price difference of Mamma.com specific factors and that's really a 9.1 percent drop, correct?

A.   Correct.

Q.   And it's your conclusion that the 9.1 percent drop is not statistically significant; is that correct?

A.   Correct.

Q.   Now, Mr. Cuban sold all 600,000 shares of Mamma.com stock for $7,946,724.87, correct?

A.   I don't have that number memorized, but ...

Q.   Do you want to look at your report, page 8, paragraph 20?

A.   Sure.
     $7,946,724.87. Yes, I see that.

Q.   If Mr. Cuban had sold those shares, 600,000 shares at the $11.99 closing price on June 30th he would have received only $7,194,000, correct?

A.   I don't recall that calculation....

Q.   I'll represent to you I did the math and it came out to $7,194,000.

A.   ... I'll believe you.

Q.   Okay.
     So if Mr. Cuban received 7.95 million dollars by actually selling his shares ... do you follow me, that's how much he actually received?

A.   Yes.

Q.   Just rounding, I'm going to call it 7.95 million dollars.

A.   Yes.

Q.   And if he had sold 'em on June 30th he would have only received we'll say 7.19 million dollars. Do you follow that?

A.   That's your assumption that that's what he would have received. You're telling me to assume that?

Q.   Sure.

A.   I will.

Q. The difference between 7.95 million, 7.19 million, is about 760,000; does that sound right?

A. Roughly, yes....

Q. Now, Professor, it's your conclusion that the price drop of 9.1 percent is not significant; is that right?

A. That's correct. I would say not statistically significant....

Q. And that's because the drop was only 9.1 percent, correct?

A. The drop was what it was. If I'm right about it, it's 9.1 percent. But Mamma.com moves enough from day-to-day that it has these types of variations in its price.

Q. And you've previously concluded in another matter that a 7.89 percent drop in a stock price is statistically significant, haven't you?

A. I don't recall it, but I may have. But nothing about the absolute number would prevent me from concluding that....

Q. Now, you testified that the information related to the PIPE was in the public arena before June 28th, 2004. That's your opinion, correct?

A. Yes.

Q. You cannot point this jury to a single document in the public arena that included the dollar amount of the PIPE, 16.6 million dollars, until Mamma.com issued its press release on June 29th, 2004, can you?

A. Well, I can point to the term sheet that came out on June 18th. It doesn't have the number 16.6 million dollars. It has the number 15 million dollars.

Q. And the term sheet, that's the term sheet that was sent from Arnie Owen at Merriman to David Goldman at Mamma.com who forwarded it to Mamma.com's lawyer. Correct?

A. Yes.

Q. ... [Y]ou haven't seen anything that suggests that document was ever transmitted to anybody outside of those three entities, have you?

A No. And the reason I cite it as support for my opinion is I have seen things that indicate that people felt they were free to share the information contained in that document.

Q. So putting aside the term sheet that was circulated ... that the only evidence is it was ever circulated between Mamma.com, Merriman, and the lawyer, ... and I'll say Sage Growth because they're on the sheet, take those four entities, you cannot point this jury to a single document in the public arena that went beyond those four entities that included the dollar amount of the PIPE, 16.6 million dollars, until Mamma.com issued the press release on June 29th, 2004, can you?

A. That's correct. I cannot point to any document that has the number 16.6 million dollars in it.

Q. You can't point this jury to a single document in the public arena that included the number of shares that were actually issued in connection with the PIPE that was announced on June 29th, 2004, correct?

A. That's correct.

Q. You cannot point this jury to a single document in the public arena that included ... the prices of the shares that were actually issued in connection with the Mamma. com PIPE until that PIPE was announced on June 29th, 2004, correct?

A. The actual dollar share price, that's correct.

Q. And that actual dollar share price in connection with Mamma.com was a discount, correct?

A. Correct.

Q. You can't point this jury to a single document in the public arena that included the number of warrants that were actually issued in connection with this transaction until Mamma.com issued that press release on June 29th, 2004, correct?

A. Now, again, when you say "in the public arena," there is the term sheet. The term sheet calls out the ratio of warrants.

Q. Okay. So this is the term sheet, again, that we're talking about that was . . . .

A. Yes.

Q. . . . that you've seen no evidence it went beyond Sage Growth, Mamma.com, Merriman, or Mamma.com's lawyer, correct?

A. That's right.

Q. Okay. So putting that document to the side . . . .

A. Fair enough.

Q. . . . you can't point the jury to a single document in the public arena that included a number of warrants that were issued in connection with the Mamma.com PIPE until Mamma.com issued its press release on June 29th, 2004, correct?

A. That's correct.

Q. And you can't point the jury to a single document in the public arena that indicated the Mamma.com PIPE was . . . certain to occur before Mamma.com issued the press release on June 29th, 2004, correct?

A. That was one hundred percent certain to occur?

Q. Right.

A. Absolutely not. I do not have . . . any document like that. . . .

MR. SCHULTZ: At this point, Your Honor, the SEC has no additional questions of Dr. Sirri.

THE COURT: Redirect?

REDIRECT EXAMINATION
[By Mr. Clark, Attorney for Mr. Cuban]

Q. . . . [A]re there other facts that support your opinion that information about the Mamma.com PIPE was public prior to Mr. Cuban's trading?

A. Yeah. There are a couple of other things that support that opinion as well.

Q. Could you tell us what they are?

A. Well, first . . . there's the volume spike that occurred on the 28th. We see that volume on the 28th is roughly 1,900 percent of what I have it was the day before. And so this volume spike I look at and . . . I infer as evidence in favor and supports my opinion that that PIPE information was public.

Q. And you and *[the SEC's expert]* Dr. Sialm both concluded that there was no news that would explain that volume spike; is that correct?

A. We looked for reasons for it and, you know, that kind of news we couldn't find news that supported that.

Q.   And is there yet another reason that supports your conclusion that information about the Mamma.com PIPE was public prior to Mr. Cuban's trading?

A.   Yes.

Q.   What's that?

A.   There ... is information about ... Mr. Owen's [of Merriman] testimony. Mr. Owen talked about the PIPE coming public, about ... he was not constrained in talking to people. And that also factored into my decision.

Q.   Are there any economic studies that support your opinion?

A.   Yes, there are.

Q.   Can you tell us about that again.

A.   ... Professor Sialm performed a[n] academic study of PIPEs and in that study he talked about the price reaction to PIPEs in advance of when the PIPEs were announced and closed. And in that he showed that the price reacts before that point, that is, the price rises before the PIPE closes. And in his academic paper he ascribes that to information about the PIPE leaking out into the market.

Q.   Let me ask you: Do you see him in the courtroom today?

A.   No.

Q.   Was ... he here on Wednesday when you testified?

A.   Yes.

Q.   He was?
     For the whole of your testimony?

A.   ... [H]e might have come in and out. When I walked in I saw him....

Q.   Okay. So he was here in the courtroom though?

A.   Yes. *[Dr. Sialm was not called by the SEC to testify at trial.]*

Q.   Okay. Do you remember on Wednesday being asked about previous cases in which you testified?

A.   Yes.

Q.   Do you remember being asked about a case called Options Express where the judge found against your client?

A.   Yes.

Q.   Was the judge in that case a federal judge, like Judge Fitzwater?

A.   No. No.

Q.   Was that judge actually an employee of the SEC?
     MR. SCHULTZ: Objection. Foundation.
     THE COURT: Would you establish how he knows?

BY MR. CLARK:

Q.   Are you aware of whether the judge was an employee of the SEC?

A.   Yes.
     THE COURT: I'll overrule the objection.

BY MR. CLARK:

Q.   And, in fact, was the judge an employee of the SEC?

A.   Yes.

Q.   Did ... the SEC raise that in your testimony?

A.   Not that I recall....

Q.   Do you know whether Guy Fauré even showed up to this trial to testify?

A.   I have some general sense he didn't.

     MR. SCHULTZ: Objection, Your Honor. Mr. Fauré has testified by video, so he has testified at trial

     THE COURT: You mean in person?

     MR. CLARK: Yes, Your Honor.

     THE COURT: All right.

     Overruled.

BY MR. CLARK:

Q.   Do you know whether Mr. Fauré showed up to testify in person in this trial?

A.   My sense is he didn't....

Q.   Dr. Sirri, you've testified about certain pay-to-hold transactions relating to Mamma.com stock that provided the market information about the impending PIPE transaction. Do you recall that?

A.   Yes.

Q.   Can you explain how that information seeps into the market?

A.   The pay-to-hold was associated with people who want to sell stock short. When you sell short stock, it's stock you don't own. So you have to borrow those shares before you sell them. And the pay-to-hold transaction is a way of going to people who have those shares who are in the business of lending them and ... paying them to keep those shares on hand for you when you want them....

Q.   As the former head of the SEC's division ... of trading and markets and an expert in securities trading, do you have an opinion about what caused this spike?

A.   Well, ... this volume spike I associate with the Mamma information coming public about the Mamma.com PIPE.

Q.   Was any of this trading on the 28th done by Mr. Cuban?

A.   No....

Q.   That ... information about the Mamma.com PIPE was publicly available before Mr. Cuban traded?

A.   Yes.

     MR. CLARK: I have no further questions, Your Honor.

     THE COURT: Recross?

RECROSS EXAMINATION
[By Mr. Schultz, Attorney for the SEC]

Q.   Dr. Sirri, you testified in response to Mr. Clark's questions that Dr. Sialm looked at the message board data on the 28th and 29th; is that correct?

A.   Yes.

Q.   Isn't it true, sir, that Dr. Sialm did not look at the message data on the 28th and 29th to see what kind of news might be out there, but in fact, he looked at the message board data to see if information about the [Mamma.com] PIPE was disclosed?

     Isn't that correct?

A.   My recollection is that in his report he talked about whether there was ... news about the Mamma.com PIPE, public news, that he reviewed a number of things, that one of the things he reviewed he said was message board traffic and that the Yahoo! message board traffic was one of the things he reviewed to conclude that there was no news about the Mamma.com transaction.

Q. There was no news about the Mamma.com PIPE, that's what his conclusion was, correct?

A. That's my recollection, yes. . . .

Q. And when you were answering questions . . . from Mr. Clark about what information existed out there on the 28th and 29th, you didn't consider this message board that talks about the SEC dropping its investigation, possibly [of Mamma. com] and that's what caused the volume spike on June 28th, correct?

A. Correct. . . .

Q. You can't point to a single document that's available in the public arena before June 29th, 2004 at 6:00 p.m. [when Mamma.com issued a press release] that indicates a PIPE was certain to occur, correct?

A. Well, I think I talked before about the information that I rely upon in coming to my opinion, I won't go through it all again: Yahoo! posting, the term sheet, the [Form] 20-F. The point is that . . . talking about my opinion of the information coming public, they were all pieces that indicated collectively that information had become public before Mr. Cuban traded.

Q. My question was a little different though: You can't point to a single document in the public arena prior to June 29th, 2004, at 6:00 p.m. that says a PIPE was certain to occur at Mamma.com, can you?

A. A single document?

    No. . . .

Q. You talked about the 20-F with Mr. Clark [Attorney for Mr. Cuban], and you've mentioned it again here, but 20-F says that a PIPE is one of multiple possibilities that might happen. Correct?

A. Well, that's in the . . . letter between Merriman Curhan and Mamma, and that letter describes the relationship between Merriman Curhan and Mamma. Merriman was engaged as an investment bank. And one of the possibilities was a capital raising transaction that was a PIPE.

Q. So one of the possibilities was a PIPE. And other possibilities were an acquisition or a sale, correct?

A. Well, they're not mutually exclusive.

Q. Right. But those are the three things that were listed. They may do a PIPE. They may do an acquisition. They may do a sale. They might do . . . some combination of all of them. Correct?

A. Correct.

Q. Doesn't say they will do a PIPE, right?

A. It definitely does not say they will do a PIPE.

Q. And nothing in the 20-F identifies the dollar amount that's going to be raised, the shares that are going to be issued, and whether discounts and warrants are going to be given to the PIPE investors as part of any potential PIPE, correct?

A. That's correct. Although I think you asked me this question before and I'll answer it the same way: It did mention warrants that were being used as a compensation in this manner.

Q. Right. The warrants that were going to be paid to Merriman, but ... those aren't talking about the warrants that are going to go to the PIPE investors, correct?

A. That's what I said, as compensation....

    MR. SCHULTZ: We have no further questions, Your Honor.

---

[4] The Trial Testimony Concludes

After Dr. Sirri completed testifying, both the SEC and Mr. Cuban rested their case. Mr. Cuban renewed his motion for a directed verdict which was denied by Judge Fitzwater. *An excerpt of the dialogue between the district court and legal counsel follows.*

    THE COURT: And does the SEC close at this time?

    MS. FOLENA: Yes, we do, Your Honor.

    THE COURT: And does Mr. Cuban close and adopt his prior motion [for a directed verdict by the court in favor of Mr. Cuban]?

    MR. MELSHEIMER: We do, Your Honor ...

    THE COURT: And the ruling of the court is the same.

    Members of the jury, the evidence in the case is now closed....

    It's very important that you follow all of my prior instructions not to talk about the case.

    I'm going to go ahead and excuse you so I can confer with counsel about scheduling.

[C] The Closing Arguments

Thereafter, the parties presented their closing arguments to the jury. During that time, the jury was provided with two documents: the court's charge to the jury as well as the stipulation of facts. These documents are addressed later in this chapter. *As excerpted, prior to the commencement of closing arguments, Judge Fitzwater directed the members of the jury as follows:*

    THE COURT: ... Members of the jury, at this time the court security officer is distributing to each of you two documents.

    One document is entitled Court's Charge to the Jury. This is a document to which I have referred several times during the course of the trial that contains the court's instructions concerning the law that governs the case, as well as some instructions that you may find helpful in making your own decisions about the facts of the case.

Additionally, you are each being provided a document entitled Stipulated Facts.[11] I will be addressing that document in the court's charge to let you know what function that document has.

In a moment you're going to hear the closing arguments in the case, and I want to give you some instructions about that as well as the court's charge before we begin.

First of all, the purpose for giving you the court's charge at the beginning of the arguments is so that you will have it to refer to if the attorneys should ask you to do so. However, as a courtesy to the attorneys I ask that you not read the charge or leaf through the charge as they are arguing. This might distract you and you need to focus on what they are saying. But if they should ask you to turn to the charge or ask you to read along, then you should feel free to do so.

After all of the arguments are completed I will read the charge aloud to you in accordance with the court rules.

In addition, the copy of the charge that you have and the Stipulated Facts is your personal and individual copy. If you wish to make notes on it, if you wish to take it home or discard it after the case is over, then you may, because it is your personal copy.

The evidence in the case has closed. This means that what the attorneys say during closing arguments is not additional evidence. If . . . an attorney should make an assertion about the evidence that you do not believe is supported by your own recollection of the evidence, then you must base your verdict upon your own determinations of the evidence and not based on what a lawyer says, if different. Because, as I have instructed you at various times during the trial, what the attorneys say is not evidence in the case.

The burden of proof, as explained in the court's charge, is on the plaintiff, the Securities and Exchange Commission. Because the SEC has the burden of proof it has the right to open and close the argument. This means that although equal time has been given to each side for closing argument, you will first hear from the SEC, then from counsel for Mr. Cuban, and then finally from counsel for the SEC in reply.

And after that process is finished then I will read the charge to you. . . .

All right. Who is arguing for the SEC?

Ms. Folena?

MS. FOLENA: I am, Your Honor.

[11.] The Stipulated Facts are set forth in the Pre-Trial Order contained in Chapter 6 of this book.

[1] The SEC's Closing Argument

Ms. Folena thereupon presented the closing argument on the SEC's behalf. *Excerpts of the Commission's closing argument follow.*

> MS. FOLENA: Thank you, Your Honor.
> May it please the court.
> Good afternoon, ladies and gentlemen.
> Well, here we are, three weeks later . . . .
> We're going to end this trial right where we started it, with the words of Mark Cuban, "Now I'm screwed. I can't sell."
> We have proven in this case through the testimony of Guy Fauré that Mark Cuban made that statement on June 28th, 2004, on a telephone call that took place at 1:00 p.m.
> During that phone call Guy Fauré gave Mark Cuban material, nonpublic information about a PIPE transaction. Mr. Cuban agreed to keep it confidential and he agreed not to trade on it.
> Ladies and gentlemen, Mr. Cuban knew he was screwed, he knew he couldn't sell, but he did it anyway. And we backed up Mr. Fauré's testimony 100 percent in this trial with an email that Mr. Fauré sent to the Mamma.com board of directors at 3:51 p.m. on June 28th, just hours after his phone call with Mark Cuban.
> And that email confirmed that Mr. Cuban was not happy about the PIPE transaction but knew that he could not sell his shares until after the public announcement.
> We have proven through Mr. Cuban's own testimony that he learned the material details of the PIPE transaction from Arnie Owen. He admitted on that witness stand that he called Mr. Owen to find out if the PIPE had discounts and warrants and that Mr. Owen confirmed that it did.
> And we also showed that Mr. Owen told Mr. Cuban that the public announcement of the PIPE would hit the tape the very next day.
> And then we showed that at 5:41 p.m., one minute after Mr. Cuban learned about those discounts and warrants he called his broker and told him to get me out, sell every share I own. And we proved that he did that just hours after he told Mr. Fauré that he was screwed and he couldn't sell.
> We have proven that the information Mr. Cuban had about the PIPE transaction, including the discounts and the warrants was information that the ordinary investor did not have, information that Mr. Cuban believed would dilute his ownership in the company and cause the value of his investment to fall.
> We have proven that despite his agreement with Mr. Fauré to keep that information confidential and not trade, he did it anyway.
> Why?
> We have proven that, too. Because he was not going to lose, not as a result of this PIPE, not as a result of this business decision that he vehemently did not agree with.
> Mr. Cuban told you on that witness stand he is always trying to win. He looks at every loss in his life as a huge failure. That desire to win, that competitive edge that makes him successful, is exactly what caused him to violate the law in this case. It's

what caused him to call his broker one minute after learning that those discounts and those warrants were going to hurt his investment. We have proven in this trial that Mark Cuban insider traded, and we've proven that he knew better.

Now, as Judge Fitzwater has explained, we, the SEC, are required to prove seven elements in this case. They're in your charge....

... Let's first talk about the information about the PIPE.

Mr. Cuban learned about that PIPE on the June 28th, 2004, telephone call with Guy Fauré. Mr. Cuban doesn't remember the call. The only person that can tell you what happened on that call is Guy Fauré.

Mr. Fauré testified that he told Mr. Cuban about the PIPE. Mr. Goldman, the president and chairman of Mamma.com confirmed that Mr. Cuban was told about the PIPE. There has been no evidence contradicting that Mr. Fauré told Mr. Cuban about the PIPE.

And, in fact, Mr. Fauré's telephone call to Mr. Cuban is backed up by Mamma.com's own internal documents....

... [W]e have proven that the PIPE transaction and its terms were material.

And you have this [jury] instruction on materiality:

Would a reasonable investor consider this information significant when considering whether to buy or sell Mamma.com stock.

Now, this is a fact issue for you. The best evidence that this PIPE and its terms were material is Mr. Cuban himself.

Remember this?

This is his blog post where he tells everybody he doesn't like the idea of selling in a private placement, stock for less than the market price, and then to make matters worse, pushing the price lower with the issuing of warrants, so I sold the stock. Those are Mr. Cuban's own words. He believed this PIPE would dilute his ownership percentage and would hurt his investment. The warrants could push the price lower.

Once Mr. Cuban found out that the company was doing a PIPE and that it had the discounts and warrants, he sold. That's materiality.

But that's not all we've shown. Mr. Owen, with years of experience selling PIPEs, confirmed that discounts and warrants were important to investors.

Mitch Kopin, one of the PIPE investors, testified that the warrants were one of the most crucial facts for him when deciding to invest.

Mr. Fauré testified that the information about the PIPE was material because it was a significant investment in a public company. And he was right....

For the entire year of 2003 this company only took in 8.9 million dollars. This PIPE is 16.6 million dollars. It's almost twice what they took in the whole previous year. But what's more, the profits for that year were only $88,000. This PIPE is 16 million. It's more than 160 times the total profit for the company for the entire year of 2003.

Here's the common sense: Here's ... what you have to ask yourselves: Wouldn't you want to know that a company that you own shares in was raising 16 million dollars through a PIPE, more than 160 times the total profit for the entire year before? ....

You see, the ordinary investor didn't have any of that information. They couldn't evaluate it. Mr. Cuban could. He had that information. He did evaluate it. And it took him one minute to sell everything he owned.

Now, the next element [focuses on whether the information was] ... nonpublic. This one is very important....

The top part [of the jury charge] reads, "Information is nonpublic, if it has not been effectively disclosed in a manner sufficient to insure its availability to the investing public. Information becomes public when disclosed to achieve a"—and here's the key—"broad dissemination to the investing public generally and without favoring any special person or group, or when, although known only by a few persons, their trading"—that's the key—"on it has caused the information to be fully incorporated into the price of the particular stock.["]

Okay. This is the paragraph that applies in this case....

Now, let's look at the press release again.

The press release. The information here was a 16 million dollar PIPE with discounts and warrants. It was announced to the public through a press release issued by Mamma.com on June 29th, 2004, at 6:00 p.m.

Okay. And you'll have this as an exhibit.

There is no evidence in this record that this press release was broadly disseminated before June 29th, 2004, at 6:00 p.m.

There is no evidence that those details that you see in this press release, the 16.6 million, the discounts and the warrants is anywhere in the public arena before that date. Even Dr. Sirri admitted that.

But there's more. The company's own internal documents, on June 23rd, about a week before it's announced to the public, the company says Mr. Cuban ... "[w]ould be privy to information not available to other shareholders" ....

But most importantly, Mr. Cuban, the largest shareholder in Mamma.com didn't know about the PIPE or its discounts or its warrants until June 28th, 2004, after his conversations with Guy Fauré and Arnie Owen. And he said that.

Now, the PIPE investors, let's talk about them for a minute. The six PIPE investors that you heard about in this trial. Yes, they were a small group. And, yes, they did know about the PIPE because they have to. Mamma.com is trying to get them to invest in the PIPE. You can't ask people to invest if you don't tell them what they're investing in. So they do know about the PIPE. But in order for you to find that their knowledge made this public, you must find according to the jury instruction that ... those six traded. They bought or sold securities in the market and caused the information about the PIPE to be fully incorporated into the price of the stock before the public announcement.

There is no evidence in this case that any of those six investors traded. There's no testimony. There's no trading records. There's no email. There's no rumors. There's not even a Yahoo! message board about that.

Even Mr. Owen, who had contact with every single one of those six PIPE investors testified he was not aware that any of them traded.

If there is no evidence that those six traded, there can be no conclusion that any trading was incorporated into the stock price. That's the law that has to be followed when you decide whether or not this information was public or not.

Even Dr. Sirri, Mr. Cuban's $900 an hour hired gun, doesn't know for sure if any of the PIPE investors, the six, traded. He never spoke to them. He testified he never saw any evidence that they traded.

And what's more, he testified that he would have no way to determine whether that trading, even if it ever existed, was incorporated into the stock price.

But here's another point. There is no evidence in this case that the PIPE investors told anybody about the PIPE. It was not broadly disseminated to the public through those six PIPE investors.

Mr. Owen testified that he had no actual recollection of telling any investors outside of those six about the PIPE. And he had not seen any document in this case that shows that anyone outside of the six PIPE investors knew about the PIPE....

Mr. Fauré and Mr. Owen gave Mr. Cuban the actual material, nonpublic information that the PIPE was going to happen, it was going to have discounts, and it was going to have warrants....

And once they confirm it to Mr. Cuban, that's the material, nonpublic information. That's what he had. That's not what the average investor had. And that's what he used to sell his shares.

Now, let's talk just for a minute, since it's relevant to this element about Dr. Erik Sirri.

This is the man that Mr. Cuban paid $900 an hour to prepare an opinion and testify for him. He was here last Wednesday from 9:00 in the morning until five in the evening and at that rate he was paid more than $7,000 for one day's work.

Now, let's look at what he says.

He says there was a volume spike on June 28th.

He claims that that volume spike likely, he's not even sure, it likely reflects information about the PIPE seeping into the market.

But he testified last Wednesday that he has no idea who those traders are or why they traded. He's never spoken to any of them. And we know that in this case the only thing that matters is whether the six PIPE investors traded. And there's no evidence that they did. But there's also no evidence that anyone outside of the six PIPE investors knew about the PIPE.

Now, last Wednesday Dr. Sirri testified that he was unable to say that that volume spike was not the result of noise trading, people trading on false information, people trading on rumors, people trading because their computers were setup with algorithms to tell them when to trade because other people were trading or it wasn't just the result of ... day traders in the market trading on momentum....

The only evidence of anybody knowing about that PIPE is the evidence that Mark Cuban knew about it. You see, Mark Cuban is the only one on June 28th that knew there was going to be a PIPE, it was going to have discounts, and it was going to have warrants. And once he found that out, he traded....

Last thing. [Dr. Sirri] talked about a 9 percent price drop after the PIPE was announced last week. And he told you that that 9 percent is not—say this one fast: Statistically significant.

But the standard is not whether it's statistically significant. The standard is what a reasonable investor would think about it. And just because Dr. Sirri doesn't think that a 9 percent price drop is statistically significant doesn't mean a reasonable investor wouldn't think that a 16 million dollar PIPE with discounts and warrants was significant to their investment decision, Mark Cuban certainly thought it was.

But even Dr. Sirri doesn't always believe that a 9 percent price drop is [not] statistically significant. 20 years ago when he was writing a paper on such things for academic purposes and not being paid $900 an hour by Mark Cuban he said that a 7.8 percent drop was statistically significant.

So which is it, Dr. Sirri?

The jury instruction that you'll get will tell you that expert opinions may be completely rejected when they're not supported by the facts or the data. And I've shown you that not one of Dr. Sirri's opinions, not one thing he said in this case is supported by the evidence.

There's no evidence the PIPE investors talked.

There's no evidence the PIPE investors traded.

There's no evidence that their trading, which didn't even exist, was incorporated into the price.

And there's no evidence that the PIPE investors broadly disseminated the information.

You see, the information Mr. Cuban had on June 28th from Guy Fauré and Arnie Owen was information the rest of the investors didn't have. It was not disseminated. And none of those PIPE investors traded on it. . . .

Mr. Cuban agreed to keep the information about the PIPE confidential and not trade on it.

So here's the jury instruction.

"The SEC must prove that Mr. Cuban expressly or implicitly agreed with Mamma.com that he would keep the material, nonpublic information confidential and that he would not trade on it or otherwise use it for his benefit."

"The existence of such an agreement can be implied from the parties' conduct and the surrounding circumstances."

Now, let's look. What has that conduct and the surrounding circumstances shown?

It shows exactly what I told you a few weeks ago that it was going to show, that Mr. Cuban and Mr. Fauré had a business relationship that was based entirely upon the fact that Mark Cuban is the single largest shareholder of Mamma.com.

You've seen emails that these two men, Mr. Fauré and Mr. Cuban, were exchanging information about the business of Mamma.com. . . .

The April 23rd, 2004 email. This email is critical. It shows Mr. Cuban is well aware that certain corporate information of Mamma.com is confidential and he obviously knows that and he will agree to keep it confidential.

Mr. Cuban testified on that witness stand that what this meant was that in relationship to acquisitions information he knows is confidential, if Mr. Fauré wanted to have a discussion about that then, yes, obviously he would keep that confidential.

Now, here's the important point about the parties' conduct and the surrounding circumstances: When you read this email note, Mr. Cuban did not have to wait for Mr. Fauré to say any magic words. You can see what Mr. Fauré said before Mr. Cuban wrote this.

Mr. Fauré did not have to ask Mr. Cuban to keep this information confidential. He didn't have to provide an elaborate explanation of what any of this meant. Mr. Cuban didn't need a written document. He didn't need any of those things to know exactly what this meant. Because Mr. Cuban had run companies before. He already knew information about acquisitions could be confidential. And he offered, he, not Mr. Fauré, Mr. Cuban offered, those are his words, that if he received confidential information, obviously, what Mr. Fauré tells him is confidential. . . .

We have proven this: That they spoke on June 28th.

We have proven that Guy Fauré said, "Mark, I've got confidential information."

We have proven that Mr. Cuban said, "Okay, uh-huh, go ahead."

And we have proven that Mr. Fauré clearly understood that that meant Mr. Cuban would hold the information in confidence, won't share it with any outside party, and will not be able to sell the stock until the public announcement.

Now, we proved that Mr. Fauré said those things right here in court. . . .

Now, Mr. Cuban sat on that witness stand and he denies that he ever said that. But how credible is that?

Mr. Cuban doesn't remember the phone call. He doesn't remember what Mr. Fauré said. He doesn't remember what he said. How could he possibly know what he didn't say?

The only person that knows and could testify about what happened on that phone call is Guy Fauré. And he did.

But Mr. Cuban meant exactly what he said.

"Now I'm screwed. I can't sell" could only mean one thing. Mr. Cuban was screwed because the PIPE was going to dilute his percent ownership in this company, make the value of his shares fall, and he couldn't sell because he agreed to keep the information confidential.

Now, Mr. Cuban says that that's just not something I would say. I would never say something like that.

But we've seen his emails. We've seen him tell Charles McKinney that what he says on message boards is bullshit. . . . We say all that colorful language he used.

Ladies and gentlemen, "Screwed. I can't sell" is exactly what Mr. Cuban would say, and that's if he didn't say worse.

We have proven the agreement of confidentiality and the agreement not to trade. . . .

... [T]hird. Mr. Cuban sold his shares because of the PIPE. Now, let's look at what this jury instruction says.

> "To prove that Mr. Cuban traded on the material, nonpublic information in the sale of his Mamma stock, the SEC must prove that Cuban used or was motivated by the material, nonpublic information in the sale of his Mamma.com stock. The SEC is not required to prove that Cuban sold his Mamma.com stock solely because of the material, nonpublic information."

Now, Mr. Cuban admitted on the witness stand in this trial that he sold because of that PIPE and he sold because of the discounts and warrants.

We have proven through Mr. Cuban's own testimony that he sold because of that private investment in public equity, and he sold because of the discounts and because of the warrants. And we have shown you in this trial all of the emails that he sent to his friends and his colleagues and members of the press saying he sold and he sold for one reason only, the PIPE. . . .

Four. The SEC must prove that before trading, this is the key, on the material, nonpublic information Mr. Cuban did not fully disclose that he planned to trade on the material, nonpublic information.

We have proven this, too. He did not disclose to anyone that he would sell before that public announcement.

"Before" is the key term.

Mr. Cuban on that stand for almost two days never testified that he told anyone that he'd sell before the public announcement. The most he ever said was that he'd sell. But he never told you when.

In fact, he specifically told Mamma.com, Guy Fauré, he wouldn't sell before the public announcement. That's what screwed can't sell means. He can't sell, and he's not going to.

Mr. Owen testified that he does not recall Mr. Cuban ever saying he would sell his shares before the PIPE was announced to the public. In fact, what Mr. Owen actually said is if a powerful investor like Mr. Cuban said "I'm selling" before the public announcement, that's something he would have remembered. And that makes sense. Of course he would have remembered this because Mr. Owen treated the PIPE information—his entire firm treated the PIPE information as confidential. He'd been selling PIPEs for years.

His company told investors that the SEC considers PIPE information material, nonpublic information, don't trade, don't disclose. . . .

So we have proven the fourth element as well. . . .

Now. The fifth element. Did Mr. Cuban act intentionally.

> "A person's state of mind can be inferred from circumstantial evidence, including the person's words, their conduct, their accounts, and all of the surrounding circumstances and the reasonable inferences that may be drawn from them."

We have proven that Mr. Cuban obtained nonpublic information about the PIPE, the discounts and warrants, and sold a minute later. We have proven the out and out deception that was involved in this conduct.

He gets the information from Mr. Fauré. He tells Mr. Fauré he's screwed, he can't sell. He gets Mr. Owen's contact information. He calls Owen to find out about the discounts and the warrants, information that the defense has not even tried to argue was public.

He finds out about the discounts and the warrants, and he sells one minute later. He knew he was screwed, he knew he couldn't sell, but he did it anyway. That's intentional conduct....

You see, insider trading happens in an office, on a telephone, in an email. In an insider-trading case you can't really run from a crime scene. All you can do is really paper your file. That's exact[ly] what Mr. Cuban did. He wasn't sending this email [to his broker Charles McKinney] because he was being conservative. He sent it because he wanted cover.

Look at that first line. He wants to make sure his trade is a hundred percent kosher. He knows his trade is no percent kosher. He knows his trade is downright illegal. He didn't ask for an email back from UBS because he didn't want one. He didn't follow-up with UBS because there was no need to follow-up on a CYA email. He just wanted to be able to say some day, in some place, that he checked. He ... just wanted cover. Those are actions of a man that knows he's done wrong. Those are not the actions of a righteous man.

The email itself lacks the information from his call with Mr. Fauré. Mr. Cuban knew this information wasn't public. When he says I'm guessing it's not public, he knew it wasn't public. Mr. Fauré told him it was confidential. He doesn't tell Mr. McKinney—and this is key—that he told Owen he would sell before the public announcement.

He says "if[.]" "If you do a PIPE, I will sell," and that's a huge point, because even in his CYA email Mr. Cuban didn't have the heart to lie to his long time broker Charles McKinney. He didn't have the heart to tell him he told Owen he was going to sell before the announcement because he never told Owen anything like that.

Now, you saw the defense try to show you all the information that Mr. Cuban gave to the SEC, but the one document he didn't give to the SEC back in 2004 was this. The CYA email. No, he didn't want the SEC to see that.

Finally, his testimony about reversing the trade. He never asked Mr. McKinney in this email or at any other time to reverse his trade.

Mr. McKinney testified he never spoke to Mr. Cuban about unwinding or reversing his trade. And he had never done that for Mr. Cuban before.

But the point is, the trade was not reversed in this case. That didn't happen. And Mr. Cuban's testimony about the fact that the trade could have been reversed can't get him out of liability in this case.

The violation of insider trading occurred when Mr. Cuban sold his shares because of the PIPE. And he can't reverse that now. Just like the bank robbery, you can't reverse it by returning the money to the bank. Once you stole it, you stole it. Once you traded, you insider traded.

But what else does the guilty man actually do?

Once Mr. Cuban received notice in 2007 that the SEC was considering suing him, his lawyer got a letter from the SEC May of 2007, six weeks later Mr. Cuban enlists his boys at Sharesleuth, a nonprofit investigative journalism site, to track down dirt on Guy Fauré in Canada, find any dirt they could find on him possible....

Mr. Cuban knows that Mr. [Fauré] is the only person that can testify about what really happened on that June 28th phone call.

So what does he do?

He sends his boys out to track 'em down, to find whatever he possibly can.

And then once he gets the telephone number for Mr. Kott, he wants his boys to call the MF-er and ask him how involved he was with Mamma ....

You are looking for dirt because Mr. Fauré is the only man that can testify about that phone call; isn't that right, Mr. Cuban? ....

Why was he sending out a band of investigators to Canada to dig something up on this guy?

Mr. Cuban admitted it right here in court. We all heard him say he wanted to crush these guys. That's his testimony. It wasn't mine.

So let's recap:

We have Mr. Cuban's feigned cooperation with the SEC. He lies to them about who's approving his trades. He doesn't tell them he told anyone he would sell before the public announcement.

The same day he sends his CYA email to his broker.

Then he learns the SEC is going [to] sue him and he sends a manhunt to Canada to dig up dirt on Guy Fauré, the only man who could testify against him.

Ask yourself: Are those the actions of a righteous man? Those are the actions of a desperate man, the man who knows he's done wrong.

We have proven element number 5, he acted with intent....

Ladies and gentlemen, we have proven every element of the offense of insider trading against Mr. Cuban. We have shown that each of those things is more likely than not. We have shown, our evidence is way stronger, than the standard that we have to meet.

Now, remember I told you in my opening statement that the defense would have reasons why we have not proven our case?

And one of those reasons will be that Guy Fauré is lying, he's lying about his conversation with Mr. Cuban and he changed his testimony.

Now, if Mr. Cuban's lawyer believed Mr. Fauré was lying and had changed his testimony, why didn't they ask him about it when he was on the videotape, when they had the chance?

Mr. Best [Attorney for Mr. Cuban] asked Mr. Fauré an hour or more of questions on that videotape, but never asked the man if he was lying. Never asked him if he had changed his testimony.

And then Mr. Melsheimer ... stood up here and read a whole bunch of documents to you, all dated before Guy Fauré's testimony on that videotape, November 2011.

But Mr. Best never asked Mr. Fauré about a single document in Mr. Melsheimer's binder. They didn't ask Mr. Fauré whether he lied. They didn't ask Mr. Fauré whether he changed his testimony. They didn't even ask ... Mr. Fauré about any of those documents, because they didn't want to know the answer.

But you know what, they didn't want you to know the answer, because they want to come in here, accuse a man on videotape of lying without ever asking him if he actually did. They want to smear him without giving him a chance to defend himself.

When my colleagues and I thought a witness on that stand was lying or changed their testimony we showed them their testimony. Right in front of you. So you could see what they would say. So you could view what their face looked like, so that you could hear their answer.

We did it with Mr. Cuban. When he changed his testimony about hunting down Guy Fauré, I asked him point-blank whether he had done that, so you could see what he'd say.

When Mr. Thompson asked Mr. McKinney about sending the CYA email with a wink and a nod he confronted Mr. McKinney with his prior testimony, so you could see what Mr. McKinney said.

And Mr. Aguilar. Who can forget the number of times we had to show Mr. Aguilar his prior testimony? We even gave Mr. Aguilar the chance to explain why he had changed his testimony.

You see, the defense's strategy in this case is to smear Guy Fauré without allowing him a chance to defend himself.

Does that resemble somebody else's conduct?

Mark Cuban.

Only his words were "I want to crush these guys," because ... once he knew the SEC was on to the fact that he had insider traded, [Mr. Cuban] was going to send his band of investigators to Canada to dig up dirt, and his lawyers were on that email. Mr. Hart, sitting in this courtroom right now, was on those emails.

But let's talk about the credibility of Mark Cuban in this case. Let's talk about the credibility of the defendant that sat on that witness stand for two days.

Was he credible when you saw him?

Whenever Mr. Cuban was confronted with a fact or a statement, in a blog, in an email, or testimony that he didn't like, he responded as follows, That's just hyperbole, it's an exaggeration. That wasn't literal. I didn't really mean that. Or that was just a stock answer. Or he just flat-out claimed not to remember.

In Mr. Cuban's world that's how you deflect. That's how you avoid admitting the facts that you don't like. That's how you avoid confronting your own words that show you're liable. . . .

When is Mr. Cuban telling the truth and when is he exaggerating?

When is he telling the truth and when is he lying?

If we look at what he said in this trial, he was not truthful. He lied when he said that Irving Kott had anything to do with his sale, a sale he made one minute after talking to Arnie Owen, a reason he never told anyone about, and is not in his blog.

He lied when he said his investment philosophy wasn't literal, when his Mamma.com purchase was completely consistent with his philosophy.

He lied when he said BS doesn't mean bullshit.

He lied when he changed his testimony right there on the stand about wanting to get to Fauré, the only man that could testify against him.

He lied when he said I know I didn't say, screwed .... He can't know he didn't say that; he doesn't remember the conversation.

Like I said three weeks ago, Mr. Cuban cannot hide from the facts. The facts don't lie.

We have proven Mr. Cuban insider-traded, and we have proven why....

I told you at the beginning, insider trading is a form of cheating. We have shown Mr. Cuban knew about information that other investors didn't, and he sold before he lost a dime.

This is not a criminal case. We're not asking you to convict Mr. Cuban of a crime. We're not asking you to send him to jail. And none of those things will happen to him.

This case is civil, and it's about, like I said, the rights and the responsibilities of all the investors in our markets, the right of every investor, every single one of us, to know that we're trading in a market that's fair, and the responsibility of every investor, every single one of us, including Mark Cuban, to play fair.

The job of the SEC is to protect investors, and we hope we've done our best in this trial to make sure that everyone that buys and sells securities in our markets does so on a level playing field, keeping the markets fair for all investors—the wealthy and the famous, the average and the ordinary—is what this case is all about.

The federal securities laws are the rules of the investment game, and they apply to everybody in the market, including Mark Cuban.

Ladies and gentlemen, find Mark Cuban liable. He didn't play by the rules. He wasn't fair. His trade was downright illegal. And above ... all of the investors in the market, Mr. Cuban knew better.

Thank you. The SEC thanks you for your service, for your patience, and for your time.

[2] Mr. Cuban's Closing Argument

As the SEC's closing argument reflected, the Commission's approach was combative. As one journalist reported, "the SEC said Cuban acted like a 'desperate man' who tried to cover up his wrongdoing, and accused him of repeatedly lying on the stand about the reasons he dumped his 600,000 shares in Mamma.com."[12] Responding to the SEC, Mr. Thomas Melsheimer presented the closing argument on Mr. Cuban's behalf. Not mincing words,

---

12. Jess Krochtengel, *Jurors Weigh Cuban Insider Case After Contentious Closings*, Law 360, *available at* https://www.law360.com/articles/4/9546/print?section=media (Oct. 15, 2013).

Mr. Melsheimer characterized the government's presentation of Mr. Fauré's recorded deposition testimony as "weak … as you will ever find in a federal courtroom" and "accused the government of covering up key evidence, making misleading arguments, name-calling and attacking the character of defense witnesses …."[13] *Excerpts of Mr. Cuban's closing argument follow.*

MR. MELSHEIMER: May it please the court, Your Honor.

Good afternoon. On behalf of Mr. Cuban and all the members of his team that have worked on this case over the last three weeks, I want to thank you for your time and attention. We know there were times that you would rather be somewhere else, but you were here, and we appreciate that very much.

As I promised you in my opening statement, we brought you all the evidence, the full story, the complete picture of what happened back in June 2004. The evidence has illustrated precisely what I promised you it would.

Number 1, the information about the Mamma.com PIPE was not confidential. It was public.

Two, that Mr. Cuban made no agreement to keep anything confidential.

Third, that Mr. Cuban made no agreement not to sell his stock.

Fourth, that Mr. Cuban disclosed his intentions to sell his Mamma stock to Mamma and its agents.

And finally—and finally, that Mr. Cuban acted like a man who had nothing to hide, because he had nothing to hide.

Now, let's review in the time I have with you what the evidence has actually shown, what it has proven over the last couple of weeks. Not what the government just told you. Not what the government said they were going to show you in [its] opening statement. Not what the government just said the evidence had proven, because I submit to you—and I'll prove this—that the government has hidden the ball.

They have hidden the ball in this trial, and they have hidden the ball in bringing this case against Mr. Cuban....

They did it throughout the trial by making misleading arguments, character attacks, name calling, and sometimes by literally trying to … white-out the evidence so you wouldn't see it.

They did it in the opening statement when they said that the … absent Mr. Fauré had no reason to lie to you, but made no mention that he had been under investigation for years by the SEC, both him and his company.

So sitting here this afternoon you know what the evidence has actually shown, the evidence in court, the testimony around the documents, the full picture, the whole story.

To understand the significance of that evidence though, you need to pay close attention to the charge that Judge Fitzwater has given you. You each have a copy of it. It's the only document in the case that you have your own personal copy of. That's how important it is.

---

13. *Id.*

Now, here is a chart with the elements that ... the SEC must prove but cannot prove.

June 28th, 2004. Let's go back. The day the Mamma PIPE was supposed to close. Mark Cuban wasn't out trying to get secret information about Mamma.

As the day began, he was at a golf tournament raising money for the Make-A-Wish Foundation. He returned to the Maverick's offices around 1:00 o'clock where he found an email. This email. This email from Mr. Fauré that asked him to call ASAP but didn't say why.

That's why Mr. Cuban said he found out about Mamma's plan for a PIPE almost by accident.

Remember these are the notes from the SEC lawyer that were admitted into evidence. "Almost by accident I found out." That's what he told them two days later, and it was the truth. . . .

As we review the evidence ... let's focus on this first element which is public.

The government must prove ... that Mr. Cuban received material, nonpublic information from Mamma concerning Mamma's impending PIPE transaction. They must prove that the information was nonpublic. . . .

Mr. Owen [at Merriman] told you they started calling potential investors and pitching them on the PIPE transaction. He testified that he and his team were out contacting potential investors. . . .

Mr. Owen did not believe that information about the PIPE was material, non-public information. He didn't seek a single agreement from any investors to keep the PIPE information confidential or to restrain trading.

How does the government respond to this?

Mr. Owen, we're going to see his testimony in great detail. They're out in the public selling this PIPE. They're talking to people all over the country. There's no restrictions with anyone they're talking to about confidentiality

The government says, well, he probably only contacted six people because those are the six investors that ended up doing the deal.

Now, does that make any sense to you at all? They're all pitching a PIPE, and based on what they suggest, all they had to do was make six phone calls?

That's not what Mr. Owen told you. That's not what your common sense tells you. . . .

So what do we know in March 2004 about the PIPE?

We know that Arnie Owen is out talking to potential investors.

We know that others on his team were out pitching the investment.

Now, during this trial the government has tried to create confidentiality agreements where none exist. . . .

They never showed you a true confidentiality agreement from anyone about the PIPE. They never played one second of testimony from any PIPE investor saying that that investor had any kind of confidentiality agreement, written or oral, about the PIPE.

What you did hear was Mr. Owen said over and over again that people did not have confidentiality agreements, he never asked investors for that and in fact people reached out to him to call him that he had not originally called.

So what happens in the marketplace when these market participants don't have confidentiality agreements?

Well, you heard from Dr. Sirri.

What did Dr. Sirri tell you last week?

"Q. Based on your experience with traders, what would traders do with information about the PIPE if they had no confidentiality obligations?

"A. Traders are free to do what they wish. They can talk, they can trade, they can talk to whomever they like."

Now, you heard the government criticize and suggest that Dr. Sirri was some kind of a hired gun making $900 an hour that didn't know what he was talking about.

This is a man that they hired not once but twice. This was a man that was one of the most senior people at the SEC. There was only one person above him in the whole organization.

But, see, when he's here saying something that they don't like he's incompetent, he's on the take. That's the kind of deceptive argument you've heard from the government throughout this case.

And we'll talk more about Dr. Sirri and his testimony.

But remember this: There's not a single expert the government brought you to contradict anything Dr. Sirri said.

They had one. They had one.

Remember . . . , Dr. Sialm?

He's in the wind. He's gone. They didn't bring him to testify. I'll suggest to you some reasons why later, but he's nowhere to be found. . . .

We know then that the PIPE's being discussed by Mr. Owen and his investors in March. We know in April it's on the Yahoo! message board. But, again, the public disclosure of this information about the PIPE didn't stop there.

What happened next?

May 27th, 2004. That is the filing [with the SEC] of the [Form] 20-F. This is the next important date in the continuing disclosure of this PIPE information. . . .

It says that Merriman is acting as Mamma's financial advisor. It says that Merriman is going to represent the company in a PIPE. It says Merriman will work together to identify acquisition transactions. And it says that Merriman will receive compensation in the form of warrants.

Now, what did the government tell you about this public document?

One word. "May." "May do a PIPE." That's the best they can do. They focused over and over on the idea since the engagement says "may" as opposed to "will" or "guarantee," that means it's somehow uncertain. They want you to believe that this word "may" takes a cloak of secrecy and drops it over this 20-F and somehow keeps it from public view.

Now, we know Merriman is the PIPE company. You go to Baskin & Robbins you get ice cream. You go to Merriman you're going to do a PIPE.

We also know that this thing was filed May 27th, 2004, had been executed in March of 2004. So this was a continuing thing. If they had decided not to do it in May, they wouldn't have attached it to their public filing in May because it no longer would have been a material agreement for the company. . . .

Every live witness who had any experience with the securities industry testified about the public nature of the information in the 20-F.

These industry witnesses all knew that PIPEs come with discounts and warrants. That's what PIPEs are. PIPEs come with discounts and warrants. They knew that because Mamma.com told the public how they were going to pay Merriman.

Remember?

They were going to pay Merriman by issuing warrants. So there's no warrants to issue to the broker unless there's warrants in the deal.

They also knew the PIPE would have discounts because every PIPE that Merriman pitched had discounts....

What happens next?

June 18th, Plaintiff's Exhibit 17th. This is the date that Sage Capital, the lead investor for this PIPE, sent around the term sheet.

Now, the argument the government makes is this was only sent to those three people, the company and their lawyers. But that's not what it says. That's not what the attachment says.

The attachment has Sage Capital Growth on it. It says June 18th, 2004. It has all the terms of the PIPE that the government claims was so secret and so nonpublic and so confidential. They're all there on the document. And there's not a hint or a whiff that this document or its terms are confidential.

If you want people to know something is confidential, it's pretty easy. You put confidential on it, do not disclose. Nowhere in this document, 18, Plaintiff's 18, does the word "confidential" appear....

So let's take a look at the summary of all this. We've got the April message board posting, talks about a PIPE. We've got the May 27th public [20-F] filing. It talks about a PIPE with warrants.

And we've got this nonconfidential term sheet that talks about PIPE, warrants, discounts, financial terms open and says it's going to close on June 28th, which in fact was the anticipated day.

So what happened? What happened?

According to the government none of this stuff is out there, this stuff is all confidential, it's nonpublic.

What happened on June 28th?

The trading spike. The trading spike happened.

You see Dr. Sirri's testimony about how information had been disseminated in the market place through rumors, through word of mouth, through potential investors in the PIPE, through SEC filings. All those things put information in the marketplace. And once it's in the marketplace and the time and the place for the PIPE transaction neared, traders traded, people bought, people sold ....

What did Dr. Sirri conclude from that? ... What's his conclusion?

"Q. Do you have a conclusion about whether the PIPE information was public before Mr. Cuban traded?

"A. Yes, I do.

"Q. What is it?

"A. My conclusion is that the information about the Mamma.com PIPE was public, was available to investors, and was incorporated into the price of the Mamma.com stock before Mr. Cuban traded."

There's not a word of testimony to contradict Dr. Sirri. Dr. Sirri is the only witness that came forth, did analysis, and made this conclusion.

Again, they had somebody, Dr. Sialm. They didn't call him. You could draw whatever conclusion about why they didn't call him, but they had him sitting in court listening to Dr. Sirri, and he hightailed it out of Dallas because Dr. Sirri's conclusions are correct. Dr. Sirri's conclusions are supported by the evidence.

All that volume, all that trading, before Mr. Cuban sold a single share of stock ....

Now, folks, the truth is that this information about the PIPE was public long before that rushed phone call between Mr. Cuban and Mr. Fauré on June 28th. And that is why you should conclude that Mr. Cuban did not receive nonpublic information, which is the first element the SEC must prove.

But the government's case fails for other reasons. Let's return to the elements the SEC must prove.

The next one is right here, number 2: They must prove that Mr. Cuban agreed to, one, keep the PIPE information confidential; and two, that he agreed that he would not trade on the information.

From the very beginning Mamma knew that Mark Cuban would never agree to do this, and he never did.

The PIPE transaction was involved at Mamma for many months, but the Mamma executives knew they had a problem. They knew that Mark Cuban didn't like PIPEs. And they knew it was going to be trouble for them if he found out about it....

So Mamma elected to keep the information about the PIPE from Mr. Cuban until the last minute.

Let's be clear about that: Many other people knew about the PIPE. That's certain. But Mr. Cuban didn't. Perhaps that's because over about four months he spent maybe 15 hours on this whole investment, which was one-half of one percent of his total investments. But as the deadline for the PIPE approached the Mamma executives must have been getting a little nervous. So they decide to approach him on June 28th, likely after he would have had any realistic chance of investing .... In the words, of Arnie Owen ... it was going to be a courtesy call.

So we're now up to June 28th, the email and Mr. Fauré's eight minute phone call with Mr. Cuban. This phone call is at the heart of the government's case because according to the government Mr. Cuban agreed to do two things on that call, agreed to keep information confidential and agreed not to sell his stock.

Here's the email. We now know though that there were actually two phone calls, a dropped call of about 26 seconds and a longer call of about eight minutes. We also know that Mr. Fauré was walking off the elevator into the lobby of a public building when he supposedly had this secret or confidential conversation with Mark Cuban....

... Mamma.com wasn't trying to get an agreement from Mr. Cuban.

Was [Mr. Fauré] instructed to get an agreement, to hold the information in confidence?

Three witnesses say no.

Was he instructed to get an agreement to restrict the ability to trade?

No.

So how in the world can he think there was implied agreement from Mr. Cuban when [Mr. Fauré] didn't even go into the call seeking to get any one of these agreements?

They want you to say, well, it's somehow implied from the circumstances. Because we know it wasn't explicit, there is no written document. They want to say, well, it's implied. But how can it be implied when the man didn't even know that he was supposed to get an agreement to hold information confidential or restrict trade?

Now, I want you to take a look at Mr. Fauré. I told you in the opening statement and that I standby this. I'd like you to look at him, study him, see if he's hesitant, see if he looks like he's a person telling the truth. We can't look at him live, because he's not here . . . .

[Mr. Cuban] offered to buy him a plane ticket. There's a nonstop from Montreal to Dallas every day. This man could be here right now watching the trial. He's not here because he, unlike Mr. Cuban, did not want to look you in the eye.

And take a look at the way he answered his most important question in his deposition about whether or not there was any agreement reached between Mark Cuban and him to keep information confidential.

Watch his eyes. Watch his shoulders. Watch what he looks like.

"Q. What was said in the phone call?

"A. Well, Mr. Cuban called me. I . . . I answered the phone. And I said, 'Mark, I've got confidential information.' He somewhat acknowledged it.

I had confidential information. Yes. I don't remember the specific words, but he said, um-hum, go ahead. Something to that effect."

Is it any wonder that the man didn't want to come down here from Montreal? He can't even look the questioner in the eye when answering this question. . . .

From that testimony? You're going to base a finding for the government on that testimony, from that witness? Who won't even show up.

But what do we know about Mr. Fauré?

Well, we know that he has reasons for making up a story or exaggerating it.

Why?

Well, we know that the SEC was investigating his company in March of 2004.

Now, before the government dropped its investigation this was his testimony. The suggestion that we didn't confront him with it, we asked him this question, this very question:

"Q. We spoke earlier about you were telling Mr. Cuban, in words or substance, I have confidential information for you.

"A. Right.

"Q. Do you recall anything Mr. Cuban said in response or replied to that statement by you?

"A. No, I do not."

Pretty simple: "A. No, I do not."

He doesn't remember anything he said.

But what happens a few days later?

He gets the letter from the SEC, the get-out-of-jail-free card from the SEC that says, we've completed the investigation as to your client against whom we do not intend to recommend any action.

Is it any surprise that eight days later, eight days later, Mr. Fauré then adds . . . that Mr. Cuban said, uh-huh, all right, somewhat acknowledged?

Mr. Fauré's testimony is not credible. . . .

Now, how do we know that Mr. Cuban did not agree to keep this information confidential?

He told you the reasons. It was plain and simpl[e]. They got up here and called the man a liar over and over again. And you're going to have to judge his credibility just like any other witness. I submit you do just that. He came here and answered all their questions, the ones that were misleading, the ones that were straight. He answered my questions. He answered the government's questions. They could still be asking him questions right now if they wanted to.

But what does he say?

Why would you not agree to keep the information confidential on that phone call?

"A. One, I'm not going to agree to keep something confidential when I don't know what the subject is," because remember Mr. Fauré did not tell him anything about the subject.

In Mr. Fauré's world he sends the email call me ASAP. Mark calls him and the first words Mr. Fauré says supposedly I have confidential information.

Now, what businessman, any businessman, certainly not one as successful as Mr. Cuban is going to say fine, I don't know what you're going to tell me, I don't know what it is, but whatever you're going to tell me I'm going to keep it confidential.

That's malarkey. That didn't happen.

But, two, he doesn't do oral confidentiality agreements.

And the testimony is uncontradicted:

"Q. Have you ever in all your years as a business person ever done an oral agreement, non-disclosure agreement?

"A. No.

"Q. Would you do that?

"A. No."

Mr. McKinney [Mr. Cuban's stock broker].

"Q. To your knowledge has Mr. Cuban ever agreed to an oral confidentiality agreement?

"A. No."

And of course we know it was Mr. Cuban's practice to do written confidentiality agreements and to have them reviewed by his attorney. . . .

So that brings us to Mr. Owen and later in the day on June 28th.

Mr. Owen is speaking to Mr. Cuban as Mamma's agent. He was asked to do so by Mr. Goldman [of Mamma.com] ....

Now, look at what [the email] from Mr. Owen [to Mr. Cuban] says and what it doesn't say.

... [T]his email says nothing about confidentiality....

... [L]et's talk about the testimony that Mr. Owen gave you, that I think is the key testimony in this whole case.

"Q. Did Mr. Cuban have any agreement to keep the information confidential?

"A. No, he didn't.

"Q. Did he have any agreement not to trade on the information?

"A. No, he didn't."

Now, remember, this is the call where he's supposedly getting the secret sauce. This is the call where he's supposedly getting that information about the PIPE that the government says is nonpublic and wasn't known to anyone....

... Mr. Owen didn't believe that information related to PIPEs was confidential. And neither he nor his team at Merriman treated it as confidential with respect to soliciting other investors.

Mr. Owen was Mamma's agent. He never sought an agreement from Mr. Cuban to keep information confidential. He never sought an agreement to restrict trade.

So what happened on the call between Mr. Cuban and Mr. Owen?

Well, no one on that call had any doubt that Mr. Cuban could sell his shares. You heard Mr. Cuban say that he said that Mr. Owen was out marketing the PIPE deal to investors, which indicates that the deal was not being treated as confidential or nonpublic.

Both Mr. Cuban and Mr. Owen agree that there was no agreement ever sought or obtained on that call.

And finally, ... Mr. Cuban told Mr. Owen that he would sell his shares just like he told Mr. Fauré....

Now, the evidence is really this. There's not a single agreement in this case shown between Mamma.com and any other person in the world to keep this information confidential and not trade on it.

The only person in the world that the SEC claims made this agreement is sitting right there. Not a lick of evidence that anyone made that agreement. And all the evidence that they argue that he made such an agreement, Mark Cuban, says just the opposite.

And [the SEC's] first live witness [Mr. Owen] ... stood up here—and that's why it's important to see people live. "I had no doubt." He had no doubt. You should have no doubt. There was no agreement not to trade. And she can say that over and over again, "I'm screwed. I can't sell." They could say that until the cows come home. That's out of Mr. Fauré's mouth. You saying it over and over again doesn't make it true, and it doesn't make it true in court, and it didn't change Mr. Owen's testimony who said that he had no doubt that there was no such restriction....

The SEC must prove that before trading on material, nonpublic information Cuban did not fully disclose to Mamma that he planned to trade on the material, nonpublic information.

The SEC can't prove this for two reasons. One, Mr. Cuban told Guy Fauré and Arnie Owen, Mamma's agent, that he was selling his shares, without qualifying that statement in any way. And Mr. Cuban did exactly what he said he was going to do.

Now, Mr. Fauré says that Mr. Cuban said "I can't sell." But what do the witnesses who spoke to him on June 28th say? Both Mr. Bertrand and Mr. Goldman were with him on the 28th. They both remember Mr. Fauré telling him that Mr. Cuban said he would sell....

There's no way Mr. Fauré can be believed when he says that Mr. Cuban says I can't sell when in fact the testimony was over and over again that he said he would sell. And in fact he did sell. So that's both evidence of no agreement, but it's also evidence of disclosure.

And remember, they got to prove nondisclosure, and there's simply no way they can make that burden here....

The next element of what the SEC has to prove to you is that Mr. Cuban acted knowingly. He acted knowingly or with severe recklessness....

Here there's no evidence that Mr. Cuban acted with intent to deceive Mamma....

There's not an email anywhere in this case where anyone from Mamma says, oh my goodness, Mr. Cuban has tricked us, he has deceived us when he sold those shares, we ... have been defrauded.

In fact, the evidence is just the opposite....

Now, look what happens. For three years no one from Mamma.com ever says a word about Mr. Cuban breaking agreements. Only in 2007 when the SEC is bearing down on Mr. Fauré and Mamma.com that Mr. Fauré first claims Mr. Cuban said I can't sell. Three years. Does that sound like someone who has been deceived or tricked when they don't complain about it or mention a word about it for three years? So there certainly can be no bad intent by Mr. Cuban....

The SEC is not trying this case based on the facts that actually existed in 2004. They're trying them off facts that they wish existed.

Is that fair?

Is that playing by the rules?

Or is that winning? Trying to win at all costs?

Now, what about Mr. Cuban's conduct in 2004?

Is it consistent with someone trying to deceive? ....

Well, this is the world that the SEC lives in. There's no guidance about whether these things are material, nonpublic in 2004, but we're going to sue you on it much later if we conclude it is.

If you talk freely and openly to the SEC lawyers you're lying because you wouldn't talk to 'em if you didn't have something to hide. That's what she said. That's what she implied, that Mr. Cuban talked to 'em and hid stuff.

And if you confirm ... if you send an email to your long-time broker saying I want to make sure this is a hundred percent kosher, that means you've done something wrong.

But the world they live in, if he hadn't sent that email they'd be up here arguing he didn't send an email to his broker seeking to confirm, he wouldn't talk to the SEC because he was guilty.

That's the world that they live in. And that's a world of unfairness. That's a world of trying to win at all costs.

Let's take a look at Mr. Cuban's cooperation. And I stand by the proverb of the guilty flee when no one gives chase but the righteous are bold.

Defendant's Exhibit 16, Mr. Cuban offers to pull a late-nighter to get the information to [SEC attorney] Mr. Turner.

Mr. Turner tells you under oath that Mr. Cuban answered all his questions.

... Mr. Turner's notes indicate that Mr. Cuban called voluntarily....

Is this the way we expect our government to act when you voluntarily speak to government lawyers for an hour and a half, they take notes, those notes are not available for nine years, we don't know where they are, and ... they didn't offer you a word of explanation as to where those notes were, and they want to criticize Mr. Cuban's recollection back in 2007 when they're sitting on notes of two interviews for an hour and a half with him?

That's the way they want to say play fair?

That's the way they want to say we're trying to win at all costs?

Mr. McKinney forwarded the email of Mr. Cuban's inquiry to compliance. He forwarded it to this man Johnny C., who was the head compliance man with ... the complete explanation. He says see below, Johnny Ciaramitaro, that's Johnny C....

And what did Mr. McKinney tell you?

If there had been a problem with that trade someone would have gotten back to you.

Yes. I believe if compliance thought something was wrong they would have let me know.

Now, we're not trying to suggest that the trade was unwound. We know it wasn't unwound. It wasn't unwound because no one told Mr. Cuban there was anything wrong with it.

We also know that Mr. McKinney testified that Mr. Cuban has never done anything improper to avoid loss in an investment.... [L]et's talk about this, because they said something in their closing that made me angry.

They said that Mr. Cuban was trying to win at all costs and he wasn't going to lose this.

You heard from Mr. McKinney that the man, Mark Cuban, has, literally lost tens of millions of dollars on stock trades without uttering a peep of complaint. Tens of millions of dollars over the years of his investments. And they're going to say now that he's such a liar and a cheat that he would do that here?

That's embarrassing and they should be ashamed of themselves....

I want to walk through the verdict form with you and the charge.

Standard operating procedure, let's walk through it.

So did the SEC prove each of its elements of the misappropriation here.

We know the SEC has the burden of proof.

So, first, that Mr. Cuban received material, nonpublic information from Mamma.com concerning Mamma's impending PIPE transaction.

They haven't proven that.

They haven't proven that it is nonpublic information. And we showed you all the reasons why.... Something can be public in one of two ways, either because the information is out in the marketplace—and we've shown you that—or because some people know about it and the trading by those people has caused the information to be incorporated in the price and volume of the stock. That's what Dr. Sirri told you. And that testimony is totally uncontradicted.

The second issue, did the SEC prove that Mr. Cuban expressly or implicitly agreed with Mamma to keep the material, nonpublic information confidential and not to trade. It can be express or implied, but there's no evidence of either one. There's no evidence of any express agreement, and we talked about that at length, and there's no evidence of any implied agreement....

But, moreover, there was nothing to imply. There was no circumstance to suggest that these individuals had a tradition of agreeing to things on the phone or that somehow they had done oral confidentiality agreements. Nothing like that.

And all you have about the agreement of confidentiality is that video testimony I played you of Mr. Fauré, which is about as weak and as inconsistent and as hesitant as you will ever find in a federal courtroom. And I submit to you that that's why he didn't come down to Dallas to testify.

Next question: That Mr. Cuban traded on the material, nonpublic information. They didn't prove that either. Because there is no material, nonpublic information that was proven by the SEC.

Number 4. Before trading on the material, nonpublic information, Cuban did not fully disclose to Mamma that he planned to trade.

We know that he did. We know that he did disclose. We know from Mr. Goldman that he disclosed. We know from Mr. Cuban's testimony that he disclosed. We know from Mr. Cuban's email to Mr. McKinney that he disclosed. He fully disclosed....

Next question: They must prove that he acted knowingly and with severe recklessness. You heard that. Intent to defraud?

No one talked about an agreement until after this case came, three-year gap between the trading and the allegation he broke some agreement.

Does that sound like someone defrauded?

Severe recklessness? You have to know that it's wrong. The SEC wouldn't tell people back [then] whether it was right or wrong. And Mr. Kopin and Mr. Aguilar told you that there simply were no rules. Those are the questions, the material questions that you'll need to answer in this case. And we submit to you that the government cannot prove any one of those.

I'm nearing the end of my time to speak with you. As I told you at the beginning of trial, the beginning of this closing, the government has the burden of proof. I will not have the opportunity to get back up and speak to you to correct any misstatements that the government makes in the next 30 minutes. They get the last word because they have the burden of proof.

I don't.

MR. MELSHEIMER: Your Honor, I've been asked to request how much time I have left.

THE COURT: You've used one hour, 44 minutes and 7 seconds.

MR. MELSHEIMER: All right. I don't know what the government is going to say when I sit down, but whatever they argue, I know they won't be able to bring you the following.

They will not be able to bring you Guy Fauré live and in person. They will not be able to show you a single document showing that Mr. Cuban clearly agreed either orally or in writing to keep information confidential or not trade.

They're not going to be able to change Mr. Owen's clear testimony. They're not going to be able to change the testimony that Mr. Cuban was free to sell his shares after his call with Mr. Owen.

They are not going to be able to change Mr. Owen's testimony that he didn't tell Mr. Cuban anything that was confidential on that call. They're not going to be able to change that. And they're not going to be able to offer you any testimony that contradicts Dr. Sirri's uncontested and unrebutted testimony that the information about the PIPE is public. They won't point to you to any expert that says the PIPE was material, nonpublic information because they didn't call one. No expert to contradict Dr. Sirri, Mr. Owen or Mr. Kopin, all of whom said that the information was nonmaterial and in fact was not nonpublic.

You now have the important job of deciding this case. And that's what so great about our jury system. It's a system like no other in the world.

As I told you in jury selection, America is the only country in the world that requires jury trials in civil lawsuits, especially in cases brought by the government.

You have an honored role in our system. You may have noticed during the last couple of weeks that you're the only people, you are the only people that everyone stands up for when they enter the courtroom, including Judge Fitzwater. He stands up for you. Just like we all do, because you're the foundation of our civil justice system.

We know that the government can sometimes be an important force for good in this country, from our nation's military to Head Start to student loans. We know the government does a lot of good things. But we also know that the government doesn't always get it right. And standing up to the government when they have got it wrong can be hard.

Mr. Cuban has been blessed with the kind of success that has made this country the envy of the world.

With those financial blessings come the ability to do something that most average citizens cannot do, stand up to the government, refuse to be bullied, refuse to be ground down in the cog of a litigation machine like the SEC that grinds on ....

But not even Mark Cuban, not even Mark Cuban has the power to make the government stop, to make the government stop pursuing a case that is utterly baseless. Not even Mark Cuban can make the SEC admit that they got it wrong.

Only you can do that.

You're more powerful than anyone in this room, more powerful than Judge Fitzwater, more powerful than Mark Cuban, more powerful than the SEC.

You, as jurors, have the ability to do what no one else can do, which is give justice, not just for Mark Cuban, but for anyone who would stand up to the government, who rightly stands up to the government and demands justice, who doesn't cave in and say I'm going to make this case go away, but stands up for what's right and refuses to be bullied.

Over the years in this country many people have needed help in many different ways from our court system, especially from jurors like yourselves who are empowered to do the right thing, and juries have been a key component of that.

You know, there's a saying that says we walk by faith and not by light. And I submit to you that we've done a little bit of both here. We've brought you the light of the evidence that shows that Mr. Cuban has done nothing wrong and he is not liable. He is not worthy of the names the government has cast upon him.

But we also have brought you our faith, our faith that as jurors you will do the right thing and tell the government finally that enough is enough.

Thank you.

Thank you for your service.

THE COURT: When we return from our break the SEC will have 27 minutes and 14 seconds remaining.

Members of the jury, at this time we're going to take a 15 minute break Please follow all of my important instructions. We'll resume in 15 minutes.

---

[3] The SEC's Final Salvo

As customary, the SEC reserved time in its closing argument to reply to the positions advocated by Mr. Melsheimer in the closing argument on Mr. Cuban's behalf. Vigorously advancing the government's case, Ms. Folena brought to a conclusion the SEC's prosecution of Mr. Cuban for illegal insider trading. *Excerpts of the SEC's conclusion of its closing argument follow.*

MS. FOLENA: May it please the court, ladies and gentlemen of the jury. You heard from Mr. Melsheimer, and I will call him and address him by his name, Mr. Melsheimer, even though he stood up here and attacked me, attacked our government, attacked the SEC, and couldn't refer to me as anything other than "she," when every other lawyer in this courtroom and the judge calls me Ms. Folena.

But I can take that. I can take those hits. But what I can't take is when he stands up here and tells you things that didn't happen in this trial.

And here's one of them. There is zero evidence in this case that anything improper occurred with the SEC staff attorney notes. Nothing. Mr. Cuban had those notes. He had them available to him. His lawyers had them available, and they used them in this trial. There's nothing improper about that. And the SEC did nothing wrong. There's no evidence of it, despite what Mr. Melsheimer wants you to believe about what happened with those notes.

Second, I won't let him come in here and smear Guy Fauré. He can smear me. He can smear my office. He can smear the government, but he's not going to smear Guy Fauré.

The instructions that you get in this case are that you are to view Mr. Fauré's testimony as if he were here live. Mr. Melsheimer played plenty of videotape testimony in this courtroom, and I never once made a suggestion about why those witnesses weren't here. You cannot view Mr. Fauré on videotape any differently than you did Mr. Cuban or Mr. Owen or Dr. Sirri. Those are the instructions from the court. That's the law. And I won't let Mr. Melsheimer tell you any differently.

But I will tell you this.

Think to yourself, if you're Guy Fauré and a United States billionaire has a nonprofit organization set up to track you down, are you going to come to trial? Are you going to walk into a United States courtroom when you live in Montreal, Canada, to face the billionaire that's using all of his resources to track you down?

I think not.

There are reasons Mr. Fauré did not testify here, but there's one thing only that you have to consider, and that is you have to consider his testimony as if he were here live. And we saw him, and he answered everyone's questions. He answered our questions. He answered the defendant's questions. And he did it honestly.

The other thing I won't let happen in this trial is for Mr. Melsheimer to suggest that Mr. Fauré lied to curry favor with the SEC when they never asked him those questions.

What we're going to do right now is we're going to show you that this currying favor business just makes no sense.

We're going to pull up a slide. 43, if we could, Mr. Duncan.

Here's what actually happened in this case.

Mr. Fauré testified consistently that Mr. Cuban said he was screwed and he couldn't sell. He testified or documented it throughout from June 28th when he tells the board that Mr. Cuban recognized he couldn't sell until after the public announcement.

December 2006, the SEC is investigating Mark Cuban for insider trading. That's Defense Exhibit 20.

January 2007, Mr. Fauré leaves his company. He leaves Mamma.com. On January 11th, he testifies that Mr. Cuban said "Now I'm screwed. I can't sell."

On September 7th, 2007, he testified Mr. Cuban said "Now I'm screwed. I can't sell."

September 19th, 2007, the SEC closes its investigation into Mamma.com. Closed. If Mr. Fauré was currying favor, why didn't he do it before the investigation is closed?

He can't help his company by saying things after the investigation is closed. It's too late at that point.

On September 27th, Mr. Fauré testified that Mr. Cuban said in response to "I have confidential information."

"Uh-huh, yeah, go ahead" and "Now I'm screwed. I can't sell."

And on November 4th, 2011, the testimony you heard in this courtroom is Mr. Fauré testified that Mr. Cuban said, "Uh-huh, yeah, go ahead" and "Now I'm screwed. I can't sell."

Why would Mr. Fauré wait until after the SEC drops it investigation against his company? He has nothing to gain at that point. If he was going to lie, he was going to do it before. And he didn't. He didn't lie before. He didn't lie after. And he certainly didn't lie in his email to the board when he said Mr. Cuban acknowledged he couldn't sell until after the public announcement.

And if the defense is trying to argue that he lied then, that is truly ridiculous.

At that point Mr. Fauré doesn't even know Mr. Cuban is going to sell his shares. And he certainly has no idea in June of 2004 that in December of 2006 the SEC is going to start investigating Mark Cuban.

So this currying favor business, now you know why they didn't ask Guy Fauré about it, because this is what he would have said. He had a perfectly logical explanation. They didn't want you to have that. They didn't want you to know.

And the other thing I'm not going to let them do is I'm not going to let them come in here and not tell you what Arnie Owen actually testified to this case. We talked about this.

... According to the defense Mr. Owen had a hundred people in this cadre of investors. Mr. Melsheimer would lead you to believe Arnie Owen called every last one of them.

Here's the actual question in this trial that was asked of Arnie Owen and here's his answer. It's on page 79 of his testimony.

"Q. So as you sit here today you can't say, can you, sir, that you contacted anyone about the Mamma PIPE other than the six investors listed in the official placement tracker, can you?

"A. That's correct."

Did the defense tell you that? NO. They want you to believe Mr. Owen contacted a hundred or more people. That is simply not true. That was not the evidence in this case.

Then they want you to believe that Mr. Owen thinks that the information about the PIPE was not confidential. But Mr. Owen testified when he was asked questions about the PIPE being made public. And here's what he said.

"Q. And with the PIPE you're soliciting private investors to make an investment in the companies, right?

"A. Yes.

"Q. You're not soliciting the general public?

"A. That's correct.

"Q. And the information about the PIPE is not made available to the general public until a press release is issued; is that correct?

"A. That's correct." ....

Mr. Owen was asked about ... the letter that his general counsel sent to all those investors. And he said ... [h]is company treated it as confidential. He treated it as confidential.

Now, did he have an explicit discussion with Mark Cuban?

No.

But here's what. He didn't have to. Guy Fauré had that conversation with Mark Cuban. Guy Fauré is a representative of Mamma.com. He controls what's confidential and what's not....

... [T]he other thing is once Guy Fauré obtained Mark Cuban's agreement to keep the information confidential and not trade on it, that is the agreement. Guy Fauré is the keeper of that confidentiality. That's his job. He is the CEO of that company. Mr. Owen is not. But regardless, Mr. Owen's firm kept PIPE information confidential. And so did Mitch Kopin.

Mitch Kopin testified in this trial that while he may have a personal belief about whether the PIPE information was material, ... he testified that he kept that information confidential at his hedge fund....

Now, why are all these people keeping the information confidential? Why is Mitch Kopin, why is Merriman?

Because they know that the SEC believes this information is material, non-public information. That's why [Merriman's General Counsel] Mr. Aguilar tells all of the PIPE investors that. They know....

This information was kept confidential. There is no evidence it was shared with anyone other than the six PIPE investors, the people that work at Mamma.com, the folks at Merriman that were selling the PIPE, and Mark Cuban. There is zero evidence that that information was broadly disseminated....

There is no information in the public arena about discounts, about warrants, or the amount of that money being raised. The information that Mark Cuban had is information that no other investor had and it is information that he admitted he used to sell his shares. And it's information that he agreed to keep confidential. That is insider trading. And it's not insider trading under some theory that Mr. Melsheimer tries to get you to believe the SEC is making up. It's insider trading according to the Supreme Court.

The instructions that Judge Fitzwater is going to give to you come from the Supreme Court of the United States of America. They recognize that when you agree to keep information confidential even if you're not an insider once you trade on that it's insider trading. So that's not my rule. That's not the SEC's rule. That's the highest court in this land's rule and we all have to follow it, even Mark Cuban....

Now, Mr. Melsheimer tried to get back to the idea that the Yahoo! message board and the 20-F made this information public, but we all know that neither of those documents said a PIPE was going to happen and neither of those documents include the warrants or the discounts.

And he put all his eggs in that Yahoo! message board basket, but he refuses to acknowledge what PX [Plaintiff Exhibit] 500 says. We know what PX 500 says. PX 500 says that on June 28th there were ... rumors that the SEC was dropping its investigation of Mamma.com. And those are the only rumors that existed on that day....

... [W]hat you would have to find is that the actual PIPE investors traded, and still, despite Mr. Melsheimer's closing statement, there is no evidence of that....

Now, why didn't the SEC call an expert?

We heard all about Dr. Sialm. We heard all about ... what he may or may not have said in an opinion that he never gave here in court.

We didn't call an expert because we didn't have to hire somebody to tell you what is painfully obvious in this courtroom, and that is that Mark Cuban insider-traded.

We didn't have to hire an expert to tell you that the … PIPE was information a reasonable investor would want to know about.

We didn't have to call an expert to tell you that the PIPE was not public.

We didn't have to call an expert to tell you that the information was not broadly disseminated.

We didn't have to call an expert to tell you no PIPE investors traded.

You know that. You can review this evidence.

We don't need a $900 an hour expert to tell you Mark Cuban insider-traded because we can show that with the actual facts, and we did.

Mr. Cuban told Guy Fauré he was screwed, he couldn't sell. He agreed not to trade. He agreed to keep it confidential. And he traded anyway. He traded on material, nonpublic information that the other investors did not have.

There's no expert in the world that we needed to tell you that. And there's no expert in the world that you have to listen to, to tell you that. You know that. That's what this evidence showed.

Then we went back to the term sheet.

Let's pull up number 22.

Mr. Melsheimer's still trying to convince you that this term sheet was somehow disseminated. There is absolutely no evidence in this trial that this term sheet left Merriman, left Mamma.com, or left Sage Capital. It just doesn't exist. It didn't happen.

The evidence is that this term sheet was kept within the parties that knew it was confidential and that were keeping it confidential.

Can we pull up slide 20, please.

This is the last part of the nonpublic jury instruction that I talked with you about this morning. I just want to reiterate, Mr. Melsheimer discussed this in his closing statement, but when you sit and you read this, this is exactly what happened here. While the 20th may have said a PIPE might happen, while the Yahoo! message board indicated there were rumors about a PIPE, what happened on June 28th is exactly what this paragraph is talking about: Guy Fauré confirmed that that PIPE would happen. Arnie Owen told Mark Cuban it was going to happen with discounts and warrants. That's the information that came from the corporate insider that is more reliable and more specific than anything that was in the public arena before that. That's what this instruction is about. It's about this case. It's what tells you that the information that Mark Cuban had was material and nonpublic.

THE COURT: One minute remains.

MS. FOLENA: Ladies and gentlemen, we've shown in this trial that Mark Cuban put himself in a position that no other investor was in. He received information no other investors received. He took that information, traded on it to his benefit. He knew the rules. He knew insider trading was illegal, but he deliberately chose not to follow them.

He knew he was screwed. He knew he couldn't sell. But he sold anyway. That's insider trading under the law of the United States Supreme Court. Mr. Cuban knew it was illegal. The Supreme Court knows it's illegal. Your jury instructions say it was illegal. Mr. Cuban insider-traded and Mr. Cuban knew better.

Thank you again for your service. Thank you for your time. Thank you for your patience.

[D] The Court's Charge to the Jury

With the arguments and testimony completed, the time had come for the jury to determine the outcome. *Prior to providing the charge to the jury, Judge Fitzwater conveyed the following admonition to the jurors.*

Normally I wait until after I have given the jury the closing instructions to remind [the jurors] of their conduct. However, as you know from the warnings I've given you and the instructions I've given you throughout the trial, because of ... the media coverage of the trial it's important that I focus on your conduct as jurors and I don't want to leave it at the end ... where you're not able to focus on it because we're getting say close to 5:00 o'clock.

So if you would please, listen carefully. I'm going to give you these instructions and then I will read the charge aloud to you and then I'll have just a handful of oral instructions at the end.

Members of the jury, the conduct rules that I am about to discuss have a common purpose, to ensure that you decide this case solely based on the evidence presented here within the four walls of this courtroom.

There are at least two important reasons for this.

First, evidence presented in court is subject to rules of evidence and rules of procedure that have been adopted after careful consideration to ensure that juries hear only evidence that will enable them to reach a just verdict.

Second, information that you obtain outside of court is not subject to testing by the parties through such means as questioning the information, cross-examining the source of the information, or offering information to dispute that information.

Keeping in mind what I have just said, you are instructed as follows:

During your deliberations you are not to discuss the case with anyone, or permit anyone to discuss it with you, other than the other members of the jury.

Second, although you may now discuss the case with your fellow jurors, you may only do so when all of you are present in the secrecy of the jury room. This means that if even one of you steps outside the jury room for any reason deliberations must stop until all of you are again present in the jury room.

It also means that even if all nine of you[14] go to the same place other than the jury room, you may not talk about the case because you are not at that point within the secrecy of the jury room.

[14.] [Note that one member of the original ten-member jury was excused due to illness.]

In saying that you must not discuss the case with anyone or permit anyone other than fellow jurors to discuss the case with you, I need to give you some specific important instructions that ... are relevant to today's electronic world.

As I've said before, I know that many of you use cell phones, smartphones, such as iPhones, Androids, Galaxy phones and Blackberries, the Internet and other tools of technology. You must not use these tools or devices to communicate electronically with anyone about this trial until the trial is completely over. This includes your family and friends.

You may not communicate with anyone about the trial on your cell phone, any kind of smartphone, through email, text messaging or on Twitter or through any blog or web site, including Facebook, Google+, MySpace, LinkedIn or YouTube. You may not use any similar technology of social media, even if I have not specifically mentioned it here.

Please advise the court security officer if you become aware that another member of the jury has violated these instructions. A juror who violates these restrictions jeopardizes the fairness of these proceedings and it may be necessary to declare a mistrial and start the trial over or retry the case. This will waste your time, the time of your fellow jurors, the parties' time and the court's time.

Third, do not read or listen to anything about this case in any way, on television, on the radio, in the newspaper, or on the Internet.

If anyone should try to talk to you about the case or if you accidently read or hear something about the trial that is more specific than simply a reference that this case is in trial, which as I said before is something you already know, bring it to my attention promptly by advising the court security officer so that I can inquire further if necessary.

Fourth, do not try to do any research or make any investigation about the case on your own. This means that during your deliberations you must not conduct any independent research about this case, the matters in the case, the Securities and Exchange Commission, and the defendant, Mr. Cuban.

In other words, you must not consult dictionaries, or reference materials, search the Internet, web sites or blogs or use any other electronic tools to obtain information about this case or to help you decide the case. Do not try to find out information from any source outside the confines of the four walls of this courtroom and the evidence that I have admitted during the trial.

Keep in mind that information that you obtain outside the courtroom is not subject to the rules of evidence and the rules of procedure that I have just mentioned and it may be information that you are not legally permitted to consider when reaching your verdict. The information is not subject to testing by the parties. And information contained in sources such as the Internet may be completely false.

If you fail to comply with this instruction it may be necessary, as I have said before, to declare a mistrial and start the trial over or to retry the case. This will waste your time, the time of your fellow jurors, the parties' time and the court's time.

Members of the jury I'll remind you at the end of my instructions that, for the first time we will be collecting cell phones, smartphones and the like from you, because by court rule jurors are not permitted to have those devices with them in the jury room during deliberations. They will be returned to you during breaks and at the end of any day, but not while you're deliberating.

I may have mentioned on the first day of trial that there have been instances in the United States where jurors, not very many, thankfully, have violated these instructions and mistrials had to be declared. So I ask you very sincerely, but I warn you very sincerely as well, to follow the instructions.

Now, if you will please, members of the jury, take out your copy of the court's charge, I will read it to you.

I remind you that this is your personal copy, you may make notes on it if you wish, you may keep it after the case is over or discard it because it's your personal copy.

I will send into the jury room the original of the court's charge and it will be on the original that the presiding juror will complete the verdict and sign and date the verdict.

In addition, you also each has a copy of the Stipulated Facts *[see Chapter 6 of this book—The Pre-Trial Order that sets forth the Stipulation of Facts]*. This is your personal copy as well.

I don't anticipate sending you another copy since you will each have a copy of the Stipulated Facts.

I will also be sending you a jury note form. I'll explain that after my other instructions. You may or may not need to use it, but just in case you do we'll have the form available.

Now the court's charge.

Thereafter, Judge Fitzwater presented the charge to the jury. *The "Court's Charge To The Jury" follows.*

COURT'S CHARGE TO THE JURY

MEMBERS OF THE JURY:

Now that you have heard all of the evidence and the argument of counsel, it becomes my duty to give you the instructions of the court concerning the law applicable to this case.

It is your duty as jurors to follow the law as I shall state it to you and to apply that law to the facts as you find them from the evidence in the case. You are not to single out one instruction as stating the law, but must consider the instructions as a whole. Neither are you to be concerned with the wisdom of any rule of law stated by me.

Regardless of any opinion you may have as to what the law is or ought to be, it would be a violation of your sworn duty to base a verdict upon any view of the law other than that given in these instructions, just as it would also be a violation of your sworn duty, as judges of the facts, to base a verdict upon anything other than the evidence in the case.

In deciding the facts of this case, you must not be swayed by bias or prejudice or favor as to any party. Our system of law does not permit jurors to be governed by prejudice or sympathy or public opinion. The parties and the public expect that you will carefully and impartially consider all of the evidence in the case, follow the law as stated in these instructions, and reach a just verdict regardless of the consequences.

This case should be considered and decided by you as an action between persons of equal standing in the community and holding the same or similar stations in life. The law is no respecter of persons, and all persons, including government agencies, stand equal before the law and are to be dealt with as equals in a court of justice.

As stated earlier, it is your duty to determine the facts, and in so doing you must consider only the evidence I have admitted in the case. The term "evidence" includes the sworn testimony of the witnesses, including deposition witnesses, the exhibits admitted in the record, and the stipulated facts.

The parties have agreed, or stipulated, to certain facts. This means that both sides agree that something is a fact. You must therefore treat each stipulated fact as having been proved. The stipulated facts are contained in a document that you will be given during your deliberations entitled, "Stipulated Facts." Please refer to that document for the stipulated facts in this case.

The term "evidence" does not include anything that I have instructed you to disregard.

Evidence admitted before you for a limited purpose may not be considered for any purpose other than the limited purpose for which it was admitted.

Remember that any statements, objections, or arguments made by the lawyers are not evidence in the case. The function of the lawyer is to point out those things that are most significant or most helpful to their side of the case and, in so doing, to call your attention to certain facts or inferences that might otherwise escape your notice. In the final analysis, however, it is your own recollection and interpretation of the evidence that controls in the case. What the lawyers say is not binding upon you. If an attorney's question contained an assertion of fact that the witness did not adopt, the assertion is not evidence of that fact.

You are not bound by any opinion that you might think I have concerning the facts of this case, and if I have in any way said or done anything that leads you to believe that I have any opinion about the facts in this case, you are instructed to disregard it. Further, nothing in these instructions to you is made for the purpose of suggesting or conveying to you an intimation as to what verdict I think you should find.

Although you should consider only the evidence in the case, you are permitted to draw such reasonable inferences from the testimony and exhibits as you feel are justified in the light of common experience. In other words, you may make deductions and reach conclusions that reason and common sense lead you to draw from the facts established by the evidence in the case.

You should not be concerned about whether the evidence is direct or circumstantial. "Direct evidence" exists when the evidence directly establishes the facts that a party asserts to be true, such as by an eyewitness or in a document. "Circumstantial evidence" is proof of a chain of facts and circumstances that, without going directly to prove the existence of an essential fact, gives rise to a logical inference that such fact does actually exist. The law makes no distinction between the weight you may give to either direct or circumstantial evidence.

Now, I have said that you must consider all of the evidence. This does not mean, however, that you must accept all of the evidence as true or accurate.

You are the sole judges of the "credibility" or believability of each witness and the weight to be given to the witness' testimony. In weighing the testimony of a witness, you should consider the witness' relationship to a particular party; the witness' interest, if any, in the outcome of the case; the witness' manner of testifying; the witness' opportunity to observe or acquire knowledge concerning the facts about which the witness testified; the witness' candor, fairness, and intelligence; and the extent to which the witness' testimony has been supported or contradicted by other credible evidence. You may, in short, accept or reject the testimony of any witness, in whole or in part.

Also, the weight of the evidence is not necessarily determined by the number of witnesses testifying as to the existence or nonexistence of any fact. You may find that the testimony of a smaller number of witnesses as to any fact is more credible than the testimony of a larger number of witnesses to the contrary.

A witness may be "impeached" or discredited by contradictory evidence, by a showing that the witness testified falsely concerning a material matter, or by evidence that at some other time the witness said or did something, or failed to say or do something, that is inconsistent with the witness' present testimony. If you believe that any witness has been so impeached, it is your exclusive province to give the testimony of that witness such credibility or weight, if any, as you think it deserves.

You should keep in mind, of course, that a simple mistake by a witness does not necessarily mean that the witness was not telling the truth as the witness remembers it, because people naturally tend to forget some things or remember other things inaccurately. So, if a witness had made a misstatement, you need to consider whether that misstatement was simply an innocent lapse of memory or an intentional falsehood, and that may depend on whether it has to do with an important fact or with only an unimportant detail.

During the trial, I have instructed you that certain earlier statements of a witness were not admitted in evidence to prove that the contents of those statements are true. You may not consider these earlier statements to prove that the content of an earlier statement is true; you may only use these earlier statements to determine whether you think the earlier statements are consistent or inconsistent with the trial testimony of the witness and therefore whether they affect the credibility of that witness.

Certain testimony has been presented to you through a deposition. A deposition is the sworn, recorded answers to questions asked a witness in advance of the trial. Before this trial, attorneys representing the parties in this case questioned the witness under oath. A court reporter was present and recorded the testimony. This deposition testimony is entitled to the same consideration and is to be judged by you as to credibility, and weighed and otherwise considered by you insofar as possible in the same way, as if the witness had been present and had testified from the witness stand.

Deposition testimony can also be introduced for the purpose of impeaching or discrediting a witness. If, in the deposition, the witness made any statements in conflict with testimony the witness gave in court, you may consider such conflicts and any explanation therefor in determining the witness' credibility.

The rules of evidence provide that if scientific, technical, or other specialized knowledge will assist the jury to understand the evidence or to determine a fact in issue, a witness qualified as an expert by knowledge, skill, experience, training, or education may testify and state an opinion concerning such matters if the testimony is based upon sufficient facts or data, the testimony is the product of reliable principles and methods, and the witness has applied the principles and methods reliably to the facts in the case.

You should consider each expert opinion received in evidence in this case and give it such weight as you may think it deserves. If you should decide that the opinion of an expert witness is not based upon sufficient knowledge, skill, experience, training, or education, or if you should conclude that the reasons given in support of the opinion are not sound, or that the opinion is not based upon sufficient facts or data, or that the opinion is outweighed by other evidence, or that the opinion is not the product of reliable principles and methods, or that the witness has not applied the principles and methods reliably to the facts in the case, then you may disregard the opinion entirely.

Certain exhibits were used during this trial for demonstrative purposes, which means they have not been admitted in evidence and will not be provided to you during your deliberations. You may consider demonstrative exhibits to the extent they help you understand the evidence admitted during the trial, but you are entitled to disregard them entirely if you find that they do not accurately reflect the evidence that they purport to demonstrate. If your recollection of the evidence differs from the exhibit, rely on your recollection.

The plaintiff has the burden of proving each essential element of its claim by a "preponderance of the evidence." A preponderance of the evidence means such evidence as, when considered and compared with that opposed to it, has more convincing force and produces in your minds a belief that what is sought to be proved is more likely true than not true. To establish a claim by a "preponderance of the evidence" merely means to prove that the claim is more likely so than not so.

If the proof fails to establish any essential element of the plaintiff's claim by a preponderance of the evidence, the jury must find against the plaintiff.

In determining whether any fact in issue has been proved by a preponderance of the evidence, the jury may consider the testimony of all the witnesses, including deposition witnesses, regardless of who may have called them, and all the exhibits received in evidence, regardless of who may have produced them.

As used in this charge, the term "SEC" means plaintiff Securities and Exchange Commission, the term "Cuban" means defendant Mark Cuban, the term "Mamma.com" means Mamma.com Inc., and the term "PIPE" means a private investment in public equity.

A corporation can act only through natural persons as its agents or employees. In general, any agent or employee of a corporation can bind the corporation by acts and declarations made while acting within the scope of the authority delegated to the agent or employee by the corporation, or within the scope of the person's duties as an employee of the corporation.

SEC'S MISAPPROPRIATION THEORY OF INSIDER TRADING CLAIM

The SEC claims that Cuban engaged in insider trading, in violation of § 17(a) of the Securities Act of 1933 ("Securities Act"), § 10(b) of the Securities Exchange Act of 1934 ("Exchange Act"), and SEC Rule 10b-5. Section 17(a) of the Securities Act, § 10(b) of the Exchange Act, and SEC Rule 10b-5 make it unlawful for a person to employ any device, scheme, or artifice to defraud someone else in connection with the purchase or sale of any security. The SEC bases this claim on what is called the "misappropriation theory" of insider trading. Cuban denies that he engaged in insider trading and denies that he violated any of these laws.

Under the "misappropriation theory" of insider trading, a person is liable for violating § 17(a) of the Securities Act, § 10(b) of the Exchange Act, and Rule 10b-5 when it is proved by a preponderance of the evidence that, in connection with a securities transaction, he knowingly or with severe recklessness misappropriates material, nonpublic information for securities trading purposes, in breach of a duty owed to the principal who is the source of the information. The person's undisclosed, self-serving use of the principal's information to purchase or sell securities, in breach of a duty to the principal, defrauds the principal of the exclusive use of that information. One way this duty to the principal can arise is when the person expressly or implicitly agrees with the principal that he will keep the material, nonpublic information confidential and that he will not trade on or otherwise use the information for his own benefit.

The "misappropriation theory" bases liability on a person's deception of the principal who entrusted the person with access to material, nonpublic information. The person's deceptive use of the information is "in connection with a securities transaction" because the person's fraud is consummated, not when he gains the material, nonpublic information, but when, without disclosure to his principal, he uses the information to purchase or sell securities. A person who trades on the basis of material, nonpublic information gains his advantageous market position through deception; he deceives the source of the information and simultaneously harms members of the investing public.

Because the duty of non-use of material, nonpublic information flows to the source of the information and not to the shareholders, a person's full disclosure to the source of the information that he intends to use the information forecloses liability under the "misappropriation theory" of insider trading. This is because the deception that is essential to the "misappropriation theory" occurs when a person secretly trades on material, nonpublic information, in violation of the source's legitimate and justifiable expectation that the recipient will not do so. If the person fully discloses to the source that he plans to trade on the material, nonpublic information, there is no "device, scheme, or artifice to defraud," and thus no violation of § 17(a) of the Securities Act, § 10(b) of the Exchange Act, or SEC Rule 10b-5.

To establish this claim, the SEC just [needs to] prove each of the following essential elements by a preponderance of the evidence:

First, that Cuban received material, nonpublic information from Mamma.com concerning Mamma.com's impending PIPE transaction;

Second, that Cuban expressly or implicitly agreed with Mamma.com to keep the material, nonpublic information confidential and not to trade on or otherwise use the information for his own benefit;

Third, that Cuban traded on the material, nonpublic information in the sale of his Mamma.com stock;

Fourth, that before trading on the material, nonpublic information, Cuban did not fully disclose to Mamma.com that he planned to trade on the material, nonpublic information;

Fifth, that Cuban acted knowingly or with severe recklessness;

Sixth, that Cuban's conduct was in connection with the sale of a security; and

Seventh, that Cuban used or caused to be used a means or instrumentality of interstate commerce in connection with the sale of a security.

First Element

The SEC must prove that Cuban received "material, nonpublic information" from Mamma.com concerning Mamma.com's impending PIPE transaction.

Information is "material" if there is a substantial likelihood that disclosure of the information would be viewed by the reasonable investor as having significantly altered the total mix of information made available. Materiality depends on the significance the reasonable investor would place on the withheld or misrepresented information. Materiality is not judged in the abstract, but in light of the surrounding circumstances. Information is material if there is a substantial likelihood that, under all the circumstances, the information would have assumed actual significance in the deliberations of the reasonable shareholder.

Information is "nonpublic" if it has not been effectively disclosed in a manner sufficient to insure its availability to the investing public. Information becomes public when disclosed to achieve a broad dissemination to the investing public generally and without favoring any special person or group, or when, although known only by a few persons, their trading on it has caused the information to be fully incorporated into the price of the particular stock.

Information is "nonpublic" if it was not available to the public through such sources as press releases, SEC filings, trade publications, analysts' reports, newspapers, magazines, rumors, word of mouth, or other sources. In assessing whether information is "nonpublic," the key word is "available." If information is available in the public media or in SEC filings, it is public. However, the fact that information has not appeared in a newspaper or other widely available public medium does not alone determine whether the information is "nonpublic." Sometimes a corporation is willing to make information available to securities analysts, prospective investors, or members of the press who ask for it, even though it may never have appeared in any newspaper publication or other publication. Such information would be public. Accordingly, information is not necessarily "nonpublic" simply because there has been no formal announcement or because only a few people have been made aware of it. For example, if Mamma.com's policy was to give out certain information to people who ask for it, that information is public information. Whether information is nonpublic is an issue of fact for you to decide.

On the other hand, the confirmation by an insider of unconfirmed facts or rumors—even if reported in a newspaper—may itself be inside information. Information from a corporate insider that is more reliable or specific than public rumors is nonpublic information despite the existence of such rumors in the media or investment community. Whether or not the confirmation of a rumor by an insider qualifies as material, nonpublic information is an issue of fact for you to decide.

Second Element

The SEC must prove that Cuban expressly or implicitly agreed with Mamma.com (a) that he would keep the material, nonpublic information confidential and (b) that he would not trade on or otherwise use the information for his own benefit. The express or implied agreement must include both aspects.

The existence of such an agreement can be implied from the parties' conduct and the surrounding circumstances.

Third Element

To prove that Cuban "traded on" the material, nonpublic information in the sale of his Mamma.com stock, the SEC must prove that Cuban used, or was motivated by, the material, nonpublic information in the sale of his Mamma.com stock. The SEC is not required to prove that Cuban sold his Mamma.com stock solely because of the material, nonpublic information.

Fourth Element

The SEC must prove that, before trading on the material, nonpublic information, Cuban did not fully disclose to Mamma.com that he planned to trade on the material, nonpublic information.

You may find that Cuban fully disclosed to Mamma.com that he planned to trade on the material, nonpublic information if he made the full disclosure to an agent of Mamma.com whose authority included receiving such notice, and who was acting within the scope of that authority when Cuban made the full disclosure. An agent is acting within the scope of the agent's authority if the agent is engaged in the performance of duties that were expressly or impliedly assigned to the agent by Mamma.com.

Fifth Element

The SEC must prove that Cuban acted "knowingly" or "with severe recklessness."

To prove that Cuban acted "knowingly," the SEC must prove that Cuban acted with an intent to deceive, manipulate, or defraud Mamma.com.

To prove that Cuban acted with "severe recklessness," the SEC must prove that Cuban engaged in conduct that involved an extreme departure from the standard of ordinary care. A person acts with reckless disregard if he knows of the danger or it is so obvious that an ordinary person under the circumstances would have been aware of it.

To prove that Cuban acted "knowingly" or "with severe recklessness," it is not enough to prove that he acted negligently, mistakenly, inadvertently, or accidentally.

A person's state of mind can be inferred from circumstantial evidence, including the person's words, conduct, acts, and all the surrounding circumstances and the reasonable inferences that may be drawn from them.

Sixth Element

It is undisputed that Mamma.com stock is a "security" within the meaning of § 17(a) of the Securities Act, § 10(b) of the Exchange Act, and SEC Rule 10b-5.

Conduct is "in connection with" the sale of a security if there is some nexus or relation between the conduct and the sale of the security. Conduct may be "in connection with" the sale of a security if you find that the conduct "touched upon" or "coincided with" the sale of the security.

Seventh Element

To use, or cause to be used, means or instrumentality of interstate commerce in connection with the sale of a security means to use or cause to be used the mails, telephone, or any facility of a national securities exchange. All that is required is that a means or instrumentality of interstate commerce be used in some phase of Cuban's sale of the security.

QUESTION

Did the SEC prove each of the essential elements of its "misappropriation theory" of insider trading claim?

> *Instruction*: The SEC has the burden of proof. If it has met its burden as to an essential element, answer "Yes;" otherwise, answer "No." Answer separately as to each element.

ANSWER

First, that Cuban received material, nonpublic information from Mamma.com concerning Mamma.com's impending PIPE transaction.

Yes _____   No _____

Second, that Cuban expressly or implicitly agreed with Mamma.com to keep the material, nonpublic information confidential and not to trade on or otherwise use the information for his own benefit.

Yes _____   No _____

Third, that Cuban traded on the material, nonpublic information in the sale of his Mamma.com stock.

Yes _____   No _____

Fourth, that before trading on the material, nonpublic information, Cuban did not fully disclose to Mamma.com that he planned to trade on the material, nonpublic information.

Yes _____   No _____

Fifth, that Cuban acted knowingly or with severe recklessness.

Yes _____   No _____

Sixth, that Cuban's conduct was in connection with the sale of a security.

Yes _____   No _____

Seventh, that Cuban used or caused to be used a means or instrumentality of interstate commerce in connection with the sale of a security.

Yes _____   No _____

Jury Deliberations

The fact that I have given you in this charge instructions about a particular claim, or that I have not so instructed you, should not be interpreted in any way as an indication that I believe a particular party should, or should not, win this case.

In order to return a verdict your verdict must be unanimous. It is your duty as jurors to consult one another and to deliberate with a view towards reaching an agreement. Each of you must decide the case for yourself, but only after an impartial consideration with each other of all the evidence in the case. In the course of your deliberations, do not hesitate to reexamine your own view and change your opinion if convinced it is erroneous. Do not, however, surrender your honest conviction as to the weight or effect of the evidence solely because of the opinion of other jurors or for the mere purpose of returning a verdict. Remember at all times that you are not partisans. You are judges—judges of the facts. Your sole interest is to seek the truth from the evidence in the case.

After I finish reading this charge, you will retire to the jury room. I will send you the exhibits that have been admitted into evidence. You will first select one member of the jury to act as presiding juror. The presiding juror will preside over your deliberations and will speak on your behalf here in court.

Do not deliberate unless all members of the jury are present in the jury room. In other words, if one or more of you go to lunch together or are together outside the jury room, do not discuss the case.

When you have reached unanimous agreement as to your verdict, the presiding juror shall fill in your answers to the questions on a copy of the charge that I will provide to you for this purpose, shall date and sign the last page of that copy of the charge, and shall notify the court security officer that you have reached a verdict. The court security officer will then deliver the verdict to me.

The court will honor the schedule you set for your deliberations and your requests for breaks during your deliberations. From time to time I may communicate with you concerning your schedule. This is done primarily for the purpose of anticipating the court's staffing needs, and is not in any way intended to suggest that your deliberations should be conducted at a different pace or on a different schedule.

During the trial, the court reporter made a verbatim record of the proceedings. The court rules do not provide for testimony to be produced for the jury in written form, or for testimony to be read back to the jury as a general aid in refreshing the jurors' memories. In limited circumstances, the court may direct the court reporter to read testimony back to the jury in open court. This is done, however, only when the jury certifies that it disagrees as to the testimony of a particular witness, and identifies the specific testimony in dispute.

If, during your deliberations, you desire to communicate with me, your presiding juror will reduce your message or question to writing, sign it, and pass the note to the court security officer, who will bring it to my attention. I will then respond as promptly as possible, either in writing or by asking you to return to the courtroom so that I can address you orally. If you do send a message or ask a question in which you indicate that you are divided, never state or specify your numerical division at the time.

October 15, 2013.

_[Signed]_____
SIDNEY A. FITZWATER
CHIEF JUDGE

After reading the court's charge to the jury, *Judge Fitzwater communicated the following instructions to the jurors.*

Members of the jury, the last page of the court's charge contains the certificate. This is the page that's to be dated and signed by the presiding juror on the original of the charge.

Now, in a moment, members of the jury, you're going to retire to begin your deliberations. I would request that you first select a presiding juror and then decide whether you want to deliberate this evening or wish to recess until the morning. That is a decision you may advise me of by advising the court security officer. You do not have to write me a note letting me know that.

I will wait until we hear from you to send the exhibits in. If you decide you want to begin your deliberations we'll have the exhibits assembled and sent in to you.

If you decide you're going to wait until the morning, we will wait and send them in to you in the morning.

If you do decide to recess until the morning, I also request that you advise the court security officer of the time that you wish to resume.

I mentioned to you a few moments ago that there is a jury note form. This is a form that you may use if you find it necessary to write me a formal note of any kind. We'll have these available. You don't have to use this form just to advise the court security officer that you're taking a break and so forth. If it is necessary for me to give you further instructions I will.

At this time, if you will please take your copies of the charge, the stipulations of fact, and your notepads, the jury is retired.

[E] The Jury Deliberates

As Judge Fitzwater informed the jurors, a jury note form was provided to enable the jury to write a formal note if a question or any other pertinent matter arose. *In its deliberations, the jury sent the following note to Judge Fitzwater.*

JURY NOTE NO. 1

TO CHIEF JUDGE FITZWATER:

Is there a "level" of detail required to determine if the information is public—is any information enough or must it be all information to make it public?

_[Signed]_____

Jane Rothman

(To be signed by Presiding Juror)

After providing counsel for the SEC and Mr. Cuban the opportunity on the record to provide their views on the appropriate response to this Jury Note, *Judge Fitzwater responded to the jury as follows.*

MEMBERS OF THE JURY:

I have received your note in which you state:

Is there a "level" of detail required to determine if the information is public— is any information enough or must it be all information to make it public?

The answer to your question is found in the court's charge, and I therefore respectfully direct you to the charge for the answer to your question.

Respectfully,

[Signed]

Sidney A. Fitzwater
United States District Judge

[F] The Jury's Verdict

The jury returned its verdict finding that Mr. Cuban was not liable of the charges alleged by the SEC. The jury answered the questions posed as follows.

QUESTION

Did the SEC prove each of the essential elements of its "misappropriation theory" of insider trading claim?

> *Instruction*: The SEC has the burden of proof. If it has met its burden as to an essential element, answer "Yes;" otherwise, answer "No." Answer separately as to each element.

ANSWER

> **First**, that Cuban received material, nonpublic information from Mamma.com concerning Mamma.com's impending PIPE transaction.
>
> Yes _____   No _____X_____
>
> **Second**, that Cuban expressly or implicitly agreed with Mamma.com to keep the material, nonpublic information confidential and not to trade on or otherwise use the information for his own benefit.
>
> Yes _____   No _____X_____
>
> **Third**, that Cuban traded on the material, nonpublic information in the sale of his Mamma.com stock.
>
> Yes _____   No _____X_____
>
> **Fourth**, that before trading on the material, nonpublic information, Cuban did not fully disclose to Mamma.com that he planned to trade on the material, nonpublic information.
>
> Yes _____   No _____X_____

Fifth, that Cuban acted knowingly or with severe recklessness.

Yes _____   No _____X_____

Sixth, that Cuban's conduct was in connection with the sale of a security.

Yes _____X_____   No _____

Seventh, that Cuban used or caused to be used a means or instrumentality of interstate commerce in connection with the sale of a security.

Yes _____X_____   No _____

The foregoing is the unanimous verdict of the jury.

Dated: <u>October 16, 2013</u>

<u>_[Signed]_____</u>
[Jane Rothman]
Presiding Juror

After *"publishing" the verdict* (namely, reading the verdict aloud in open court), Judge Fitzwater asked each of the jurors individually whether this was his or her verdict—called *"polling" the jury*. As Judge Fitzwater informed the jurors, "the purpose of polling the jury is to ensure that the verdict is unanimous. If the verdict is unanimous, it will be accepted and ordered filed with the clerk."

After publishing the verdict and polling each member of the jury, *Judge Fitzwater communicated these final words to the members of the jury.*

Members of the jury, you're almost finished with your service, but before I excuse you, I want to give you some final instructions and also offer sincere thanks for your service.

First of all, now that you have completed your service, you are released from your secrecy. You are now free to talk about the case with anyone. You are also free to decline to discuss the case if you wish.

Your deliberations are secret. You never have to explain or justify your verdict to anyone.

Under the local rules of our court, we have a Rule 47.1 entitled Contact with Jurors. It provides that a party, attorney or representative of a party or attorney shall not before or after trial contact any juror, prospective juror or the relatives, friends or associates of a juror or prospective juror, unless explicitly permitted to do so by a presiding judge. Because I have not given that permission you should not … expect to be contacted by any party or attorney or representative of a party or attorney for any reason.

There are two important exceptions to this.

First of all, you, as jurors, have the right to initiate contact if you wish. That's your decision. And you have the right to either initiate contact or not, as you prefer.

Second, members of the media have a right under the First Amendment to approach you and ask if you want to talk about your service and about the case.

The rules of our court cannot prevent members of the media from doing this. And, indeed, we respect the rights of the media under the First Amendment. You as individuals have the right either to speak to the media or not to speak to the media. In other words, they have the right to approach you and then it's your decision to decide whether you want to talk with the media or not.

Members of the jury, it's customary for the court to thank those who have served on a jury for their important service. And I can assure you that although it is customary, it is in no way insincere. We could not honor the right of trial by jury in our country if we did not have people such as yourself who honored your summonses and came here to be present for jury service.

I have found over the years that jurors have two different reactions when they receive the jury summons and when they finish their service. When they receive the summons it's often a, oh, no, I've been summoned for jury duty. But when they finish they realize how important a part of the system of justice they have been and they are grateful to have had that opportunity, and I hope that you feel that way.

Now that you are released from your secrecy and have completed your service, you are, of course, free to read any media coverage of the case, anyone who's been saving it up for you, that sort of thing, and you're free to talk about the case, but, as I indicated, you don't have to if you don't wish.

I thank counsel for their professionalism in the trial of the case. I thought both sides were very professional in how they presented the case, and I do thank you for a very good trial.

I will be entering a judgment on the verdict in favor of the defendant.

At this time the court will stand in recess.

[G] The Judgment

At the conclusion of the case, Judge Fitzwater entered judgment in favor of Mr. Cuban. *The district court's order of judgment follows.*

JUDGMENT

This civil action was tried to a jury beginning on September 30, 2013. On October 16, 2013 the jury returned a verdict in favor of the defendant.

Accordingly, it is ordered and adjudged that this civil action is dismissed with prejudice.

Done at Dallas, Texas October 16, 2013.

[Signed]
SIDNEY A. FITZWATER
CHIEF JUDGE

CHAPTER 8

Concluding Comments and Conjectures

This concluding chapter offers comments and conjectures to ponder regarding this contentious litigation. For several of these comments, there are no clear answers. Indeed, with respect to a number of points that I make, the reader may well disagree with me. That is all well and good—as this litigation was both unusual and tenacious.

I. WHY DID THE SEC FILE THIS LAWSUIT IN DALLAS?

Mr. Cuban is well known in Dallas, nationally, and globally—as an astute entrepreneur and investor, key participant on the program "Shark Tank," owner of the NBA's Dallas Mavericks, and celebrity on "Dancing with the Stars." Being the owner of the Dallas Mavericks and an avid basketball hoopster, Mr. Cuban well knows the distinct advantage of playing on one's home court. Ordinarily, in any athletic contest, ranging from high school tennis to collegiate football to NBA basketball, the "home" team is more likely to perform better in its "friendly confines" than playing its opponent on "enemy turf." As applied to this Matter, the inquiry is: "Why did the SEC sue Mr. Cuban in federal district court in the city of Dallas Texas?" This inquiry becomes more pressing in view that this case was pursued by the SEC staff in the Commission's "home office" situated in Washington D.C. rather than by the Commission's staff located in its Fort Worth Texas regional office. Customarily, a case investigated and tried by regional office staff will be litigated in those federal courts that are in that region. By contrast, "home office" cases, with some frequency, are filed in any eligible jurisdiction that the SEC deems attractive.

Given that Mamma.com was not a Texas-based company and that Mr. Cuban's trades of Mamma.com stock were not consummated in Texas, it appears that the Commission could have brought suit elsewhere, perhaps in New York City, New Jersey, or San Francisco. With some frequency, for example, the SEC has filed suit in federal district court in the Southern District of New York even when the defendant's residence and alleged misconduct occurred to a significant degree in another jurisdiction.[1]

In Dallas, Mr. Cuban maintains an excellent reputation as being an outstanding sports franchise owner and benefactor to the enhancement of the Dallas community.[2] Outside of Dallas, he may or may not be viewed as positively. At the time of trial, Mr. Cuban had been levied money fines by the NBA in over a dozen incidents.[3] Accordingly, a New York City, San Francisco, or New Jersey jury may have been more to the liking of the SEC.

Nonetheless, Dallas clearly was the venue with the closest nexus to the conduct that transpired. In this respect, while in Dallas or in close proximity, Mr. Cuban: resided; received and transmitted the subject emails; engaged in the subject telephone calls; and ordered the selling of his Mamma.com stock. This sell order was communicated to Mr. Cuban's broker whose office likewise was in Dallas who thereupon transmitted the order from his Dallas brokerage office.

By contrast, Mamma.com was a Canadian company and had no U.S. headquarters. The only significant nexus to the Northern District of California was that Mr. Arnold Owen of Merriman was situated in San Francisco when he engaged in the telephone conversation with Mr. Cuban regarding the Mamma.com PIPE transaction. With respect to the Southern District of New York, Mr. Cuban's sales of Mamma.com stock were effected on the Nasdaq Stock Market whose market site is situated at Times Square, New York City. In addition, Mr. Cuban's trades may have been routed through the New York City offices of UBS. And in regard to New Jersey, that state is the home of Nasdaq's Data Center (Carteret, New Jersey). Hence, with respect to each of

---

1. See, e.g., SEC v. Wyly, Civ. No. 10-05760 (S.D.N.Y. 2010) (Complaint), 788 F. Supp. 2d 92 (S.D.N.Y. 2011) (denying motion to dismiss); SEC v. Morton, Civ. No. 10-1720 (S.D.N.Y. 2010) (Complaint), 2011 WL 1344259 (S.D.N.Y. 2011) (denying motion to dismiss); SEC v. 800America, Inc., Civ. No. 02-9046 (S.D.N.Y. 2002) (Complaint), 2006 WL 3422670 (S.D.N.Y. 2006) (denying motion to dismiss and granting SEC's motion for summary judgment).

2. See, e.g., Mark Cuban Foundation, in Dallas, Texas, www.nonprofitfacts.com (2013). During the past year, Mr. Cuban and the Dallas Mavericks have been criticized for their alleged lack of adequate oversight regarding acts of sexual harassment by a number of Mavs' employees. See Scott Cacciola, *Mavericks and Mark Cuban Sanctioned by N.B.A. Over Handling of Sexual Harassment*, N.Y. Times (Sept. 19, 2018), *available at* https://www.nytimes.com/2018/09/19/sports/mark-cuban-mavericks-nba.html.

3. See Jodie Valade, *Mark Cuban Does the Unexpected*, ESPN W (June 2, 2011) (that as of June 2011, Mr. Cuban had been fined about $1,665,000 for 13 incidents as Mavericks owner), *available at* http://www.espn.com/espnw/news/article/6615266/nba-finals-dallas-mavericks-owner-mark-cuban-does-unexpected. Mr. Cuban's incurrence of NBA fines has continued. See, e.g., Michael Blaustein, *Mark Cuban Finally Pushed NBA Referees Too Far*, NY Post (Jan. 13, 2017) ("Billionaire Mavericks owner Mark Cuban's mouth has gotten so big that NBA refs think he's a threat to the game itself."); Andrew Powell-Morse, *Mark Cuban: King of NBA Fines* (April 25, 2013), *available at* https://bleacherreport.com/1614612-mark-cuban-king-of-nba-fines.

these locales, there arguably transpired sufficient conduct to enable the Commission to bring the action in each such jurisdiction.

Pursuant to Section 27 of the Securities Exchange Act, the Commission may institute suit in any federal judicial district "wherein any act or transaction constituting the violation occurred...."[4] Arguably, the SEC could have elected to bring this action against Mr. Cuban in the Southern District of New York (where the Nasdaq market site is situated), New Jersey (where the Nasdaq Data Center is located), or in the Northern District of California (where Mr. Owen engaged in the telephone discussion with Mr. Cuban regarding the Mamma.com PIPE transaction)—assuming that "any act or transaction constituting the violation occurred" in each such respective jurisdiction.

Assuming that the SEC was authorized and had elected to file the case in federal district court in any of the above jurisdictions, Mr. Cuban likely would have sought a change in venue under 28 U.S.C. §1404(a) to the Northern District of Texas.[5] It is uncertain whether Mr. Cuban would have succeeded.[6] Nonetheless, Dallas—the Northern District of Texas—clearly was the locale in the United States where nearly all of the key events transpired. Accordingly, the SEC acted consistently with the statutory directives in its determination to institute this litigation in the Northern District of Texas. While the Commission may be commended for selecting the district wherein by far the most significant contacts and events allegedly occurred, SEC critics proffer a less gentle rationale: The Commission wanted to inflict as much pain and embarrassment upon Mr. Cuban as practicable when bringing suit, thereby perhaps inducing him to settle the proceeding—and the Northern District of Texas clearly met that objective. Irrespective of the SEC's motives, acting consistently with its usual pattern of "not gaming the system," the SEC's election to institute the action in Dallas was appropriate and consistent with notions of "fair play."

The foregoing discussion is not meant to imply that the SEC would have been victorious if it had sued Mr. Cuban in New York City, New Jersey, or San Francisco. That is a question which cannot be definitively answered. As

---

4. 15 U.S.C. §78aa. The SEC also alleged a violation of Section 17(a) of the Securities Act, 15 U.S.C. §77q. Pursuant to Section 22 of that Act, 15 U.S.C. §77v, the SEC's action could have been brought in federal district court where Mr. Cuban resided, transacted business, or "where the offer or sale took place, if [Mr. Cuban] participated therein ...." Under this statute, the Southern District of New York, District of New Jersey, Northern District of California, and the Northern District of Texas arguably were the eligible districts. See §2(a)(3) of the Securities Act, 15 U.S.C. §77b(a)(3) (defining the term "offer to sell" broadly).

5. 28 U.S.C. §1404(a) states that "for the convenience of parties and witnesses, in the interest of justice, a district court may transfer any civil action to any other district where it might have been brought."

6. See, e.g., SEC v. Alpine Securities Corp., 2018 WL 3377152 (S.D.N.Y. 2018) (denying motion for improper venue); SEC v. Kearns, 2009 WL 2030235 (S.D.N.Y. 2009) (granting motion to transfer action to District of New Jersey); SEC v. Thrasher, 1993 WL 37044 (S.D.N.Y. 1993) (denying motion for improper venue); SEC v. Capt. Crab, Inc., 655 F. Supp. 615 (S.D.N.Y. 1986) (granting motion to transfer action to Southern District of Florida).

addressed below, there existed additional fundamental reasons why the Commission did not succeed. Nonetheless, for reasons not publicly known, to its credit, the SEC opted to play on Mr. Cuban's turf. As frequently occurs, the "home team"—here, Mr. Cuban—prevailed as the "winner."

II. GOING TO TRIAL WITH THE GOVERNMENT—AN EXPENSIVE ORDEAL

An overwhelming percentage of SEC enforcement actions are settled with the defendant neither admitting nor denying the allegations set forth in the Commission's Complaint.[7] From the SEC's perspective, the relief procured in these settlements ordinarily is what the Commission largely seeks, including the ordering of injunctions, disgorgement of ill-gotten gains, money penalties, and at times even more drastic measures such as the imposition of officer and director bars.[8] These sanctions are levied without the Commission going through the travails of trial, thereby enabling the SEC to utilize its personnel to pursue other suspected wrongdoing.[9] From the defendant's standpoint, relatively expeditious resolution of the SEC's action—without admitting or denying the Commission's allegations—enables such defendant to move forward, lessens the specter of the Commission making a criminal referral to the U.S. Department of Justice, drastically reduces the financial costs incurred in litigating with the SEC, alleviates to some degree the anxiety and distractions that would arise, and prevents complainants in private litigation to utilize offensive collateral estoppel as a strategy to recover damages against the subject defendant.[10]

Not all defendants opt to settle and several who have elected to proceed to trial have emerged victorious.[11] To take this route in an effective manner

---

7. See Marc I. Steinberg and Ralph C. Ferrara, *Securities Practice: Federal and State Enforcement* § 3.60 (2d ed. 2001 and 2018-2019 supp.) ("A large number (as high as 90%) of enforcement actions initiated by the SEC are settled rather than contested.").

8. See, e.g., Aaron v. SEC, 446 U.S. 680 (1980) (setting forth standards for issuance of injunction); SEC v. Jasper, 678 F.3d 1116 (9th Cir. 2012) (levying of money penalties and director-officer bar); SEC v. Mayhew, 121 F.3d 44 (2d Cir. 1997) (ordering of disgorgement); SEC v. Posner, 16 F.3d 520 (2d Cir. 1994) (imposition of officer and director bar).

9. See Steinberg and Ferrara, *supra* note 7, at §§ 3:60-3:66.

10. See Parklane Hosiery Co., Inc. v. Shore, 439 U.S. 322 (1979) (authorizing use in appropriate cases of offensive collateral estoppel in private litigation following an adverse finding in an SEC litigated proceeding); Marc I. Steinberg, *Understanding Securities Law* 451 (7th ed. 2018); Frank Razzano, *To Cooperate with the Securities and Exchange Commission or Not to Cooperate—That Is the Question*, 31 Sec. Reg. L.J. 410 (2003).

11. See, e.g., Flannery v. SEC, 810 F.3d (1st Cir. 2015); SEC v. Shanahan, 646 F.3d 536 (8th Cir. 2011); *SEC Loses Latest Insider Trading Trial to Former STEC Chief Executive Officer* [SEC v. Moshayedi], 46 Sec. Reg. & L. Rep. (BNA) 1165 (C.D. Cal. 2014); Joel M. Cohen, *SEC v. Obus: A Case Study on Taking the Government to Trial and Winning*, 47 Rev. Sec. & Comm. Reg. 247 (2014).

will "take plenty of money"[12]—hundreds of thousands—if not millions—of dollars. The wherewithal to undertake this journey generally is available only for those defendants who are wealthy or who have adequate insurance coverage—as only they will have sufficient financial resources to mount an effective defense.[13] Mr. Cuban's litigation with the SEC illustrates the costs entailed in presenting an impressive defense. As reported, retaining premier legal counsel and support personnel, Mr. Cuban incurred roughly $12 million of legal fees in this litigation.[14] Hence, proceeding to trial with the government is a daunting task—both from an emotional and financial perspective.

III. THE MURKY INSIDER TRADING LAW IN THE UNITED STATES

To prove its case against Mr. Cuban, among other things, the SEC was required to show that the information regarding the Mamma.com PIPE transaction was both material and nonpublic. Perhaps surprising to some as seen by the jury findings set forth in Chapter 7, the Commission failed in this quest. More precisely, in response to the questions: Whether Mr. Cuban received or traded on material, nonpublic information regarding Mamma.com's forthcoming PIPE transaction, the jury answered "No".

Nonetheless, the SEC's theory in bringing its case against Mr. Cuban illustrates the murkiness of U.S. insider trading law. It was not disputed that Mr. Cuban received the information regarding the impending Mamma.com PIPE transaction from two sources: (1) the company's CEO Mr. Guy Fauré; and (2) Mr. Arnold Owen of Merriman that served as Mamma.com's placement agent for the PIPE transaction. In developed markets outside of the United States, if an individual knowingly receives material and nonpublic information from an insider, such as a corporate executive, he or she cannot trade the subject securities until that information is adequately disseminated to the investing public.[15] This broad prohibition is widely embraced in developed markets throughout the world—but not in the United States.[16]

---

12. George Harrison, *Got My Mind Set On You* (1987).

13. See Steinberg and Ferrara, *supra* note 7, at §3:62; Jon Eisenberg, *Litigating with the SEC—A Reasonable Alternative to Settlement*, 21 Sec. Reg. L.J. 421 (1994).

14. See Dina ElBoghdady, *Billionaire Mark Cuban Takes on the SEC*, Wash. Post (Nov. 20, 2013) (reporting that in post-trial interviews, Mr. Cuban stated that he "paid $12 million in legal fees to defend himself").

15. See, e.g., Australia Corporations Act 2001 (Cth) §1043A; Regulation (EU) No. 596/2014 of the European Parliament and Council (Market Abuse Regulation), Articles 7, 8, 10, 14, 17 (16 April 2014); Directive (EU) 2014/57/EU of the European Parliament and Council (Criminal Sanctions for Market Abuse), Article 3 (16 April 2014); Ontario Securities Act, ch. S-5, §76 (1990).

16. The author has elaborated on this subject in several other works. See, e.g., Marc I. Steinberg, *International Securities Law—A Contemporary and Comparative Analysis* (Kluwer Law International 1999); Marc I. Steinberg, *Insider Trading Regulation—A Comparative Analysis*, 37 Int'l Law. 153 (2003); Marc I. Steinberg, *Texas Gulf Sulphur at Fifty—A Contemporary and Historical Perspective*, 71 SMU L. Rev. 625 (2018). See also, *Market Abuse Regulation—Com-*

Prior to restrictive U.S. Supreme Court decisions in the insider trading area that commenced in 1980, liability was imposed under the federal securities laws' anti-fraud provisions in a far more expansive manner. Utilizing the parity of information[17] or equal access rationale,[18] the law of insider trading that then existed resembled the framework that today is embraced by developed markets outside of the United States. In this country, the more expansive approach of yesteryear remains viable only when insider trading occurs in connection with a tender offer.[19] In that setting, SEC Rule 14e-3 imposes liability based on a parity of information approach.[20] Mr. Cuban's trading of Mamma.com stock was related to a prospective PIPE transaction, clearly not involving a tender offer.

Accordingly, the SEC was constrained by U.S. Supreme Court precedent[21] to establish that Mr. Cuban "misappropriated" the allegedly material and nonpublic information he received from Mr. Fauré and Mr. Owen and thereupon sold his Mamma.com stock. As held by the Supreme Court, one who breaches a fiduciary duty or a relationship of trust and confidence to the *source* of the information engages in such misappropriation.[22] Seeking to expand the contours of the misappropriation theory, the SEC adopted Rule 10b5-2 whereby one is deemed to breach such a duty of trust and confidence by trading the

---

mentary and Annotated Guide (Marco Ventoruzzo and Sebastian Mock eds. Oxford Univ. Press 2017).

17. See, e.g., SEC v. Texas Gulf Sulphur, 401 F.2d 833, 848 (2d Cir. 1968) (en banc) (stating that "anyone in possession of material inside information must either disclose it to the investing public, or if he is disabled from disclosing it in order to protect a corporate confidence, or he chooses not to do so, must abstain from trading in or recommending the securities concerned while such information remains undisclosed").

18. *Id.* (stating that the "essence" of the insider trading prohibition "is that anyone who, trading for his own account in the securities of a corporation, has access, directly or indirectly, to information intended to be available only for a corporate purpose and not for the personal benefit of anyone may not take advantage of such information knowing it is unavailable to those with whom he is dealing, i.e., the investing public").

19. Generally, a tender offer is "a means frequently used to acquire control of a corporation characterized by active solicitation to purchase a substantial percentage of the target's stock from the target's shareholders at a premium over the market price, offered for a limited period of time and that may be contingent upon the tender of a specific number of shares." Marc I. Steinberg, *Understanding Securities Law* 500 (7th ed. 2018).

20. 17 C.F.R. §240.14e-3. With certain exceptions, Rule 14e-3 prohibits "insider and tippee trading in the tender offer context by applying the disclose-or-abstain provision where an individual is in possession of material information relating to a tender offer which he/she knows or has reason to know that such information is nonpublic and was obtained directly or indirectly from the offeror, the subject corporation, any of their affiliated persons, or any person acting on behalf of either company." *Id.* at 517.

21. See United States v. O'Hagan, 521 U.S. 642 (1997); Dirks v. SEC, 463 U.S. 646 (1983); Chiarella v. United States, 445 U.S. 222 (1980); discussion in Chapter 2 herein.

22. See United States v. O'Hagan, 521 U.S. 642 (1997). This rationale was invoked by the U.S. Court of Appeals in this case. See SEC v. Cuban, 620 F.3d 551 (5th Cir. 2010) (contained in Chapter 2 herein).

subject securities after agreeing to maintain the confidentiality of the material and nonpublic information.[23] The SEC sought to invoke this rationale against Mr. Cuban.[24]

Nonetheless, the question arises how an oral or written confidentiality agreement becomes a litmus test for the recognition of a relationship of trust and confidence. Indeed, parties customarily enter into non-disclosure agreements because they deal at arms-length and do *not* trust one another. To elevate a non-disclosure agreement to the status of constituting a relationship of trust and confidence between the contracting parties belies economic reality. Noncompliance with such an agreement may well constitute a breach of contract; but a contractual breach is distinctly different from fiduciary transgression. The SEC thus is in a "pickle;" yet, the lower federal courts at present, as illustrated by the Fifth Circuit's decision in *SEC v. Cuban*, are accommodating the Commission by permitting these allegedly contractual breaches to state a viable claim under the misappropriation theory.[25]

All of this points to the unacceptable status of U.S. insider trading law. The insider trading parameters in developed markets elsewhere are far more straight-forward and protective of market integrity—namely, if one knowingly receives or has unequal access to material and nonpublic information regarding a subject company or the market for its securities, one cannot trade such securities until such information is adequately disseminated to the investing public.[26] The *SEC-Cuban* saga thus poignantly illustrates the deficient U.S. insider trading framework.

IV. THE FAILED SETTLEMENT NEGOTIATIONS

Prior to trial, settlement negotiations between the SEC and Mr. Cuban failed to resolve the Matter. Although all of the terms offered by the Commission are not publicly known, Mr. Cuban publicly commented that he rejected the SEC's proposal that he pay $2 million in disgorgement and money penalties.[27] In all probability, the Commission also sought Mr. Cuban to settle,

---

23. Rule 10b5-2(b)(1), 17 C.F.R. §240.10b5-2(b)(1) (stating that a person has "a duty of trust and confidence" under the misappropriation theory when such person "agrees to maintain information in confidence").

24. See SEC v. Cuban, 620 F.3d 551, 555 (5th Cir. 2010).

25. *Id.* at 557 (Illustrating the contractual, not fiduciary, nature of the alleged agreement, the Fifth Circuit stated: "We say only that on this factually sparse record, it is at least equally plausible that all sides understood there was to be no trading before the PIPE....").

26. See *supra* notes 15-16 and accompanying text; discussion in Chapter 2 herein. See generally Marc I. Steinberg and William K.S. Wang, *Insider Trading* (Oxford Univ. Press 3d ed. 2010).

27. See Dina ElBoghdady, *Billionaire Mark Cuban Takes on the SEC*, Wash. Post (Nov. 20, 2013).

neither admitting nor denying, the government's allegations that he engaged in fraudulent conduct and to the imposition of an injunction.[28]

With the benefit of hindsight, the SEC should have been more flexible in its negotiations with Mr. Cuban. Although there is no assurance that Mr. Cuban would have accepted the SEC's offer of settlement, the Commission would have been prudent to invoke a liability provision based on negligent, rather than intentional, misconduct. In view of Mr. Cuban's stature and financial ability to defend his reputation, the prospect of accepting a settlement accusing him of securities fraud was untenable. The SEC should have recognized the difficulty of its case, particularly in view that: (1) its key witnesses were to testify by video rather than live at trial; and (2) Mr. Cuban had a sound explanation why he would never have agreed to the alleged confidentiality agreement: namely, as an astute entrepreneur and investor, Mr. Cuban as a matter of customary practice would never become a party to such an agreement without being provided with significantly more background information, conferring with his legal counsel, Mr. Robert Hart, and the agreement being in writing. That Mr. Cuban would spontaneously agree to the confidentiality agreement per Mr. Fauré's video testimony may seem far-fetched. With the SEC having the burden of proof, these problematic aspects of the case should have persuaded the Commission to bargain for a settlement premised on Mr. Cuban's alleged negligence.

Significantly, in this situation, the SEC had a readily available provision it could have sought to utilize—Section 17(a)(3) of the Securities Act which imposes liability for negligent conduct in the offer or sale of securities.[29] Here, Mr. Cuban sold his Mamma.com stock upon learning of the impending Mamma.com PIPE transaction. Accordingly, the following settlement terms could have been offered by the SEC to Mr. Cuban which he may or may not have accepted: Without admitting or denying the SEC's allegations, Mr. Cuban would settle and agree to the following: (1) a violation of Section 17(a)(3) of the Securities Act premised on allegedly negligent conduct; (2) disgorgement of the monetary amount of the losses he avoided (approximately $750,000) due to his sales of Mamma.com stock; (3) payment of prejudgment interest on this $750,000 amount; (4) with no injunction being imposed.

Occasionally, the SEC has invoked Section 17(a)(3) to combat negligent insider trading.[30] Being accused of negligent conduct by a zealous regulatory

---

28. The provisions that the SEC normally invokes in these types of settings are Section 17(a) (1) of the Securities Act, Section 10(b) of the Securities Exchange Act, and SEC Rule 10b-5. All of these provisions require that the defendant act with reckless or intentional misconduct in order for there to be a violation.

29. 15 U.S.C. §77q(a)(3). See Aaron v SEC, 446 U.S. 680 (1980) (holding, inter alia, that §17(a)(3) encompasses negligent conduct).

30. See, e.g., In re Bolan, Securities Exchange Act Release No. 75066 (2015). The author has written on this subject. See Marc I. Steinberg and Abel Ramirez, Jr., *The SEC's Neglected Weapon: A Proposed Amendment to Section 17(a)(3) and the Application of Negligent Insider Trading*, 19 U. Penn. J. Bus. L. 239 (2017).

enforcement agency and settling without admission of fault may be viewed by some defendants as an acceptable outcome. After all, when going to trial, there are no certainties and a truly adverse outcome impugning one's reputation remains a distinct possibility. Here, the Commission swung for the fences rather than strategizing for a solid base hit, albeit a single. In this endeavor, the Commission struck out swinging.

V. THE SEC'S "STAR" WITNESSES

The SEC's "premier" witness was Mr. Guy Fauré, the chief executive officer of Mamma.com, who allegedly entered into the confidentiality agreement with Mr. Cuban. To corroborate Mr. Fauré's testimony, the government called Mamma.com's executive chairman, Mr. David Goldman. The SEC's case against Mr. Cuban largely depended on witness credibility. Mr. Fauré testified that Mr. Cuban entered into a confidentiality agreement prior to Mr. Fauré informing Mr. Cuban of the impending Mamma.com PIPE transaction. While Mr. Cuban did not remember the contents of the conversation with Mr. Fauré, he testified that he was certain that he would not have entered into a confidentiality agreement under such circumstances.

The SEC's dilemma, of course, was that Mr. Fauré and Mr. Goldman refused to come to Dallas to testify at trial and were not subject to being subpoenaed. The consequence was that the testimony of the Commission's star witnesses were shown to the jury by means of video. Understandably, the Commission's task was made significantly more arduous due to the physical absence of these witnesses at trial. Although it sought (as did Mr. Cuban) to induce these witnesses to testify in person, they declined to do so. This eventuality was a situation which the SEC must have envisioned.

VI. THE JURY CHARGE

As set forth in Chapter 7 and earlier in this chapter, the jury answered "No" to the questions whether Mr. Cuban received or traded on material, nonpublic information regarding Mamma.com's forthcoming PIPE transaction. As essential requirements, in order for Mr. Cuban to be found liable, a finding that this information was *both* material and nonpublic was necessary. Why these *two elements were combined* in the questions presented to the jury is perplexing. With the jury's verdict, it remains unclear whether the jury found that the information: (1) was neither material nor nonpublic; (2) was material but public; or (3) was nonpublic but not material. Merging these two elements also created a risk that the jurors would not focus adequately on each of these elements or would be confused regarding the separate nature of the inquiries. Moreover, if an appeal had been taken, the basis for deciphering the jury's verdict would have been more challenging.

VII. THE SEC CALLING MR. CUBAN IN PRESENTING ITS CASE

As addressed in Chapter 7, the SEC elected to call Mr. Cuban as a witness in presenting its case to the jury. For the reasons set forth in that earlier discussion, this strategy in a civil case of calling the defendant as a witness in the plaintiff's direct case is frequently utilized. As such, it would be unfair to criticize the SEC for engaging in this strategy. Nonetheless, the question may be raised whether the Commission should have ended its direct case with the testimony of its premier witness, Mr. Guy Fauré. Such a strategy may have resulted in the SEC presenting a significantly stronger direct case to the jury. As effectuated, the Commission's direct case was materially diminished by Mr. Cuban's solid demeanor and testimony when questioned on the stand. The SEC may well have chosen a different path—namely, cross-examining Mr. Cuban when he was called as a witness by the defense. Proceeding in this manner would have enabled the Commission to present a largely unimpeded direct case against Mr. Cuban, thereby perhaps putting the "Cuban Team" on the defensive and adversely impacting its strategy in presenting its case.

VIII. WHERE WAS DR. SIALM?

The greatest mystery of the case is the SEC's decision not to call its expert witness Dr. Clemens Sialm to rebut the expert testimony given by Dr. Erik Sirri, Mr. Cuban's expert. As addressed in Chapter 7, Dr. Sirri gave two important opinions: first, the information regarding the impending Mamma.com PIPE transaction was publicly known; and second, that a drop of over nine percent in Mamma.com's stock price after the company publicly announced the consummation of the PIPE transaction was not statistically significant (and, hence, by implication, that the information regarding the PIPE transaction was not material). These opinions were of fundamental importance in this litigation. In practical effect, Dr. Sirri testified that the information Mr. Cuban received relating to the impending Mamma.com PIPE transaction was neither material nor nonpublic.

Instead of calling Dr. Sialm to rebut Dr. Sirri's testimony, the SEC sought to impeach Dr. Sirri's credibility and the basis for his opinions. A tactic used by the Commission was to emphasize to the jury that Dr. Sirri was being compensated at the rate of $900 per hour. Why the SEC opted to resort to this tactic is puzzling as Dr. Sirri had been employed by the Commission in high level positions on two separate occasions. The jury may have thought that the Commission's strategy was one of desperation and an affront to the integrity of a distinguished professional.

Only the Commission and Dr. Sialm know for certain why he was not called to testify. Conjecture prevails to understand why. Possibilities include: (1) Dr. Sialm in fact agreed with Dr. Sirri's expert opinions; (2) although Dr. Sialm would opine that information relating to the impending Mamma.com PIPE transaction was material and nonpublic, his previous writings may have contained contrary analysis that would subject him to considerable impeach-ment on cross-examination; (3) the SEC believed that Dr. Sirri's testimony was ineffective and that there was no need to have Dr. Sialm testify; or (4) for reasons known only by the SEC and Dr. Sialm, Dr. Sialm was unable to testify. Whatever the actual reason, Dr. Sirri's expert opinions were not refuted by any witness at trial.

With the benefit of hindsight, unless Dr. Sialm in fact agreed with Dr. Sir-ri's expert opinions or was unable to testify, the SEC made a huge mistake in not calling Dr. Sialm to testify. There was no expert witness disagreeing with Dr. Sirri's opinions with respect to the subjects of whether the impending Mamma.com PIPE transaction was material and was publicly known. These issues may be viewed as being of a technical nature, particularly for layper-sons who comprised the jury. It is understandable why the jurors would heav-ily rely on Dr. Sirri's expertise in their deliberations. The lack of an expert to rebut Dr. Sirri's opinions proved detrimental and perhaps catastrophic to the SEC's case.

IX. DECLINING TO APPEAL THE JURY VERDICT AND JUDGMENT

The SEC declined to appeal the adverse judgment to the U.S. Court of Appeals. In declining to do so, the Commission's determination was correct. This was not a situation where the jury decided against the SEC on one or two key issues. Rather, with respect to every significant question posed, the jury found in Mr. Cuban's favor. In its verdict, the jury found that Mr. Cuban: (1) did not receive material, nonpublic information from Mamma.com regard-ing the impending PIPE transaction; (2) did not agree to maintain the con-fidentiality of this information; (3) did not agree not to trade or otherwise use this information for his benefit; (4) did not sell his Mamma.com stock on material, nonpublic information; (5) fully disclosed to Mamma.com that he planned to sell his Mamma.com stock; and (6) did not act with knowing or reckless misconduct.

In view of this jury verdict, the SEC wisely elected not to appeal. Although perhaps it could have challenged the correctness of some of Judge Fitzwa-ter's rulings as a basis for reversal, this effort in all probability would have been futile. The SEC had its day in court and lost. Rather than incurring more negative publicity and an adverse appellate court decision, the Commission prudently folded its tent.

X. CONCLUSION

With the jury returning a verdict in Mr. Cuban's favor after only three hours of deliberation,[31] the question may be posed whether the Commission

---

31. See Renae Merle, *Cuban on His Crusade Against the SEC—And When He'll Be Satisfied,* Wash. Post (March 17, 2016).

acted appropriately in bringing this case. Not surprisingly, opinions differ. Certainly, some events went against the Commission's way at trial, such as the refusal of Mr. Fauré and Mr. Goldman to testify live at trial. But the Commission must have been aware of this possibility. And some of the events were the SEC's own doing, such as its failure to call Dr. Sialm to rebut the opinions of Dr. Sirri and its decision to bring the case in the Northern District of Texas. All in all, the Commission's case was far from formidable. It nonetheless opted to proceed with this litigation—and incurred a significant defeat.